EFFICIENCY AND RUSSIA'S ECONOMIC RECOVERY POTENTIAL TO THE YEAR 2000 AND BEYOND

To my parents,

Roslyn Seitzman Rosefielde
and
Louis Rosefielde

in memoriam

Efficiency and Russia's Economic Recovery Potential to the Year 2000 and Beyond

Edited by
STEVEN ROSEFIELDE
University of North Carolina
Chapel Hill

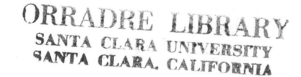
Ashgate

Aldershot • Brookfield USA • Singapore • Sydney

© Steven Rosefielde 1998

Published by
Ashgate Publishing Ltd
Gower House
Croft Road
Aldershot
Hants GU11 3HR
England

Ashgate Publishing Company
Old Post Road
Brookfield
Vermont 05036
USA

British Library Cataloguing in Publication Data
Efficiency and Russia's economic recovery potential to the
    year 2000 and beyond
    1. Russia (Federation) - Economic conditions - 1991-
    2. Russia (Federation) - Economic conditions - 1991- -
    Forecasting
    I. Rosefielde, Steven
    330.9'14'00112

Library of Congress Cataloging-in-Publication Data
Efficiency and Russia's economic recovery potential to the year 2000 and beyond
    / Steven Rosefielde, editor.
        p.   cm.
    Includes bibliographical references and index.
    ISBN 1-84014-411-4 (hardbound)
    1. Industrial productivity--Russia (Federation) 2. Industrial
productivity--Soviet Union. 3. Economic forecasting--Russia
(Federation) 4. Russia (Federation)--Economic conditions--1991- -
-Economic models. 5. Production functions (Economic theory)
I. Rosefielde, Steven.
HC340.12.Z9I5234   1998
    338.5'44'0947--dc21   98-20664
                                                                CIP

ISBN 1 84014 411 4

Printed in Great Britain by The Ipswich Book Company, Suffolk

Contents

PART I: PRODUCTION POTENTIAL AND EFFICIENCY: THEORY AND MEASUREMENT

v

List of Figures

List of Tables

List of Contributors

Mikhail Iu. Afanas"ev
Doctor of Sciences
Department of CEMI RAN
Central Economics and
  Mathematics Institute
Russian Academy of Sciences
Moscow, 117418, ul.
Krasikova, 32, Russia

M.V. Antonov
Senior Researcher
Central Economics and
  Mathematics Institute
Russian Academy of Sciences
Moscow, 117418, ul.
Krasikova, 32, Russia

Slava V. Brover
Researcher of CEMI RAN
Central Economics and
  Mathematics Institute
Russian Academy of Sciences
Moscow, 117418, ul.
Krasikova, 32, Russia

Vyachaslav Danilin
Professor of Economics
Central Economics and
  Mathematics Institute
Russian Academy of Sciences
Moscow, 117418, ul.
Krasikova, 32, Russia

Cliff J. Huang
Professor of Economics
Vanderbilt University
Nashville, TN 37235 USA

George B. Kleiner
Professor of Economics
Central Economics and
  Mathematics Institute
Russian Academy of Sciences
Moscow, 117418, ul.
Krasikova, 32, Russia

Joseph M. Nowakowski
Assistant Professor of
  Economics
Department of Economics
Muskingum College
New Concord, OH 43762
USA

Ralph W. Pfouts
Emeritus Professor of
  Economics
Department of Economics
CB# 3305, Gardner Hall
University of North Carolina
Chapel Hill, NC 27599-3305
USA

A.B. Pomansky
Professor of Economics
Department of Finance Analysis
National Credit Bank
Moscow, Russia

Steven S. Rosefielde
Professor of Economics
CB# 3305, Gardner Hall
University of North Carolina
Chapel Hill, NC 27599-3305
USA

G. Yu. Trofimov
Senior Researcher
Central Economics and
  Mathematics Institute
Russian Academy of Sciences
Moscow, 117418, ul.
Krasikova, 32, Russia

Robert S. Whitesell
Assistant Professor
Department of Economics
University of Redlands
Redlands, CA 92373
USA

Preface

This volume is the outgrowth of a long term research project begun in the late seventies funded variously by the National Academy of Sciences, the National Science Foundation and the International Research Exchange Board, which sought to assess the comparative production potential and efficiency of the Soviet socialist economy and its western market rivals using stochastic production frontiers and other methods. The initial results cast Soviet performance in a favorable light until new data acquired after the fall of communism made it clear why the original findings were mistaken.

The new information suggests that Soviet economic performance, efficiency and production potential were far poorer than previously thought and that the causes of these deficiencies persist despite significant changes in the post-Soviet economic system, constraining Russia's economic recovery potential. Although post-Soviet capitalism, vitalized by foreign assistance could still propel rapid modernization, a deeper appreciation of Russia's profound misdevelopment, and lingering communist legacy suggests that the path to free enterprise, whether along Anglo-American, European social democratic or Japanese corporatist lines is likely to be challenging.

The volume is divided into three parts. Part I elaborates the fundamentals of contemporary production function based efficiency theory as they bear on the assessment and measurement of Russia's economic recovery potential, including procedures for investment decisionmaking during the transition period. Part II presents econometric case studies using a variety of techniques, especially stochastic production frontier analysis, quantifying the efficiency and production potential of Russia and the Soviet Union from different perspectives. The performance of enterprises, sectors and the nation are studied statically, intertemporally and intersystematically at various stages of production, in a multiproduct context, sectorally and in the aggregate to assess open and concealed inefficiencies, and occasional sources of strength.

Part III utilizes these materials to appraise Russia's economic prospects taking account of the obsolescence and infungibility of embodied technologies, efficiency potential, and the legacy of socialist policies like egalitarianism. It demonstrates that Russia is beginning its renewed historical quest for economic modernization in the upper tail of the fourth tier of the global development hierarchy, below Thailand, and that its near term economic recovery potential is slight compared with the old benchmarks which placed it in the first tier. It is hoped that this finding, and the other technical aspects of the study will contribute to the development of improved ways of expediting Russia's transition, recovery and modernization.

Research Summary

From the outset of the Bolshevik revolution when Lenin nationalized the means of production and abolished free enterprise, comparative economic efficiency has been a central focus of Soviet, and now Russian studies. The direst predictions of Ludwig von Mises, Frederick Hayek and Lionel Robbins who thought that the extreme inefficiency of planned chaos would swiftly destroy the Soviet economy, as well as the utopian forecasts of those who saw the future and were sure it worked were gradually dispelled by the USSR's mixed accomplishments, but a consistent assessment of socialism's comparative merit proved more illusive. Casual observers relying on market theory, or political inclination were not shy about taking strong stands, but matters were more complicated for specialists who somehow had to balance statistical and planning theoretic claims against visible realities. The consensus which developed conceded that the command economy was an effective engine for rapidly industrializing and catching up with the west initially, but not over the longer term as microeconomic inefficiencies sapped its vitality. Although few forecast the Soviet Union's imminent collapse, most specialists believed that comparative socialist economic performance had plateaued, and was glacially eroding despite advances in planning and market oriented reforms because of socialism's inherently inferior efficiency characteristics.

The theoretical and econometric research elaborated in this volume corroborate the widely held surmise that Soviet efficiency had been sufficiently high to ensure its survival in the absence of political discord, even though the command economy was better suited to extensive than intensive development. But, it qualifies the consensus by showing that Soviet economic performance was poorer than previously supposed, and has bequeathed Russia with an infungible capital stock which complicates the twin tasks of transition and industrial modernization. The evidence suggests that Russia's comparative size is much smaller than past purchasing power parity estimates indicate and that it is unrealistic to expect rapid convergence to the European standard of living even if the economy soon recovers to its pre-depression level.

This view is consistent with the widely accepted premise in the international community that competitive markets are superior to controlled economies, but conflicts with the surprisingly optimistic judgment voiced by many official agencies assisting Russia's transition that the attainment of European consumption norms will be largely accomplished by the year 2000 when post-Soviet economic recovery is complete. Part of this divergence of course reflects the imperatives of managing global relations with Russia, but as this volume makes plain it is also the consequence of prior measurement error. The essentials are illustrated with the aid of a few summary statistics presented in Table S1. The first panel displays CIA purchasing power parity estimates for 1989; the second Goskomstat's purchasing power parities for 1995; and the third estimates calculated at Russia's 1994 exchange rate before the government managed 40 percent appreciation of 1995. The disparity between the first and the third is large: 4.6:1, and by construction is unaffected by the 50 percent decline in Russia's GDP from 1989 through the first quarter of 1995 calculated by the United Nations, or any other alternative including the smaller contraction recomputed by a team of Goskomstat-World Bank specialists (Rossiiskaia Federatsiia, 1995). A further 9 percent contraction ensued through the fourth quarter of 1996. On the CIA's reckoning Russia was the second largest economy in the world in 1989, ahead of Japan, Germany (west only) and France with GDPs respectively of 2,309, 2,044.2, 1,143.5 and 993.7 billion dollars expressed in 1991 prices (CIA, 1992), with a per capita income of $15,631 placing it in the top tier of the world's development hierarchy (Table 12.2). These statistics cast the performance of the Soviet economic system in a favorable light, given Russia's frequently noted historical backwardness, and acknowledged systemic deficiencies. Somehow, despite these obstacles, Russia seems to have caught up to its rivals achieving a per capital GNP just below the European community average in 1989. Based on this experience, it appears plausible to infer that once the macroeconomic dislocations associated with transition are behind her, even though GDP per capita in 1995 based on the old parities is in the third development tier, Russia should be able to quickly recover its pre-crisis global standing, and converge to the U.S. norm as marketization enhances efficiency (cf. Bulatov, 1995).

The alternative estimates paint a drastically different picture. They indicate that the deficiencies of administrative command planning kept Russia from rising out of the lower tail of the third development tier despite decades of mass investment, and that hyperdepression has consigned it to the fourth tier. The theoretical and empirical analysis of Soviet economic efficiency undertaken in this volume support this revised assessment of past attainments and suggest that Russia's modernization will be more arduous than some optimistic recovery forecasts imply. Systemic issues aside, the heart of the problem appears to repose in Russia's warped technological base, which is not only obsolete, but infungible. If this diagnosis is correct, Russia cannot salvage much of its capital stock for the production of globally competitive manufactures, and will be forced to comprehensively recapitalize (cf. Ericson, 1994, 1996). From the long term perspective Hayek's predictions about socialist inefficiency seem closer to the mark than his critics. Although the Soviet Union survived longer than anticipated it underperformed capitalism even during Stalin's forced industrialization (Harrison, 1994), but has left Russia with a poisoned legacy that is proving difficult to overcome.[1]

Bibliography

Åslund, Anders, *How Russia Became a Market Economy*, Washington, D.C.: Brookings Institute, 1995.

Åslund, Anders, Peter Boone, and Simon Johnson, "How to Stabilize: Lessons from Post-Communist Countries", paper prepared for the Brookings Panel on Economic Activity, March 28-29, 1996.

Bulatov, A.S., *Ekonomika vneshnykh sviazei Rossii*, Beck, Moscow, 1995.

CIA, *Handbook of International Economic Statistics*, CPAS 92-10005, September 1992.

Ekonomicheskii Monitoring Rossii: global'nye tendentsii i kon"iunktura v otrasliakh promyshlennosti, Bulletin 7, first half 1996, Institut Narodnokhoziaistvennovo Prognozirovaniia RAN (Russian Academy of Sciences), Moscow, April 1996.

---

[1]As of the summer of 1997 there is mixed evidence that Russia's GDP may have finally bottomed out after eight years of continuous decline. President Yeltsin is forecasting a sustained recovery, but many sober specialists still believe that it will take decades for Russia to attain the living standards currently enjoyed in the developed west.

Ericson, Richard, "Cost Trade-Offs in Activity Shutdowns: A Note on Economic Restructuring During Transition", in R. Campbell and A. Brzeski, ed., *Issues in the Transformation of Centrally Planned Economies*, Bloomington, IN: Indiana University Press, 1994, pp. 195-217.

_____, "Note on the Input-Output Tables of Centrally Planned Economies", preprocessed, March 1996.

Harrison, Mark, "National Income" in R.W. Davies, Mark Harrison and S.G. Wheatcroft, *The Transformation of the Soviet Union* 1913-1945, Cambridge, MA: Cambridge University Press, 1994.

OECD, *The Russian Federation 1995*, OECD Economic Surveys, November 1995.

Russian Economic Trends 1995, Vol. 4, No. 4, Russian European Center for Economic Policy, Whurr Publishers, 1995.

Rossiiskaia Federatsiia: Doklad o natsional'nykh schetakh, Goskomstat and World Bank, Moscow, October 1995.

_____, "The Russian Economy-Stabilization at Last?", *Transition*, 6, 5-6, May-June 1995b.

Table S1   Changed Perceptions of Russia's Production Potential (Billions of 1991 Dollars)

	1989	1995
I. CIA		
GNP	2,309	1,154.5
Percent of U.S.	40.8	17.9
GNP per Capita	15,631	7,722
Percent of U.S.	68	31.5
II. PURCHASING POWER PARITY (1995)		
GNP	1,402	701
Percent of U.S.	24.8	10.9
GNP per Capita	9,491	4,689
Percent of U.S.	41.3	19.1
III. EXCHANGE RATE		
GNP	500	250
Percent of U.S.	8.8	3.9
GNP per Capita	3,388	1,672
Percent of U.S.	14.7	6.8

SOURCES: CIA, *Handbook of International Economic Statistics*, CPAS92-10005, September 1992, Tables 7 and 21, pp. 25 and 39. "The Russian Economy-Stabilization at Last?", *Transition*, World Bank, Vol. 6, No. 5-6, May-June, 1995, p. 20. *Russian Economic Trends 1995*, 1996, Table A1, p. 112 and Table 27, p. 35. *Economic Survey of Europe in 1993-1994*, Economic Commission for Europe, United Nations, New York and Geneva, 1994, Table 2.2.1, p. 33. *Economic Survey of Europe in 1994-1995*, Economic Commission for Europe, United Nations, new York and Geneva, 1995, Table 3.1.1, p. 70. *Survey of Current Business*, U.S. Department of Commerce, Vol. 75, No. 5, May 1995, Table 7.1, p. 23. *Survey of Current Business*, Vol. 74, No. 8, August 1994, Table 7.1, p. 32.

METHOD:

CIA

GNP: The CIA reported its geometric mean estimate of Soviet GNP in 1989 valued in 1991 prices at approximately .50 which converts to a dollar estimate of about 67 percent. The dollar figure is .67 (5,659.3) = 3,791.7 dollars. Russia's ruble share of Soviet GNP was .609, implying a dollar value of 0.609 (3,791.7) = 2,309 billion dollars in 1991 prices.

According to the figures published in the *Economic Survey of Europe in 1993-1994*; *Economic Survey of Europe in 1994-1995*, and "The Russian Economy-Stabilization at Last?", Russia's GNP fell precisely 50 percent from 1989 through the first quarter of 1995. Russia GDP in 1995 can be estimated at 0.5 (2,309) = 1,154.5 billion dollars. Cf. *Rossiiskaia Federatsiia: Doklad o natsional'nykh schetakh*, Goskomstat and World Bank, Moscow, October 1995.

The American GNP (GDP) in 1989 and 1995 valued in 1991 prices were respectively 5,659.3 and 6,432.9 billion dollars. The percent of U.S. entries were calculated with these figures.

GNP per Capita: Population statistics derived for Russia are taken and estimated from CIA data for 1989 and after. The American figure is from the same source for 1989 and the *Survey of Current Business* for 1995. The 1989 figure is 22,982; for 1995 it is 24,514.

GOSKOMSTAT: Russia's GDP in 1995 was 1,655,000 billion rubles. The average monthly purchasing power parity exchange rate was 2,224 rubles per dollar. The dollar value of the GDP therefore was 744 billion in 1995 prices and 701 in 1991 prices. The corresponding capita figure in 1991 prices is 4,689. The 1989 GNP by construction is double the 1995 estimate, and per capita GNP is 9,491 adjusted for the intervening population growth (the population in 1989 was 147.6 million, in 1995 149.5 million).

EXCHANGE RATE: Russian GDP in 1995 was 96 percent of 1994 (586,580 billion rubles). The exchange rate for 1994 was 2,250, before the government began intervening in the Spring of 1995. The dollar GDP is 266 billion dollars, in 1994 prices and 250 billion adjusted for comparability to 1991 prices. The 1989 figure is double this by construction.

N.B.: The GNP decline 1989-1995 reported in *Russian Economic Trends, 1995* is 39 percent in line with the revisions detailed in *Rossiiskaia Federatsiia: Doklad o natsional'nykh schetakh*, Goskomstat, October 1995, Tables 1-3, pp. xx-xxi. If the revised figure is substituted for the 50 percent contraction previously reported, the comparative size of the 1989 GNP is further *diminished*.

Table S2 **European Transition Countries: Economic Activity, 1991-95 (Percentage Change over Same Period of Preceding Year)**

	NMP or GDP[a]					Gross Industrial Output			1994				
	1991	1992	1993	1994	1995 Forecast	1991	1992	1993	Jan.-March	Jan.-June	Jan.-Sept	Jan.-Dec	1995 Forecast
Albania	-27.7	-9.7	11.0	7.4[b]*	6	-41.9	-30.1	2.5	-28.3	-20.2	-21.8	-18.6	2
Bulgaria	-11.7	-5.7	-1.5	0.2	2.0-2.2	-22.2	-15.9	-10.0	-3.4	-2.8	1.1	2.0	..
Bosnia-Herzegovina						-16.2							
Croatia	-20.9	-9.7	-3.7	0.8	4	-28.5[c]	-14.6	-5.9	-8.0	-6.4	-4.5	-2.7	2
Czech Republic	-14.2	-6.4	-0.9	2.6*	3.7	-24.4	-7.9	-5.3	-0.6	0.8	2.0	2.3	..
Hungary	-11.9	-4.3	-2.3	2.0	0-1	-19.1	-9.8	3.9	9.0	7.6	8.7	9.1	4.6
Poland	-7.0	2.6	3.8	5	5	-11.9	3.9	7.3	10.8	10.2	12.7	13.0	..
Romania	-12.9	-8.2	1.3	3.5	4.2	-22.8	-21.9	1.3	-1.4	-0.9	2.1	3.3	..
Slovakia	-11.2	-7.0	-3.2	4.8	4-5.5	-17.6	-14.1	-10.6	2.3	4.5	6.0	6.4	..
Slovenia	-8.1	-5.4	1.3	5.0	5.0	-12.4	-13.2	-2.8	3.4	7.4	7.5	6.4*	5.5
The FYR of Macedonia[d]	-12.1	-13.4	-14.1	-7.2	0.8	-17.2	-15.8	-14.6	-15.7	-13.8	-11.1	-9.0	0.7
Yugoslavia	-11.2	-26.2	-27.7	6.5	7.0	-17.6	-22.4	-37.4	-25.5	-14.5	-6.2	1.2	9.0
Eastern Europe	-11.5	-6.0	-1.7	3.7	4.2	-18.5	..	-3.0	0.8	2.2	4.8	6.0*	..
CETE-4	-9.5	-1.1	1.3	4.1	4.1	-16.0	..	2.4	7.3	7.3	9.3	9.6*	..
SETE-8	-13.4	-12.1	-5.9	3.2	4.4	-21.6	..	-9.6	-7.5	-4.5	-0.9	1.3	..
Armenia	-8.8	-52.3	-14.8	-2	..	-7.7	..	-10.3	-9.5	4.7	0.3	6.9	..
Azerbaijan	-0.7	-22.6	-23.1	-22	..	4.8	..	-7.0	-24.3	-25.3	-26.7	-24.8	..
Belarus	-1.2	-9.6	-9.5	-20	(-5-7)	-1.0	..	-7.4	-34.7	-31.5	-25.4	-19.3	(-6.9)
Georgia	-20.1	-40.3	-39.4	-30	..	-22.6	..	-26.6	-71.6	-49.5	-47.1	-39.7	..
Kazakhstan	-11.8	-13.0	-12.9	-25	..	-0.9	..	-14.8	-30.9	-29.4	-28.7	-28.5	..
Kyrgyzstan	-4.2	-16.4	-16.4	-26	..	-0.3	..	-25.3	-33.0	-31.8	-25.8	-24.5	..
Republic of Moldova	-18.7	-28.3	-4.8	-30	..	-11.1	..	-10	-28.0	-30.0	-31.3	-29.9	..
Russian Federation[e]	-12.8	-19.2	-12	-15	-9	-8.0	..	-14.1	-24.9	-25.8	-23.1	-20.9	-13
Russian Federation[f]	-14.3	-22.0	-13	-16									
Tajikistan	-8.4	-31.0	-17.3	-12	..	-3.6	..	-19.5	-17.3	-20.0	-25.9	-30.8	..
Turkmenistan	-4.7	35.8	10.0	..	..	4.8	..	4.0	-20.2	-33.2	-28.4	-25.0	..
Ukraine	-11.6	-13.7	-14.2	-19	..	-4.8	..	-22.4	-38.4	-36.0	-31.2	-27.7	..
Uzbekistan	-0.5	-11.1	-2.4	-4		1.5	..	-7.0	-8.4	-4.0	-0.8	1.0	..
CIS	-11.5	-17.8	-11.5	-16		-7.8	..	-12.5	-27.5	-27.6	-25.4	-23	
Estonia	-10.0	-14.2	-8.6	.8	..	-7.2	..	-26.6	-3.3	-5.5	-6.2	-7.0*	..
Latvia	-10.4	-34.9	-14.9	-2.2[b]	..	-0.7	..	-38.1	-11.1	-10.2		-7.0*	..
Lithuania	-13.1	-39.3	-27.1	-6.5[b]		-3.5	..	-34.2	-32.5	-34.1	-33.7	-27.8	
Baltic States	-11.5	-32.5	-17.5	-3.7	..	-3.4	..	-33.9	-19.3	-20.4	-19.9	-16.6	
Total Transition Economies	-11.6	-15.2	-9.4	-10.2	..	-9.0	..	-12.7	-21.0	-20.6	-17.5	-15.3	
Ex-GDR Länder	-19.2	7.8	5.8	8.9	9	-49.1	..	5.8	14.5	16.5	15.5	15*	

SOURCES: *Economic Survey of Europe in 1994-1995*, Economic Commission for Europe, United Nations, New York and Geneva, 1995; national statistical publications and statistical office communications to UN/ECE; IMF estimates for Albania; non-governmental forecasts. Aggregates for eastern Europe, the Baltic states and total transition economies are UN/ECE secretariat computations based on 1992 weights and some estimates for missing components. Forecasts for 1995 are forecasts of national conjunctural institutes.

NOTES: Aggregates are *Eastern Europe* (the 12 countries above that line), with sub-aggregates *CETE*-4 ("central European transition economies":

Czech Republic, Hungary, Poland, Slovakia) and *SETE*-8 ("south European transition economies": Albania, Bulgaria, Romania, and the 5 Yugoslav successor states); *CIS* (12 member countries of the Commonwealth of Independent States); *Baltic states* (Estonia, Latvia, Lithuania), and *total transition countries*.

---

[a]Gross domestic product unless otherwise noted.

[b]January-September only.

[c]Enterprises with 25 or more employees.

[d]Gross material product (value added of the material sphere including depreciation).

[e]Sample of physical output indicators. Since March 1993, the Ukrainian Ministry of Statistics has published two industrial output indicators: one based on deflated gross output value analogous to those shown for other CIS countries, and one based on an aggregation of physical indicators. The former shows much more moderate rates of output contraction in 1993 (8 percent for January-December), but may be affected by inadequate deflation procedures during a period of rapidly accelerating inflation. Similar alternative indicator are also computed by the Republic of Moldova and Uzbekistan.

[f]Net material product (produced).

[g]UN/ECE estimate based on preliminary indications from the Estonian Central Statistical Office, 10 March 1995; January-September GDP was .3 percent.

[h]All enterprises (-9.5 percent in enterprises with 50 or more employees, to which quarterly figures refer).

Introduction

The Russian economy today is in the trough of a hyperdepression. Its gross national product and industrial production have fallen proportionally well below the lowest levels experienced in America's Great Depression of 1929, although the exact magnitude of the catastrophe cannot be precisely fixed. This behavior stands in sharp contrast with the Soviet record, where growth was unbroken for more than three decades 1945-1989, and raises a variety of troubling questions about the economic unravelling of the Soviet Union, and Russia's economic recovery prospects.

Was Soviet economic performance as authoritatively recomputed in the west really as good as it seemed? Was its production potential, productivity and efficiency really on a par with Italy's and other countries of the developed west as often suggested, and if so why were these achievements vitiated by the introduction of markets. Does not theory teach that competitive processes enhance production potential, productivity and efficiency rather than diminishing them? Is the positive correlation between market building and hyperdepression transitory, or are there institutional and historical forces at work preventing Russia from recovering to the Soviet standard, or moving beyond it to capitalist prosperity?

This volume addresses these issues by revisiting the theories and methods used to appraise Soviet economic performance; carrying out new calculations using stochastic production frontier and other econometric techniques, and by showing how the accumulated distortions of the past have caused Russia's hyperdepression and are shaping its recovery potential. The analysis reveals that Russia's post-Soviet economic crisis is a direct result of the Soviet Union's warped production potential which could only be sustained and concealed as long as the government was prepared to serve as a purchaser of last resort. The inferiority of its products, misassortments, factor misallocation and command inefficiencies constraining production did not seem to matter while the state assured that everything produced was sold, but when enterprises were forced to fend for themselves the worthlessness of their wares, and the capital generating them was exposed.

Russia's recovery potential, it will be shown, is tied to the Soviet past. Current low levels of production which put it in the fourth tier of the international development hierarchy can be augmented by further improvements in variable factor allocation, management, entrepreneurship and macroeconomic regulation. But overcoming the operating inefficiencies of administrative command planning is unlikely to restore per capita GDP to the European community average, authoritatively thought to apply as late as 1989, due to the obsolescence of its goods and the infungibility of its embodied technologies. It should therefore be expected that Russia will remain in the ranks of less developed nations into the twenty-first century and that convergence to the western norm will depend primarily on the specifics of its systemic transformation.

A full appreciation of these concepts and conclusions requires careful consideration of the evidence. While descriptive literature abounds with aphorisms about the inferiority of Soviet goods, factor misallocation and other omnipresent inefficiencies, another more authoritative empirical literature suggests that their aggregate consequence were relatively small. The dollar value of Soviet GNP in 1989 computed by the CIA was two thirds that of America's and the postwar growth of the superpowers was remarkably similar. How can it be claimed under these circumstances that Russia's hyperdepression is a direct consequences of the failures of an administrative command planning system which succeeded nearly as well as American market capitalism?

The answer is both simple and complex. The obvious explanation, at least with respect to comparative size, is that the composite dollar/ruble ratios used to compute the dollar value of Soviet goods were not adequately adjusted for their inferior engineering and demand characteristics. The first lapse overstated input costs and hence value added; the second their competitive international worth.

The extent to which these methodological deficiencies might seriously distort Soviet accomplishments while formally acknowledged was not fully comprehended because it was claimed that product qualities were correctly matched, that Soviet data could be adjusted to reliably measure production potential, and that the characteristics of the USSR's goods validly reflected socialist preferences regardless of their worthlessness on the international market.

These nuances are investigated in chapters 1 and 2 where the relationships between capitalist and command production potentials are systemically surveyed, and the errors sustaining the assertion that adjusted ruble factor cost pricing reliably measures production potential are identified. Chapters 3-6 probe the theoretical and specificational foundations for estimating Soviet and Russian production potential and efficiency with stochastic production frontier, and other production function based techniques.

The application of these methods in chapters 7-10 verifies the hypothesis that aggregation disguised the blemishes of Soviet value statistics by disclosing the presence of severe inefficiencies at various stages of production, and in multiproduct firms which usually go unobserved. The documentation of these inefficiencies makes it clear that the relatively high degree of efficiency displayed by individual Soviet sectors and by production in the aggregate is merely a consequence of misevaluation and inappropriately narrow conceptions of potential. Although the relationship of the average firm's output to the computed frontier did not differ much at the sectoral level in the USSR and the US, the Soviet production frontier itself lay well beneath Paretian possibilities because of the efficiency constraints imposed by administrative command planning. The underproductivity of the Soviet economy, concealed by exaggerated dollar valuation in this perspective is shown to be an endemic consequence of the command mechanism, rather than being primarily attributable to historical backwardness or other obstacles beyond the Soviet leadership's control. This insight makes it possible to appreciate that Russia's hyperdepression is not merely connected to the Soviet past because GNP had been less than previously estimated, or technologies were backward, but because the inefficiencies of administrative command planning resulted in the production of goods that failed to satisfy demand, and the choice of infungible embodied technologies that make these errors partly irreversible.

Chapter 11 carries the story forward by demonstrating that a significant sample of firms in Moscow during the postcommunist transition are not profit maximizing. The precise explanation for this aberrant behavior is unclear, but the finding provides concrete evidence that Russian markets are malfunctioning, complicating recovery.

The remaining chapters elaborate the various meanings of economic recovery in a disequilibrium context, and explore Russia's options constrained as they are by the legacy of the Soviet past. Special attention is given to the obsolescence and infungibility of the residual Soviet era capital stock, the efficiency implications of socialist policies like egalitarianism, improving foreign trade efficiency, and aspects of communism's institutional legacy. This investigation is not comprehensive, but it does confirm that Russia's recovery, transition and modernization remain problematic because communism saddled it with inappropriate, inflexible embodied technologies and transmuted institutions that continue to severely impair economic efficiency.

List of Abbreviations

AFC	adjusted factor cost
BEA	American Bureau of Economic Analysis
CD	Cobb-Douglas production function
CDMP	constant disparate mobility of factor productivity
CEMP	constant equal mobility of factor productivity
CES	constant elasticity of factor substitution production function
CIA	American Central Intelligence Agency
CMP	constant mobility of factor productivity
CMS	constant marginal shares production function
CNMP	constant nonzero mobility of factory productivity
CUMP	constant unitary mobility of factor productivity
ELMC	egalitarian labor managed community
ELMF	egalitarian labor managed firm
GDP	gross domestic product
GNP	gross national product
Goskomstat	Soviet State Statistics Committee
Gossnabsbyt'	Soviet State Procurement and Distribution Agency
GPF	grand production frontier
GVO	gross value of output
H-O	Heckscher-Ohlin theory
khozraschyot	Soviet enterprise economic cost accounting
MBMW	machinebuilding and metalworking
MFP	marginal factor productivity
MITI	Japanese Ministry of International Trade and Industry
MP	marginal productivity
OLS	ordinary least squares
Roskomstat	Russian State Statistics Committee
RSFSR	Russian Soviet Federated Socialist Republic
sebestoimost'	prime cost
VES	variable elasticity of factor substitution production function

List of Abbreviations

Part I Production Potential and Efficiency: Theory and Measurement

Steven S. Rosefielde

Synopsis

Prior assessments of Russia's economic performance and recovery potential have been called into question by reestimating GNP at the prevailing market rate of exchange. It had been previously thought that Russia's per capita GNP was close to the European community average, and that recovery potential should be calibrated relative to this norm.

The essays in Part I provide a foundation for assessing whether Russia's production potential really placed it in to first tier of the world's development hierarchy in the last days of perestroika, and for evaluating the factors determining its post-Soviet efficiency and recovery potential. The first two chapters explain why administrative command planning systems would be extremely inefficient compared with the west, even though they may appear efficient with respect to internal norms, and how the erroneous association of production potential with adjusted ruble factor costing gives the misleading impression that some aspects of Soviet Russian economic performance were more reliably estimated than was the case. The remaining chapters provide a link between efficiency theory and socialist valuation on one hand, and the specificational requirements of efficiency estimation on the other. Inefficiency takes many forms, can be defined with respect to multiple optima, and is conditioned by the characteristics of prevailing technologies. The analysis of these subtleties both illuminates the difficulties of rigorously specifying the productive environment shaping Russia's economic potential, and its accurate estimation. Although, as will soon become clear, these studies do not provide an unambiguously best specification for estimating inefficiency, they do show that inefficiency of various kinds can be estimated with sufficient precision to broadly gauge the likely dimensions of Soviet comparative international performance and Russia's economic recovery potential.

1

1 Production Potential and Efficiency: Concepts, Methods and Statistics

Steven S. Rosefielde

Introduction

The terms "efficiency" and "production potential" are commonplaces in economics, but definitions often vary with the context. To avoid unnecessary confusion this chapter lays out the general concepts and explains how the definitions most pertinent to the assessment of Russian economic performance and recovery potential are related to neoclassical theory.

Concepts

Theoretical discussions of production potential and efficiency usually take generally competitive neoclassical economics as their point of departure and apply it to the analysis of specific issues such as the performance of capitalist firms. Supply potential is described by the unit's production possibilities frontier. Output is efficient if it lies on the frontier and inefficient if it lies below. Inefficiencies, where they exist, are classified either as "economic" when the mix of goods produced is wrong from a Paretian perspective, and "technical" when demand is disregarded and potential is measured in physical or price weighted terms. It is also widely understood in applied research that the data used to estimate inefficiency may not reflect best practice, causing production potential and hence inefficiency to be understated. Thus while discussions of capitalist production potential and efficiency which logically underpin any analysis of recovery potential are typically conducted in Paretian terms, estimates normally are predicated on processes and data that depart in complex ways from the neoclassical ideal. The same problem can easily generate confusion when other types of potentials involving technology choice, managerial performance and foreign trade are addressed, and can only be avoided by paying careful attention to the nature of the arguments, methods and evidence in question.

These difficulties are compounded when the units of observation are controlled economies, enterprises or other pertinent decisionmaking bodies. Markets by definition in these environments are severely constrained or supervened, invalidating the assumptions on which neoclassical efficiency theory rests. Some adjustment is obviously required, but the literature does not provide any systematic guidance. Analysts sometimes invoke the chimera of perfect planning but more plausibly have been inclined either to make ad hoc allowances, or to rely on the neoclassical standard (Bergson, 1953). As a consequence, production potential and efficiency in socialist and capitalist economies have tended to be treated identically, except insofar as the distinctive systemic shortcomings of the Soviet interenterprise and intersectoral factor allocation mechanisms are said to have constrained potential to an inferior production feasibility frontier (Bergson, 1961).

The list of systemic efficiency impediments however is easily expanded. First, state trading constrained production potential by impeding the efficient acquisition of foreign factor supplies and technologies. Second, factor prices were fixed and non-competitive, impairing intraenterprise input allocations and implying that the feasibility frontier cannot represent a second best set of equilibrium points on the contract curve in an Edgeworth-Bowley box where it is assumed that input prices normally vary with output shares.

Third, enterprise managers even under khozraschyot (self-financing requiring inputs to be purchased from the proceeds of product sales) were not able to freely minimize costs and maximize revenue, but were restricted by plan directives in the form of line item budgetary constraints, and minimum assortment targets causing inputs and outputs to be misemployed. Factors were not paid the value of their accounting marginal products and output prices were not approximately proportional to the marginal rate of transformation as required by technical efficiency (Bergson, 1953), necessarily diminishing production potential.

Fourth, the notorious deficiencies of gossnabsbyt, the state wholesale procurement and distribution system, compelled Soviet managers to hoard large intermediate input reserves and maintain expensive facilities for the internal manufacture of critical inputs (the safety factor) normally available from other suppliers. Had parts been deliverable on a "just in time" basis, and resources not diverted to ancillary activities, observed output could have been far higher. But the command system precluded these gains, constraining production below its counterpart capitalist potential.

Fifth, the more general failures of planning disrupted the smooth flow of interenterprise supply and forced managers to interrupt their normal routines to produce assigned goods on an emergency basis.

Sixth, the characteristics of Soviet goods, including the capital stock were inferior. Both were designed to produce large output volumes, without regard to demand, imparting an exaggerated impression of enterprises' ability to manufacture goods competitively marketable domestically and in the west. This deficiency has often been disregarded on the dubious grounds that Soviet characteristics reflected socialist preferences, but now that concern has shifted toward the virtues of transition this artifice is transparent.

Seventh, and last, a miscellany of factors stultified effort including egalitarianism, the under-remuneration of managers and workers, and a growing sense of despair that the system would never prosper.

These seven sources of technical inefficiency and Bergson's concept of allocative technical inefficiency can be collectively subsumed under the rubric of command constrained production potential, although, for some purposes, it may be useful to keep them distinct. The magnitudes of the losses implied individually and in the aggregate cannot be precisely calibrated, but the descriptive literature makes it clear that they were enormous, severely degrading production potential compared with the workably competitive capitalist standard.

Estimates of technical inefficiency in the Soviet Union and other controlled economies are inevitably computed with respect to all the command constraints on production potential. The magnitude of perceptible technical inefficiency will depend on the degree to which various firms underperform inferior Soviet best practice. If the deviation is small, these enterprises will appear to be relatively efficient, even though their absolute performance pales when contrasted with the workably competitive capitalist standard. Judged from this perspective, Soviet performance is indisputably poor, but the high efficiency relative to the command constrained potential also merits attention from some standpoints. For the purposes of this study it can be interpreted as an indicator of general managerial competence. If most managers are able to harness the resources at their disposal under adverse conditions to attain results near the command constrained best practice maximum, then it can plausibly be inferred that they are masters of their trade and are doing a good job. This inference is not unimpeachable because low command constrained technical inefficiency could merely mean that Soviet managers were equally incompetent, but the contributors to this volume are inclined toward the first interpretation because on-site inspections have persuaded them that the Soviets accomplished a great deal given the limits of the system.

Ideally, empirical studies should quantify each form of inefficiency identified, and sum them to create a composite picture of the sources and magnitudes of Soviet underpotential and inefficiency from a multitude of perspectives. In practice all we are really able to directly observe are deviations from command constrained best practice, and the workably competitive standard in the west, filtered through the prism of purchasing power parity. This provides a crude basis for appraising Russia's recovery potential, which should suffice for the purposes of this investigation, but the limitations of the exercise should also be borne carefully in mind when deciphering results and implications. The force of these various considerations can be conveniently summarized in tabular form. Table 1.1 lists eleven different standards of production potential. Those which are demand responsive are classified under economic efficiency or the welfare standard; those that disregard demand are categorized as technically efficient. The concept of Soviet production potential applicable in this study is the tenth command constrained variant. The eleventh entry represents observed production adjusted for managerial inefficiency, and can be notionally equated with achieved production in the Russian Soviet Federated Socialist Republic (RSFSR) in 1989.

Russia's economic recovery potential conceptually is the difference between the peak production potential achieved in 1989, adjusted downward for the deterioration of the capital stock, and the current level. This gap can be computed with respect to various product mixes. Two are especially interesting, one reflecting the standard Soviet assortment, the other a superior output bundle that might be competitive in the west. Russia's economic recovery potential is large with respect to the first, and small with respect to the latter. Finally Russia's production potential appraised with both product mixes can be compared with the workably competitive standard described in Table 1.1, entry 4. It turns out to be small on either measure (Table S1).

Valuation

The statistics used to measure efficiency in the empirical chapters of this volume use price weights to value outputs and inputs whenever more than one product or factor is involved. Ruble or dollar prices are utilized as weights depending on the problem under consideration. In the first instance as is widely understood, turnover (sales) taxes and subsidies could seriously distort the weightings, but this is seldom the case here because the firms and industrial sectors studied are valued at enterprise or industrial wholesale prices before the turnover taxes applied at retail. Subsidies likewise are comparatively slight.

Dollar prices may be biased to the extent purchasing power parity ratios misindicate characteristic values among products, or between supposedly identical goods when observations are cross nationally pooled. The appropriate remedy for the latter distortion is to be sure that characteristics are properly matched, but the attainment of this goal is often problematic.

In the past it was also important to point out that in principle dollar prices reflected both the marginal rate of American transformation and substitution as well as correctly measuring purchasing power parity. This is still so, but the inability of the Russians to sell their manufactures after communist trade barriers were dismantled suggests that qualitative differences between systems were greater than previously conceded for purposes of international comparison. The neoclassical implications of dollar weighted values used to compute productive efficiency therefore must be interpreted accordingly.

The situation regarding ruble values is less satisfactory. Although it is generally recognized that established ruble prices fixed by the Soviet State Price Committee on Marxian labor value criteria reflected neither consumer demand nor marginal socialist factor cost, specialists long contended that the appropriate adjustment protocol could make them approximately proportional to the marginal rate of transformation on a production feasibility frontier given input price fixing. It will be shown in chapter 2 however that assortment constraints and restrictions on enterprise input normally prevent managers from combining inputs and transforming products as required by the efficiency ideal postulated in adjusted factor costing both with respect to established and adjusted ruble prices. This means that even though the efficiency measures computed in this volume are not broadly distorted by turnover taxes and subsidies, they still do not have the ideal characteristics traditionally missupposed in the discipline, and could not attain them through the imputation of competitive interest charges and land rents. The command constraints that diminish Russian/Soviet productivity, unfortunately also obscure assessment of efficiency potential.

Table 1.1   **Standards of Production Potential and Efficiency**

Welfare Standard	Technical Efficiency
1. Universal Long Run Economic Efficiency: All nations use global best practice technologies, allocating factors optimally intra-firm, nationally and internationally in accordance with competitive consumer demand, resulting in global Pareto optimality and zero excess profits.	5. Universal Long Run Technical Efficiency: Same as 1. without consumer welfare equilibrium. Factor prices are those which should be in effect if 1 were satisfied.
2. Universal Short Run Economic Efficiency: Same as 1, but with some non-zero profits.	6. Universal Short Run Technical Efficiency: Same as 5, but with some non-zero profits.
3. National Long Run Economic Efficiency: Same as 1, but with some international factor and technological immobilities, and profits associated therewith.	7. National Long Run Technical Efficiency: Same as 5, but with some international factor and technological immobilities, and profits associated therewith.
4. National Short Run Economic Efficiency: Same as 3, but with some non-zero profits.	8. National Short Run Technical Efficiency: Same as 7, but with some non-zero profits.
	9. National Short Run Bergsonian Technical Efficiency: Same as 8, but without interenterprise allocative factor efficiency.
	10. National Short Run Command Constrained Technical Efficiency: Same as 9, but with degraded productivity arising from a) inefficient foreign trade, b) factor and output price fixing, c) plan constraints on input use and product assortment, d) hoarded resources (the safety factor), e) systemic supply disruptions, f) utility insensitive design practices intended to maximize output volumes, g) undercompensation, h) egalitarianism, i) stagnant real consumption.
	11. National Short Run: The Achieved Level Same as 10, but takes account of inefficiency attributable to managerial incompetence.

Moreover, sensitivity analysis cannot rectify this conceptual problem. While it is wise to occasionally compute enterprise efficiency at alternative prices to gauge the effects of index number relativity, none of the measures calculated correspond with the constrained or unconstrained neoclassical ideals, nor can they collectively illuminate what the outcome might be if the relevant equilibrium prices were available.

Application

These complications place stringent limits on the analysis and assessment of Russia's recovery potential. Ideally, we would like to know how much output can be increased from its current level under the post-Soviet system, given the existing capital stock and other factor supplies. This potential could then be compared to various other standards like the command constrained best achieved level, western best practice, or superior fully efficient variants of both in order to gauge the accomplishment. In practice however we do not know the untested potential of the transition system, the opportunity costs of the old system, or the full potential of either administrative command planning, or western capitalism.

The best that can be accomplished under these circumstances is to use the peak achieved levels of the Soviet period variously valued as a benchmark, together with estimates of command constrained inefficiency, and fungibility to evaluate how Russia might fare if it chose two interesting alternative paths: replicating the Soviet output bundle, or supplying a product mix responsive to market demand.

This study focuses on both these possibilities, expressed in dollars to facilitate international comparison. The results allow us to appraise Russia's recovery prospects on the supposition that the impact of systemic change is strongly restricted by infungible embodied technologies and human skills. Weaker assumptions permit better outcomes.

Although, the jury is still out on this important matter, the performance of Russia's markets reported in this volume does not provide strong support for believing that the new system has substantially augmented production potential. Leontief statistics do signal some improvement in foreign trade efficiency, but econometric estimates suggest that at least some sampled firms are not profit maximizing.

Bibliography

Bergson, Abram, 1961.

_____, *Soviet National Income and Product in 1937*. New York, NY: Columbia University Press, 1953.

2 The Misspecification of Soviet Production Potential: Adjusted Factor Costing and Bergson's Efficiency Standard

Steven S. Rosefielde and Ralph W. Pfouts

Introduction

The standards, and methods for measuring Soviet economic performance, and by extension the behavior of other controlled economies are well known. They were first elaborated by Abram Bergson in the early fifties based on the general equilibrium theories and accounting practices elaborated by Paul Samuelson, Sir John Hicks and Simon Kuznets.

The principle conclusion drawn from these analytical investigations was that Soviet national income and product statistics could provide an intelligible perception of economic performance if they were consistently recalculated at adjusted factor cost, even though prices were fixed by the State Price Committee, and planned chaos superseded the market. Adjusted factor costing it was asserted made prices approximately proportional to the marginal rate of transformation for composite goods reflecting long run opportunity costs not as in the efficiency standard in each and every industry, but 'on the average in the economy generally', and hence measured production potential.[1]

It was freely acknowledged that production potential was an indicator of technical efficiency, given interenterprise and intersectoral factor misallocation, and that it did not imply consumer satisfaction. Supply in the Soviet Union was unresponsive to demand by institutional design, precluding the possibility that national product statistics could reflect economic efficiency in the Paretian sense applicable in competitive market economies. This did not rule out the possibility that established, or even adjusted factor prices might reflect planners' marginal rates of substitution, but no one conversant with the mechanics for Soviet price formation could take a proposition of this sort seriously.

Despite the lucidity of this neoclassical concept, the production potential standard was clearly a second best because it bore no coherent relationship to value. Even if production were technically efficient as Bergson's theory assumed nothing assured that the outputs produced were "goods" instead of "bads", or worthless things. Nor could it be persuasively argued that there was some sort of equivalence between adjusted factor costing and competitive value added because factor prices were set administratively by the state. All that really could be inferred was the comparative size of two or more technically efficient, adjusted factor cost weighted bundles of goods, as distinct from these same goods weighted with established ruble prices. From time to time comparisons were made in dollars, but they were deemed to be unreliable indicators of Soviet production potential and consumer preferences.

This chapter examines the limitations of the Bergsonian concept of production potential for composite goods and inputs as a standard for evaluating Russia's economic recovery potential. It will be shown that the concept has to be modified because adjusted factor costing cannot reliably generate approximate estimates of technical efficiency as has long been wrongly maintained, and that the imputation of interest changes and land rents does not enhance the accuracy of efficiency estimates from a neoclassical standpoint. The deficiencies of ruble prices in the Soviet context constitute an insuperable barrier to measuring competitive production potential, even on average for the economy at large in the long run.[2] Production potential can still be calculated, but it is necessarily clouded by all the arbitrary constraints of administrative command planning which not only allocate factors inefficiently, but force firms onto lower production feasibility frontiers because directives prevent managers from using their inputs optimally at prevailing factor prices. Command constrained production potential should be computed at enterprise ruble wholesale prices net of retail turnover taxes and subsidies in accordance with adjusted factor costing practice because these prices determine the choices of bonus maximizing managers, but further adjustments for imputed interest (in lieu of profits), and land rents are unwarranted because they misindicate prevailing opportunity costs.

Soviet Command Constrained Production Potential

The twin assertions that Soviet production potential cannot be reliably approximately estimated in a strict neoclassical sense by revaluing national product at adjusted factor cost, and consequently that all ruble measures merely provide clouded impressions of command constrained technical efficiency can be formally evaluated by analyzing whether the ratio of adjusted average factor cost prices can reliably and approximately equal the negative of the producer's marginal rate of transformation under Soviet conditions.[3] According to Bergson, if we let p_i denote the established price of good i and p_i^* the adjusted factor cost price of the same good then

$$\frac{p_j^*}{p_i^*} = - \frac{\partial x_i}{\partial x_j}. \tag{2.1}$$

Parenthetically it may be noted that the notation above for the marginal rate of transformation is used to denote both the firm and the economy. We have not distinguished the two believing that the meaning is clear.[4]

The implications of (2.1), even in the soft, approximative terms in which it is cast, we will argue cannot be correct except under circumstances so special that they are irrelevant for all practical purposes. Hence we will contend that Bergson has no grounds for claiming that adjusted factor costing for subsidies, turnover taxes and profits captures opportunity costs. Also observe that the same kind of problem arises in post-communist economies where production is constrained, p_i, the observed transition price is formed from disequilibrium factor prices and differs significantly from p_i^*, due to turnover taxes (pseudo value added taxes) and inadequate capital charges.

The case for asserting that there is more than a mere hypothetical and/or accidental correspondence between relative adjusted factor cost prices and the marginal rate of transformation in an administratively controlled economy requires that production be responsive to prices either through bonus incentive optimization or optimal plan directives because the marginal rate of transformation is an engineering datum that is unobservable in official Soviet statistics and cannot be reconstructed *a priori* from neoclassical factor cost theory. If production is not responsive to prices at the managerial or planning levels then no mechanism exists to reliably connect prices, official, adjusted or otherwise with the marginal rate of transformation.[5] Soviet firms it could be argued may have satisfied this requirement because plans were "computopic", but this is confuted by the literature.   More plausibly Soviet managers like their capitalist twins may have served this function because bonuses were related to profits (or revenues), and maximizing involved price taking.[6]   The prices that serve as data to the managers however were the established prices not the adjusted prices. They had no knowledge of the prices adjusted according to the Bergson procedure. To the extent firms profit maximized the correct relation requires that the unstarred prices replace the starred prices in (2.1). If the firms were not profit maximizers no form of (2.1) will hold.

For later reference we also note that in a price taking, profit maximizing model the following equilibrium conditions hold

$$p_j \, \frac{\partial x_j}{\partial v_{jk}} = w_k, \quad \forall_{j=1,k=1}^{m \quad n} \tag{2.2}$$

Here the derivative is the marginal product of good j generated by a small increase of factor k including variable capital used in producing j and w_k is the price of factor k. These equations make it possible to write[7]

$$\frac{p_j}{p_i} = \frac{\dfrac{\partial x_i}{\partial v_{ik}}}{\dfrac{\partial x_j}{\partial v_{jk}}} = -\frac{\partial x_i}{\partial x_j} \tag{2.3}$$

It is clear that (2.3) is the condition that prevailed simply because the p's represent the price that firms actually used. It is equally clear that (2.1), which is the condition necessary to Bergson's contentions, is quite different from (2.3).

We will now argue that Soviet firms labored under constraints that forced them into a second best position and made it impossible for (2.3) to be fulfilled by either the established prices or the prices adjusted by Bergson's procedure.

To facilitate exposition we focus on the case of a multi-product firm in which the product mix is determined by bonuses paid for profit maximizing. This criterion has been chosen because it implies behavior that is most likely to equate prices to the marginal rate of transformation. If (2.1) is not satisfied with bonuses determined by profit maximizing, it will be violated even more by the substitution of other criteria such as quantity maximizing because prices will not determine assortments (Rosefielde and Pfouts, 1988). Assume further that the production functions expressed in conventional notation are strictly concave, or in the linear homogeneous case quasi concave

$$x_j = f_j\left(v_{j1}, v_{j2}, \ldots, v_{jn}\right). \quad \forall_{j=1}^m \tag{2.4}$$

In addition there is an overall budget constraint equal to the receipts from sales by the firms in the last operating period plus a limited amount of credit which shows that the total expenditure on resources must not exceed the amount of money available to the firm. This sum minus fixed capital costs,[8] is denoted by M, and the constraint takes the form

$$\sum_{k=1}^n w_k v_{jk} - M \leqq 0. \tag{2.5}$$

Finally, because of the multiproduct nature of the firm, the planning authorities can require that a particular assortment of products be produced. If they require that a minimum amount of each product be produced, then the profit maximizing Lagrangian is

$$L = \sum_{j=1}^m p_j x_j - \sum_{j=1}^m \sum_{k=1}^n w_k v_{jk} - \sum_{j=1}^m \lambda_j \left(\overline{x}_j - f_j\left(v_{j1}, \ldots, v_{jn}\right)\right)$$

$$\tag{2.6}$$

$$- \theta\left(\sum_{j=1}^m \sum_{k=1}^n w_k v_{jk} - M\right)$$

The assortment constraints show $\overline{x}_j$ as the minimum amount required and thus can be written as

$$\overline{x}_j - f_j \left(v_{j1}, \ldots, v_{jn}\right) \leqq 0. \quad \forall_{j=1}^m$$

The Kuhn-Tucker conditions are

$$\frac{\partial L}{\partial v_{jk}} = p_j \frac{\partial f_j}{\partial v_{jk}} - w_k + \lambda_j \frac{\partial f_j}{\partial v_{jk}} - \theta w_k \leqq 0, \quad \forall_{j=1,k=1}^{mn} \tag{2.7}$$

$$\frac{\partial L}{\partial \lambda_j} f_j \left(v_{j1}, \ldots, v_{jn}\right) - \overline{x}_j \geqq 0, \quad \forall_{j=1}^m,$$

$$\frac{\partial L}{\partial \theta} = M - \sum_{j=1}^m \sum_{k=1}^n w_k v_{jk} \geqq 0.$$

An assortment constraint is binding if the quantity of the product produced by unconstrained profit maximizing is less than the amount required in the assortment. In this case (2.7) can be shown as

$$\left(p_j + \lambda_j\right) \frac{\partial f_j}{\partial v_{jk}} = (1 + \theta) w_k, \quad \forall_{kj} \tag{2.7a}$$

These results show that managers in multiproduct firms will acquire and allocate factors to best internal use, among all product lines, given the assortment constraints imposed by the planning authorities. The equilibrium requirement (2.7a) which conditions the volume of production for each good differs from the Pareto condition since it clearly is not the equivalent of (2.2), and shows that established factor prices do not accurately measure equilibrium marginal factor cost.

The marginal rate of transformation will not equal the negative of the ratio of adjusted factor cost prices due to the impact of the dual variables λ_j. Forming the ratio of the efficiency conditions for the production of any two goods yields

$$\frac{\left(p_j + \lambda_j\right)}{\left(p_i + \lambda_i\right)} = \frac{\dfrac{\partial f_i}{\partial v_{ik}}}{\dfrac{\partial f_j}{\partial v_{jk}}}. \tag{2.8}$$

We cannot in general deduce (2.3) from the last equation, unless the assortment constraints are ineffective. Moreover if λ_i, $\lambda_j = 0$, and the assortment constraints are not binding then firms are producing the proper mix of goods and services required by the rules of Soviet enterprise optimization. Insofar as p_i, $p_j \neq p_i^*$, p_j^* when λ_i, $\lambda_j = 0$, this implies that another optimum might be found if the systems directors required the price authorities to set enterprise accounting prices in accordance with the nostrums of adjusted factor costing, but this is not assured because the constraints for the new assortment might be binding. Ironically, insofar as prices determine production choice without constraint in multiproduct firms it is the ratio of official enterprise wholesale prices not adjusted factor cost prices which should hold because it alone reflects the prevailing marginal rate of transformation and derivatively "production potential" on the production feasibility frontier. And of course, it goes without saying that neither official accounting prices, nor Bergson's prices adjusted for mandated profit differentials and other rents reflect competitive efficiency.

This means that average adjusted factor cost prices can only serve as unambiguous indicators of prevailing efficiency if λ_i, $\lambda_j = 0$ and $p_i = p_i^*$. If λ_i, $\lambda_j \neq 0$, then adjusted prices can only be coincidentally proportional to the marginal rate of transformation regardless of the relationship between p_i and p_i^*. It does not matter whether adjusted prices are derived from *average* or *marginal* Marxian labor cost data. If λ_i, $\lambda_j \neq 0$, no amount of theory normed accounting (as distinct from dual variables) adjustment can satisfactorily illuminate production potential (feasibility) given the realities of administrative command planning even under khozraschyot. However there is one case in which all neoclassical sensibilities can be approximately satisfied, but it only serves to highlight the restricted applicability of adjusted factor cost.

Suppose that Soviet national product is valued throughout in enterprise wholesale prices, which are relatively free of turnover taxes. Bergson's price adjustment protocol with respect to turnover taxes in this instance merely requires that final purchaser sales data be revalued in enterprise wholesale prices, before taxes.

Suppose further that profit markups above labor value prime cost (sebestoimost') fortuitously equal the imputed neoclassical capital charges required by Bergson's method, and that labor compensation is close to its competitive value added. Then if enterprise profit maximization over the relevant domain of input choice is only slightly constrained, the ratio of official enterprise wholesale prices, and adjusted factor cost prices will approximately equal the competitive marginal rate of transformation.

Moreover, if production functions are linear homogeneous, the average factor cost convention underlying both the official and the corrected prices will be consistent with marginal cost pricing, and "production potential" will correspond still more closely with competitive possibilities subject to other systemic inefficiencies.

These relationships can be shown formally by minimizing cost,

$$\hat{L} = \sum_i \sum_k w_k^* v_{ik} - \sum_i \alpha_i \left(f_i \left(v_{ij}, \ldots, v_{in} \right) - \bar{x} \right)$$

$$(2.9)$$

$$- \beta \left(\sum_i \sum_k w_k^* v_{ik} - M \right),$$

where w_r^* are the near competitive equilibrium adjusted factor cost prices assumed above. The Kuhn-Tucker theorem yields

$$\frac{\partial \hat{L}}{\partial v_{jr}} = w_r^* - \alpha_j \frac{\partial f_j}{\partial v_{jr}} - \beta w_r^* \gtreqless 0, \quad \forall_{j=1,r=1}^{m \quad n}$$

$$(2.10)$$

$$\frac{\partial \hat{L}}{\partial \alpha_j} = \bar{x}_j - f_j \left(v_{j1}, \ldots, v_{jn} \right), \lesseqgtr 0$$

$$\frac{\partial \hat{L}}{\partial \beta} = M - \sum_i \sum_k w_k^* v_{rk} \lesseqgtr 0.$$

From (2.10) we have

$$\frac{\alpha_i}{\alpha_j} = \frac{\dfrac{\partial f_j}{\partial v_{jr}}}{\dfrac{\partial f_i}{\partial v_{ir}}} = - \frac{\partial x_j}{\partial x_i}.$$

$$(2.11)$$

It is widely understood that α_i, as used in (2.9), represents the marginal cost of good i.

If production functions are homogeneous of degree one marginal and average factor costs will be the same. To see this multiply (2.10) by $\dfrac{\overline{v}_{jr}}{x_j}$ and sum on r. The superior bars indicate optimum values. This yields

$$\sum_r w_r^* \frac{\overline{v}_{jr}}{x_j} - \alpha_j \sum_r \frac{\partial f_j}{\partial v_{jr}} \frac{\overline{v}_{jr}}{x_j} - \beta \sum_r w_r^* \frac{\overline{v}_{jr}}{x_j} = 0, \qquad (2.12)$$

assuming that each factor is used. Now since

$$p_j^* = \sum_r w_r^* \frac{\overline{v}_{jr}}{x_j},$$

we obtain from (2.12) by virtue of Euler's theorem on homogeneous functions

$$p_j^* (1 - \beta) - \alpha_j = 0.$$

Thus using (2.11) and the last equation it is possible to write

$$\frac{p_j^*}{p_i^*} = \frac{\alpha_j}{\alpha_i} = - \frac{\partial x_i}{\partial x_j} \qquad (2.13)$$

which demonstrates that the ratio of average adjusted factor cost prices could approximately equal the ratio of marginal costs and the technically efficient marginal rate of transformation so long as factor supplies are not significantly restricted in different activities, and Bergson's accounting cost adjustments accurately estimate official average costs before turnover taxes and subsidies.

Clearly the importance of this result depends on a) the assumption that line item budgetary constraints on inputs excluded from (2.9) are non binding; b) the number of firms in the Soviet Union and its post-Soviet successor states that have homogeneous production functions of degree one; c) the correspondence between official profit markups, Bergson's capital imputations and the marginal cost of capital necessitated by the production function; d) the appropriateness of labor compensation, and consequently the extent to which the ratios of computed average adjusted factor cost prices happen to approximate the ratios of marginal cost. The likelihood that these conditions will be satisfied to any meaningful degree is negligible on institutional and engineering grounds, and because imputed capital charges often deviate markedly from accounting profits.[9]

Ruble and Adjusted Ruble Factor Cost

The preceding analysis makes it clear that Soviet command constrained production potential should be computed with the prices managers employ to determine product assortment and input use because they will approximately coincide with opportunity costs whenever constraints are weak or non-binding. This means in the Soviet context that researchers should use enterprise wholesale ruble prices before turnover taxes and subsidies levied at the wholesale and retail levels whenever possible. These prices are usually referred to as ruble factor cost prices, and are distinguished from adjusted ruble "enterprise wholesale" factor cost prices because the latter use imputed interest charges in lieu of enterprise profits, and sometimes include imputed land rents. Our investigation has demonstrated that these adjustments are counterindicated because they are arbitrary, have no bearing on managerial decisionmaking, and do not reflect relative marginal productivities for the economy at large in the long run. The factor cost standard implies that inputs are compensated in accordance with the value of their short run marginal products, otherwise as is in fact the case, the distinction between factor cost and arbitrary nonfactor payments loses its cogency.[10]

The quantitative consequence of computing production potential at ruble factor cost instead of the previously preferred valuation at adjusted ruble factor cost could be significant in specific cases, but the CIA growth estimates presented in Table 2.1 reveal that it is apt to be remarkably small. This of course does not mean that ruble factor price calculations somehow closely approximate opportunity costs in the technical efficiency sense defined by Bergson. It merely shows that measurements of command constrained inefficiency may be insensitive to various alternative sets of disequilibrium price weights.[11]

Composite Goods

The validity of the modeling and mathematical analysis elaborated above has been accepted by Bergson, without conceding the inference that adjusted factor costing fails to measure prevailing Soviet efficiency because among other things it is contended that AFC reflects the opportunity costs of composite goods in the economy on average, even though prices are not proportional to marginal productivities in each and every industry.

We accept the distinction. Although Bergson's average efficiency standard degrades economywide productivity because factors by assumption are intra and interindustrially misallocated, it does not preclude uniform adjusted factor cost prices from conforming with average (composite) relative marginal productivities on a lower production feasibility frontier. But how does Bergson know that the intra-firm, intra-industrial and interindustrial disproportionalities between uniform adjusted factor cost prices and marginal rates of transformation he acknowledges, average out so that they are proportional to the uniform composite good adjusted factor cost prices he computes? He does not. There are no theoretical principles pointing to his conclusion. If the command economy misallocates factors within firms, across firms in individual industries and intersectorally from the standpoint of the Pareto rule, what mechanism causes them to be "efficiently" employed in the aggregate? There is no mathematical connection between adjusted factor cost price setting and "averaged inefficiencies" however computed, and therefore there is no basis for supposing anything about their proportionalities. This does not preclude the discovery of such regularities, but no one including Bergson has ever undertaken the requisite quantitative computations to substantiate his intuition.

Bergson's "efficiency" hypothesis thus stands or falls solely on the intuition that "averaged micro-inefficiency" somehow serviceably approximates "composite efficiency", rather than on the properties of the unspecified "average" which might make uniform adjusted factor cost composite good prices proportional to the unobserved marginal rate of transformation.

It is not the averaging which is important, but the marginal rates of enterprise product transformation and their relationship to prices that count in determining the composite good average marginal rate of transformation and their relationship to adjusted factor composite good prices. Bergson's assertion that the composite good rate of transformation is proportional to uniform adjusted factor cost prices thus can only be known to be true on theoretical grounds (absent comprehensive empirical verification) if the Pareto conditions are satisfied because this is the only instance in which the relationship between industrial and aggregate marginal productivities is clearly defined.[12]

To demonstrate this relationship, let

$$x_k = f_k\left(v_{1k}, \ldots, v_{nk}\right), \quad k = 1, \ldots, m$$

be the production functions of m firms (industries) and let

$$f_{ki} = \frac{\partial x_k}{\partial v_{ik}} > 0. \qquad \begin{array}{l} \forall_n^m \\ k=1 \cdot \\ i=1 \end{array}$$

Bergson claims that "on the average" the adjusted factor price ratio equals the ratio of marginal products or that

$$\frac{\sum_k w_k \dfrac{f_{ki}}{f_{kj}}}{\sum_k w_k} = \frac{\zeta_i}{\zeta_j}, \tag{2.14}$$

where the ζ are adjusted factor prices and w_k is the weight for enterprise or industry k used in averaging. The w's are all positive and may all be equal to unity.

If (2.14) holds, since the choice of numerator and denominator on the right side is arbitrary, we can write

$$\frac{\sum_k w_k \dfrac{f_{kj}}{f_{ki}}}{\sum_k w_k} = \frac{\zeta_j}{\zeta_i}.$$

Consequently we can write

$$\frac{\sum_k w_k \dfrac{f_{ki}}{f_{kj}}}{\sum_k w_k} = \frac{\sum_k w_k}{\sum_k w_k \dfrac{f_{kj}}{f_{ki}}}$$

or

$$\sum_k w_k \frac{f_{ki}}{f_{kj}} \sum_k w_k \frac{f_{kj}}{f_{ki}} = \left(\sum_k w_k\right)^2.$$

There are m^2 terms on each side of the last equation.

The last equation may be rewritten as

$$\sum_{k=1}^{m} w_k^2 + \sum_{r=2}^{m} w_1 w_r \frac{f_{1j}}{f_{1i}} \frac{f_{ri}}{f_{rj}} + \sum_{r\neq2}^{m} w_2 w_r \frac{f_{2j}}{f_{2i}} \frac{f_{ri}}{f_{rj}} + \ldots$$

$$+ \sum_{r=1}^{m-1} w_m w_r \frac{f_{mj}}{f_{mi}} \frac{f_{ri}}{f_{rj}} = \sum_{k=1}^{m} w_k^2 + \sum_{r=2}^{m} w_1 w_r + \sum_{r\neq2}^{m} w_2 w_r + \ldots$$

$$+ \sum_{r=1}^{m-1} w_m w_r$$

Canceling and collecting terms we can rewrite the last equation as

$$\sum_{r=2}^{m} w_1 w_r \left(\frac{f_{1i}}{f_{1j}} \frac{f_{rj}}{f_{ri}} + \frac{f_{ri}}{f_{rj}} \frac{f_{1j}}{f_{1i}} - 2 \right)$$

$$+ \sum_{r=3}^{m} w_2 w_r \left(\frac{f_{2i}}{f_{2j}} \frac{f_{rj}}{f_{ri}} + \frac{f_{ri}}{f_{rj}} \frac{f_{2j}}{f_{2i}} - 2 \right) \tag{2.15}$$

$$+ \ldots + w_{m-1} w_m \left(\frac{f_{m-1,i}}{f_{m-1,j}} \frac{f_{mj}}{f_{mi}} + \frac{f_{mi}}{f_{mj}} \frac{f_{m-1,i}}{f_{m-1,i}} - 2 \right) = 0$$

It will be sufficient for the last equation to hold if the quantities in parentheses are all equal to zero. For example we may consider

$$w_s w_r \left(\frac{f_{si}}{f_{sj}} \frac{f_{rj}}{f_{ri}} + \frac{f_{ri}}{f_{rj}} \frac{f_{sj}}{f_{si}} - 2 \right) = 0$$

Dividing the last equation by $w_s w_r \dfrac{f_{ri}}{f_{rj}} \dfrac{f_{sj}}{f_{si}}$ yields

$$\left(\frac{f_{si}}{f_{sj}} \frac{f_{rj}}{f_{ri}} \right)^2 - 2 \frac{f_{si}}{f_{sj}} \frac{f_{rj}}{f_{ri}} + 1 = 0$$

or

$$\left(\frac{f_{si}}{f_{sj}} \frac{f_{rj}}{f_{ri}} - 1 \right) \left(\frac{f_{si}}{f_{sj}} \frac{f_{rj}}{f_{ri}} - 1 \right) = 0. \tag{2.16}$$

Thus $\dfrac{f_{si}}{f_{sj}} = \dfrac{f_{ri}}{f_{rj}}$ and Bergson's average rule can be satisfied only if the neoclassical conditions are satisfied. It is also clear that this result is independent of the weighing scheme used since the weights cancel in the step leading to (2.16).

It may seem that equation (2.15) could be satisfied if at least one but not all of the quantities in parentheses were negative thus opening the possibility of the terms offsetting each other. In this event the left side of (2.16), for example, would have to be negative. But this is clearly impossible.

It is obvious that $f_{si}/f_{sj} = f_{ri}/f_{rj}$ is sufficient for (2.15) to be satisfied and (2.16) shows that it is also necessary. Consequently in saying that the efficiency conditions are satisfied "on the average", Bergson also must be saying that they are satisfied for each enterprise or industry, if he desires to rest his case on anything more than unsubstantiated intuition.

It follows directly that it cannot be scientifically claimed that uniform adjusted factor prices objectively conform to their relative marginal products, if as previously shown in (Rosefielde and Pfouts, 1995) adjusted factor costs do not normally determine enterprise production, and are not proportional to shadow prices. The only escape from this conclusion is to switch grounds treating adjusted factor prices as approximately representing hypothetical relative marginal productivities as they might be if the Soviet Union were nearly competitively Pareto efficient, rather than as they actually were under planning, but such a stance we believe concedes our basic point.

Conclusion

Assessment of Soviet efficiency and production potential have tended to exaggerate real accomplishments in the past because adjusted factor costing theory misleadingly suggested that deleting turnover taxes, adding subsidies, imputing interest in lieu of profits and imputing land rents would assure accurate measurement of growth and productivity because the resulting ruble values would be proportional to opportunity costs.[13] Reconsideration of this important matter reveals that production potential should be computed at the enterprise wholesale ruble prices used by managers to determine product assortment and input utilization. Whenever value statistics are reported in industrial wholesale or retail ruble prices, turnover taxes should be deleted and subsidies added, without further adjustment for interest in lieu of profits, or land rents. This protocol is not only correct, but has the welcome benefit of saving an enormous amount of superfluous and misleading ruble factor costing adjustment.

**Table 2.1   Soviet Economic Growth by Sector of Origin
(CIA Estimates: Established Price Weights)**

Growth Rates (compound annual rates)	1960-65	1965-70	1970-75	1975-80
GNP (established prices)	5.0	5.4	4.0	2.8
GNP (factor costs)	5.0	5.3	3.7	2.7

SOURCES: CIA, *USSR: Measures of Economic Growth and Development, 1950-80*, Joint Economic Committee of Congress, Washington, D.C., December 8, 1982, Table 11, p. 41, Table A5, pp. 63-4.

Notes

1.   In a recent article commenting on our critique of adjusted factor costing Bergson explains that we misunderstood his initial intention in contending that his adjustments were designed "to make the results conform to the so called 'efficiency standard' of economic theory, and so provide observations on Russian production potential of the well known kind that theory shows can be obtained with such valuation". He points out, as we noted that he only claimed that this was approximately so. "The AFC standard might be viewed as an attempt on the average for many commodities to conform more nearly than prevailing ruble prices do to the transformation rates actually prevailing. And that I still venture to think was achieved..." He then asserts that our demonstrations do not address this issue because "under AFC the uniform factor prices conform to their relative marginal productivities, not as in the efficiency standard in each and every industry, but 'on the average in the economy generally'".

      This rebuttal is misleading. Average productivities for either industry or the economy are weighted aggregates of individual outputs and their corresponding inputs "actually occurring". For the ratios of any two average composite productivities to be proportional to composite prices, this same requirement must be satisfied for every pairing of the subaggregate in the full technically efficient case, and if this requirement is softened for the "weak" technically efficient case, it must still be true that marginal productivities are maximized for factors in all uses between the composities. We demonstrate that neither is likely to be so except by happenstance because of enterprise level line item budget constraints on outputs and inputs.

Also, Bergson's strictures on the long run are inconsistent with his assertion that adjusted factor cost prices are approximately proportional to prevailing marginal productivities which always pertains to the short run. Bergson does however obliquely parry our assertion about planning constraints by maintaining that "As is usually so with the efficiency standard, however, AFC properly refers to the 'long run' where constraints such as those R-P consider often cease to be binding, and in the case of the USSR agencies above the enterprise level become relatively influential. That is especially important in the sphere of investment allocation". We find this rejoinder perplexing. AFC is merely a price adjustment convention. The degree to which any set of estimates reflect the short or long term efficiency standard are solely a matter of construction. The simple procedures Bergson employs of subtracting turnover taxes and adding subsidies to national income data appear to us pertinent only to the short run, since no explicit adjustments for rents and changes in capital stocks are made (Bergson, 1995).

2.   Bergson has acknowledged that uniform factor prices are not proportional to relative marginal productivities for firms and industries in the short run and hence do not conform to the efficiency standard in this sense (Bergson, 1995). But he counter-argued that adjusted factor cost prices are approximately proportional to opportunity costs on average for the economy as a whole in the long run. This qualification however is inadequate. As Samuelson showed long ago the efficiency standard is only meaningful if it holds in the short run, and separately it can be demonstrated that the economywide average Bergson invokes can only reflect opportunity costs if it holds for all firms forming the average (Rosefielde and

Pfouts, 1997).

3. The negative sign today is understood and not mentioned in stating the equilibrium conditions. We retain the older convention here following Bergson.

4. The set of enterprise production possibilities frontiers as Bergson correctly explained does not map into the nation's production possibilities frontier because factor prices are not competitively efficient with respect to interenterprise and intersectoral factor allocation. The economy wide frontier represents production feasibilities given this constraint.

5. Neoclassical theory does not strictly require a price mechanism for the equilibrium conditions to be met, although the Austrians take this position. The correspondence could be accidental or due to perfect planning, neither of which however is appropriate for the purposes at hand. Bergson rejects perfect planning, and therefore without the requisite price mechanism any approximate equality between relative adjusted factor cost prices and the marginal rate of transformation must be coincidental. From a mathematical viewpoint equations such as (2.3) arise from the first order conditions which are necessary but not sufficient. Sufficiency is attained by specifying the shape (concavity) of the objective function and of the constraints.

6. For the purposes at hand it does not matter if enterprise managers maximized profit, GVO, or even physical output subject to a self-financing constraint as long as bonus incentives induced them to economize costs and maximize revenue. Obviously, Bergson's case is weakened under GVO (revenue) or physical output maximizing because output and input prices have less effect on their behavior. (See Rosefielde and Pfouts, 1988.) Hidden inflation raises the problem of whether established prices of new goods and "improved" products are closely related to accounting factor cost as Bergson supposes. Soft budget constraints may allow managers to weaken input constraints and behave in ways that are incompatible with bonus maximizing tied to profit maximizing. These complications may further degrade Bergson's case for adjusted factor costing.

7.   The marginal rate of transformation for the firm in equilibrium
        holds economywide:

$$\frac{\partial x_i}{\partial x_j} = \frac{d x_i}{d x_j}.$$

8.   Capital is valued here like all other goods at Marxian accounting
        cost, not ideally from the standpoint of production potential at
        competitive market prices. Bergson reprices capital by deleting
        turnover taxes, adding subsidies, deleting profits on durables and
        adding back imputed capital service charges. If as was the case
        until the sixties firms acquired fixed capital gratis factor prices and
        factor proportions would be distorted, constraining production
        potential.

9.   Bergson correctly asserts in the passage quoted in note 2 that if
        equation 3 does not hold exactly, the economy will not be on its
        production possibility frontier, operating instead on a feasibility
        locus.   But this does not assure that relative prices correspond
        variously with factor productivities in different industries and hence
        on average for the economy as a whole. They never, except by
        happenstance, correspond with factor productivities in any use.

10.   Bergson counterargues that the distinction between factor cost and
        arbitrary non-factor payments does not lose its cogency "so long as
        the turnover levies and budgetary subsidies do not depend on the
        inputs of one or another factor, and that is often the case with the
        levies and subsidies considered".   His point appears to be that
        turnover taxes and subsidies are arbitrary and hence different than
        factor cost.   But this distinction ignores our demonstration that
        factor costs do not measure value added when prices are dispropor-
        tional to marginal productivities, and hence are no less arbitrary
        than subsidies or turnover taxes however determined (Bergson,
        1995).

11.   Bergson, setting aside the theoretical issues correctly observes that
        we could not know that CIA estimates of Soviet growth were
        virtually unaffected by adjusted factor costing without undertaking
        the calculation. We of course concur, but the observation disregards
        the effect this corroboration had on professional judgment about the

reliability of Soviet growth statistics. Most professionals were inclined to discount official growth claims, but became more acquiescent when they were confirmed by adjusted factor costing (Bergson, 1995). The overestimation of value added attributable to adjusted factor costing is examined in (Rosefielde and Pfouts, 1997).

12.   If the Soviet composite good marginal rate transformation actually means anything under conditions of micro-input misallocation, there may be some set of quantity weights that makes uniform composite good prices proportional to the composite MRT, but there is nothing in Bergson's method assuring that his weights satisfy this requirement.

13.   Bergson resists the proposition that adjusted factor costing mislead professional opinion about the real magnitude of Soviet accomplishments (Bergson, 1995).

Bibliography

Åslund, Anders, "How Small Is Soviet National Income?". In Henry Rowen and Charles Wolf, Jr. Eds., *The Impoverished Superpower: Perestroika and the Soviet Military Burden*, pp. 13-62. San Francisco, CA: ICS Press, 1988.

Bergson, Abram, "Neoclassical Norms and the Valuation of National Product in the Soviet Union and Its Postcommunist Successor States: Comment", *Journal of Comparative Economics*, Vol. 21, No. 3, December 1995, pp. 390-393.

_____, "The Communist Efficiency Gap: Alternative Measures". *Comparative Economic Studies* XXXVI, 1:1-12, Spring 1994.

_____, *Planning and Performance in Socialist Economies*, Boston: Unwin Hyman, 1989.

_____, "Comparative Productivity: the USSR, Eastern Europe and the West", *American Economic Review*, Vol. 77, No. 3, June 1987a, pp. 342-357.

_____, *Productivity and the Social System--The USSR and the West*, Harvard University Press, Cambridge, Massachusetts, 1978a.

_____, *Soviet Postwar Economic Development*, Almqvist and Wiksell, Stockholm, 1978b.

_____, "National Income". In Bergson and Simon Kuznets, Eds., *Economic Trends in the Soviet Union* pp. 1-37. Cambridge, MA: Harvard University Press, 1963.

_____, "Reliability and Usability of Soviet Statistics: A Summary Appraisal". *American Statistician* 7, 5:13-16, June-July, 1953a.

_____, *Soviet National Income and Product in 1937*. New York, NY: Columbia University Press, 1953b.

Bergson, Abram and Herbert Levine, *The Soviet Economy: Toward The Year 2000*. London: George Allen and Unwin, 1983.

CIA, *Measuring Soviet GNP: Problems and Solutions*. SOV90-10038, September 1990.

_____, *USSR: Measures of Economic Growth and Development, 1950-80*. Joint Economic Committee of Congress, pp. 175-250, December 8, 1982.

Moorsteen, Richard and Raymond Powell, *The Soviet Capital Stock 1928-1962*, Homewood, IL: Richard D. Irwin, 1966.

Rosefielde, Steven, "Russia's Economic Recovery Potential: Optimizing the Residual Productivity of the Soviet Capital Stock", *Comparative Economic Studies*, Vol. XXXVI, No. 4, Winter 1994, pp. 119-142.

_____, "The Soviet Economy in Crisis: Birman's Cumulative Disequilibrium Hypothesis". *Soviet Studies* XL, 1:23-43, April 1988.

_____, *The Transformation of the 1966 Soviet Input-Output Table from Producers to Adjusted Factor Cost Values*, G.E. TEMPO, Washington, D.C., 1975b.

Rosefielde, Steven, and R.W. Pfouts, "Value Imputed: Adjusted Factor Cost and the Overstatement of Soviet Economic Performance", unpublished ms., May 1997.

_____, "Neoclassical Norms and the Valuation of National Product on the Soviet Union and Its Postcommunist Successor States", *Journal of Comparative Economics*, Vol. 21, No. 3, December 1995, pp. 375-389.

_____, "Economic Optimization and Technical Efficiency in Soviet Enterprises Jointly Regulated by Plans and Incentives", *European Economic Review* 32, 6:1285-1299, 1988.

3 Production Potential, Production Functions and Efficiency

Ralph W. Pfouts and Cliff J. Huang

Introduction

The maximum supply producible by any economic unit from a firm to the nation, given prevailing technologies, resources and other associated conditions is referred to as production potential. The attainment of the maximum presupposes the existence and efficient use of production functions, but does not predetermine their form. If any particular production potential is achieved, the characteristics of the underlying production function are of subsidiary importance, but this is not the case otherwise. The degree to which units fail to realize their potential may be strongly affected by the characteristics of the production function. For this reason it is essential to understand the properties of production functions conventionally applied to appraise efficiency, and to appreciate their common origins as mean value estimators.

This chapter addresses these issues by demonstrating how the Cobb-Douglas (CD), the constant elasticity of substitution (CES), the Leontief, the constant marginal share (CMS), the variable elasticity of substitution (VES), and other functions are all members of a general class of mean value functions which are equally plausible on a priori grounds, and do not exclude the possibility of yet other non-mean value alternatives. The demonstration implies that the true specification cannot be determined solely on mathematical grounds, and must be ascertained insofar as possible statistically. If conventional least squares techniques are applied the frontier of the true specification must lie below the efficiency frontier, and for this reason other methods for stochastically and deterministically identifying production potential have been devised. These procedures illuminate aspects of the problem, but it should be clearly understood seldom settle disputes about true functional forms, or more subtly the limitations of the data used to estimate potentials.

The Power Means

The first type of mean value function that we will use is the power mean (Hardy, Littlewood and Polya, 1951, pp. 12-15). This may be written as

$$M_\tau = \left(\sum_{i=1}^{n} q_i a_i^\tau \right)^{\frac{1}{\tau}}, \tag{3.1}$$

where $a_i \geq 0$, $q_i > 0$ for all i and $\sum q_i = 1$. It is evident that M_1 is the arithmetic mean, M_2 the root mean square and M_{-1} the harmonic mean. It can be demonstrated that

$$M_0 = \lim_{\tau \to 0} M_\tau = \prod_{i=1}^{n} a_i q_i, \tag{3.2}$$

if $a_i > 0$ for all i. Thus M_0 is the geometric mean. Similarly it can be shown that

$$M_{-\infty} = \lim_{\tau \to -\infty} M_\tau = \text{Min} \ (a_i). \tag{3.3}$$

We note that the power means are homogeneous of degree one; indeed the power means are the only homogeneous mean value functions.

If (3.1) is restated as a production function, using conventional notation, it becomes

$$P = \left[(1 - \delta) \ K^\tau + \delta L^\tau \right]^{\frac{1}{\tau}}. \tag{3.4}$$

This is clearly a CES function (Arrow, Chenery, Minhas and Solow, 1961). If $\tau = 1$, (3.4) becomes
$$P = (1 - \delta)K + \delta L,$$

a linear production function. In the event that $\tau \to 0$, reference to (3.2) shows that (3.4) becomes
$$P = K^{(1-\delta)} L^\delta,$$

which is of course the CD function, and it is assumed that K, L > 0. In the case in which $\tau \to -\infty$ (3.4) becomes

$$P = \text{Min } (K, L),$$

which is the Leontief function.

Composite Power Means

We now introduce a variant of the power mean. We write

$$P_i = \left[(1 - \delta_i)K^{\tau_i} + \delta_i L^{\tau_i}\right]^{\frac{1}{\tau_i}}, \quad i = 1, 2. \tag{3.5}$$

We further write

$$P = \left[(1 - \delta_0)P_1^{\tau_0} + \delta_0 P_2^{\tau_0}\right]^{\frac{1}{\tau_0}}. \tag{3.6}$$

It is apparent that (3.6) is a valid use of the power mean formula. Reference to (3.1) shows that the only restriction on the arguments of the power mean is that they be non-negative. The usual economic preconceptions would assure that P_1 and P_2 have the desired characteristic.

Equation (3.6), which we will call the composite power mean, is an extremely flexible general form of the power mean class of production functions, which can be specialized to obtain various types of production functions. That is, by assigning particular values to the constants in (3.5) and (3.6) we may obtain a number of production functions that have proved to be of interest.

Thus if we let $\tau_1 = 1$, $\tau_2 \to 0$ and $\delta_1 = 0$ in (3.5) and (3.6), we obtain

$$P = \left[(1 - \delta_0)K^{\tau_0} + \delta_0 K^{\tau_0(1-\delta_2)} L^{\tau_0\delta_2}\right]^{\frac{1}{\tau_0}} \tag{3.7}$$

from (3.6). It may be seen that (3.7) is the generalization of the CES function which was suggested by Bruno (1962). Quite clearly (3.7) is a power mean of a CD function and a fixed capital-output function. If S_k represent capital's share, the elasticity of substitution for (3.7) is

$$\sigma = \cfrac{1}{1 - \tau_0 + \cfrac{\tau_0(1-\delta_2)}{S_k}}.$$

Similarly by letting $\tau_0 = 1$, $\tau_1 \to 0$, $\tau_2 = 1$ and $\delta_2 = 1$, we get from (3.5) and (3.6),

$$P = \left(1 - \delta_0\right)K^{(1-\delta_1)} L^{\delta_1} + \delta_0 L, \tag{3.8}$$

which is the CMS production function which was proposed by Bruno (1968). Obviously (3.8) is a combination of a CD function and fixed labor-output function. The elasticity of substitution for (3.8) is

$$\sigma = 1 + \frac{\delta_0(1-\delta_1)}{\delta_1} \frac{L}{P},$$

which will always be at least as great as unity under the usual assumptions about the numerical values of the constants. It should also be noted that if $\delta_1 = 1$, (3.8) becomes $P = L$ and the elasticity of substitution is not defined.

If we let $\tau_0 \to 0$, $\tau_1 \to 0$, $\tau_2 = 1$, and $\delta_1 = 0$, we have from (3.5) and (3.6),

$$P = K^{(1-\delta_0)} \left[\left(1 - \delta_2\right)K + \delta_2 L\right]^{\delta_0}. \tag{3.9}$$

This is a VES production function of the type which was developed by Revankar (1971). It is clear that the VES function is a CD function of a fixed capital-output production function and a linear production function. The elasticity of substitution for (3.9) is a function of the capital-labor ratio:

$$\sigma = 1 + \frac{(1-\delta_2)}{\delta_2(1-\delta_0)} \frac{K}{L}.$$

A generalized form of the composite power mean can be used to obtain a "two-level" CES function which was first used by K. Sato (1967). In addition the same type of composite power mean can be used to obtain Uzawa's production function (1962).

We assume the presence of factors of production indicated by a_j, $j = 1, ..., n$. We suppose further that

$$P_i = \left(\sum_{j=1}^{n} q_j a_j^{\tau_i} \right)^{\frac{1}{\tau_i}}, \quad i = 1, \ldots, m.$$

A power mean of these last functions may be shown as

$$P = \left(\sum_{i=1}^{m} \alpha_i P_i^{\tau_0} \right)^{\frac{1}{\tau_0}}, \quad \Sigma \alpha_i = 1. \tag{3.10}$$

This is Sato's two-level CES function. It is clearly a CES function of CES functions.
        If we set

$$\tau_0 = \tau_1 = \ldots = \tau_m = \tau$$

then

$$P_i = \left(\sum_{j=1}^{n} q_j a_j^{\tau} \right)^{\frac{1}{\tau}}, \quad i = 1, \ldots, m$$

and from (3.10) we obtain

$$P = \left(\sum_{i=1}^{m} a_i P_i^{\tau} \right)^{\frac{1}{\tau}},$$

which is the "pedestrian" CES function of Sato. This last is a CES function of sub-CES functions each having the same elasticity of substitution.
        Equation (3.10) can also be used to generate Uzawa's production function. If, in (3.10), we let $\tau_0 \rightarrow 0$, we have

$$P = \prod_{i=1}^{m} \left(\sum_{j=1}^{n} q_j a_j^{\tau_i} \right)^{\frac{\alpha_i}{\tau_i}}. \tag{3.11}$$

This is Uzawa's production function. It is a CD function of CES functions. Uzawa shows that all homogeneous production functions of degree one having constant partial elasticities are functions of the type of (3.11). It may be added that (3.11) also includes linear, homogeneous production functions with variable elasticities of substitution. The VES function is a particular case of (3.11) and has a variable elasticity of substitution.

Mean Values with Arbitrary Functions

Power means are a special case of a more general type of mean value function. It can be shown (Hardy, Littlewood and Polya, 1951, pp. 65-67) that if

(a) $\Phi(x)$ is continuous, differentialable and strictly monotonic in $H \leq x \leq K$,

(b) $H \leq a_i \leq K$, $i = 1, ..., n$.

(c) $q_i > 0$, $\Sigma q_i = 1$

then there is a unique M in the closed interval [H, K] such that

$$\Phi(M) = \Sigma q_i \, \Phi(a_i).$$

Thus a mean with arbitrary function Φ can be written as

$$M_\Phi = \Phi^{-1} \left[\Sigma q_i \, \Phi(a_i) \right]. \tag{3.12}$$

It is evident that (3.1) is a special case of (3.12) with $\Phi(a_i) = a_i^\tau$.

This more general type of mean value function can be used to obtain a class of production functions of the type developed by Zellner and Revankar (1969). These writers postulate a neo-classical production function $f(L, K)$ which is homogeneous of arbitrary degree. They introduce a monotonic transformation function g and write $P = g(f)$, which is a generalized production function. They also obtain an equation

$$L \, \frac{\partial g}{\partial L} + K \, \frac{\partial g}{\partial K} = \alpha(P) \, P.$$

In this equation $\alpha(P)$ is a returns to scale function.

A GPF may be developed using a mean with arbitrary function. To do this we first write two production functions

$P_1 = f_1 (L, K)$

$P_2 = f_2 (L, K)$,

which are homogeneous of degrees β_1 and β_2 respectively. We now form a mean value function making use of an increasing monotonic function

$$P = \Phi^{-1} \left[(1 - \delta) \Phi (P_1) + \delta \Phi (P_2) \right]. \tag{3.13}$$

This last equation can be viewed as representing a class of the GPF functions.

Returns to scale can be examined by forming the equation

$$K \frac{\partial P}{\partial K} + L \frac{\partial P}{\partial L} = K D (\Phi^{-1}) \left[(1 - \delta) \frac{d\Phi}{dP_1} \frac{\partial P_1}{\partial K} + \delta \frac{d\Phi}{dP_2} \frac{\partial P_2}{\partial K} \right]$$

$$+ L D (\Phi^{-1}) \left[(1 - \delta) \frac{d\Phi}{dP_1} \frac{\partial P_1}{\partial L} + \delta \frac{d\Phi}{dP_2} \frac{\partial P_2}{\partial L} \right], \tag{3.14}$$

where D represents the differential operator. After straightforward manipulations of (3.14), we obtain

$$K \frac{\partial P}{\partial K} + L \frac{\partial P}{\partial L} = D (\Phi^{-1}) \left[(1 - \delta) \frac{d\Phi}{dP_1} \left(K \frac{\partial P_1}{\partial K} + L \frac{\partial P_1}{\partial L} \right) \right.$$

$$\left. + \delta \frac{d\Phi}{dP_2} \left(K \frac{\partial P_2}{\partial K} + L \frac{\partial P_2}{\partial L} \right) \right].$$

Because of the homogeneity of f_1 and f_2, the last equation may be shown as

$$K \frac{\partial P}{\partial K} + L \frac{\partial P}{\partial L} = D (\Phi^{-1})$$

$$\left[(1 - \delta) \beta_1 \frac{d\Phi}{dP_1} P_1 + \delta \beta_2 \frac{d\Phi}{dP_2} P_2 \right]. \tag{3.15}$$

It is quite evident that (3.15) is capable of showing increasing, decreasing or constant returns to scale depending on the relative values of the variables involved.

To consider a special case let $\beta_1 = \beta_2 = \beta$. Then (3.15) becomes

$$K \frac{\partial P}{\partial K} + L \frac{\partial P}{\partial L} = \beta D (\Phi^{-1}) \left[(1 - \delta) \frac{d\Phi}{dP_1} P_1 + \delta \frac{d\Phi}{dP_2} P_2 \right].$$

If we now assume, as a further specialization, that Φ is homogeneous, we are in effect also assuming that the generalized mean becomes a power mean which is homogeneous of degree one. This is the case because the power means are the only homogeneous mean value functions and they are always homogeneous of the first degree. If the assumption that Φ is homogeneous of degree one is invoked we have from the last equation above

$$K \frac{\partial P}{\partial K} + L \frac{\partial P}{\partial L} = \beta D (\Phi^{-1})$$

(3.16)

$$\left[(1 - \delta) \Phi (P_1) + \delta \Phi (P_2) \right] = \beta D (\Phi^{-1}) \Phi (P).$$

Because of the complementary degrees of homogeneity of $D (\Phi^{-1})$ and Φ, (3.16) becomes

$$K \frac{\partial P}{\partial K} + L \frac{\partial P}{\partial L} = \beta P,$$

and the returns to scale depend only on the degree of homogeneity of f_1 and f_2 in this special case. In this case β is the returns to scale function.

Equivalent Mean Value Functions

The mean value function M_Φ is established when Φ is chosen. It is natural to inquire as to whether $M_\Phi = M_\psi$ requires that Φ and ψ be the same function. It can be proved that the necessary and sufficient condition that $M_{\Phi(a)} = M_{\psi(a)}$ is that $\Phi = \tau \psi + t$ where τ and t are constants and $\tau \neq 0$ (Hardy, Littlewood and Polya, 1951, pp. 66-67).

The theorem is of interest in the theory of production functions because it shows that the function Φ is not unique and that in this sense the production function is not unique. A linear function of Φ will obtain the same result as Φ. In the approach that we have employed, Φ represents the rule for combining sub-production functions in the cases of the composite power mean and the mean with arbitrary function. Thus the theorem fundamentally relates to the process of aggregation by showing that the aggregation rule is not unique when the production function is a mean value function; a linear function of the rule will yield the same result.

Conclusion

As was stated at the outset, the purpose of this paper is to provide relationships among some of the production function forms thus offering a more unified view of the various forms. This was done by showing that the production functions under consideration are particular cases of mean value functions. The most general mean value function is the mean value with an arbitrary function. It was demonstrated that this type of function provides a class of GPF. The next most general form of the mean function was the composite power mean. This type of mean value function in various forms offers Sato's two-level CES function, Uzawa's function, the VES, the CMS and the generalized CES. The direct power mean generates the CES, the CD, the linear and the Leontief production functions. Thus relationships between the various production function forms are established.

Bibliography

Arrow, K.J., H.B. Chenery, B.S. Minhas, and R.M. Solow, "Capital-Labor Substitution and Economic Efficiency", *Review of Economics and Statistics*, 43, 1961, pp. 225-250.

Bruno, M., "A Note on The Implications of an Empirical Relationship Between Output Per Unit of Labor, the Wage Rate and the Capital-Labor Ratio", unpublished mimeo, Stanford, July 1962.

_____, "Estimation of Factor Contribution to Growth Under Structural Disequilibrium", *International Economic Review*, 9, 1968, pp. 49-62.

Hardy, G.H., J.E. Littlewood, and G. Polya, *Inequalities*, 2nd ed., Cambridge, 1951.

Revankar, N.S., "A Class of Variable Elasticity of Substitution Production Functions", *Econometrica*, 39, 1971, pp. 61-71.

Sato, K., "A Two-Level Constant Elasticity of Substitution Production Function", *Review of Economic Studies*, 34, 1967, pp. 201-218.

Uzawa, H., "Production Functions with Constant Elasticities of Substitution", *Review of Economic Studies*, 29, 1962, pp. 291-299.

Zellner, A., and N.S. Revankar, "Generalized Production Functions", *Review of Economic Studies*, 36, 1969, pp. 241-250.

4   Efficiency Frontiers and Homothetic Production Functions

M.V. Antonov, A.B. Pomansky and G. Yu. Trofimov

Introduction

The efficiency characteristics of single output, multifactor enterprises with variable returns to scale was first analyzed by Ragnar Frisch [Frisch, 1965] for a class of concave-convex production functions (which satisfy the ultra passim law), where the efficiency frontier is a surface in the factor space because the functions are convex for small outputs and concave otherwise.

This paper extends Frisch's research by examining the properties of the efficiency frontier for general (monotonically increasing) and homothetic production functions. It is shown that the set of optimal scale combinations is equivalent to the set of Pareto-efficient points in the input coefficient space. Optimal scale combinations satisfy Euler's theorem, which requires that efficient factor combinations are determined by marginal productivities. The homotheticity assumption permits the application of this principle to pricing factors for non-optimal scales of production. An important result of the paper for the homothetic case is that optimal scale combinations must lie on a Pareto-efficient isoquant.

Our investigation follows the frontier production functions approach developed in [Forsund, Hjalmarsson, 1988], and assumes that frontier production functions reflect best-practice technology.   Estimates are computed with respect to this best practice empirical efficiency frontier for the cotton-refining industry of Turkmenia by filtering all inefficient sub-best practice observations. Inefficient micro-units, accordingly do not influence the estimation.   Our findings suggest that cotton refining production functions may be homothetic because output variances are small. Also the iterative inefficient observation search procedure devised may be generally helpful for mitigating the "outlier" problem associated with computing deterministic production frontiers.

The Efficiency Frontier

Consider a production function $y = f(x)$ mapping the positive orthant of inputs $x \in R_n^+$ into the interval of positive real numbers. The function $f(x)$ is monotonically increasing and continuously differentiable.

    The optimal scale for the factor combination x is defined as the positive real number:

$$\mu(x) = \underset{\mu}{Argmax} \; \frac{f(\mu x)}{\mu}.$$

The function $\mu(x)$ indicates the scale of production maximizing average returns to scale along the factor ray $f(\mu x)/\mu$, $\mu > 0$. For a linear homogeneous production function the optimal scale coincides with the interval $(0, \infty)$ for each x. For homogeneous production functions with diminishing (increasing) returns the optimal scale is $0(\infty)$ for all combinations of inputs.

    The optimal scale for the input vector x_0 is $\mu(x_0)x_0$. *The efficiency frontier* $E[f(x)]$ for the production function $f(x)$ is the locus of optimal scale points corresponding to all combinations of inputs $x \in R_n^+$. The mapping $R_n^+ \to E[f(x)]$ is, in general, not well defined. In the case of linear homogeneous production functions $E[f(x)]$ coincides with R_n^+. The efficiency frontier is the origin of the factor space for strictly convex production functions. It is a surface of dimension n-1 if the production function is convex-concave (convex for small outputs and concave otherwise).

    Theorem 1: *The efficiency frontier coincides with the set of Pareto-efficient combinations maximizing average factor returns $f(x)/x_i$, i = 1, ..., n.*

    Proof: (i) Let x^0 be an optimal scale point. Suppose it is not Pareto-efficient: there exists a vector x^1 such that $f(x^1)/x_i^1 \geq f(x^0)/x_i^0$ for all $i = 1, ...,$ n with at least one strict inequality. Since x^0 is an optimal scale point, $f(x^0)/x_i^0 \geq f(tx^0)/tx_i^0$ for all $t > 0$. Choose t such that $f(x^1) = f(tx^0)$. Then, by the assumption, $f(x^1)/x_i^1 \geq f(tx^0)/tx_i^0$ or $tx_i^0 \geq x_i^1$ which holds as strict inequality for some i. This contradicts the equality of outputs.

    (ii) Let x^0 be Pareto-efficient. Suppose it is not the optimal scale point. Then there exists $t > 0$ satisfying $f(tx^0)/t > f(x^0)/tx_j^0$, contradicting the Pareto-efficiency of x^0.

    Define *the Euler operator* as $D_e\left[f(x)\right] = \sum_{j=1}^{n}\left(\partial f(x)|\partial x_j\right)x_j.$

It measures the value of output with factors priced according to their marginal productivities. The Euler theorem holds for production functions homogeneous of degree λ.

$$\lambda\, f(x) = \sum_{j=1}^{n} \frac{\partial f(x)}{\partial x_j}\, x_j.$$

In other words the Euler operator is represented by a product of output $f(x)$ and the homogeneity degree λ. The effect of each factor is evaluated through the marginal productivity multiplied by $1/\lambda$.

In general factors are priced exactly through marginal productivities for combinations belonging to the efficiency frontier.

Theorem 2: *If $x \in E[f(x)]$ then $D_e[f(x)] = f(x)$.*

Proof: If $x \in E[f(x)]$ then $f(\mu x)/\mu$ reaches a maximum at $\mu = 1$. The first order condition is $\sum x_i\, \partial\, f(\mu x)/\partial\, x_i - f(\mu x) = 0$. Inserting $\mu = 1$ yields the result.

Theorem 2 suggests *the efficiency frontier equation*. The converse of Theorem 2 is true under the regularity conditions implying that $\mu(x)$ is unique for each ray x in the factor space.

Homothetic Production Functions

Let us now consider the efficiency frontier for homothetic production functions $f(x) = F(g(x))$, where $g(x)$ is a linear homogeneous (kernel) function and $F(\cdot)$ is a strictly monotonic function. The homotheticity of a production function closely relates to the "homotheticity" of the Euler operator on this function.

Theorem 3: *The function $f(x)$ is homothetic if and only if $D_e[f(x)] = h(f(x))$, where $h(\cdot)$ is a continuous mapping $R_1^+ \to R_1^+$.*

Proof: (i) For homothetic functions

$$D_e\left[f(x)\right] = F'(g)\, g(x), \tag{4.1}$$

where $g = g(x)$. Since $y = F(g)$ is strictly monotonic, g is a continuous function of y: $g = z(y)$. Inserting it into the right-hand side of (4.1) proves the "only if" part.

(ii) Consider a function satisfying the non-homogeneous partial differential equation:

$$D_e\left[f(x)\right] = h(f(x)), \tag{4.2}$$

where $h(\cdot)$ is a positive continuous function. The corresponding system of ordinary differential equations is

$$\frac{dx_1}{x_1} = \frac{dx_2}{x_2} = \ldots = \frac{dx_n}{x_n} = \frac{dy}{h(y)}.$$

It has n independent first integrals:

$$\frac{x_1}{x_n} = c_1, \quad \frac{x_2}{x_n} = c_2, \quad \ldots, \quad \frac{x_{n-1}}{x_n} = c_{n-1}, \quad \frac{e^{p(y)}}{x_n} = c_n,$$

where $p(y)$ is a primitive function for $1/h(y)$. It is monotonically increasing, because $h(y)$ is positive.

Consider the equation

$$\Phi\left(\frac{x_1}{x_n}, \frac{x_2}{x_n}, \ldots, \frac{x_{n-1}}{x_n}, \frac{e^{p(y)}}{x_n}\right) = 0, \qquad\qquad (4.4)$$

where $\Phi(\cdot)$ is an arbitrary differentiable function. It includes all solutions to (4.2) and determines y as a function of $x_1, \ldots, x_n$ satisfying (4.2). Solving (4.3) with respect to the last argument of $\Phi(\cdot)$ we have: $p(y) = \ln g(x)$, where

$$g(x) = x_n \Psi\left(\frac{x_1}{x_n}, \frac{x_2}{x_n}, \ldots, \frac{x_{n-1}}{x_n}\right) \text{ is a linear homogeneous function.}$$

Since $p(y)$ is monotonically increasing, $y = f(x)$ is represented as $y = F(g(x))$, where $F(g)$ is strictly monotonic, and $g(x)$ is homogeneous of degree one.

Theorems 2 and 3 imply a Corollary which is important for our empirical studies.

Corollary: *The efficiency frontier of a homothetic production function is an isoquant of this function: $f(x) = const$ for $x \in E[f(x)]$.*

Proof: Theorems 2 and 3 imply that $f(x) = D_e[f(x)] = h(f(x))$ for $x \in E[f(x)]$. Hence, for each vector of inputs $x \in E[f(x)]$ output is a unique solution to the equation $y = h(y)$.

The corollary helps to derive analytically the efficiency frontier for homothetic production functions (see examples below). The converse statement is not true. The production function given implicitly as $y^3 = x_i$ −

by) [Johansen, 1972] is non-homothetic with efficiency frontier $E[f(x)] = \{0\}$ which is trivially an isoquant.

Theorem 3 extends the Euler theorem to the case of homothetic functions, but it does not help to measure factor productivity in the multifactor case. In order to price factors one should use the function $H(x) = \int_0^1 \frac{f(\lambda x)}{\lambda} \, d\lambda$ which represents cumulative returns to scale along the ray λx. (This function was introduced in [Pomansky, Trofimov, 1989] to derive a Lyapunov function for the multisectoral dynamic model of capital accumulation.)

For homothetic production functions $f(x) = D_e[H(x)]$, the factor i price is $\partial H(x)/\partial x_i$. To see this note that $f(\lambda x) = F(\lambda g(x)\}$ and $H(x) = \int_0^1 \frac{F(\lambda g(x))}{\lambda} \, d\lambda$. Differentiating implies $\partial H \, | \, \partial x_i = \int_0^1$ $F'(\lambda g(x)) \, g_i'(x) \, d\lambda$. Changing variables: $u = \lambda g(x)$ results in $\partial H \, | \, \partial x_i =$ $g_i'(x) \int_0^{g(x)} \frac{F'(u)}{g(x)} \, du = \frac{g_i'(x)}{g(x)} F(g(x))$, and $D_e[H(x)] = F(g(x)) = f(x)$.

The following examples illustrate these concepts.

Example 1: Convex-concave exponential function: $y = 1 - \exp(-g(x)^2)$, $g(x) = x_1^a x_2^{1-a}$. The Euler operator is represented as

$$D_e[f(x)] = F'(g) \, g(x) = 2g(x)^2 \exp(-g(x)^2).$$

According to the corollary, the efficiency frontier is an isoquant and, hence, it satisfies:

$$1 - \exp(-g_0^2) = 2g_0^2 \exp(-g_0^2)$$

The (unique) positive solution to this equation roughly equals $g_0 \approx 1.12$. The efficiency frontier is represented by the surface: $x_1^a x_2^{1-a} = g_0$.

$$\text{Cumulative returns to scale are } H(x) = \int_0^1 \frac{f(\lambda x)}{\lambda} \, d\lambda = \{u = \lambda g\} = \int_0^g$$

$$F(u) \, du = \int_0^g (1 - \exp(-u^2)) \, du = g(x) - \sqrt{2\pi} \left[\Phi\left(g(x)\sqrt{2}\right) - 0.5 \right], \text{ where}$$

$\Phi(\cdot)$ is the standard normal distribution function.

    Example 2.   Zellner-Revankar function [Zellner and Revankar, 1969]: $y^\alpha e^{\beta y} = g(x)$, $g(x) = x_1^a x_2^{1-a}$. By the implicit function theorem

$$\frac{\partial f(x)}{\partial x_1} = \frac{a f(x)}{(\alpha + \beta f(x)) x_1}, \quad \frac{\partial f(x)}{\partial x_2} = \frac{(1 - a) f(x)}{(\alpha + \beta f(x)) x_2}$$

The Euler operator is $D_e\left[f(x)\right] = \dfrac{f(x)}{\alpha + \beta f(x)}$. The efficiency frontier

equation is:

$$\alpha + \beta f(x) = 1, \tag{4.6}$$

and the optimal scale output is $y_0 = (1 - \alpha)/\beta$. Optimal scale combinations explicitly satisfy: $g(x) = y_0^\alpha \exp(\beta y_0)$.

    To calculate $H(x)$ use the equalities: $f(\lambda x)^\alpha e^{\beta f(\lambda x)} = \lambda g(x) = \lambda f(x)^\alpha e^{\beta f(x)}$. Denote $f(x)^\alpha e^{\beta f(x)} = C^{-1}(x)$ and change variables for a fixed x: $\lambda = C(x) y^\alpha e^{\beta y}$, $d\lambda = C(x) [\alpha y^{\alpha-1} e^{\beta y} + \beta y^\alpha e^{\beta y}] \, dy$. Note that $y = f(x)$ for $\lambda = 1$, and $y = 0$ for $\lambda = 0$. Thus we have $H(x) = \int_0^{f(x)}$

$$\frac{y \left[\alpha y^{\alpha-1} + \beta y^\alpha\right] e^{\beta y}}{y^\alpha e^{\beta y}} \, dy =$$

$$\int_0^{f(x)} \left[\alpha + \beta y\right] dy = \alpha f(x) + \frac{\beta}{2} f(x)^2 = f(x) \left[\alpha + \frac{\beta}{2} f(x)\right].$$

Frontier Production Functions

Consider an industry producing a single homogeneous good and populated with N firms. The technological possibilities of each firm are given by the (micro-) production function $y^k = f^k(x^k)$, $y^k \in R^+$, $x^k \in R_m^+$, $k = 1, ..., N$. The deterministic *frontier production function* $f_0(x)$ indicates maximal outputs that could be obtained if combinations of inputs x were used in the best-practice firm: $f_0(x) = \max_k f^k(x)$.

The frontier production function of the industry can be estimated directly without estimating micro- production functions $f^k(x)$. This approach was developed in [Forsund, Hjalmarsson, 1988]. Suppose there are N observations of input-output combinations $\{x^k, y^k\}$ and the deterministic frontier production function depends on the vector of unknown parameters a: $f_0(x, a)$. The estimation procedure minimizes the distance between the frontier and observations which must lie on, or below it, as Figure 1 demonstrates. The best estimation a^* solves the problem:

$$\min_a \Sigma_k |f_0(x_k, a) - y_k|$$

subject to: $\qquad f_0(x_k, a) \geq y_k, \quad k = 1, \ldots, N.$

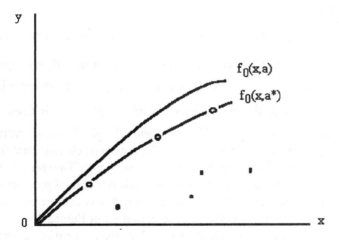

Figure 4.1   The Aggregate Industrial Efficiency Frontier

The standard criticism of deterministic frontiers is that inefficient observations ("outliers") may have too much influence on the estimated function. The deterministic approaches [e.g., Timmer, 1971; Thiry and

Tulkens, 1988] try to eliminate inefficient observations and recompute a frontier for residual observations. The stochastic frontier approach [Schmidt and Lovell, 1979; Greene, 1980; Forsund and Hjalmarsson, 1988] allows for some observations to be above the frontier due to uncontrolled factors. Inefficiencies are treated in probabilistic terms as if they are caused by random events.

　　　Our empirical analysis focuses on the efficiency frontier rather than the frontier production function. The former reflects information about the best-practice plants with optimal scale of production. We use the deterministic approach by filtering out all inefficient observations before numerically estimating the efficiency frontier. Inefficient micro-units, thus, do not influence estimates. The iterative search procedure proposed below may be helpful in mitigating the "outlier" problem in the case of deterministic frontier production functions.

Empirical Efficiency Frontier

Suppose that the technology at each micro-limit is fixed and represented by a Leontief production function

$$f^k(x) = \min_i \left[x_i^k \mid \xi_i^k \right], \text{ where } \xi_i^k, \; i = 1, \ldots, n, \text{ are input coefficients.}$$

Each observation is, thus, given by a point in input coefficient space $\Xi^k = \left(\xi_1^k, \ldots, \xi_n^k \right)$, $k = 1, \ldots, N$. *The empirical efficiency frontier* is a Pareto-efficient subset of the observation set $\Theta = \left\{ \Xi^k \right\}_{k=1}^N$. It does not include all dominated observations: if $\Xi^l \geq \Xi^k$ and $\Xi^k \neq \Xi^l$, then observation l does not belong to the empirical frontier. This concept closely relates to the above (theoretical) efficiency frontier. According to Theorem 1, the empirical frontier indicates micro-units with the optimal scale of production, given that the frontier production function of the industry is convex-concave. The empirical frontier in the two-factor case is plotted in Figure 2.

　　　The iterative search procedure is based on the sequential selection of efficient observations. Each iteration includes two stages. In the first state the Θ_1 with minimal input coefficients (coordinates) $\xi_1, \xi_2, \ldots, \xi_n$ is selected from the initial set Θ. Obviously, the subset Θ_1 belongs to the efficiency frontier. In the second stage all observations dominated by those from the subset Θ_1 are removed from the initial set. Denote the set of dominated points as Θ_1'. In the next iteration the same procedure is repeated with the remainder subset $\Theta/\left(\Theta_1 \cup \Theta_1'\right)$ and the subset of efficient points selected in the second iteration is Θ_2. The empirical efficiency frontier is the subset $\Theta^* = \overset{T}{\underset{t=1}{\cup}} \Theta_t$, where T is the number of iterations.

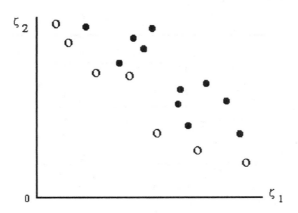

Figure 4.2   Aggregate Efficiency Frontier: The Two Factor Case

Figure 3 illustrates the search procedure for the case of two factors and six observations. In the first iteration the points $\Theta_1 = \{\Xi^1, \Xi^6\}$ with minimal input coefficients are selected and the dominated observation $\Theta_1' = \{\Xi^2\}$ is removed. The second (and the last) iteration selects the efficient subset $\Theta_2 = \{\Xi^3, \Xi^4\}$ and filters out the inefficient point Ξ^5.

The procedure differs from the method of filtering inefficient observations according to the criterion of "free-disposal domination" [Thiry, Tulkens, 1988]. It was applied for the empirical analysis of the cotton-proceeding industry of Turkmenia. The main production factors are labor, capital and energy. The data set comprises annual input coefficients for 22 plants over 10 years (1970-1980). The initial sample, thus, consists of 220 observations. The selection of the empirical efficiency frontier required 14 iterations and the number of efficient points is 14. The absolute majority of inefficient observations (146) was filtered out in the first iteration. This is the typical feature of the procedure for the case of large number of observations and small number of factors.

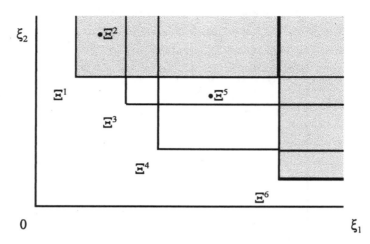

Figure 4.3   Efficiency Frontier Search Technique

Numerical Estimates

The standard deviation of output for efficient units is 10 percent to the average optimal scale. Only two of those observations deviate significantly from the average. Hence, there are no compelling reasons to reject the assumption of homotheticity for the industry's frontier production function.

The latter is supposed to be of the generalized Zellner-Revankar type [Zellner and Revankar, 1969]:

$$y^\alpha e^{\beta y} = A \, K_{\alpha_K} \, L_{\alpha_L} \, E_{\alpha_E},$$

where y is output; K, L, E are factors: production capital, labor inputs and energy consumption; α and β are positive parameters of scale, A is a numeraire constant, α_K, α_L, α_E are factor elasticities, $\alpha_K + \alpha_L + \alpha_E = 1$.

Since this is a homothetic function, the efficiency frontier is an isoquant:

$$\alpha_K \ln K + \alpha_L \ln L + \alpha_E = B,$$

where $B = \alpha \ln y_0 + \beta y_0 - \ln A$, and y_0 is the optimal scale. The OLS estimates for scale elasticities and parameter B are obtained for efficient observations (14 points) as the solution to:

$$\min \Sigma_j \; [\alpha_K \ln K_j + \alpha_L \ln L_j + \alpha_E \ln E_j - B]^2,$$

and $j = 1, ..., 14$ is the observation number. The estimated values are: $\alpha_K = 0.310$, $\alpha_L = 0.354$, $\alpha_E = 0.336$, $B = -0.005$. Figure 4 illustrates the estimation of frontier in the two factor case.

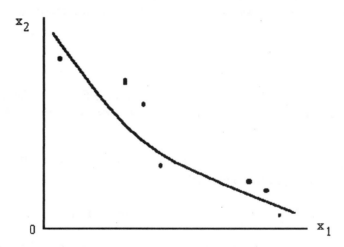

Figure 4.4   The Homothetic Efficiency Frontier

The estimated frontier is a surface in the three factor space. It constitutes a class of frontier production functions which satisfy (4.4):

$$\alpha + \beta \bar{y}_0 = 1,$$

where $\bar{y}_0$ is the estimate of optimal scale for the industry as the average output of efficient plants.

Conclusion

The paper has examined optimal scale combinations of factors. We used the equivalence between optimal scale points in the factor space and the efficiency frontier, and focused on the latter in the empirical part of the paper. The analysis of empirical efficiency frontier can be applied in various areas beyond production theory and its applications. The search procedure elaborated here was used by the authors for optimal selection of banking projects. Efficient portfolios of projects were selected from the initial set according to expected returns, risk and term. As above, the frontier of the admissible portfolio set was estimated numerically. The ultimate choice among efficient portfolios depended on financial constraints faced by the bank.

Bibliography

Antonov, M. and A. Pomansky, "Credit Rationing and the Efficient Allocation of Loan Funds", *Economics and Mathematical Methods*, 30, 1994, pp. 111-126.

Forsund, F. and L. Hjalmarsson, *Analysis of Industrial Structure: A Putty-Clay Approach*, Stockholm: IUI, 1988.

Frisch, R., *Theory of Production*, Dordrecht: D. Reidel, 1965.

Greene, W.H., "Maximum Likelihood Estimation of Econometric Frontier Functions", *Journal of Econometrics*, 13, 1980, pp. 27-56.

Johansen, L., *Production Functions*, Amsterdam: North-Holland, 1972.

Pomansky, A. and G. Trofimov, "Dynamic Aggregation in Models of Capital Allocation", *Economics and Mathematical Methods*, 25, 1989, pp. 1042-1052.

Schmidt, P. and C.A.K. Lovell, "Estimating Technical and Allocative Inefficiency Relative to Stochastic Production and Cost Functions", *Journal of Econometrics*, 9, 1979, pp. 343-366.

Thiry, B. and H. Tulkens, "Allowing for Technical Inefficiency in Parametric Estimates of Production Functions", Louvain: CORE, 1988.

Timmer, C.P., "Using a Probabilistic Frontier Function to Measure Technical Efficiency", *Journal of Political Economy*, 79, 1971, pp. 776-794.

Zellner, A. and N. Revankar, "Generalized Production Functions", *Review of Economic Studies*, 36, 1969, pp. 241-250.

5 Hyperbolic Technical Efficiency: Axiomatic Foundations and Extensions

George B. Kleiner and Slava V. Brover

Introduction

The literature on efficiency measurement is extensive. It covers a broad range of theoretical (L'vov, 1990; Baltrushevich, 1992), and methodological issues (Fare, 1985). This chapter focuses on one aspect of the subject; technological attainment, the degree to which technologies approximate best practice (Forsund and Hiallmarsson, 1987; Antonov, Pomansky and Trofimov, 1991; Kleiner, 1986), assuming that factors are employed at minimum cost, and output potentials for the superior and inferior technologies are fully realized. Attainment (efficiency) is understood here as supply potential, without further regard to demand. The concept is analogous to Abram Bergson's well known distinction between technical efficiency (producing at any point on a production possibility frontier) and the "welfare standard" where production is Paretian optimal (Bergson, 1953). The best practice frontier amounts to the same thing as the Paretian frontier when factor prices and uses are competitively determined. Otherwise, the frontier generated by the technology may lie elsewhere. To avoid confusion, it also needs to be made clear that "technological inefficiency" (inferior technologies) as we use the term does not involve shortfalls from the potential of a specific production frontier as it does in the stochastic enterprise production frontier analysis because the comparisons considered are between efficiently employed technologies, given prevailing input prices.

The general axiomatic foundations of enterprise production functions and the measures of technological attainment associated with them are discussed in (Fare, Grosskopf and Lovell, 1985; Bergson, 1953; Kleiner, 1988; Russell, 1990). In the Soviet period these methods were often employed in making centralized investment decisions, especially regarding innovation and were sometimes used to assess managerial performance

(Afanas"ev, 1992).   They were also utilized in designing managerial incentives for the efficient introduction and use of new machinery and equipment.   These indicators and incentives have become increasingly obsolete, and are being replaced by market criteria, but they still serve a useful purpose in an inflationary environment that complicates the estimation of present value.   Optimal physical technology indicators like Farrell's "Hyperbolic Technical Efficiency" index defined in (Fare, Grosskopf and Lovell, 1985) are well known measures of this type:

$$F_g \left(x, u \right) = \inf \left\{ \lambda \geq 0: \ \left(\lambda x, \lambda^{-1} u \right) \in G \right\} \tag{5.1}$$

where   x, u are input and output vectors (the technology);
G is a set of possible (comparable) technologies.
The potential (or rather inefficiency) of a base technology A = (x, u) is defined as the "path length" from A to the periphery of G along a hyperbolic curve, and is sufficiently general to include the production of goods and bads (Russell, 1990).   The axiomatic foundations of (5.1), however are inadequate.   Farrell's index is often rank inconsistent with respect to the metric chosen (Euclidean distance, the city block distance, Boolean coordinates); the selection criterion for the hyperbolic path is deficient and it has been criticized for being incompatible with profit maximizing.   Also, results depend only on point A = (x, u) belonging to the hyperbolae $\Gamma = \left\{ (y, v) \in G: \ (y, v) = \left(\lambda x, \lambda^{-1} u \right) \right\}$ for different λ. Points in G that do not satisfy this criteria cannot be compared with A, limiting its applicability when $G \cap \Gamma$ is small or empty.
This article attempts to ameliorate these deficiencies by devising better technology indices, and improving the axiomatic foundations of Farrell's index.   During the course of the analysis it will also be shown how Farrell's index can be made compatible with profit maximizing.

The Formulation of the Problem

Any technology index must have a few basic characteristics (Fare, 1985):
G - a set of technologies;
A∈G - a designated initial (base) technology;
$\rangle$ - a binary basis for comparing technological efficiency on G: Y > Z, if Y, Z∈G, the technology Y is more efficient than technology Z.

The set G can be either finite or infinite, include real technologies or those under development, and have any configuration. The relation $\rangle$ should be consistent with the structure of G in the sense that in any non-trivial case the technologies compared should include a large subset of G x G.

The relative efficiency of the two technologies may depend on the initial (base) point. That is why the relation $\rangle$ is generally deemed to depend on the point A: $\rangle = \rangle_A$.

The problem in the general case is to construct a technological efficiency scale (in the sense of (Farrell, 1957)).

Let us specify the structure of the set of technologies G and the efficiency relation $\rangle_A$, starting with G. Each technology $Y \in G$ is supposed to be completely defined by the input vector (y) and output vector (v) used or produced during a specified interval. There are two non-overlapping finite classification sets containing non-exchangeable inputs and outputs for the technologies in G. Additionally, a system of quantification is defined to measure of inputs and outputs. This allows inputs and outputs to be represented as elements of two, fixed dimensional, vector spaces. The operation of addition in each of these spaces corresponds to the union of the sets, and the operation of positive scalar multiplication corresponds to the proportional increase or decrease of elements in the set. Each technology $Y \in G$ is thus representable as a couple of non-negative vectors $Y = (y, v)$, $y \in R_+^n$, $v \in R_+^m$, where n is the number of inputs, and m the number of outputs.

The set of technologies G consists of homogeneous elements: the sets of inputs and outputs used by these technologies are the same size, and are expressed in the same units.

Let us now specify the characteristics of the strict and loose technological efficiency relatives $\rangle_A$. The efficiency of technologies Y, $Z \in G$ are comparable only if they can be compared with the base technology $A \in G$. When describing a production technology as a transformation of an input vector into an output vector, productivities should be explicitly considered (the existence of such structures and proportions between inputs and outputs is well-known (Pfanzagl, 1971)). Generally this structure can be represented by two binary relationships (η and θ) on the input and output sets. Let (i_1, i_2) $\in \eta$, if inputs y_{i_1} and y_{i_2} are proportional for a given technology. Analogously, let (j_1, j_2) $\in \theta$ if two outputs j_1 and j_2 are proportionally dependent for a given technology.

Evidently, η and θ are equivalence relations on the sets $\{1, ..., n\}$ and $\{1, ..., m\}$ respectively splitting them into non-overlapping subsets: $\{1, ..., n\} = N_1 \cup ... \cup N_k$, $\{1, ..., m\} = M_1 \cup ... \cup M_l$, denoting the sets of equivalent indices (from the point of view of η and θ). Now if $i_1, i_2 \in N_t$ for t, $1 \le t \le k$, then for each possible input vectors y, $y' \in R^n$ $y'_{i_1}/y'_{i_2} = y_{i_1}/y_{i_2}$. But if i_1, i_2 $(1 \le i_1, i_2 \le n)$ belong to different sets N_t, then y_{i_1} and y_{i_2} are functionally independent. Let ω denote the coupled equivalence relations $\omega = (\eta, \theta)$, and consider ω as a binary relation on the sets of couples $(y, v) \in R^n_+$ x R^m_+. Let us call this relation ω, the scheme of technological proportions, and the technology vectors $y = (y, v)$ and $z = (z, w)$ ω-parallel, if $y_{i_1}/y_{i_2} = z_{i_1}/z_{i_2}$ for each $(i_1, i_2) \in \eta$ and $y_{i_1}/y_{i_2} = w_{i_1}/w_{i_2}$ for each $(j_1, j_2) \in \theta$. Let ω-parallel vectors Y and Z be denoted by $Y\|_\omega Z$.

Evidently, if $Z = (z, w)$ where $z \ne 0$, $w \ne 0$, then the vectors Y and Z are ω-parallel iff the non-zero numbers $\lambda_1, ..., \lambda_n, \mu_1, ..., \mu_m$ exist such that $y_i = \lambda_i z_i, i = 1, ..., n$; $v_j = \mu_j w_j, j = 1, ..., m$, where $\lambda_i = \lambda_{i'}$, if i, i' $\in N_t$ for some t, $1 \le t \le k$, and $\mu_j = \mu_{j'}$, if j, j' $\in M_s$ for some $1 \le s \le l$. The strongest form of ω-parallelism occurs when $\eta = \{1, ..., n\}$ x $\{1, ..., n\}$, $\theta = \{1, ..., m\}$ x $\{1, ..., m\}$; in this case all inputs are functionally dependent, and so are all outputs, and each vector Y ω-parallel to Z is $Y = (y, v) = (\lambda z, \mu w)$, where $\lambda, \mu \ne 0$. Let us assume that ω consists of any η and θ satisfying the following property: if $x_i = 0$ then η contains any couple like (i, k) where $1 \le k \le n$, and if $u_j = 0$ then θ contains any couple like (j, l) where $1 \le l \le n$. These properties ensure the coincidence of the distribution of zero elements of the base vector A and all vectors Y ω-parallel to it. The corresponding relation ω will be the weakest variant of ω-parallelism. These two extreme forms were used in (Fare, 1985) when constructing Farrell's and Russell's technological efficiency indices.

It means that technological efficiency is only comparable for those vectors that are ω-parallel to each other and to the base vector A. The structure of ω is defined either apriori using the information about the whole set of technologies or--in the minimal variant--the condition of ω-parallelism ensures the coincidence of zero elements in the vectors compared.

Let Π^A_ω denote the set of the vectors $Y \in R^n_+$ x R^m_+ which are ω-parallel to the vector A. Then technological efficiency is only comparable for the elements in $G^A_\omega = G \cap \Pi^A_\omega$: $Y \rangle_A Z \rightarrow Y, Z \in G^A_\omega$.

Any transitive binary relation can be used as a base for comparing the efficiency of the elements Y, $Z \in G_\omega^A$. In this context let us define the strict relation of efficiency $\rangle$ according to (Fare, 1985) by a component-wise comparison of the technological factors: Y is strictly more efficient than Z if Y, $Z \in G_\omega^A$ and

$$y_i < z_i \quad \text{or} \quad y_i = z_i = 0, \quad i = 1, \ldots, n,$$

$$(5.2)$$

$$v_j > w_j \quad \text{or} \quad v_j = w_j = 0, \quad j = 1, \ldots, m.$$

(Let us denote the relation $\rangle_A$ defined by $>_{A\omega}$.)

Loose technological efficiency is derived from the above: $Y \geq_{A\omega} Z$ if either $Z = Y \in G_\omega^A$ or $Y >_{A\omega} Z$. The relation $>_{A\omega}$ is the intersection of the relation $\rangle_A$ and that of the membership to Π_ω^A. Let us call it the efficiency relationship jointly based on technology A and the dependence ω.

Each technological efficiency measure thus is defined by the following list:

$$S = < G, A, \omega, >_{A\omega} >,$$

where   G is a subset $R^n \times R^m$ (the set of technologies analyzed);
    A is a designated element in G (the base technology);
    $\omega = (\eta, \theta)$ is a couple of two equivalence relations, $\eta \subset \{1, \ldots, n\} \times \{1, \ldots, n\}$, $\theta \subset \{1, \ldots, m\} \times \{1, \ldots, m\}$ (the configurations of technological proportions);
    $>_{A\omega}$ is a transitive binary relation on G_ω^A of type (5.2) based on the technology A and proportions ω.

Under these conditions the technology index computed for base technology A, compared with a set of technologies G will be a function F defined on the set of subsets $R_+^n \times R_+^m$ containing A. This implicit truncation is frequently encountered when firms evaluate themselves (the point A). Central authorities are more likely to take a broader perspective.

Axiomatic Description and Interpretation of Technology Indices

Let us consider the characteristics of function F more thoroughly. This is best accomplished with the aid of two sets of axioms. The first (Axioms A1-

A3, A6) are general (see also Forsund, 1987; Antonov, 1991; Kleiner, 1986); the second (Axioms A4, A5, A7) are specific. Other axioms are more restrictive. These axioms are not unique, but these have the virtue of simplicity and are relatively unrestrictive.

The core relationships required to define a homomorphic scale between two systems (Farrell, 1957), are elaborated below and include a unitary relationship (the designated point A) and four binary relationships (efficiency, proportionality, inclusivity and superiority).

1. The Domain and the Range of the Function F.

Let $B^A (R_+^n \times R_+^m)$ denote a set of all subsets $G \subset R_+^n \times R_+^m$ containing the point $A \in R_+^n \times R_+^m$. The function F generally depends on A, is defined on $B^A (R_+^n \times R_+^m)$ and ranges on 0 to 1:

$$A1: \quad F = F_A: \quad B^A \left(R_+^n \times R_+^m \right) \to (0, 1] \tag{5.3}$$

2. F on a One-Element Set.

As $G \in B^A (R_+^n \times R_+^m)$, the only possible case is $G = \{A\}$. Defining F_A for $G = \{A\}$ yields the measure unit and makes the scale absolute. The technology index of A with respect to itself is 1:

$$A2: \quad F_A (\{A\}) = 1 \tag{5.4}$$

The specification of units and scales in Axioms A1 and A2 are conventional and do not need any special justification. The condition $0 < F(G) \leq 1$ means that each set of technologies G contains the "test" point A. Property (5.4) refers to the reflexivity of loose efficiency.

3. The Behavior of the Function F on a Two-Element Set G.

This group includes four properties, the first two of which concern the monotonic continuity of the efficiency index, and the last the local homogeneity of the index, i.e. its behavior when the technological vector is changed proportionally (but restrictively).

Let us assume that $F_A (\{Y, A\})$, where $Y \neq A$, describes the degree to which technology Y is more efficient than the technology A (if the technology Y is really more efficient than A, $Y \geq_{A\omega} A$), and $F_A (\{Y, A\}) = 1$ if the relation $Y \geq_{A\omega} A$ does not hold.

The first axiom of this group defines the "direction" of efficiency (the greater the efficiency the lower the value of the index $F_A (\{Y, A\})$), and the relationship between the technology index and actual efficiency (the non-strict monotonic continuity of the index for the relation $\geq_{A\omega}$):

A3: $F_A(\{Y, A\}) \leq F_A(\{Z, A\})$, if $Y \geq_{A\omega} Z \in G$ (5.5)

The first property is related to Axioms A1 and A2, the second is a minimal requirement for a well behaved efficiency index.

When a strictly more efficient technology is compared with the base technology, the function should have sufficient "resolution" to discriminate all better technologies from the base:

A4: $F_A(\{Y, A\}) < 1 \leftrightarrow Y >_{A\omega} A$ (5.6)

This property is not essential but without it the relative efficiency of part of the technologies set may be indiscernible. The efficiency index thus should be strictly monotonic to distinguish the efficiency rank of all technologies with respect to the base.

Axioms A3 and A4 reflect the behavior of the function F with regard to the binary efficiency relationship $>_{A\omega}$ on the set G. As these technologies are described by couples of vectors, there is one other binary relationship that should be noted, associated with multiplication on a vector space.

Let us note first that if y, $\dot{y}' \in R_+^n$ are input vectors and $y' = \alpha y$, where $\alpha < 1$, then it can be assumed that y' is "better" (is more efficient) than y by α^{-1} times. Similarly, if v, $v' \in R_+^m$ are output vectors and $v' = v/\alpha$, where $\alpha < 1$, then v' is also "better" than v by α^{-1} times. The significance of Axiom A5 elaborated below is that it requires that technology $Y' = (y', v')$ consisting of input vector y' and output vector v' should be "better" than technology $Y = (y, v)$ by $\alpha^{-1} > 1$ times. This implies that efficiency is calculated for each coordinate of the technological vector, and that an equiproportional "improving" of all coordinates by $\alpha^{-1} > 1$ times makes the whole technology proportionally "better". This property should not be dismissed as counterfactual because there are no grounds for assuming that different coordinates of the technological vector have different weights or there are non-linear dependencies between the outputs and scale (intensity).

Finally, it is reasonable to assume that if a technology Y is more efficient than the base by $\beta > 1$, and the technology αY is more efficient than Y by $\alpha^{-1} > 1$ then αY is more efficient than A by $\alpha^{-1} \beta > 1$ (αY, where $\alpha > 0$, here and below denotes a technological vector $\alpha Y = (\alpha y, \alpha^{-1} v)$). Thus, for equiproportional technologies more efficient than the base $\alpha Y >_{A\omega} Y >_{A\omega} A$ are transitive where $\alpha < 1$. This property can be formulated as follows:

$$F_A (\{\alpha Y, A\}) = \alpha F_A (\{Y, A\}), \text{ where } \alpha < 1, Y >_{A\omega} A \qquad (5.7)$$

By A4 the property $Y >_{A\omega} A$ is equivalent to $F (\{Y, A\}) < 1$. It also is not difficult to show that if A4 is true then property (5.7) is equivalent to:

$$F_A (\{\alpha Y, A\}) = \alpha F_A (\{Y, A\}), \text{ if } F_A (\{\alpha Y, A\}) < 1 \qquad (5.8)$$

In other words, the efficiency index of a given technology with regard to the base is assumed to be a linearly homogeneous function differing by a scale coefficient, but due to the boundedness of the index (Axiom A1) this property is true only if the initial technology and the scaled one are strictly more efficient than the base.

We assume additionally that given Y and A, $F (\{\alpha Y, A\})$ depends continuously on α. This assumption can be relaxed if technological efficiency changes discretely when the technology changes equiproportionally and continuously.

Axiom A5 therefore can be formulated as follows:

A5: $F_A (\{\alpha Y, A\})$ is a continuous function $\qquad$ (5.9)
for $\alpha > 0$ for each $Y \in R_+^n$ x R_+^m, where
$F_A (\{\alpha Y, A\}) = \alpha F_A (\{Y, A\})$,
if $F_A (\{Y, A\}) < 1$ and $F_A (\{\alpha Y, A\}) < 1$

4. The properties of the function F with respect to the structures of the set $B^A (R_+^n x R_+^m)$.

On the set of subsets $G \subset R_+^n$ x R_+^m there are two basic types of structures: set-theoretic operations and efficiency relationships connected with the base set R_+^n x R_+^m. The principal example of set-theoretic operations is inclusivity. It is reasonable to suppose that the larger the set, the greater the possibility of finding an efficient technology:

$$A6: \quad F_A (G') \le F_A (G), \text{ if } G \subseteq G' \subset R_+^n \times R_+^m \qquad (5.10)$$

The efficiency relationships can be illuminated by defining a binary domination relationship on the set B^A ($R_+^n \times R_+^m$). Let a set G' dominate the set G (it is more efficient) if there is an epimorphism φ: $G \to G'$ such that F ($\{\varphi (Y), A\}$) $\leq F$ ($\{Y, A\}$) for each $Y \in G$ (denoted as $G' \therefore G$).

The property $G' \therefore G$ means that each element $Y \in G$ is dominated by an element in G', providing a superior efficiency reading. $G' \therefore G$ requires the function F to be monotonically continuous.

A7: $F_A(G') \leq F_A(G)$, if $G' \therefore G$ (5.11)

Indeed, if each element $Y \in G$ has a lower efficiency value than some element $Y' \in G'$ compared to the base technology then the index of the whole set G should not exceed the index of set G'. The contrary would imply that the index of a set is not a function of the indices of its elements, but depends on the relations between them.

Properties (5.3)-(5.11) comprise a system of axioms reflecting normal attributes of a technology index. Theorem 1 below describes the general form of the index valued with prices. The index of two technologies satisfying properties A1-A5 is described in Theorem 2.

Before turning to these theorems it is necessary to introduce one more special operation for comparing scalar indicators. Let a and b be positive or negative real values of an indicator during some time interval (e.g., the profit or loss per unit of time). Let us assume that the greater the value of the indicator the better. The comparison of two values a and b can be undertaken either with (the multiplicative, index approach) or difference (the additive approach). The multiplicative approach is adopted here.

It is usually assumed that a is "greater" than b by k times if $a/b = k$, where $a \geq b$, iff $k \geq 1$. However, this measure is possible only if a and b are positive. If a, b < 0 then for the multiplicative comparison, the relationship is reversed: a is k times "greater" than b, if $b/a = k$; then $a \geq b$ iff $k \geq 1$. If $a > 0$, $b < 0$ then it is evident that a is infinitely greater than b.

Let us introduce a special binary operation of directed division on R, that can be interpreted without regard to the signs of the operands as "the frequency with which one value is better than the other". Let $a|b$ denote this operation and

$$a \mid b = \begin{cases} a/b, \text{ if } a, b > 0 \\ b/a, \text{ if } a, b < 0 \\ \infty, \text{ if } a \geq 0, b < 0 \text{ or } a > 0, b = 0 \\ 0, \text{ if } a \leq 0, b > 0 \text{ or } a < 0, b = 0 \end{cases}$$

Because this operation is zero degree homogeneous relative to its arguments, the comparison pertains to scale.

The operation defined on the set of numbers normally involves an operation on the set of functions. If $f(x)$ and $g(x)$ are functions defined on a set D and ranging in $R \cup \infty$ then the function $h(x) = f(x) \mid g(x)$ for each $x \in D$ fixed shows the degree to which $f(x)$ is "better" than $g(x)$. Under some conditions a function can be defined comparing f and g on the whole set D. Let

$$f \mid g = \inf_{x \in D} f(x) \mid g(x).$$

If $f(x)$ and $g(x)$ measure the behavior of two different entities under the same conditions defined by the vector $x \in D$ (e.g., $f(x)$ and $g(x)$ are the estimated profits of the two enterprises with externally imposed input and output prices), $f \mid g$ shows the degree to which the first outperforms the second (given price-fixing).

We can expound Theorems 1 and 2 by describing the structure and properties of the technology index using the following notation. Let $p \in R_+^n$ be an input price vector, $q \in R_+^m$ an output price vector, $p = (p, q)$, and $Y = (y, v) \in R_+^n \times R_+^m$ an arbitrary technology. Let

$$\pi (P, Y) = \Sigma \, q_j v_j - \Sigma \, p_i y_i$$

denote the profit generated by technology Y and prices P. Let $\pi(Y)$ denote the profit generated by technology Y, given price vector P. Let us also assume that if $y = (y_1, \ldots, y_n)$, $z = (z_1, \ldots, z_n) \in R^n$ then $y \circ z = (y_1 z_1, \ldots, y_n z_n) \in R^n$. The result of the directed division $\pi(Y) \mid \pi(A)$ denotes the minimal (over all possible prices) profit ratio of technologies Y and A.

Theorem 1. Let $x \in R_+^n$ be a non-zero input vector, $u \in R_+^m$ a non-zero output vector, $A = (x, u)$ a base technology, $w = (\eta, \theta)$ a scheme of technological dependence, $>_{A\omega}$ a technological efficiency relationship with the base technology A and the scheme ω, $G_\omega^A \subset R_+^n \times R_+^m$ a set of technologies comparable with A. Let $F:B^A (R_+^n \times R_+^m) \to [0, 1]$ be some function. Then

1) The following assertions (a), (b) and (c) are equivalent:

a) The function F satisfies the Axioms A1-A7.
b) The function F is representable as

$$F(G) = \inf_{(y,v)\in G_\omega^A} \max_{\substack{x_i \neq 0 \\ u_j \neq 0}} \left\{ y_i/x_i,\ u_j/v_j \right\}, \quad G\in B^A \left(R_+^n \times R_+^m \right) \qquad (5.12)$$

c) $$F(G) = \left(\sup_{Y\in G_\omega^A} \pi(Y) \,|\, \pi(A) \right)^{-1} \text{ for each } G\in B^A \left(R_+^n \times R_+^m \right) \qquad (5.13)$$

2) For each $G\in B^A$ ($R_+^n \times R_+^m$), each technology $Y = (y, v)\in G$ contains all technologies $Y' = (y', v')\|_\omega Y$ such that $y' \geq y$ and $v' \leq v$; the function F satisfying the properties (a)-(c) coincides with Farrell's hyperbolic efficiency index:

$$F(G) = F_g (x, u) = \inf \left\{ \lambda \geq 0 \colon \left(\lambda x, \lambda^{-1} u \right) \in G \right\} \qquad (5.14)$$

The first part of Theorem 1 establishes a one to one correspondence between the structural form of the technological efficiency index (5.12) and the system of properties A1-A7, and enables the inverse function to be interpreted as the maximum ratio of profits for all comparable technologies with respect to the base technology (this ratio being calculated at non-Paretian prices for each producer). The lower/greater the technological efficiency index of the set G, the greater (lower) is the profit generated by the technologies in G.

Let us note that if the inputs (extended to include "bads") of the technological vector Y∈G are denoted by negative numbers, and vectors Y are represented as functions Y(i) over the set of component numbers $1 \leq i \leq n + m$ then the formula (5.12) for the technology index satisfying the Axioms A1-A7 can be rewritten using directed division | as:

$$F(G) = \left(\sup_{(y,v)\in G_\omega^A} Y \,|\, A \right)^{-1}, \quad G\in B^A \left(R_+^n \times R_+^m \right)$$

The second part of Theorem 1 establishes the correspondence between the generalized technology index and Farrell's hyperbolic index for sets containing all "inferior" technologies based on componentwise comparisons of input and output technology vectors (e.g., is strongly disposable).

The characterization of the above technology index for the case comparing two technologies Y and A (which corresponds to a one- or two-element set G) is given by the following theorem.

Theorem 2. 1) In the notation of Theorem 1 the following properties are equivalent:

> a) The function $F(\{Y, A\})$ satisfies the Axioms A1-A5.
>
> b) For each $Y\|_\omega A$

$$F\left(\{Y, A\}\right) = \min \left\{ \max_{\substack{x_i \neq 0 \\ u_j \neq 0}} \{y_i/x_i, u_j/v_j\}, 1 \right\} \tag{5.15}$$

> c) For each $Y\|_\omega A$

$$F\left(\{Y, A\}\right) = \left(\max \{\pi(y) \mid \pi(A), 1\}\right)^{-1} \tag{5.16}$$

> 2) If $Y \geq_{A\omega} A$ then

$$1/F\left(\{Y, A\}\right) = \min_{\substack{x_i \neq 0 \\ u_j \neq 0}} \{x_i/y_i, v_j/u_j\} = \pi(Y) \mid \pi(A) \tag{5.17}$$

The equivalence of the assertions (b) and (c) of Theorem 1 as well as Theorem 2 can be interpreted as an equivalence between technical and "economic" efficiency for a set of inferior non-Paretian prices. When prices are unstable and unpredictable, managers may prefer to maximize technological attainment in physical terms rather than profit.

Conclusion

We have found that a technology index satisfying conventional axioms can be formulated as a function of the ratios of the components of the technologies, given zero elasticities of factor substitution. Non factor substitutability is the consequence of the componentwise definition of relative efficiency and the Axiom A4; the non-substitutability of inputs and outputs is due to the Axiom A5.

This result can be interpreted as follows. The system of Axioms A1-A5 (along with the property $Y \geq_{A\omega} A$) provide a conceptual basis for input output systems of the Leontief type with rectangular isoquants (the linearly homogeneous concave function with zero elasticity of factors substitution) that can be arranged as component ratios of vectors Y and A or of their inverse values (for the input components). Its representation as

$$1/F \left(\{Y, A\}\right) = \inf_{p \geq 0} \left(\pi(P, Y) \mid \pi(P, A)\right) \tag{5.18}$$

is analogous to representing a production function as a lower bound of a ratio of observed minimum cost to optimal minimum unit cost over the set of possible prices. Such a representation for the case of linearly homogeneous concave production functions can be obtained by the duality theory of the production functions and minimal cost per unit functions (Bergson, 1953). If $n = 0$, equation (5.18) immediately follows from the duality theorem of production functions and minimal unit cost. The reciprocal assertion is also true: if the efficiency index of a technology Y is defined by a Leontief function of component ratios of two vectors, and the profit generated by technology Y is a linear homogeneous function of prices, input and output vectors, then the profit generated by technology A can be formulated in the same manner. In a general case, comparative technological efficiency defined as a lower bound of the directed ratio of corresponding profits over a price set appears to have no clear economic interpretation.

The efficiency index (5.12) and, Farrell's index possess the simplest functional structure, which can be considered a virtue for some purposes. They provide a basis for constructing more sophisticated indices, where factor substitution and input-output elasticities are variable and diverse. The use of axiomatics for these and other extensions should help illuminate their full economic implications.

Bibliography

Afanas"ev, M., "Methods of Estimating Productive Efficiency for the Enhancement of Plan Decisionmaking", *Atlantic Economic Journal*, Vol. 20, No. 1, March 1992, pp. 1-14.

Antonov, M.B., A.B. Pomansky, and G. Yu. Trofimov, "Homothetic Production Functions and Efficiency Bounds Analysis", *Economics and Mathematical Methods*, Vol. 27, 4, 1991 (in Russian).

Baltrushevich, T.G. and V.N. Liefshits, "Innovation Efficiency Assessment: "Old" and "New" Problems", *Economics and Mathematical Methods*, V. 28, 1, 1992 (in Russian).

Bergson, A., *Soviet National Income and Product in 1937*, Columbia University Press, New York, 1953.

Dmitruk, A.V. and G.A. Koshevoy, "On the Existence of a Technical Efficiency Criterion", *Journal of Economic Theory*, 55, 1991.

Fare, R., S. Grosskopf and C.K. Lovell, *The Measurement of Efficiency of Production*, 1985, Boston: Kluwer-Nijhoff Publishing.

Fare, R., S. Grosskopf, C.K. Lovell, and C. Pasurka, "Multilinear Productivity comparisons When Some Outputs are Undesirable", *The Review of Economics and Statistics*, 93, 1989.

Farrell, M.J., "The Measurement of Productive Efficiency", *Journal of the Royal Statistical Society*, Ser. A, General, 120, Part 3, 1957.

Forsund, F.R. and Hiallmarsson, L., *Analyses of Industrial Structure: A Putty-Clay Approach*, Stockholm, 1987.

Kleiner, G.B., *Production Functions: Theory, Methods, Application*, Moscow: Finansy i Statistika Publishers, 1986 (in Russian).

_____, *Ensuring a Balanced Plan for a Corporation*, Moscow: MIPK Minpribora SSSR Publishers, 1988 (in Russian).

L'vov, D.S., *Effective Management of Technical Development*, Moscow: Ekonomika Publishers, 1990 (in Russian).

Mathematical Economic Models in the Enterprise Management System, Moscow: Nauka Publishers, 1983 (in Russian).

Pfanzagl, J., *Theory of Measurement*, 2nd ed., Wirzburg, Wien: Physica-Verl., 1971.

Russell, R., "Continuity of measures of Technical Efficiency", *Journal of Economic Theory*, August 1990, 51 (2).

6 Average and Marginal Factor Productivity: Interdependencies and Efficiency

George B. Kleiner

Introduction

Efficient production requires that prices be equated with competitive minimum marginal cost. Often this requirement may not be met, but this is difficult to ascertain with the kind of output and input cost data employed in production function studies. This limitation can be overcome in some cases with the aid of a new concept, the "mobility of factor productivity" that allows investigators to determine whether enterprises are operating in stage 1, 2, or 3, and hence profit maximizing. Whenever it can be shown that profit maximizing is incomplete, this constitutes proof certain that enterprises are inefficient.

This chapter analyzes various classes of production functions with constant and variable mobilities of factor productivity that can be estimated to ascertain the stage of production firms are operating at, and derivatively whether profit maximization is incomplete. An empirical test of the methodology on contemporary Russian enterprises is provided in chapter 11.

The Mobility of Factor Productivity

The mobility of factor productivity caused by a unit change in the employment of factor i, all other factors impounded can be defined as the elasticity of average and marginal products, for the production function $y = f(x_1, ..., x_n)$, that is

$$MFP_i = \frac{dAP_i}{dMP} / \frac{AP_i}{MP_i}, \ x_1, \ \ldots, \ x_{i-1}, \ x_{i+1}, \ \ldots, \ x_n$$

(6.1)

$$= Const; \quad i = 1, \ \ldots, n$$

MFP_i are second order characteristics of production functions with respect to the factor space (Kleiner, 1986b). The mobility induced by unit factor changes will be denoted as $MFP_i[f](x)$ if both the function for which MFP_i and the point calculated need to be jointly identified. The mobility of factor productivity is a property of a production function in the same sense as the marginal rate of factor substitution and the elasticity of factor substitution reflect input-output relationships.

$MFP_i(x)$ approximately shows the percentage change in average productivity if marginal productivity changes one percent in response to a unit variation in the ith factor (cross factor elasticities are analyzed in section 5).

The direction of change in total productivity for a prescribed input level with variable efficiency is indicated by the sign of MFP_i; if $MFP_i > 0$, total productivity declines when marginal productivity falls, and increases if $MFP_i < 0$. If the absolute value of MFP_i is small, then the average productivity may be relatively stable under the same circumstances. If $|MFP_i(x)|$ is large total productivity is likely to be more sensitive to technological change. In models in which $MP_1(x_1, \ldots, x_n)$ pertains to value (utility) with respect to its price, or rent, MFP_i is the elasticity of factor productivity divided by its price (that is, the elasticity of labor productivity divided by the wage). It should be noted that the properties of the production function under discussion are evaluated locally and are interpretable only for small changes in input use. By contrast MFP_i may reflect small or large changes in factor employment over time because the interpretation of μ_1 at point x depends on small changes of MP_i, not on small changes in the ith input per se. Unlike the marginal rate of factor substitution and the elasticity of factor substitution, the mobility of factor productivity is sensitive to the volume of factors employed, including $n = 1$.

The relationship between average and marginal productivity has been extensively examined in the literature (Intriligator, 1971; Brown, 1971). In (Intriligator, 1971) this relationship was used to form an "economic domain"--a set of points in the resource space satisfying neoclassical criteria. The first explicit investigation of the interdependencies between marginal and average productivity, however, was probably undertaken in Kleiner (1986a, 1988).

Before proceeding with an analysis of the relationship between $MFP_i(x)$ and the elasticity of factor substitution, $MFP_i(x)$ needs to be more precisely defined. The following transformation was considered in (6.2): $x_k \rightarrow x_k$, where $x_k = x_k$ under $k \neq i$, $x_i' = df/dx_i$. $MFP_i(x)$ as expressed in (6.2) is correct, if the transformation where the Jacobian is d^2f/dx_i^2 is non zero at point x. The general definition of μ_i is as follows:

$$MFP_i(x) = \begin{cases} \dfrac{d(f/x_i)}{df_i'} \Big/ \dfrac{f}{x_i f_i} & \text{if} \quad f_{ii}''(x) \neq 0, \\[2ex] 1 & \text{if} \quad f_{ii}''(x) = 0, \left(f_i'(x)x_i - \right. \\ & \qquad \left. - f(x)\right) f_i'(x) \neq 0, \\[2ex] \infty & \text{if} \quad f_{ii}''(x) = 0, \left(f_i'(x)x_i - \right. \\ & \qquad \left. - f(x)\right) f_i'(x) = 0. \end{cases}$$

(6.2)

Thus $MFP_i[f] \equiv \infty$ for a linear function f.

From this we can get the following formula for $MFP_i(x)$:

$$MFP_i[f](x) = \frac{x_i f_i'(x)^2 - f(x)f_i'(x)}{x_i f(x)f_{ii}''(x)}$$

(6.3)

$$= -\frac{f_i'(x)}{x_i f_{ii}''(x)} \left(1 - \frac{x_i f_i'(x)}{f(x)}\right)$$

For homogeneous production functions with two factors the mobility of factor productivity $MFP_1(x)$, $MFP_2(x)$ and elasticity of their substitution $\sigma_{12}(x)$ are functionally related as described in the following theorem.

Theorem 1: Let $f(x_1, x_2)$ be a homogeneous production function of degree γ. Then MFP_1, MFP_2 and σ_{12} are connected by the identity

$$(\gamma - 1)^2 \left(1 - MFP_1(x)\right) \left(1 - MFP_2(x)\right) = \left(1 - \frac{MFP_1(x)}{\sigma_{12}(x)}\right)$$

$$\left(- \frac{MFP_2(x)}{\sigma_{12}(x)}\right).$$

If $\gamma = 1$, then the mobility of factor productivity for both inputs is identical and coincides with elasticity of their substitution:

$$MFP_1 = MFP_2 = \sigma_{12}.$$

This identity for linear homogeneous functions in the two factor case is considered in (6.6) in a different form. If $\gamma \neq 1$ then $MFP_1(x)$ and $MFP_2(x)$ are functionally independent.

The relationship between the mobility of factor productivity and the elasticity of their substitution can also be characterized in the following way. Let f be a production function of n arguments. Consider function $\phi(t, x_1, ..., x_n)$ of $n + 1$ arguments, which is determined as

$$\phi(t, x_1, ..., x_n) = tf(x_1/t, x_2, ..., x_n).$$

If t is interpreted as time, then $tf(x_1/t, x_2, ..., x_n)$ can be considered as total output during t periods under the condition that the first resource x_1 was distributed equally among periods and the other resources were invariant. If t is interpreted as set of firms, and the resource x_1 is equally distributed among them then $tf(x_1/t, x_2, ..., x_n)$ will equal total output. Proportion ϕ/f shows efficiency for an equal distribution of the first resource among t identical firms instead of concentrating them in a single enterprise (usually $\phi/f > 1$ if $t > 1$). The function ϕ is homogeneous of degree one for t, x_1. (The proofs of this and other theorems are not considered in this paper).

It can be shown that mobility of the factor productivity of the first input for production function f at points $x_1, ..., x_n$ equals the direct partial elasticity of factor substitution with respect to t and u for the function $\phi(t, u, x_2, ..., x_n)$ at the point t, $tx_1, x_2, ..., x_n$, where $t > 0$ is an arbitrary number:

$$MFP_1\big[f(x_1, \ldots, x_n)\big]\,(x_1, \ldots, x_n) = \sigma_{tu}\big[tf(u/t, x_2, \ldots, x_n)\big]$$

$$(t, tx_1, x_2, \ldots, x_n)$$

(6.4)

Since for homogeneous functions employing two inputs the elasticities of factor substitution depend only on their proportion, we can take $t = 1$ in (6.5):

$$MFP_1\big[f(x_1, \ldots, x_n)\big]\,(x_1, \ldots, x_n) = \sigma_{tu}\big[tf(u/t, x_2, \ldots, x_n)\big]$$

$$(1, x_1, x_2, \ldots, x_n).$$

Analogous formulas can be written for MFP_i under any $i = 1, \ldots, n$.
Let's consider the proportion (6.5) in the case of $n = 1$:

$$MFP_1\big[f(x_1)\big]\,(x_1) = \sigma_{tu}\big[tf\,(u/t)\big]\,(t, tx_1) = \sigma_{tu}\big[tf(t)\big]\,(1, x_1). \quad (6.5)$$

Any linear homogeneous function of two variables $F(t, u)$ can be expressed as $t^*f(u/t)$, if we take $f(u/t) = F(1, u/t)$. Hence for any linear homogeneous nonnegative function $F(x_1, x_2)$ the following equality is true:

$$\sigma_{12}\big[F(x_1, x_2)\big]\,(x_1, x_2) = MFP_1\big[F(1, x_2/x_1)\big]\,(x_1). \quad (6.6)$$

This means that the correspondence between the mobility of factor productivity in the one-factor case and elasticity of factor substitution for linear homogeneous function where two factors are utilized is due to the one-to-one correspondence between these functions

$$F(x_1, x_2) \leftrightarrow F(1, x_2/x_1).$$

Thus the mobility of factor productivity is a natural extension for $n = 1$ of the definition of elasticity of factor substitution, which is inapplicable for a production function employing a single factor.

It should be noted that the expression (6.4) was suggested by P. Samuelson (1968) as an alternative "vector" definition of elasticity of factor substitution in n-factor case if $n > 2$. Let us consider this question more closely (see also Sato and Koizumi, 1973a,b; Samuelson, 1973).

P. Samuelson defined

$$\sigma_i = - \frac{f_i'(x)}{x_i f_{ii}''(x)} \left(1 - \frac{x_i f_i'(x)}{f(x)} \right)$$

and noticed that if $f'(x_1, x_2)$ is a linear homogeneous bivariate function, then 1) $\sigma_i = \sigma_{12}$, the elasticity of substitution, 2) $\sigma_i = x_i f_i/f$ are income shares, 3) sign (σ_i/dx_i) = sign $(\sigma_i - 1)$. This is why Samuelson suggested interpreting σ_i, $i = 1, ..., n$ as a generalization of elasticity of substitution for the n-factor case with $n > 2$. But if we take any arbitrary multifactor function, only the third proposition is valid. The connection between σ_i and the substitution indexes when $n > 2$ is less obvious than the case where $n = 2$. Therefore we suggest that $MFP_i = \sigma_i$ be considered an n-factor generalization of the elasticity of substitution not for the case $n > 2$, but in the case $n = 1$. As we saw MFP_i has the clear economic interpretation and can be useful in the multifactor case not as a "substitute" for different indices of the elasticity of substitution, but as a "complement". The functional form, where these elasticities are constant is discussed next section.

Production Functions with Constant Mobility of Factor Productivity

Let us first define the general form of a production function with fixed mobility for one of its factors. For this purpose we shall choose the general form of a homogeneous production function employing two factors and constant elasticity of factor substitution. According to (6.11) a homogeneous function $f(x_1, x_2)$ of degree γ with an elasticity of factor substitution $\sigma_{12}(x_1, x_2) = \sigma(x_1/x_2)$, where $\sigma(x_1/x_2)$ is a given function, can be expressed as:

$$f(x_1, x_2) = c_1 x_1^\gamma$$

$$\exp \left(-\int \frac{d(x_1/x_2)}{\dfrac{x_1}{x_2} + \dfrac{x_1^2}{x_2^2} c_2 * \exp \left(-\int \dfrac{d(x_1/x_2)}{(x_1/x_2) \sigma(x_1/x_2)} \right)} \right), \quad (6.7)$$

where c_1, c_2 are constant (this formula generalizes Sato-Hoffman's (1968) formula for an arbitrary γ and if $\gamma = 1$ it coincides with (6.8)). Formula

(6.8) can be interpreted in a more general sense if f is considered to be a function not of two but of n variables under the condition that f is a homogeneous function of degree γ for two first arguments. In this case constants c_1 and c_2 should be interpreted as functions of variables $x_3, ..., x_n$, and elasticity σ_{12} as a function of all variables $x_1, ..., x_n$ (for two first variables it depends on the proportions x_1/x_2). Function $\psi(t, u, x_2, ..., x_n) = tf(u/t, x_2, ..., x_n)$ of $n + 1$ arguments t, u, $x_2, ..., x_n$ is linear homogeneous of the two first arguments, allowing ψ to be represented in the following form

$$\varphi\left(t, u, x_2, ..., x_n\right) = c_1\left(x_2, ..., x_n\right) * t *$$

$$\exp\left(-\int \frac{d(t/u)}{t/u + (t^2/u^2)\, c_2\left(x_2, ..., x_n\right) \exp\left(-\int \frac{d(t/u)}{(t/u)\, \sigma\left(t/u, x_2, ..., x_n\right)}\right)}\right),$$

where $c_1(x_2, ..., x_n)$, $c_2(x_2, ..., x_n)$ are functions that permit the elasticity of t, u substitution $\sigma_{tu}(t, u, x_1, ..., x_n)$ and the function $\sigma(t/u, x_2, ..., x_n)$ to be equivalent.

Taking (6.7) into account we obtain a general form of function $f(x_1, ..., x_n)$ with constant mobility of productivity for the first factor $MFP_1[f](x_1, ..., x_n) = \mu(x_1, ..., x_n)$:

$$f\left(x_1, ..., x_n\right) = c_1\left(x_2, ..., x_n\right) *$$

$$\exp\left(\int \frac{dx_1}{x_1 + c_2\left(x_2, ..., x_n\right) * \exp\left(\int \frac{dx_1}{x_1 * \mu\left(x_1, ..., x_n\right)}\right)}\right),$$

where $\mu(x_1, ..., x_n)$ is given, $c_1(x_2, ..., x_n)$, $c_2(x_2, ..., x_n)$ are arbitrary twice differentiable functions.

Let us now define the general form of a function with constant mobility of factor productivity for all factors. We shall call the function $f(x_1, ..., x_n)$ a CMP function (Constant Mobility of Factor Productivity), if $MFP_i = const_i$, $i = 1, ..., n$. It has three subclasses: a set of CDMP functions (Constant Disparate Mobility of Factor Productivity), for which $MFP_i =$

const, $MFP_i \neq MFP_j$, when $i \neq j$; a set of CEMP functions (Constant Equal Mobility of Factor Productivity), for which $MFP_1 = ... = MFP_n = const \neq 1$, and a set of CUMP functions (Constant Unitary Mobility of Factor Productivity), for which $MFP_1 = ... = MFP_n = 1$. Functions with arbitrary variable arguments $MFP_1(x), ..., MFP_n(x)$ are classified as VMP (Variable Mobility of Factor Productivity).

The forms of CDMP, CEMP and CUMP functions are described by the following theorem.

Theorem 2: The CUMP class consists of functions of the following form:

$$f(x_1, ..., x_n) = \exp(a_0 + a_1 \ln x_1 + ... + a_n \ln x_n + a_{12} \ln x_1 \ln x_2$$
$$+ ... + a_{n-1,n} \ln x_{n-1} \ln x_n + ... + a_{1...n} \ln x_{1...} \ln x_n), \tag{6.8}$$

where $a_0, a_1, ..., a_{1...n}$ are nonnegative constants.[1]

2. The CEMP class contains functions of the type:

$$f(x_1, ..., x_n) = \left(a_0 + a_1 x_1^c + ... + a_n x_n^c + a_{12} x_1^c + ...\right.$$
$$\left. + a_{n-1,n} x_{n-1}^c x_n^c + ... + a_{1...n} x_1^c ... x_n^c\right)^{1/c}, \tag{6.9}$$

where $a_0, a_1, ..., a_n$ are nonnegative constants, and $c = 1 - 1/MFP_i$.[2]

3. The CDMP class consists of functions of the form:

$$f(x_1, ..., x_n) = \left(a_1 + b_1 x_1^c 1\right)^{1/c} 1 ... \left(a_n + b_n x_n^c n\right)^{1/c} n$$
$$\left(\text{if } MFP_i \neq MFP_j, MFP_i \neq 1, \quad i, j = 1, ..., n\right) \tag{6.10}$$

where $a_0, ..., a_n, b_1, ..., b_n$ are positive constants, $c_i = 1 - 1/MFP_i$, $i = 1, ..., n$, and of functions of the form:

$$f(x_1, ..., x_n) = a_0 x_1^c 1 \left(a_2 + b_2 x_2^c 2\right)^{1/c} 2 ... \left(a_n + b_n x_n^c n\right)^{1/c} n$$
$$\left(\text{if } MFP_i = 1, MFP_i \neq MFP_j, \quad i, j = 2, ..., n\right) \tag{6.11}$$

where $a_0, ..., a_n, b_2, ..., b_n$ are positive constants, $c_i = 1 - 1/MFP_i$, $c_i \neq c_j$, $c_i \neq 0$, $i, j = 2, ..., n$.[3]

The general form of the CMP functions is described by the following theorem.

Theorem 3: Let $f(x_1, ..., x_n)$ be a nonnegative twice differentiable function, defined over the positive orthant R_+^n.

The following conditions are equivalent: (a) the mobility of the productivity of the i-th factor, $MFP_i[f]$ is a nonzero constant, $i = 1, ..., n$; (b) there exists a partition of indices set $\{1, ..., n\}$ into nonintersecting subsets $N_1, ..., N_s$ and constants a_{0k}, $a_{i1...ir} \geq 0$, $c_2, ..., c_s$, such that the f function can be written as

$$f(x_1, ..., x_n) = \left[\exp\left(a_{01} + \sum_{r=1}^{|N_1|} \sum_{i_1<...<i_r N_1} a_{i_1...i_r} \ln x_{i_1} \cdots \ln x_{i_r} \right) \right]$$

$$* \prod_{k=2}^{s} \left(a_{0k} + \sum_{r=1}^{|N_k|} \sum_{i_1<...<i_r N_k} a_{i_1...i_r} x_{i_1}^{c_k} \cdots x_{i_r}^{c_k} \right)^{1/c_k} \tag{6.12}$$

where $|N_k|$ is a number of elements of a set N_k, $k = 1, ..., s$. In this case subsets $N_1, ..., N_s$ and the constants $c_2, ..., c_s$ are connected by $MFP_1[f], ..., MFP_n[f]$.

$MFP_i[f] = 1$, if $i \in N_1$ (if all $MFP_i[f]$ are not equal to one, coefficients $a_{i_1...i_r}$, where $i_1 < ... < i_r \in N_1$, are equal to zero);[4]

$MFP_i[f] = MFP_j[f]$, if $i, j \in N_k$ for some k, $1 \leq k \leq s$;
$MFP_i[f] \neq MFP_j[f]$, if i, j do not belong to a set N_k, $i \leq k \leq s$;
$c_k = 1 - 1/MFP_i[f]$ if $i \in N_k$, $k = 2, ..., s$.
In symbolic form we can write the theorem alternatively as
$$CMP = CUMP\,(N_0) \star CEMP\,(N_1) \star ... \star CEMP\,(N_s),$$
where $CEMP\,(N_i)$ is a CEMP function of variables x_k, $k \in N_i$.

It follows that for any set of nonzero constants $\alpha_1, ..., \alpha_n$ there exists a function $f(x_1, ..., x_n)$ of n variables, for which $MFP_i[f] = \alpha_i$, $i = 1, ..., n$.

To construct this function simply divide $\alpha_1, ..., \alpha_n$ into groups of equal values, calculate the number of groups s and define sets $N_1, ..., N_s$, and apply a CDMP function with $c_k = 1 - 1/\alpha_i$, $i \in N_k$, $k = 1, ..., s$, so that $MFP_1(x), ..., MFP_n(x)$ are functionally independent.

Let us restrict our attention to functions exhibiting constant mobility of factor productivity, and consider the extreme cases where $MFP_i(x) \equiv \infty$ and $MFP_i(x) \equiv 0$.

If $MFP_i(x) \equiv \infty$, then $f_{ii}'' \equiv 0$, $x_i f_i'^2 - f_i' f \neq 0$. This means that

$$f(x) = a\left(x_1, \ldots, \hat{x}_i, \ldots, x_n\right) + b\left(x_1, \ldots, \hat{x}_i, \ldots, x_n\right) \star x_i,$$

where a, b $\neq 0$ are functions of the other variables. If all MFP_1, ..., MFP_n are equal to infinity then

$$f\left(x_1, \ldots, x_n\right) = a_0 + a_1 x_1 + \ldots + a_n x_n + a_{12} x_1 x_2 + \ldots$$

$$+ a_{n-1,n} x_{n-1} x_n + \ldots + a_{1\ldots n} x_1 \ldots x_n$$

where $a_0, a_1, \ldots, a_{1\ldots n}$ are nonnegative constants and for each $i = 1, \ldots, n$ there exists a nonzero coefficient, containing i among indexes, and a nonzero coefficient, which does not contain i among its indexes. Sometimes functions of this form are called quasilinear, because they are linear in each variable.

We can obtain a similar functional form using the CEMP function. If we work with CDMP functions, then when $MFP_i \to \infty$ we get a class of functions

$$f\left(x_i, \ldots, x_n\right) = \left(a_{01} + a_1 x_1\right) \star \ldots \star \left(a_{0n} + a_n x_n\right),$$

where $a_{0i}, a_i > 0$, $i = 1, \ldots, n$. This is a more restricted form of the functions with constant infinite mobility of factor productivity.

The second extreme case is connected with the condition $MFP_i(x) \equiv 0$. We can easily show that there does not exist a function among twice differentiable functions for which $MFP_i(x) \equiv 0$ for all x under domain of the function f.

However the class of functions with zero constant mobility of factor productivity can be represented as a limit case of the class of functions with constant mobility of factor productivity (the elasticity of factor substitution, where σ_1 is defined only for twice differentiable functions also cannot be identical to zero). The limit of the CMP function

$$f\left(x_1, \ldots, x_n\right) = \prod_{k=1}^{S} \left(a_{0k} + \sum_{r=1}^{|N_k|} \sum_{i_1 < \ldots < i_r \, N_k} a_{i_1 \ldots i_r} x_{i_1}^{c_k} \ldots x_{i_r}^{c_k} \right)^{1/c_k} \tag{6.13}$$

under $c_k \to \infty$, $k = 1, ..., s$ (corresponding to $MFP_i \to 0^+$) is equal to

$$f(x_1, ..., x_n) = \prod_{k=1}^{S} \min_{1<r<|N_k|} \min_{i_1<...<i_r N_k} \left(1, \xi_{i_1...i_r} x_{i_1} ... x_{i_r}\right) \qquad (6.14)$$

where $\xi_{i_1...i_r} = 0$ if $a_{i_1...i_r} = 0$; $\xi_{i_1...i_r} = 1$ if $a_{i_1...i_r} \neq 0$.

As in the case of the class of functions with zero constant elasticity of factor substitution (Kleiner, 1980), here it is reasonable to begin with the form of the function with constant mobility of factor productivity, differing slightly from (6.13), by entering coefficients $a_{i_1...i_r}$ into the parenthesis with variable products and representing the constant terms as $a_{0k} = b_k^{c_k}$:

$$f(x_1, ..., x_n) = \prod_{k=1}^{S} \left(b_k^{c_k} + \sum_{r=1}^{|N_k|} \sum_{i_1<...<i_r N_k} \left(a_{i_1...i_r} x_{i_1...i_r}\right)^{c_k} \right)^{1/c_k} \qquad (6.15)$$

(for finite c_k and nonnegative $a_{i_1...i_r}$ formulas (6.13) and (6.16) are equivalent). The limit of function (6.16) under $c_k \to -\infty$, $k = 1, ..., s$ is

$$f(x_1, ..., x_n) = \prod_{k=1}^{S} \min_{1<r<|N_k|} \min_{i_1<...<i_r N_k} \left(b_k, a_{i_1...i_r} x_{i_1}... x_{i_r}\right).$$

It is the class of functions with arbitrary nonnegative parameters b_k, $a_{i_1...i_r}$ and arbitrary divisions $N_1, ..., N_s$ of the set $\{1, ..., n\}$ that we shall define as the class of *functions with nonzero constant mobility of factor productivity CNMP*.

Note that the absence of a single functional form of CMP functions with zero mobility of factors productivity is not unique to this class of functions. The same is true for multifactorial CES functions.

The full list of two-factor CMP functional forms is given in Table 6.1.

Table 6.1   **Constant Mobility of Factor Productivity: Functional Forms**

Functional Form	Symbol	Mobility of Factor Productivity
1. $y = a_0 \, e^{a_{12}\ln x_1 \ln x_2} \, x_1^{a1} \, x_2^{a2}$	CUMP	$MFP_1 = MFP_2 = 1$
2. $y = \left(a_0 + a_1 x_1^c + a_2 x_2^c + a_{12} x_1^c x_2^c\right)^{1/c}$	CEMP	$MFP_1 = MFP_2 = 1/(1-c)$, $c \neq 0$
3. $y = a_0 x_1^{a_1} \left(a_{02} + a_2 x_2^c\right)^{1/c}$	CDMP	$MFP_1 = 1$, $MFP_2 = 1/(1-c)$ $c \neq 0; c \neq 1$
4. $y = \left(a_{01} + a_1 x_1^{c_1}\right)^{1/c_1} \left(a_{02} + a_2 x_2^{c_2}\right)^{1/c_2}$	CDMP	$MFP_1 = 1/(1-c_1)$, $MFP_2 = 1/(1-c_2)$, $c_1 \neq c_2 \neq 0$
5. $y = \min\left(a_0, a_1 x_1, a_2 x_2, a_{12} x_1 x_2\right)$	CNMP	$MFP_1 = MFP_2 = 0$

Let us briefly examine the relationship between CMP and other functions. We shall begin with CUMP functions (6.9). Functions with unit mobility of factor productivity look like translog functions (Christensen, 1971)

$$y = \exp\left(a_0 + a_1 \ln x_1 + \ldots + a_n \ln x_n + \sum_{i,j=1}^{n} a_{ij} \ln x_i \ln x_j\right), \quad (6.16)$$

The set of CUMP production functions with two factors are a subset of the translog set (there are no diagonal elements $a_{ii}(\ln x_i)^2$ in CUMP functions). If $n \geq 3$, CUMP and translog functions do not belong one to another, because in (6.17) there are no multiplicative terms with more than two multipliers.

CUMP functions can be considered generalizations of Cobb-Douglas functions

$$y = \alpha_0 x_1^{\alpha_1} \ldots x_n^{\alpha_n}, \quad (6.17)$$

where constancy of some coefficients $\alpha_1, \ldots, \alpha_n$ is relaxed. If we take

$$\alpha_1 = a_1 + a_{12}\ln x_2 + \ldots + a_{1\ldots n}\ln x_2 \ldots \ln x_n,$$
$$\alpha_2 = a_2 + a_{23}\ln x_3 + \ldots + a_{2\ldots n}\ln x_3 \ldots \ln x_n,$$
$$\ldots \ldots \ldots \ldots \ldots \ldots \ldots \ldots \ldots \ldots \ldots \ldots,$$
$$\alpha_n = a_n$$

then CUMP function (6.9) can be expressed by (6.18).

Analogously CEMP functions can be considered as generalization of linear homogeneous functions with constant and equal elasticity of factor substitution (Kleiner and Sirota, 1975)

$$y = \left(\alpha_1 x_1^c + \dots + \alpha_n x_n^c \right)^{1/c} \tag{6.18}$$

(if α_i depends on inputs as follows:

$$\alpha_1 = a_1 + a_{12} x_2^c + \dots + a_{1\dots n} x_2^c \dots x_n^c,$$
$$\alpha_2 = a_2 + a_{23} x_3^c + \dots + a_{2\dots n} x_3^c \dots x_n^c,$$
$$\dots\dots\dots\dots\dots\dots\dots\dots\dots\dots,$$
$$\alpha_n = a_n)$$

CDMP functions are similar to "multiregime two-factor functions" (Kleiner, 1976) of the form

$$y = \left(a_1 x_1^{\beta_1} + b_1 x_2^{\beta_1} \right)^{\gamma_1/\beta_1} \dots \left(a_s x_1^{\beta_s} + b_s x_2^{\beta_s} \right)^{\gamma_s/\beta_s}. \tag{6.19}$$

If $\gamma_1 = \dots = \gamma_s = 1$, the S-regime function (6.20) can be obtained from the S-factorial CDMP functions

$$f\left(x_1, \dots, x_s \right) = \left(a_1 + b_1 x_1^{\beta_1} \right)^{1/\beta_1} \dots \left(a_s + b_s x_s^{\beta_s} \right)^{1/\beta_s}$$

as

$$y = x_1^s f\left(x_2/x_1, \dots, x_2/x_1 \right).$$

The general structural form of the CMP function is reminiscent of the general form of a homogeneous function with constant elasticity of factor substitution derived by Allen (CESA)

$$y = \alpha_0 x_1^{\alpha_1} \dots x_m^{\alpha_m} \prod_{k=2}^{s} \left(\sum_{j}^{N_k} \alpha_j x_j^{\beta_k} \right)^{\rho_k/\beta_k} \tag{6.20}$$

from Uzawa (1962). In general the case neither CMP class nor CESA class belong to one another, but if $\rho_2 = \rho_3 = \dots = \rho_s = 1$ then the function (6.21) can be obtained from (6.13) if we take $a_{02} = \dots = a_{0s} = 0$, $a_{i_1 \dots i_r} = 0$ when $r \geq 2$.

As a rule the CMP functions are nonlinear because of the constant terms and variable products generated by the various factors. But, homogeneous CMP functions do exist. The relationship between classes of homogeneous functions and CMP functions are described by the following theorem.

Theorem 4: 1) The following conditions are equivalent:

(a) $f(x_1, \dots, x_n)$ is a homogeneous CMP function of degree γ.

(b) function $f(x_1, \dots, x_n)$ is of the form

$$f\left(x_1, \ldots, x_n\right) \prod_{k=1}^{|N_1|} x_k^{a_k} \prod_{k=2}^{s} \sum_{i_1 < \ldots < i_{r_k} N_k} \left(a_{i_1 \ldots i_{r_k}} x_{i_1}^{c_k} \ldots x_{i_{r_k}}^{c_k} \right)^{1/c_k}$$

where $1 \le r_k \le n-1$, $a_0, a_1, \ldots, a_{i_1 \ldots i_{r_k}}, c_2, \ldots, c_s$ are constants, and

$$\gamma = \sum_{i=1}^{|N_1|} a_i + r_2 + \ldots + r_s.$$

2) Among CEMP functions there are functions of the following form, which are homogeneous of degree γ

$$f(x_1, \ldots, x_n) = \left(a_{1 \ldots r} x_1^c \ldots x_r^c + a_{2 \ldots (r+)} x_2^c \ldots x_{r+1}^c + \ldots + a_{(n-r+1) \ldots n} x_{n-r+1}^c \ldots x_n^c \right)^{1/c},$$

where $1 \le r \le n - 1$, $a_{i_1 \ldots i_r} \ge 0$, c are arbitrary constants; here $\gamma = r$.

3) There are no homogeneous functions in class of CDMP functions.

4) The Cobb-Douglas function is the only homogeneous CUMP function.

It is worth noting that the homogeneous CMP function can only be homogeneous of some specific degree when it is either a Cobb-Douglas function or includes a Cobb-Douglas function as part of a multiplier.

If $n = 2$ the Cobb-Douglas and CES functions are the only homogeneous CMP functions. For $n = 3$ a homogeneous CMP function can have one of the following forms:

$$y = a_0 x_1^{a_1} x_2^{a_2} x_3^{a_3} \qquad \text{(degree of homogeneity is } \gamma = a_1 + a_2 + a_3 \text{)},$$

$$y = x_1^{a_1} \left(a_2 x_2^c + a_3 x_3^c \right)^{1/c} \qquad \text{(degree of homogeneity is } \gamma = a + 1 \text{)},$$

$$y = \left(a_1 x_1^c + a_2 x_2^c + a_3 x_3^c \right)^{1/c} \qquad \text{(degree of homogeneity is } \gamma = 1 \text{)}.$$

$$y = \left(a_{12} x_1^c x_2^c + a_{13} x_1^c x_3^c + a_{23} x_2^c x_3^c \right)^{1/c} \text{(degree of homogeneity is } \gamma = 2 \text{)}.$$

Let us consider the output elasticity of input i of a CDMP function as an example of the behavior of CMP functions.

The elasticity

$$\epsilon_i \left(x_i \right) = 1 - \frac{a_{oi}}{a_{oi} + a_i x_i^{c_i}}$$

depends only on the level of input i. In the case where $a_{ai} > 0$, $a_i > 0$, it is between zero and one, and declines monotonically (if $c_i > 0$) or increases (if $c_i < 0$).

A Generalization: Cross Mobilities of Factor Productivities

The definition of the mobility of factor productivity MFP_i permits two generalization. The first concerns the influence of changes in marginal productivity of all factors on the average productivity of the ith factor: $AP_i = f/x_i$. The second concerns technological progress.

In this article we consider two types of input variation: 1) when quantities of all but one factor are constant, 2) when input proportions are constant. The indexes for these cases are

$$MFP_{ij}^k = \frac{d(f/x_i)}{df_j'} \Big/ \frac{f/x_i}{f_j'} \text{ with } x_1, \ldots, x_{k-1}, x_{k+1}, \ldots, x_n = const,$$

(6.21)

$$i, j, k = 1, \ldots, n$$

$$M\tilde{F}P_{ij}^k = \frac{d(f/x_i)}{df_j'} \Big/ \frac{f/x_i}{f_j'} \text{ with } \frac{x_1}{x_k}, \ldots, \frac{x_{k-1}}{x_k}, \frac{x_{k+1}}{x_k}, \ldots, \frac{x_n}{x_k} = const,$$

(6.22)

$$i, j, k = 1, \ldots, n$$

In both instances the average elasticity of factor i with respect to the marginal product of factor j is dAP_i/dz,
$$z_1 = x_1, \ldots, z_{k-1} = x_{k-1}, x_k = f_j', z_{k+1} = x_{k+1}, \ldots, z_n = x_n,$$
for MFP_{ij}^k,
and
$$z_1 = x_1/x_k, \ldots, z_{k-1} = x_{k-1}/x_k, x_k = f_j', z_{k+1} = x_{k+1}/x_k, \ldots, z_n = x_n/x_k,$$
for MFP_{ij}^k
If $i = j = k$ then MFP_{ij}^k coincides with mobility of productivity MFP_i, for the ith factor.

The value of MFP_{ij}^k shows the percentage change of average productivity with respect to factor i, when the marginal productivity with respect to factor j changes by 1 percent holding all factors, except factor k constant. Thus we are interested in how changes in the usage of input k associated with the marginal productivity of factor j influence f_i. The increase in x_k normally leads to a decrease in marginal productivity x_j. This is why $MFP_{ij}^k \leq 0$ must be true in the neoclassical case.

The value of MFP_{ij}^k shows the percentage change in the average productivity of factor i when the marginal productivity of factor j changes by 1 percent given constant factor proportions.

It is clear that the assumption of x_i/x_k = const, $i \neq k$, $i = 1, ..., n$ is equivalent to x_i/x_1 = constant, $i \neq 1$, $i = 1, ..., n$. This is why μ_{ij}^k does not depend on k. The upper index of this symbol can be ignored, because as will be established below, MFP_{ij}^k can also be defined by two indexes.

Let us write the formulas for calculating MFP_{ij}^k, $M\tilde{F}P_{ij}^k$ as (without proofs)

$$MFP_{ij}^k = \begin{cases} \dfrac{f_i' f_k'}{f f_{jk}''} = \left(\dfrac{df}{dx_k} \middle/ \dfrac{f}{x_k} \right) \middle/ \left(\dfrac{df_j'}{dx_k} \middle/ \dfrac{f_j'}{x_k} \right) & \text{if } k \neq i, \\[4mm] \dfrac{(f_i' x_i - f) f_j'}{x_i f f_{ij}''} = \left(\dfrac{d(f/x_i)}{dx_i} \middle/ \dfrac{f/x_i}{x_i} \right) \middle/ \left(\dfrac{df_j'}{dx_i} \middle/ \dfrac{f_j'}{x_i} \right) & \text{if } k = i \end{cases}$$ (6.23)

$$M\tilde{F}P_{ij}^k = \dfrac{\sum\limits_{l=1}^{n} (f_i' x_1 - f) f_j'}{\left(\sum\limits_{l=1}^{n} f_j'' x_1 \right) f} = \left(\dfrac{df}{dx_j} \middle/ \dfrac{f}{x_j} \right)$$

$$\middle/ \left(\dfrac{d\left(\sum\limits_{l=1}^{n} f_i' x_1 - f \right)}{dx_j} \middle/ \dfrac{\sum\limits_{l=1}^{n} f_i' x_1 - f}{x_j} \right)$$ (6.24)

If $f > 0$, $f_i' > 0$, then the formulas for MFP_{ij}^k, $M\tilde{F}P_{ij}^k$ can be rewritten in a more compact form:

$$MFP_{ij}^k = \dfrac{d\ln f}{d\ln x_k} \middle/ \dfrac{d\ln f'}{d\ln x_k} \qquad k \neq i,$$ (6.25)

$$M\tilde{F}P_{ij}^k = \dfrac{d\ln f}{d\ln x_j} \middle/ \dfrac{d\ln \left| \sum\limits_{l=n}^{n} f_i' x_1 - f \right|}{d\ln x_j}, \qquad i, j, k = 1, ..., n$$ (6.26)

It follows from these formulas, first, that if $i \neq k$, $l \neq k$, then

$$MFP_{ij}^k = M\tilde{F}P_{ij}^k, \qquad k, j = 1, ..., n$$ (6.27)

This means that a change in marginal productivity with respect to factor j caused by a change in factor k, influences all factor productivities equally, except for factor k itself. Second, MFP_{ij}^k does not depend on i. This means that the influence of the marginal productivity of factor j on the average productivity of other factors is the same as that with fixed factor proportions. In this case we will use the lower index to denote MFP_{ij}^k: $MFP_{ij}^k = MFP_j$. Third, according to (6.26) the MFP_{ij}^k expresses the proportionality between the output elasticity of factor j and elasticity of the marginal product of factor k. Equality (6.27) can be interpreted in the same way. Notice from (6.24) that the expression for μ_{ij}^k when $k \neq 1$ is the same as the formula for the elasticity of factor substitution.

$$\sigma = \frac{f_1' f_2'}{f f_{12}''},$$

developed by Hicks (1932) for linear homogeneous production functions in the two factor case. The same expression was examined (Sato and Koizumi, 1973b) as one of the indexes of factor substitution for any production functions employing two inputs. Thus equalities (6.24), (6.26) provide alternative independent interpretations of "Hicksian elasticities of substitution"

$$\sigma = \frac{f_j' f_k'}{f f_{jk}''}$$

for arbitrary production functions of several variables.

Next, let us consider the structural form of the production functions where MFP_{ij}^k, MFP_{ij}^k are constant for all i, j, k. We begin with the case $MFP_{ij}^k = const, k \neq i, k \neq j$.

Since it follows from (6.28) that MFP_{ij}^k "is almost independent" from i, the definition of the general form of functions with specified constants can be expressed with different formulas representing MFP_{ij}^k (two formulas are included in (6.24); two others are obtained from them when $k = j \neq i$, $k = j = i$):

1) MFP_{ij}^k are given, $k \neq j$, $i = k$;
2) MFP_{ij}^k are given, $k \neq j$, $i = j$;
3) MFP_{ij}^k are given, $k \neq j$, $i \neq k$;
4) MFP_{ij}^k are given, $k \neq j$, $i = j$.

As for $k = j = i$ $MFP_{ij}^k = MFP_i$, the last case is described by theorem 3.

The cases (6.1)-(6.3) are described in theorems 5-7, which are addressed below.

Let us assume that the sign $\star$ can take any value for observations in the set $\star$; these values are assigned to (Intriligator, 1971, n) unless explicitly stated otherwise.

Theorem 5: Let $f(x_1, ..., x_n)$ be a production function. If there exists even one pair of indexes $k \neq j$ that $MFP_{kj}^k \neq MFP_{jk}^j$, then $MFP_{k1}^k = ... = MFP_{kn}^k = MFP_{k\star}^k$, and f is the Cobb-Douglas function

$$f\left(x_i, ..., x_n\right) = \alpha_0 x_1^{\alpha_1} ... x_n^{\alpha_n},$$

where $\alpha_0, \alpha_1, ..., \alpha_n$ are constants, and $\alpha_k = 1 - \dfrac{1}{MFP_{k\star}^k}$, $k = 1, ..., n$. If for

any unequal k, j we have $MFP_{kj}^k = MFP_{jk}^j$, then all MFP_{kj}^k are equal, $MFP_{kj}^k = MFP_{\star\star}^\star$, and the function has the following form:

$$f\left(x_1, ..., x_n\right) = \left(\alpha_0 + \alpha_1 x_1^\beta ... x_n^\beta\right)^{1/1+\beta},$$

where $\alpha_0, \alpha_1, \beta$ are constants, and $\beta = -\dfrac{1}{MFP_{\star\star}^\star}$.

Theorem 6: Let $f\left(x_1, ..., x_n\right)$ be a production function. The following conditions are equivalent:

(a) MFP_{jj}^k are constant for $k \neq j$;

(b) there exists a partition of the set $\{1, ..., n\}$ into nonintersecting subsets $N_0, N_1, ..., N_s$, such that f has the following form

$$f\left(x_1, ..., x_n\right) = \prod_{j \; No} a_j \left(x_j\right) \prod_{r=1}^{s} \left(\sum_{i \; Nr} a_i \left(x_i\right)\right)^{\alpha_r}, \tag{6.28}$$

where $\alpha_1, ..., \alpha_s$ are constants; and $a_1\left(x_1\right), ..., a_n\left(x_n\right)$ are one-factor functions.

Subsets $N_0, ..., N_s$ and constants $\alpha_1, ..., \alpha_s$ are determined by MFP_{jj}^k as follows:

$$N_0 = \left\{k, j \mid MFP_{jj}^k = 1\right\}$$

$$N_r = \left\{k, j \mid MFP_{jj}^k = \frac{\alpha_r}{\alpha_r - 1}\right\}, \qquad r = 1, ..., s$$

(if $N_0 = 0$, then $\prod_{i \; No} a_j\left(x_j\right)$ is equal to 1).

Theorem 7: Let $f(x_1, ..., x_n)$ be a production function. The following conditions are equivalent:

(a) $MFP_{*1}^1, ..., MFP_{*n}^n$ (where $\star$ in MFP_{*k}^k is any value, except k, $k = 1, ..., n$) are constant;

(b) there exists a partition of the set $\{1, ..., n\}$ into nonintersecting subsets $N_0, N_1, ..., N_s$, such that f has the following form

$$f(x_1, ..., x_n) = \exp\left(\alpha_0^0 + \sum_{l=1}^{|N_0|} \sum_{i_1 < ... < i_l N_0} \alpha_{i_1...i_l}^0 x_{i_1} \cdots x_{i_l}\right)$$

(6.29)

$$\star \prod_{r=1}^{s} \left(\alpha_0^r + \sum_{l=1}^{|N_r|} \sum_{i_1 < ... < i_l N_r} \alpha_{i_1...i_l}^r x_{i_1} \cdots x_{i_l}\right)^{\beta_r},$$

where α_0^r, $a_{i_1...i_l}^r$, β_r are constants, and subsets $N_0, ..., N_s$ and constants $\beta_1, ..., \beta_s$ are determined by $MFP_{*1}^1, ..., MFP_{*n}^n$ in the following way:

$$N_0 = \left\{k \mid MFP_{*k}^k = 1\right\},$$

$$N_r = \left\{k \mid MFP_{*k}^k = \frac{\beta_r}{\beta_r - 1}\right\}, \quad r = 1, ..., s$$

(if $N_0 \neq 0$. then $\alpha_0^0 = 1$, $\alpha_{i_1...i_l}^0 = 0$).

Finally, the form of production functions with given and constant $MFP_{ij}^k = MFP_j$ is described by the following theorem.

Theorem 8: Let $f(x_1, ..., x_n)$ be a production function, for which $MFP_1, ..., MFP_n$ are constant. Then there are no more than two different values among $MFP_1, ..., MFP_n$, and only one of the following outcomes is possible:

a) $MFP_1 = ... = MFP_n \neq 1$, and the function f has the form

$$f = \left(\varphi^{\alpha_1} + \alpha_0\right)^{1/\alpha_1},$$

(6.30)

where φ is an arbitrary linear homogeneous function of $x_1, ..., x_n$, $\alpha_0 \neq 0$ and $\alpha_1 = 1 - 1/MFP_*$ are constants;

b) $MFP_1 = ... = MFP_n = 1$, and the function f has the form

$$f = \psi^{\alpha_2},\qquad\qquad (6.31)$$

where ψ is an arbitrary linear homogeneous function, and α_2 is a constant;
  c) $MFP_{i1} = ... = MFP_{ik} = v \neq MFP_{j1} = ... = MFP_{jn-k} = 1$, where $\{i_1,$
$..., i_k, j_1, ..., j_{n-k}\} = \{1, ..., n\}$, and the function has the form

$$f = \left(\varphi^{\alpha_1} + \alpha_0\right)^{1/\alpha_1} \varphi^{\alpha_2},\qquad\qquad (6.32)$$

where ψ is a linear homogeneous function of $x_{i_1}, ..., x_{i_k}$, ψ is a linear homogeneous function of the other variables, $\alpha_0 \neq 0, \alpha_1 \neq 0, \alpha_2 \neq 0$ are constants, and

$$\frac{\alpha_1 v}{v - 1} + \alpha_2 = 1.$$

Conversely, if the function f has the form (6.31), (6.32) or (6.33), then the conditions for $MFP_1, ..., MFP_n$, assumed in (a), (b), (c) are fulfilled.

Concluding Remarks

The analysis of the characteristics of MFP_{ij}^k, MFP_{ij}^k has three purposes. It provides a richer understanding of the full effects of marginal input variations, facilitates empirical analysis of partial elasticities of factor substitution (McFadden, 1963; Blackorby and Russell, 1981, 1989) and provides a basis for evaluating whether enterprise profit maximizing is complete.

In the course of elaborating these properties we have also identified several classes of production functions with interesting economic interpretations.

Let us review them from the standpoint of estimation. The CUMP function

$$y = \exp\left(a_0 + a_1 \ln x_1 + ... + a_n \ln x_n + a_{12} \ln x_1 \ln x_2 + ...\right.$$

$$\left. + a_{n-1,n} \ln x_{n-1} \ln x_n + ... + a_{1...n} \ln x_1 ... \ln x_n\right)$$

can be made log linear, becoming a generalized Cobb-Douglas function, linear in parameters. In principle, all the parameters of CUMP functions have precise economic meanings. For $n = 2$, since

$$a_1 = \frac{d\ln f}{d\ln x_1}\left(x_1, 1\right), \qquad a_2 = \frac{d\ln f}{d\ln x_2}\left(1, x_2\right), \qquad a_{12} = \frac{d\left(\dfrac{d\ln f}{d\ln x_1}\right)}{d\ln x_2},$$

a_1 can be interpreted as the percentage change of output caused by a one percent increase of the first factor (the point (x_1, x_2), $x_2 = 1$ was our initial point), given various assumptions about the first and the second order condition (Kleiner, 1986b). Similarly a_2 shows the percentage change of output, caused by a one percent increase of the second factor (the point (x_1, x_2), $x_1 = 1$ was our initial point). Parameter a_{12} measures the effect of a one percent change of the first (second) factor on the level of the elasticity of output of the second (first) factor.

The following equalities, determining the influence of a_0, a_1, a_2, a_{12} on elasticities of output for all factors associated with points $x_1, x_2 = 0; 1$ can be used as a basis for interpretating the parameters of CEMP function in the two factor case.

$$y = a\left(a_0 + a_1 x_1^c + a_2 x_2^c + a_{12} x_1^c x_2^c\right)^{1/c}$$

if $a_0 + a_1 + a_2 + a_{12} = 1$:

$$\frac{d\ln f}{d\ln x_1}(1, 1) = a_1 + a_{12}, \qquad \frac{d\ln f}{d\ln x_2}(1, 1) = a_2 + a_{12},$$

$$\frac{d\ln f}{d\ln x_1}(1, 0) = \frac{a_1}{a_0 + a_1}, \qquad \frac{d\ln f}{d\ln x_2}(0, 1) = \frac{a_2}{a_0 + a_2},$$

The interpretation of parameters a_{0i}, a_i of the n-factor function CUMP

$$y = a\left(a_{01} + a_1 x_1^{c_1}\right)^{1/c_1} \dots \left(a_{0n} + a_n x_n^{c_n}\right)^{1/c_n}$$

is also derived from the output elasticity of factor i. Assuming $a_{0i} + a_i = 1$, $i = 1, ..., n$,

$$a_i = \frac{d\ln f}{d\ln x_1}\left(x_1, ..., x_{i-1}, 1, x_{i+1}, ..., x_n\right), \qquad i = 1, ..., n$$

which shows percentage change of output caused by a one percent increase of factor i if $x_i = 1$ is the initial value.

In the general case the number of estimated parameters is 2^n for CUMP functions and $2^n + 1$ for CEMP functions. When $n \geq 4$ it is difficult to obtain consistent estimates for all parameters (but it does not prevent the use of the function for forecasting). For this reason we recommend using the following special CMP functional form as a compromise between the simplicity of interpretation and the complexity of a functional form

$$y = a_0 x_1^{a_1} ... x_k^{a_k}\left(a_{0, k+1} + a_{k+1}x_{k+1}^{c_{k+1}}\right)^{1/c_{k+1}}$$

$$... \left(a_{0n} + a_n x_n^{c_n}\right)^{1/c_n}$$

(6.33)

where $a_0, ..., a_n, a_{0\,k+1}, ..., a_{0n}, c_{k+1}, ..., c_n$ are parameters assuming $a_{0i} + a_i = 1$, $i = k + 1, ..., n$. The estimated $2n - k + 1$ parameters of this function c_{k+1}, ..., c_n are not assumed to have any particular values and are therefore compatible with both CEMP and CDMP functions. But since it is unlikely that c_i and c_j will be the same it is possible to assume from the beginning that $c_i \neq c_j$, $i, j = k + 1, ..., n$. In this case it can be shown that the function (6.34) can be completely defined within CMP class if

a) the mobility of factor x_1, ..., x_k productivity is equal to 1;

b) the mobility of factor x_{k+1}, ..., x_n productivity is constant, not equal 1 and differs from one another.

c) for $i = 1, ..., k$, the output elasticity of factor x_i does not depend on other factors.

Each pair of these conditions are independent even if the third condition is satisfied.

The division of variables into groups x_1, ..., x_k and x_{k+1}, ..., x_n is done apriori. It is based on information about the role of each factor in production: if x_i cannot equal zero given nonzero output, then x_i is included in first k variables.

The interpretation of the parameters of function (6.34) is not complicated: a_i reflects the percentage output increase in response to a one percent increase in factor i, $i = 1, ..., n$. Here the point $x_i = 1$ is initial point (if $i \leq k$ then the initial point can be any value).

As theorems 5, 6 and 8 show we have no parametric production functions to simultaneously estimate all MFP_{ij}^k, MFP_{ij}^k if they are assumed constant. The class of functions obtained in theorem 7 for $MFP_{*k}^k = \text{const}$ is similar to the CMP class. The function with $MFP_{*k}^k = 1$ is the analogue of the CUMP function:

$$y = \exp \left(a_0 + a_1 x_1 + ... + a_n x_n + a_{12} x_1 x_2 + ... \right.$$

$$\left. + a_{n-1,n} x_{n-1} x_n + ... + a_{1...n} x_1 ... x_n \right). \tag{6.34}$$

Among these functions there are functions $y = a_0 a_1^{x_1} ... a_n^{x_n}$, which can be distinguished from (6.35) by the condition

$$\frac{d \ln y}{d \ln x_i} = \text{const}, \quad i = 1, ..., n.$$

There are also functions which are analogous to the CEMP class

$$y = \left(a_0 + a_1 x_1 + ... + a_n x_n + a_{12} x_1 x_2 + ... \right.$$

$$\left. + a_{n-1,n} \ln x_{n-1} \ln x_n + ... + a_{1...n} x_1 ... x_n \right)^\beta, \tag{6.35}$$

where $\beta \neq 0$. They involve degrees of linear functions from the CUMP class

$$y = \left(a_{01} + a_1 X_1 \right)^{\beta_1} ... \left(a_{0n} + a_n X_n \right)^\beta, \tag{6.36}$$

for which $MFP_{*k}^k = \dfrac{\beta_k}{\beta_k - 1}$, $k = 1, ..., n$ ($*$ can have any value, so long as it is not equal to k).

Consider the class of functions (6.29) with $MFP_{ij}^k = \text{const}$ (theorem 6). The power of the set of these functions f is larger than the power of parametric classes of functions (6.30) and (6.13), because f depends on the indeterminate functions $a_1(x_1), ..., a_n(x_n)$. Uzawa's function with constant elasticities of factor substitution and CUMP functions belong to this class. The class is wide enough to include various block-multiplicative functions.

As far as functions with constant MFP_{ij}^k are concerned (which are determined by theorem 8), the following points are worth observing. The characteristics of the homogeneous functions $(MFP_{ij}^k \equiv 1)$ and of other functions obtained from them can be assessed by adding a constant term or raising them to a power. Both linear homogeneous functions with constant and equal elasticities of substitution (6.19), and their nonhomogeneous counterparts

$$y = \left(a_1 x_1^\alpha + \dots a_n x_n^\alpha + a_0\right)^{1/\alpha}$$

belong to this group.

As theorem 5 shows, the strongest constancy condition for MFP_{ij}^k, MFP_{ij}^k is MFP_{ij}^k const under $k \neq j$. The Cobb-Douglas function is the only function among all functions used for modeling purposes that satisfies this condition. This function also satisfies all other conditions of theorems 2-8 (in theorem 8 it is necessary to substitute $z_i = \exp x_i$, $i = 1, \dots, n$).

Notes

1.   There are multiplications of three, four and more multipliers in formulas (6.9) and (6.10) after double multiplications of logarithms and degrees of variables.

2.   See note 1.

3.   For functions of the CUMP class there is only one mobility equal to one among $\mu_1, \dots, \mu_n$; we shall take $MFP_1 = 1$.

4.   If all variables x_i, for which $MFP_i \equiv 1$, are united into a single class N_1, then for each i N_k, where $k > 1$, there are a coefficient among nonzero coefficients $a_{i\dots i}$ with indexes from N_k, which contains i among the indexes, and a coefficient which does not contain i.

Bibliography

Blackorby, C. and R.R. Russell, "The Morishima Elasticity of Substitution: Symmetry, Constancy, Separability and Its Relationship to the Hicks and Allen Elasticity", *Review of Economic Studies*, 48, 1,1981.

_____, "Will the Real Elasticity of Substitution Please Stand Up?", *The American Economic Review*, Vol. 79, No. 4, September 1989, 882-888.

Brown, M., *Theory and measurement of Technological Changes*, Moscow: Statistics Publishers, 1971.

Christensen, L.R., D.W. Jorgensen, and L.J. Lau, "Conjugate Duality and the Transcendental Logarithmic Production Function", *Econometrica*, 30, 1971, 255-256.

Hicks, J.R., *The Theory of Wages*, London: Macmillan, 1932.

Intriligator, M., *Mathematical Optimization and Economic Theory*, New York: , 1971.

Kleiner, G.B., "Neoclassical Production Functions and Duality", *Economics and Mathematical Methods*, Vol. XVI, 5, 1980.

_____, "Methodology of Production Function Choice in Modelling of Automated Management System Objects", *All-Union Conference on Management Problems*, Moscow: Institute for Control Problems Publishers, 1986a.

_____, *Production Functions: Theory, Methods, Application*, Moscow: Finance and Statistics Publishers, 1986b.

_____, "Production Functions with Variable and Constant Mobility of Factors Productivities", *Some Questions of Analysis and Modelling of National Economic Processes*, Moscow: Central Institute of Economics and Mathematics Publishers, 1988.

Kleiner, G.B. and B.N. Sirota, "On Production Functions with Constant and Variable Elasticities of Factors Substitution", *Economics and Mathematical Methods*, Vol. XI, 3, 1975.

_____, "On One Class of Production Functions", *Economics and Mathematical Methods*, Vol. XII, 2, 1976.

McFadden, D., "Constant Elasticity of Substitution Production Functions", *Review of Economic Studies*, 30, 1963, 73-83.

Samuelson, P.A., "Two Generalization of Elasticity of Substitution", *Value, Capital and Growth*, Chicago, 1968.

_____, "Relative Shares and Elasticities Simplified: Comment", *American Economic Review*, September 1973, 63.

Sato, R. and R.H. Hoffman, "Production Function with Variable Elasticity of Factor Substitution", *Review of Economics and Statistics*, 50, 4, 1968.

Sato, R. and T. Koizumi, "The Production Function and the Theory of Distributive Shares", *American Economic Review*, June 1973, 63.

_____, "Relative Shares and Elasticities Simplified: Reply", *American Economic Review*, September 1973, 63.

Stolerue, L., *L'equilibre et le Croissance Economique*, Paris: Dunod, 1969.

Uzawa, H., "Production Functions with Constant Elasticity of Substitution", *Review of Economics and Statistics*, 29, 1962, 291-299.

Part II Estimates of Soviet and Russian Production Potential and Efficiency

Steven S. Rosefielde

Synopsis

The chapters in Part II empirically confirm the hypothesis that prior authoritative estimates exaggerated Soviet Russian economic performance. Chapter 7 provides a benchmark by analyzing the improbable behavior implied by past adjusted ruble factor cost, and purchasing power parity dollar estimates. Chapter 8 uses the specificational studies in Part I to estimate aggregate and industrial sectoral efficiency in Soviet Russia and America. This study appears to validate traditional performance estimates because efficiency is similar in both systems. Chapters 9 and 10 however reveal that these similarities mask profound microeconomic inefficiencies predicted by administrative command planning theory at different stages of production and in multiproduct firms. Factors are both technically and economically misallocated. Although parallel studies of American firms are not reported, the evidence of Soviet microeconomic inefficiency is compelling. Finally, Chapter 11 demonstrates that these problems have not yet been surmounted by Russia's transitional system because the enterprises investigated did not profit maximize.

7 Comparative Production Potential in the USSR and the West: Pre-Transition Assessments

Steven S. Rosefielde

Introduction

The concepts, specifications and techniques elaborated in Part I are reflected in varying degrees in past assessments of Soviet economic performance that still shape many current appraisals of Russia's economic recovery potential. The accepted view was that while the Soviet Union had the world's second largest GNP, and Russia's per capita income was just below the European Community average, factor productivity was far less impressive, reflecting the comparative systemic inefficiency of administrative command planning. Likewise, while postwar Soviet economic growth was conspicuously rapid through the mid sixties, it subsequently slowed, culminating in 1991 in the USSR's collapse (Table 7.1).

This characterization suggests that the Soviet Union had accumulated a large capital stock with potent embodied technologies, creating an enormous production potential that was increasingly unrealized because of the cumulative deficiencies of state economic control. It therefore might seem to follow that Russia should be able to recover to or beyond prior achieved levels merely by substituting the market for administrative command planning.

Doubts about the reliability of the data sustaining this inference and the underlying paradigm however are raised by the counterindicative performance of the industrial sector and comparative productivity growth which show the Soviet Union rivaling and sometimes outperforming the United States. This behavior is simply too good to be true and serves a much needed caveat against the assumption that adjusted ruble factor costing and dollar purchasing power parities applied to Soviet statistics provided

101

dependable measures of Russia's past economic performance and production potential.

Comparative Potential and Efficiency

Soviet economic performance was usually evaluated in comparison with the American standard, with the west taken as an alternative reference point. These comparisons were computed in dollars, rubles and as geometric means, but dollars were the most frequent choice to facilitate comparison with other nations.

The primary measures of comparative potential, GNP and per capita national income were computed straightforwardly by transforming official Soviet Marxian ruble accounts into American GNP categories, converting them with dollar-ruble ratios and where appropriate dividing by the population. The CIA put Soviet GNP at 3.8 trillion dollars, and Russian per capita national income at 15,631 dollars in 1989, valued at 1991 prices. These figures were respectively 67 and 68 percent of the American standard. A lower GNP figure in the vicinity of 51 percent was sometimes presented as the dollar parity, but was actually the geometric ruble and dollar mean.[1]

The per capita dollar figure placed Russia just behind the Netherlands and Italy in the international rankings, a surprisingly high accomplishment given the inefficiencies associated with administrative command planning. This suspect result was attributed to Russia's massive capital accumulation which enabled it to produce at the western level by substituting capital for productivity (Table 7.1). Russia's subpar performance on this score was interpreted as evidence of its systemic inefficiency. Table 7.2 provides estimates of this type for the year 1960 computed by Abram Bergson. They are described as "coefficients of factor productivity", and assume that the underlying technologies are linear homogeneous, and Cobb-Douglas. The metric is gross domestic material product (except in Soviet/American comparisons where gross national material product is employed) and excludes output originating in selected final services: health care, education, government administration, defense and housing. Labor is adjusted for nonfarm hours, and together with reproducible fixed capital is defined conformably with output.

Soviet coefficients of factor productivity are only 31 and 41 percent of the US level calculated respectively on a per worker, or combined factor basis. This poor showing may have diverse technical causes. The linear homogeneous Cobb-Douglas production function used for the US, for example, could ignore economies of scale in the Soviet Union, but it seems more likely that the Soviet underproductivity (underefficiency) should be primarily attributable to the shortcomings of the economic system.

Table 7.1   Soviet Economic Growth 1965-88 Key Indicators

Official Series	1965-70	1970-75	1975-80	1980-85	1985-88
1. GNP	7.6	6.2	4.8	3.6	3.9
2. New Capital Formation	7.3	6.3	3.5	3.1	4.9
3. Employment (workers, and kolkhozniki)	2.5	1.9	1.4	0.7	-0.3

SOURCES: *Narkhoz SSSR, 1988*, pp. 8, 34; *Narkhoz SSSR, 1985*, p. 390.

Table 7.2   Coefficients of Factor Productivity Comparative Static Estimates for 1960 (US = 100)

	Gross Material Product Per Employed Worker	Gross Material Product Per Unit of Factor (Labor and Reproducible Capital) Inputs		
	DOLLARS (1)	DOLLARS (2)	RUBLES (3)	FISHER IDEAL (4)
United States	100	100		
France	51	63		
Germany	51	65		
United Kingdom	49	64		
Italy	34	47		
USSR	31	41	31	36

SOURCES: Abram Bergson, *Productivity and the Social System - The USSR and the West*, Table 6.1, pp. 76-7, Table 7.1, p. 93, Appendix Tables 11, p. 236 and 18, p. 241.

DATA: Gross material product represents gross domestic product exclusive of output originating in selected final services: health care, education, government administration, defense and housing. Dollar estimates are valued at prevailing 1960 US prices. Ruble estimates are computed at 1970 Soviet factor cost, and reflect national as distinct from domestic product. US data is conformably defined in calculating the US/USSR coefficient of factor productivity. Major inputs refer to labor and reproducible fixed capital. Employment is adjusted for differences in nonfarm hours; capital is calculated as the average of two relatives one with fixed capital included gross of depreciation and the other with such capital included net of depreciation. The Fisher ideal estimate is computed with dollar estimates that are defined analogously with the ruble estimates. Combined inputs are aggregated logarithmically according to the Cobb-Douglas specification.

METHOD: The coefficients of factor productivity are computed according to the formula:

$$\theta = (y_i/y_j)/[(k_i/k_j)^\alpha (v_i/v_j)^\beta (\ell_i/\ell_j)^{1-\alpha-\beta}]$$

where the ith subscript refers to the Soviet Union, or a specific European country and the jth to the United States. y,k,v, and l are output, fixed capital, inventories and labor, and the exponents are factor shares based on American dollar weights.

This finding is confirmed by subsequent calculations for 1975. Bergson applies the same conceptual apparatus, and data conventions to assess comparative factor productivity but alters his approach in two ways. The sample is expanded to include additional capitalist and socialist countries, and the systems underproductivity (underefficiency) effect is estimated directly using various econometric techniques.

The selection of supplementary socialist observations is not restricted to command regimes. In addition to Poland which at the time closely adhered to the Soviet paradigm he includes Hungary and Yugoslavia. The performance of both these economies is significantly influenced by competitive market processes, and in the latter case by collective enterprise management. As a consequence, the updated estimates shed light broadly on the comparative merit of all types of socialist economies.

The specification employed to estimate socialist underproductivity is:

$$\log y = A \log k + B \log l + Md + Q \qquad (7.1)$$

where A,B,M and Q are constants; y is output per worker relatively to that in the United States, k and l are capital and land per worker, similarly calculated; and d is a dummy variable denoting socialism, or its absence. The constants in (7.1) are evaluated by regressing y on k, l and d. A and B are not forced to equal 1 (the function is not linearly homogeneous), and the Cobb-Douglas specification is not adjusted to allow for economies of scale. The marginal productivity (and income elasticity) of labor are not explicitly estimated, but by construction can be assumed constant.

The principal feature of the regressions run on these data is the sign of the coefficient M on the dummy variable d representing socialism. It indicates that socialist countries are underproductive and/or underefficient. The magnitude of the coefficient is high in all variants. In the standard case it is .351 implying that output per worker under socialism is 29.6 percent below the capitalist norm. Supplementary regressions using country specific dummy variables suggest that the Soviet Union was the least efficient socialist country followed by Hungary, Poland and Yugoslavia.

As with most econometric research it is easy to fault these results. The assumption of a Cobb-Douglas production function is arbitrary. The sample size is small. With the exception of Spain, the levels of development between socialist and capitalist countries diverge noticeably. The unifying factors that make the Soviet Union, Poland, Hungary and Yugoslavia socialist, and presumably cause their underefficiency are neither clearly explained, nor convincingly defended. Nonetheless, the findings do confirm the expectation that administrative command planning and other forms of socialism were underproductive and inefficient, despite their aggregate accomplishments.

This assessment however is incomplete because it omits developments after 1975, prior dynamic growth and disregards sectoral asymmetries. The Russian economy manifested a distinct duality since the late 19th century. Industry generally, and heavy industry in particular were markedly more productive than other components of gross material product, and it would be surprising if this had ceased to be the case. Perhaps Soviet performance approached the American standard in these regards, evaluated with standard western data.

Soviet dynamic productivity can be evaluated by comparing its relative position in 1960 and 1975. Table 7.3 provides the desired information.   It presents coefficients of factor productivity based on Bergson's original 1960 study.   A parallel computation derived from the 1975 production function could also be undertaken, but comparable data on land in 1960 are unavailable.   The productivity statistics in Table 7.3 are displayed in two variants, one based on employment, the other combined factors properly weighted conceptually with American dollar valued factor shares.   The improvement in relative Soviet factor productivity (efficiency) on both scores is remarkable.   Gross material product per employed worker is 87 percent higher in 1975 than in 1960.   The gain in gross material product per unit of factor (labor and reproducible capital) inputs is less pronounced, but still an impressive 34 percent.   The magnitude of these advances are in line with the European mean and suggest that whatever productivity/efficiency disparities separated the USSR and the US in 1975, they may have been reduced further in the late seventies and eighties.

Table 7.3   Coefficients of Factor Productivity Comparative Static Variations (US = 100)

	Gross Material Product Per Employed Worker		Gross Material Product Per Unit of Factor (Labor and Reproducible Capital) Inputs	
	1960	1975	1960	1975
United States	100	100	100	100
France	51	94	63	96
Germany	51	91	65	92
United Kingdom	49	69	64	73
Italy	34	71	47	77
USSR	31	58	41	55

SOURCES: Table 7.A1. Bergson, *Productivity and the Social System*, Table 7.1, p. 93, Table A18, p. 241.

METHOD: Labor and reproducible inputs are aggregated logarithmically respectively with weights of .7415, .2278 and .0307 reported by Bergson for American factor income shares in 1960.   See pp. 71, 95 note 3, and

Appendix Table 18, p. 241. Bergson includes inventories in his calculations for 1960. See Appendix Table 12, p. 238.

The coefficient of factor productivity is $\theta = (y_i/y_j)/[(k_i/k_j)^\alpha (v_i/v_j)^\beta (\ell_i/\ell_j)^{1-\alpha-\beta}]$ where the ith subscript refers to the Soviet Union, or a specific European country, and the jth to the United States. y, k, v and ℓ are output, fixed capital, inventories and labor, and the exponents are factor shares based on American dollar weights.

The duality of the Soviet economy also manifests itself in his data. Table 7.4 reproduces Bergson's estimates of gross industrial product per employed worker and per unit of factor inputs in selected countries in 1960. They are calculated as before, but omit agriculture as well as selected services. Relative Soviet industrial factor productivity is clearly higher than in agriculture. Instead of conspicuously lagging the pack Soviet industrial factor productivity is more or less on a par with Italy and the United Kingdom and not glaringly below France and Germany.

Table 7.4   Gross Industrial Product per Employed Worker and per Unit of Factor Inputs, Selected Countries, 1960

	Gross Industrial Product Per Employed Worker	Gross Industrial Product per Unit of Factor (Labor and Reproducible Capital) Inputs
United States	100	100
France	60	71
Germany	54	69
United Kingdom	48	61
Italy	46	60
USSR	50	58

SOURCES: Bergson, *Productivity and the Social System*, Table 7.5, p. 108.

DATA: Gross industrial product represents essentially the gross output originating in manufacturing, mining, power, construction, transport and communications, and trade. In the calculation of output per worker and per composite unit of factor inputs, reference is to employment and capital stock used in the same sector. Valuation of output and inputs is as in Table 7.1 (Table 7.1 this paper). Employment is also adjusted for hours in the same way as in Table 7.2. Combined inputs are aggregated logarithmically according to the Cobb-Douglas specification. The coefficient of factor productivity (column 2) is specified in Table 7.1.

Bergson has not published counterpart statistics for 1975, but official Soviet and CIA ruble data can be used to show that the sectoral duality of the Soviet economy persisted and intensified. Table 7.5 reports estimates of aggregate and industrial factor productivity growth 1965-85. The output series other than industry are adopted from CIA estimates, as are the statistics on employment, and capital. Industry (excluding construction, transport, communications and trade) is calculated with CIA weights and official Soviet growth data. Inputs are combined according to the Cobb-Douglas specification with Bergson's income share weights. Industrial total factor productivity measured in this way decisively outstrips the aggregate rate for the entire period 1965-85 and for each quinquennial subperiod. The differential exceeds 60 percent. Although analogous estimates for the US and the West are not at hand, this disparity suggests that the Soviets not only significantly diminished their relative aggregate underproductivity, but their industrial underproductivity as well.

Table 7.5   Official Estimates of Soviet Factor Productivity Growth 1965-85 (Adjusted CIA Statistics)

	1965-70	1970-75	1975-80	1980-85	1965-85
Gross National Product	6.2	4.3	3.1	2.8	4.1
Combined Inputs	3.8	3.8	3.1	2.5	3.3
Workhours	2.0	1.7	1.2	0.7	1.4
Capital	7.4	8.0	6.9	6.3	7.1
Total Factor Productivity	2.4	0.5	0	0.3	0.8
Industrial Output	8.4	7.5	4.4	3.7	6.0
Combined Inputs	4.9	3.8	3.4	2.6	3.6
Workhours	3.1	1.5	1.4	0.5	1.6
Capital	8.8	8.7	7.7	7.0	8.0
Total Factor Productivity	3.5	3.7	1.0	1.1	2.4

Compound annual rates of growth

SOURCES: *Allocation of Resources in the Soviet Union and China - 1985*, JEC, March 19, 1986, Table 4, p. 80 and Table 5, p. 81; Rosefielde, *Economic Foundations of Soviet National Security Strategy*, unpublished manuscript 1987, Tables 9.4 and 9.14; Bergson, *Productivity and the Social System*, Appendix Tables 11, p. 236.

METHOD: Factors are combined, following Bergson, according to the Cobb-Douglas specification (see Bergson, 1978, p. 159-60 note 8). The income elasticities (shares) imputed to capital (.328 GNP, .317 industry) are provided in (Bergson 1978), Appendix Tables 11. Labor is .672 GNP, and .683 industry. Cf. Appendix Table 22, p.245. The input data are taken from CIA sources; industrial output is based on official statistics; and GNP combines the CIA's nonindustrial series, with official Soviet industrial data. Total factor productivity growth for aggregate output and industry

$$\theta = \mathring{y}/[\alpha \mathring{R} + (1-\alpha)\mathring{l}]$$

where $\mathring{y}$, $\mathring{R}$, and $\mathring{l}$ are output, capital, and labor growth, and α, β and $(1-\alpha-\beta)$ are the output elasticities of these factors measured in 1955 rubles (GNP) and 1959 rubles (industry). Capital weights are net of depreciation.

Industry is not a homogeneous activity. The Soviets have long accorded higher priority to producer durables than nondurable and durable consumer goods. This preference is reflected in their productivity behavior. Tables 7.6 and 7.7 derived from official Soviet statistics reveal that productivity growth was fastest in the military machinebuilding, and civilian machinebuilding sectors and relatively sluggish in the light and food processing industries. Presumably relative Soviet static machinebuilding and metalworking productivity was unusually high. This deduction cannot be tested in the case of military machinebuilding because the volume of reproducible fixed capital utilized in this sector is not precisely known. Bilateral comparisons of Soviet and American machinebuilding factor productivity computed in dollars can be made however with the assistance of input-output data converted with CIA dollar-ruble ratios similar to those Bergson employs, but differing in some particulars. Tables 7.8 and 7.9 report these findings in four variants. Soviet machinebuilding productivity exceeds the US standards in 1975 in three of the four alternatives. It is 8 percent smaller using the series that most closely approximates Bergson's, but the output figure for 1970 on which it is predicated was tacitly repudiated by the CIA in 1982. Table 7.8 places these findings in an intertemporal perspective. It reveals in line with our previous analysis that the Soviets narrowed the gap with the US in the early seventies, in this instance overtaking it, but leveled off thereafter. Using official Soviet MBMW growth indices and either official or CIA final product data for 1972 and 1970 respectively, the 1985 coefficient of Soviet machinebuilding factor productivity surpasses the US by 12 to 35 percent. Soviet machinebuilding production is not only higher than the US's, (Table 7.A10) but its machinebuilding industry is more productive (efficient).

Table 7.6   Official Estimates of Soviet Industrial Combined Factor Productivity Growth by Sector 1965-1985

	1965-70	1970-75	1975-80	1980-85	1965-85
Electric	3.0	3.7	2.6	0.3	2.4
Fuels	5.4	3.0	-0.5	-2.4	1.3
Ferrous Metals*	1.4	2.3	1.2	--	1.6
Chemicals	5.5	6.0	1.3	2.5	3.8
Machinebuilding	5.8	6.4	4.0	3.3	4.9
Wood, Pulp, Paper	2.8	3.1	-0.6	1.8	1.8
Construction Materials	3.4	3.6	0	0.9	2.0
Light Industry	3.5	2.0	0.6	-0.1	1.5
Food	1.3	2.5	-0.2	1.6	1.3

SOURCES: Table 7.A3.

METHOD: Total factor productivity is defined in Table 7.4. The capital weight is .33; labor is .67.

*The employment series for 1980-85 includes nonferrous metallurgy. Factor productivity growth in the ferrous metals sector therefore has not been computed for this subperiod. The figure for 1965-85 is extrapolated from the subperiod 1965-80.

Table 7.7   **Soviet Industrial Combined Factor Productivity Growth by Sector 1974-82 (Including Military Machine Building)**

Sector	θ (1)	$\hat{y}$ (2)	$\hat{k}$ (3)	$\hat{l}$ (4)
Electric Power	2.72	4.63	5.94	1.20
Fuels	-0.42	2.89	8.21	1.07
Ferrous metals	-0.12	1.93	6.35	0.24
Chemicals	2.23	6.00	8.77	1.41
Machinery and Equipment	3.83	7.86	9.00	1.69
Military Machine Building	4.88	9.54	10.73	2.02
Construction Materials	-0.06	2.65	6.39	0.98
Light Industry	0.52	3.00	6.63	0.52
Food	0.16	2.42	5.71	0.64

SOURCES: Rosefielde, *Annotated Compendium of Soviet Economic Statistics 1950-80; Narodnoe khoziaistvo*, 1982, pp. 117, 127, and 131; Rosefielde, *East-West Trade and Postwar Economic Growth*, SRI, 1976, p. 59. Rosefielde, *False Science: Underestimating the Soviet Arms Buildup*, Second Edition, 1987, Appendix 8, note 34.

METHOD: $\theta = \hat{y}/(\alpha \hat{k} + \beta \hat{l})$ where $\alpha = .32$ and $\beta = .68$. The coefficients are factor shares derived from the 1966 Soviet input-output table, with capital services computed at a 12 percent annual rate of interest.

Table 7.8   **Coefficients of Machine Building and Metalworking Factor Productivity Comparative Static Variations in 1975 (US = 100)**

	Output Per Employed Worker	Output Per Unit of Factor (Labor and Reproducible Capital) Inputs
United States	100	100
USSR A. (Soviet Quantity Weights)		
1. Official: 1966 I-O Table	98	113
2. Official: 1972 I-O Table	107	124
3. CIA/Official Purchasers I	79	92
4. CIA/Official Purchasers II	89	103

SOURCES: Table 7.A10.

DATA: The derivation of the data underlying the statistics in this table is explained in Tables A4-A10. Also see note 11. They differ conceptually from Bergson's aggregate estimates in two ways: capital is not adjusted for uncompleted construction (Bergson, 1987b, pp. 40-46), and labor is measured in man years, not manhours. Also in aggregating factors Bergson's industry weights (inventories treated as capital) are used rather than his figures for all sectors excluding selected final services. The labor weight is .7750; capital .2250. See Bergson, *Productivity and the Social System*, Appendix Table 18, p. 241.

METHOD: Combined factors are aggregated logarithmically according to the Cobb-Douglas specification $x = k^{\alpha}l^{1-\alpha}$. The coefficient of factor productivity is specified in Table 7.2.

COMMENTS: Of the two official series, the one derived from the 1972 input-output table should be preferred because it is closest to Bergson's 1975 base year. The CIA figure for 1975 is lower partly because of its handling of weapons, and partly because of its arbitrary adjustments for "hidden inflation". It is the least reliable estimate. See Rosefielde, *False Science*, Table A12, p. 298, and footnote 11 this paper.

Soviet output and capital data are converted from rubles to dollars using CIA estimated purchasing power parity ratios calculated alternatively with Soviet and American quantity weights. Since Bergson seeks to compute the dollar value of the Soviet product mix, the dollar-ruble ratios based on Soviet quantity weights are the most appropriate for the purpose at hand.

Apparently, if the authoritative data are reliable it follows illogically that the Soviets not only outproduced America in machinebuilding, but were more efficient as well.

Economic Inefficiency

The suspicion cast on the reliability of the CIA's and Bergon's statistics is increased by the introduction of two straightforward adjustments. First, the data are cleansed by restoring the official Soviet output series before the CIA's dubious corrections for inflation and weapons production. Table 7.10 reveals that this augments the Soviet coefficient of factor productivity in 1975 by 33 percent, placing it on a par with Great Britain. It also raises Soviet GNP to 95.3 percent of the American level. Both figures are preposterous and confirm the theoretical inference that the value of Soviet output is exaggerated because production and characteristics are not optimized with respect to consumer demand.

Table 7.9   Coefficients of Machine Building and Metalworking Factor Productivity Comparative Static Variations 1970-85 (Output per Unit of Combined Inputs) (US = 100)

	1965	1970	1975	1980	1985
United States	100	100	100	100	100
USSR (Soviet Quantity Weights) 1. Official 1972: I-O Table 2. CIA/Official: Purchasers II	77 64	97 81	124 103	139 116	135 112

SOURCES: Table 7.A10.

METHOD: See Table 7.7.

Table 7.10   Coefficients of Factor Productivity (US=100)

	Gross Material Product Per Unit of Factor (Labor and Reproducible Capital) Inputs	
	1960	1975
United States	100	100
United Kingdom	64	73

USSR
  Official
  Bergson
  Belkin/Shukhgal'ter
	
	41
	41
	13
		
		73
		55
		18

SOURCES: Abram Bergson, *Productivity and the Social System-The USSR and the West*, Table 6.1, pp. 76-7, Table 7.1, p. 93, Appendix Tables 11, p. 236 and 18, p. 241; Bergson, "Comparative Productivity: USSR, Eastern Europe and the West: Appendix Sources and Methods for Basic Data", unpublished manuscript, 1987. *Narodnoe khoziaistvo 1965*, p. 55; *Narodnoe khoziaistvo 1975*, p. 48. Imogene Edwards, Margaret Hughes and James Noren, "U.S. and U.S.S.R.: Comparisons of GNP", *Soviet Economy in a Time of Change*, JEC, Vol. 1, pp. 369-401. Viktor Belkin, "Vlianie razlichii rynochnovo i nerynochnovo khoziaistvennovo mekhanizma na sopostavleniia makroekonomicheskikh pokazateli", paper presented at the Conference on Comparing the Soviet and American Economies, American Enterprise Institute, April 19-22, 1990; Maya Shukhgal'ter, "Capital Stock in the USSR and USA: Problems of Comparison", paper presented at the Conference on Comparing the Soviet and American Economies, American Enterprise Institute, April 19-22, 1990; Steven Rosefielde, "The Illusion of Material Progress: The Analytics of Soviet Economic Growth Revisited", *Soviet Studies*, Vol. XXXIII, No. 2, July 1991.

DATA: Gross material product represents gross domestic product exclusive of output originating in selected final services: health care, education, government administration, defense and housing. The material components of these activities such as weapons are retained. Dollar estimates are valued at prevailing 1975 US prices. The Soviet data are derived primarily from (Edwards, et. al., 1979). These data are in 1976 prices, and have been adjusted to a 1975 base using the Department of Commerce's implicit price deflator. Soviet output reflects gross national, as distinct from gross domestic material product. Major inputs refer to labor and reproducible fixed capital. Employed is adjusted for differences in nonfarm hours; capital is calculated as the average of two relatives one with fixed capital included gross of depreciation and the other net of depreciation. Soviet output in the official variant has been computed by adjusting Bergson's estimate for 1975 812.5 billion dollars upwards by a coefficient Ω reflecting the ratio of Soviet growth (proizvedennyi natsional'nyi dokhod: net material product) 1960-75 shown in *Narodnoe khoziaistvo* and the GNP rate given in (Edwards, et. al., 1979) both valued in rubles. The later source does not provide estimates for 1960. The long period rates 1955-75 therefore were compared and computed for fifteen years to estimate the growth differential 1960-75:

$$\Omega = (y_{75}/y_{55})^{15/20}/(y_{75}^{E}/y_{55}^{E})^{15/20} = 1.33$$

The adjusted dollar GNP figure thus is 1.33 (812.5) = $1,080.6, which is 95.3 percent of the US figure, in contrast to Bergson's estimate of 71.7 percent. This estimate assumes reasonably that official Soviet NMP and Bergson's GNP are similarly defined, and that the ratio Ω valued in dollars and rubles are alike. The later assumption is supported by the close correspondence between the dollar and ruble GNP growth reported 1955-75 (2.80 in rubles; 2.59 in dollars) in (Edwards, et al, 1979), p. 391. All other factor values are taken from (Bergson, 1987). The revised Soviet index numbers of factor inputs and outputs for 1975 are: $y_i/y_j = 95.3$; $k_i/k_j = 79.1$; $v_i/v_j = 154.3$; $\ell_i/\ell_j = 150.7$.

The third variant of Soviet output has been calculated by applying a coefficient formed as the ratio of Viktor Belkin's estimate of the comparative size of Soviet GNP in 1987 and the CIA's estimates for 1989: $\lambda = .14/.66 = .21$. The Soviet fixed capital is calculated by applying a coefficient formed as the ratio of Maya Shukhgal'ter's estimate of the comparative size of the Soviet capital stock in 1987 and Bergson's estimate for 1975: $\mu = .15/.80 = .18$. No attempt has been made to appraise intertemporal changes in comparative size. These ratios have been applied directly to Bergson's data for both 1960 and 1975.

The Soviet Index numbers of factor inputs and output for 1975 are y_i/y_j = 15.1; k_i/k_j = 14.2; v_i/v_j = 27.8; ℓ/ℓ = 150.7. Those for 1960 are y_i/y_j = 10.6; k_i/k_j = 9.8; v_i/v_j = 14.0; ℓ_i/ℓ_j = 162.5.

METHOD: Labor and reproducible inputs are aggregated logarithmically. The weights reported by Bergson for American factor income shares in 1960 are labor .7415, fixed capital .2278, and inventories .0307. See *Productivity and the Social System*, pp. 71, 95 note 3, Appendix Table 18, p. 238.

The coefficient of factor productivity is $\theta = (y_i/y_j)/[(k_i/k_j)^{\alpha}(v_i/v_j)^{\beta}(\ell_i/\ell_j)^{1-\alpha-\beta}]$ where the ith subscript refers to the Soviet Union, or a specific European country, and the jth to the United States. y, k, v and ℓ are output, fixed capital, inventories and labor, and the exponents are factor shares based on American dollar weights.

The magnitude of the loss caused by this economic inefficiency is not easily appraised. Nonetheless its order can be sensed by modifying Bergson's data to reflect the perception of comparative size of two eminent Soviet economists. According to Viktor Belkin's calculations Soviet GNP is roughly 21 percent of Bergson's estimate for 1975, making allowances for diverse factors. Likewise, Maya Shukhgal'ter contends that the Soviet capital stock is only 15 percent of Bergson's figure. Ceteris paribus, these modifications generate a monumental decline in the coefficient of factor productivity ranging from two thirds in 1960 to three quarters in 1975 of Bergson's estimate, with even larger reductions judged in terms of the official standard. Clearly, the statistical distortion caused by command constrained economic inefficiency directly perceived by knowledgeable Soviet professionals may be enormous, far beyond anything suggested by index number relativity theory, rendering aggregate international comparison nearly indeterminant.

Economic Inefficiency: Sectoral Aspects

The adjustments advocated by Belkin and Shukhgal'ter assume that the principal cause of the low standard of Soviet living is the poor quality of its goods. They therefore increase the CIA's ruble dollar ratio by the degree they deem sufficient to make Soviet goods saleable on the world market. This expedient is to the good, but it does not make further allowance for the fact that even if quality in some general sense were up to world standards, neither characteristics, nor assortments would be responsive to demand. Factor productivity judged from the standpoint of economic efficiency thus could be even lower in most activities than they estimate.

However, there is at least one important exception that warrants special recognition: the military machinebuilding sector. Most weapons in the Soviet Union were built to competitive international standards, and were responsive to the demands of the Ministry of Defense. The dollar prices computed for these goods by the CIA despite numerous deficiencies therefore are apt to be much more accurate measures of real economic value than its prices for civilian goods. Some allowance for this duality should be taken into account by adjusting output and capital data upward for sectoral variations in demand responsiveness and international competitiveness. If it is crudely assumed that the Belkin/Shukhgal'ter revisions should only cover seventy five percent of output and capital then the Soviet coefficient of factor productivity doubles from 18 to 36,[2] using the official output data as the base.

Post Mortems

The collapse of the USSR has added credence to Belkin's and Shukhgal'ter's criticism of most Western Soviet productivity, growth and efficiency estimates, but the old assessments remain largely unaltered. The CIA continues to assert that official Soviet data were reliable subject to a variety of minor modifications, without appreciating that its factor cost adjustments for imputed interest and land rents were conceptually flawed.

Bergson has been somewhat more forthcoming. He acknowledges that official data, statistics derived from them both in rubles and dollars may have seriously overstated Soviet performance, but holds out the possibility that his estimates and the CIAs were essentially right by observing that the claims of Belkin, Åslund and others have not been proven (Bergson, 1994, 1995). As a consequence, estimates of Russia's recovery potential tend to be more sanguine than the evidence appears to warrant.

Notes

1.　　CIA, *Handbook of International Economic Statistics*, **CPAS** 92-10005, September 1992, Tables 7, 21, 31, pp. 24, 38 and 54. The U.S. GNP in 1989 valued at 1991 dollars was 5,659.2 billion dollars. The Soviet figure was 67 percent of this or 3,791.7 billion dollars. Russia accounted for 60.9 percent of Soviet GNP valued in rubles in 1989, implying a dollar GNP of 2,309 billion dollars.

2.

$$\theta = \left[(.25(95.3) + .75(95.3)(.21))/\left[(.25(79.1) + .75(79.1)(.18))\right.\right.^{.2278}.$$

$$(.25(154.3) + .75(154.3)(.18))^{.0307} (162.5)^{.7415}$$

$$= 38.83/\left[(30.45)^{.2278} (59.40)^{.0307} (162.5)^{.7415}\right.$$

$$38.83/(2.1775)(1.1336)(43.5861)$$

$$= .36$$

Bibliography

Allocation of Resources in the Soviet Union and China - 1985, *JEC*, March 19, 1986.

Belkin, Viktor, "Vlianie razlichii rynochnovo i nerynochnovo khoziaistvennovo mekhanizma na sopostavleniia makroekonomicheskikh pokazateli", paper presented at the Conference on Comparing the Soviet and American Economies, American Enterprise Institute, April 19-22, 1990.

Bergson, Abram, "Neoclassical Norms and the Valuation of National Product in the Soviet Union: Comment", *Journal of Comparative Economics*, Vol. 21, No. 3, December 1995, pp. 390-393.

_____, "The Communist Efficiency Gap: Alternative Measures", *Comparative Economic Studies*, Vol. XXXVI, No. 1, Spring 1994, pp. 1-12.

_____, "The USSR Before the Fall: How Poor and Why?", *Journal of Economic Perspectives*, No. 5, Fall 1991, pp. 29-44.

_____, "Comparative Productivity: The USSR, Eastern Europe and the West", *American Economic Review*, Vol. 77, June 1987, pp. 342-357.

_____, *Productivity and The Social System - The USSR and The West*, Cambridge, Massachusetts, Harvard University Press, 1978.

_____, *Planning and Productivity Under Soviet Socialism*, New York, Columbia University Press, 1968.

CIA, *USSR: Gross National Product Accounts, 1970, Research Aid*, Washington, DC, 1975.

_____, *USSR: Measures of Economic Growth and Development, 1950-80, JEC*, 1982.

DIA, *Gorbachev's Modernization Program: A Status Report*, DDB-1900-140-87, August 1987.

Edwards, Imogene, Margaret Hughes, and James Noren, "U.S. and U.S.S.R.: Comparisons of GNP", *Soviet Economy in a Time of Change*, *JEC*, Vol. 1, 1982, pp. 369-41.

Gallik, Dmitri, Barry Kostinsky, and Vladimir Treml, *Input-Output Structure of the Soviet Economy in 1972*, Foreign Economic Report, No. 18, April 1983.

Hanson, Philip and Keith Pavitt, *The Comparative Economics of Research Development and Innovation in East and West: A Survey*, Harwood, New York, 1987.

Kravis, Irving, Alan Heston, and Robert Summers. *World Product and Income*. Baltimore, Md., Johns Hopkins University Press, 1982.

Rosefielde, Steven, *The Transformation of the 1966 Soviet Input-Output Table from Producers to Adjusted Factor Cost Values*, GE75TMP-47, Washington, DC, 1975.

_____, *East-West Trade and Postwar Economic Growth*, SRI, 1976.

_____, *False Science: Underestimating the Soviet Arms Buildup*, 2nd edition, Transaction, 1987a.

_____, *Economic Foundations of Soviet National Security Strategy*, unpublished manuscript 1987b.

_____, "The Illusion of Material Progress: The Analytics of Soviet Economic Growth Revisited", *Soviet Studies*, Vol. 43, No. 4, 1991, pp. 597-611.

_____, *Annotated Compendium of Soviet Economic Statistics*, unpublished manuscript 1985.

_____, "Russia's Economic Recovery Potential to The Year 2000", in Ronald Hill, ed., *Fifth World Congress Conference Volume*, Macmillan, forthcoming 1996.

Shukhgal'ter, Maya, "Capital Sock in the USSR and USA: Problems of Comparison", paper presented at the Conference on Comparing the Soviet and American Economies, American Enterprise Institute, April 19-22, 1990.

U.S. Department of Commerce, *Survey of Current Business*, Vol. 45, No. 7, July 1965.

_____, *Survey of Current Business*, Vol. 49, No. 7, July 1969.

_____, *Survey of Current Business*, Vol. 51, No. 7, July 1971.

_____, *Survey of Current Business*, Vol. 54, No. 7, July 1974.

_____, *Survey of Current Business*, Vol. 59, No. 7, July 1979.

_____, *Survey of Current Business*, Vol. 63, No. 7, July 1983.

_____, *Survey of Current Business*, Vol. 64, No. 7, July 1984.

_____, *Survey of Current Business*, Vol. 66, No. 7, July 1986.

_____, *Fixed Reproducible Tangible Wealth in the United States 1925-85*, Bureau of Economic Analysis, Washington, DC, June 1987.

Appendix

Table 7.A1   **Index Numbers of Factors and Output, Total Economy (Exclusive of Selected Services), Selected Countries, 1960 and 1975**

	Employment Adjusted for Hours (1)	Reproducible Fixed Capital (2)	Gross Material Product (3)
I. 1960			
United States	100.0	100.0	100.0
France	30.1	13.4	15.4
Germany	43.2	15.4	21.9
United Kingdom	40.2	14.1	19.8
Italy	33.8	8.6	11.4
USSR	162.5	54.6	50.5
II. 1975			
United States	100.0	100.0	100.0
France	25.1	19.4	22.8
Germany	28.0	31.6	26.3
United Kingdom	25.7	19.6	17.6
Italy	22.6	15.5	16.0
USSR	150.7	79.1	71.7

SOURCES: Bergson, *Productivity and the Social System - the USSR and the West*, Appendix Table 12, p. 238. Table A2 this paper.

Table 7.A2 Derivation of Bergson's 1975 Output and Input Statistics

	GDMP Per Capita (1975 US Dollars)	Population Mid-Year (Millions)	GNMP Millions (US Dollars)	Index US=100
	(1)	(2)	(3)	(4)
I. Output				
USA	5307.3	213.566	1133.5	100.0
Germany	4825.0	61.829	298.3	26.3
	4894.8	52.748	258.2	22.8
France	3255.0	55.830	181.7	16.0
Italy	3565.1	55.981	199.6	17.6
UK	3194.0	254.4	812.5	71.7
USSR				

	Workers in Non-Farm Sectors	Average Weekly Hours	Workers in Non-Farm Sectors Adjusted for Non-Farm Hours	Agricultural Workers	Workers in Material Sectors Adjusted for Non-Farm Hours	
	Thousands (1)	US=100 (2)	Thousands (3)	Thousands (4)	Thousands (5)	Index (6)
II. Employment						
USA	64,940	100.0	64,940	3,476	68,416	100.0
Germany	18,268	94.8	17,318	1,823	19,141	28.0
France	14,837	101.6	15,074	2,104	17,178	25.1
Italy	12,449	97.8	12,175	3,274	15,449	22.6
UK	17,633	95.9	16,910	668	17,578	25.7
USSR	79,096	94.4	74,667	28,453	103,120	150.7

	Reproducible Fixed Capital	
	Dollars (Billions) (1)	Index (US=100) (2)
III. Gross Stock of Reproducible Fixed Capital, Material Sectors, July 1, 1975 in 1975 US Dollars		
USA	2752.6	100.0
Germany	868.9	31.6
France	533.5	19.4
Italy	426.8	15.5
UK	539.5	19.6
USSR	2176.0	79.1

	Inventories	
	Dollars (Billions) (1)	Index (US=100) (2)
IV. Inventories, Material Sectors, Specified Countries, July 1, 1975 in 1975 US Dollars		
USA	332.4	100.0
Germany	89.7	27.0
France	99.3	29.9
Italy	70.2	21.1
UK	84.3	25.4
USSR	513.0	154.3
	Reproducible Capital	
	Dollars (Billions) (1)	Index (US=100) (2)
V. Reproducible Capital, Material Sectors, Specified Countries, July 1, 1975 in 1975 US Dollars		
USA	3085.0	100.0
Germany	958.6	31.1
France	632.8	20.5
Italy	497.0	16.1
UK	623.8	20.2
USSR	2689.0	87.2

SOURCES: Abram Bergson, "Comparative Productivity: USSR, Eastern Europe and the West: Appendix Sources and Methods for Basic Data", unpublished manuscript, 1987.

Panel I (Output):	Table 1 and 2, pp. 1a and 1b.
Panel II (Employment):	Tables 6 and 7, pp. 14 and 20a.
Panel III (Fixed Capital):	Table 9, p. 30.
Panel IV (Inventories):	Table 10 p. 50.
Panel V (Capital):	Panel III plus panel IV.

Table 7.A3   Soviet Factor Productivity Growth 1965-85 (Official Statistics)

	1965-70	1970-75	1975-80	1980-85
ELECTRIC				
Output	9.0	7.1	5.0	3.6
Combined Inputs	6.0	3.4	2.4	3.3
Labor	3.8	1.5	0.7	2.2
Capital	10.4	7.3	6.0	5.4
FUELS				
Output	5.7	5.1	2.9	1.3
Combined Inputs	0.3	2.1	3.4	3.7
Labor	-1.6	-0.5	1.1	1.3
Capital	4.3	7.4	8.2	8.6
FERROUS METALS				
Output	5.7	5.0	1.9	2.0
Combined Inputs	4.3	2.7	0.7	3.0
Labor	2.1	0.4	-2.0	1.8
Capital	8.8	7.4	6.2	5.5
CHEMICAL				
Output	12.2	10.6	5.7	5.0
Combined Inputs	6.7	4.6	4.4	2.5
Labor	4.0	2.2	2.0	0.5
Capital	12.1	9.6	9.2	6.7
MACHINEBUILDING AND				
METALWORKING	11.7	11.6	8.2	6.2
Output	5.9	5.2	4.2	2.7
Combined Inputs	3.9	2.8	1.7	0.8
Labor	10.0	10.0	9.4	7.2
Capital				
WOOD, PULP, PAPER				
Output	5.5	5.2	1.5	3.5
Combined Inputs	2.7	2.1	2.1	1.7
Labor	0.3	-0.6	0	0
Capital	7.5	7.7	6.5	5.3
CONSTRUCTION MATERIALS				
Output	8.6	7.5	2.5	2.9
Combined Inputs	5.2	3.9	2.5	2.0
Labor	3.4	1.4	0.6	0.5
Capital	8.9	9.0	6.4	4.9
LIGHT INDUSTRY				
Output	8.6	4.6	3.4	1.4
Combined Inputs	5.1	2.6	2.8	1.5
Labor	3.0	0.1	1.1	-0.5
Capital	9.4	7.7	6.4	5.7

	1965-70	1970-75	1975-80	1980-85
FOOD				
Output	5.9	5.4	1.5	3.3
Combined Inputs	4.6	2.9	1.7	1.7
Labor	3.1	0.7	-0.2	0
Capital	7.7	7.4	5.6	5.2

SOURCES: Rosefielde, *Annotated Compendium of Soviet Economic Statistics 1950-85*, unpublished manuscript, September 1987, Tables K2 and L8. Table 9.9 this volume. Bergson, *Productivity and the Social System*, Appendix Table 22, p. 245.

DATA: Labor is measured in manhours.

METHOD: Following Bergson the capital share is set at .33 and the labor share at .67. Inputs are combined arithmetically with these income shares in accordance with the usual interpretation of the exponents of the Cobb-Douglas production function as income elasticities. The ruble price weights are in 1959 prices. Capital is gross of depreciation. Comparable weights derived from the 1966 I-O table are .32 and .68.

Compound annual rates of growth.

Table 7.A4   Factor and Product Series for the Soviet Metalworking and Machine Building Sector 1965-85

		1965	1970	1975	1980	1985
Output (Billions of 1970 Rubles)						
1.	Official: 1966 I-O Table	28.8	50.2	86.8	128.5	173.5
2.	Official: 1972 I-O Table	31.4	54.9	94.9	140.4	189.6
3.	CIA: 1970 Purchasers I	29.0	40.6	59.4	77.1	84.1
4.	CIA: 1970 Purchasers II	32.7	45.8	67.1	87.0	94.9
5.	CIA: 1970 AFC	27.5	38.5	56.4	73.2	79.8
6.	CIA: 1982 AFC	33.0	46.1	64.0	77.3	84.3
7.	CIA/Official Purchasers I	23.2	40.6	70.2	103.8	140.2
8.	CIA/Official Purchasers II	26.2	45.8	79.2	117.1	158.2
Fixed Capital (Billions of Rubles)						
	Book Value: 1972 I-O Table	33.3	53.5	86.1	135.1	191.7
Labor (Millions)						
	Man Years: 1972 I-O Table	9.9	12.0	13.8	15.1	15.8

SOURCES: Steven Rosefielde, *The Transformation of the 1966 Soviet Input-Output Table From Producers to Adjusted Factor Cost Values*, GE75TMP-47, Table A6, pp. 89-90; Rosefielde, *False Science: Underestimating the Soviet Arms Buildup*, Transaction, 1987, Tables A11, p. 294 and A12, pp. 297-8; Rosefielde, *Annotated Compendium of Soviet Economic Statistics 1950-85*, Unpublished manuscript, 1987, Tables Y2, K2, and L2; Dmitri Gallik, Barry Kostinsky and Vladimir Treml, *Input-Output Structure of the Soviet Economy in 1972*, Foreign Economic Report, No. 18, April 1983, Table B3, pp. 104-6; CIA, *USSR: Gross National Product Accounts, 1970, Research Aid*, CIA, Washington, D.C., 1975; DIA, *Gorbachev's Modernization Program: A Status Report*, DDB-1900-140-87, August 1987, Table A1, p. 26, Table B2, p. 32; CIA, *USSR: Measures of Economic Growth and Development, 1950-80*, JEC, 1982, Table A1, pp. 53-4, and Table D7, p. 143.

DATA: Output

1.   Official: 1966 I-O: The 1966 MBMW statistic published in the 1966 I-O table (32.3 billion rubles), valued at 1967 purchasers prices is converted to 1970 prices and extrapolated to 1970 as

explained in Rosefielde, *False Science*, Table A12. Official Soviet MBMW real growth indices are used to estimate output in other years.

2. Official: 1972 I-O: The 1972 MBMW statistic published in the 1972 I-O table (64.7 billion rubles), valued at 1972 purchasers price is extrapolated to other years with the official MBMW growth index, and then converted to 1970 prices with the industrial wholesale price index (including turnover tax). See *Narkhoz 72*, p. 198.

3. CIA: 1970 Purchasers I: The 1970 MBMW figure was computed by the CIA in *USSR: Gross National Product Accounts* in 1975, and valued at 1970 purchasers prices. It is extrapolated to other years with official CIA growth statistics including those using 1982 price weights for the subperiod 1980-85 (see *Gorbachev's Modernization Program: A Status Report*, Table B2, p. 32).

4. CIA: 1970 Purchasers II: The 1970 MBMW statistic valued at 1970 purchasers prices is taken from *USSR: Measures of Economic Growth and Development*, Table D7 and extrapolated to other years with the CIA's MBMW growth statistics including those using 1982 price weights for the subperiod 1980-85 (see *Gorbachev's Modernization Program: A Status Report* Table B2, p. 32).

5. CIA*: 1970 AFC: These data are valued at 1970 adjusted factor cost and are obtained directly from *USSR: Measures of Economic Growth and Development* Table A-1. The 1985 estimate is extrapolated from *Gorbachev's Modernization Program: A Status Report*, Table A1, p. 26.

6. CIA*: 1982 AFC: The statistics valued at 1982 adjusted factor cost are taken directly from *Gorbachev's Modernization Program: A Status Report*, Table B2, p. 32. The values are higher because they partially embody the CIA's estimate of Soviet hidden machine-building inflation.

7. CIA/Official: Purchasers I: same as 3 except growth is extrapolated with the official MBMW real GVO index.

8. CIA/Official: Purchasers II: same as 4 except growth is extrapolated with the official MBMW real GVO index.

---

*For a discussion of the shortcoming of these data see (Rosefielde, 1987a).

Fixed Capital: These statistics are derived from the 1972 input-output table, extrapolated to other years with official Soviet statistics (Table K2). According to (Gallik et al., 1983 p. 16), they are computed at original book value.

Labor: These statistics are derived from the 1972 input-output table, extrapolated to other years with official Soviet statistics. The 1972 estimate is consistent with Rapawy's series.

Table 7.A5 **Dollar Value of Soviet Metalworking and Machine Building Output and Capital 1965-85**

		1965	1970	1975	1980	1985
I. Billions of 1976 Rubles Output						
Output						
1.	Official: 1966 I-O Table	24.5	42.7	73.8	109.2	147.5
2.	Official: 1972 I-O Table	26.7	46.7	80.7	119.3	161.2
3.	CIA: 1970 Purchasers I	24.7	34.5	50.5	65.5	71.3
4.	CIA: 1970 Purchasers II	27.8	38.9	57.0	74.0	80.5
5.	CIA/Official: Purchasers I	23.2	40.6	70.2	103.8	140.2
6.	CIA/Official: Purchasers II	26.2	45.8	79.2	117.1	158.2
Fixed Capital		31.3	50.2	80.8	126.8	179.9
II. Billions of 1976 Dollars (Soviet Quantity Weights)						
Output						
1.	Official: 1966 I-O Table	92.1	160.5	277.4	410.5	554.5
2.	Official: 1972 I-O Table	100.4	175.6	303.4	448.5	606.0
3.	CIA: 1970 Purchasers I	92.9	129.7	189.3	246.2	268.0
4.	CIA: 1970 Purchasers II	104.5	146.2	214.3	278.2	302.6
5.	CIA/Official: Purchasers I	74.2	129.7	224.1	331.3	447.6
6.	CIA/Official: Purchasers II	83.6	146.2	252.6	373.4	503.8
Fixed Capital		86.0	137.9	222.0	348.4	494.2
III. Billions of 1976 Dollars (US Quantity Weights						
Output						
1.	Official: 1966 I-O Table	56.5	98.4	170.0	251.6	339.9
2.	Official: 1972 I-O Table	61.5	10.6	185.9	274.9	371.4
3.	CIA: 1970 Purchasers I	56.9	79.5	116.4	150.9	164.3
4.	CIA: 1970 Purchasers II	64.1	89.6	131.3	170.5	185.5
5.	CIA/Official: Purchasers I	45.4	79.5	137.4	203.1	274.4
6.	CIA/Official: Purchasers II	51.2	89.6	154.8	228.9	309.3
Fixed Capital		66.0	105.9	170.5	267.5	379.5

SOURCES: Table A4; Imogene Edwards, Margret Hughes, and James Noren, "U.S. and U.S.S.R.: Comparisons of GNP", *Soviet Economy in a Time of Change*, JEC, Vol. 1, 1979, pp. 372, 379; CIA; *USSR: Measures of Economic Growth and Development, 1950-80*, JEC, 1982, Table B3, p. 87; *Narodnoe khoziaistvo 1977*, p. 143.

METHOD: Panel I: The output series in Table A4 are converted from 1970 to 1976 ruble prices using the official Soviet industrial wholesale price index including turnover tax (1976=85; 1970=100). The fixed capital series in Table A4 is converted from 1970 to 1976 ruble prices with a composite index of construction and machinery prices. The construction index in 1976 is 102.7; 1970=100 (See *USSR: Measures of Economic Growth and Development*, Table B3, p. 87). Both indexes are equally weighted. Cf. "U.S. and U.S.S.R.: Comparisons of GNP", Table 2, p. 379 on new fixed investment. The composite index in 1976 is 93.9; 1970=100.

Panel II: Dollar-ruble ratios (the inverse of the ruble-dollar ratios) based on Soviet quantity weights for machinery and investment (computed at purchasers prices) are taken from "U.S. and U.S.S.R.: Comparisons of GNP", Table 2 and applied respectively to the output and fixed capital series in Panel I.

Panel III: Dollar-ruble ratios based on US quantity weights for machinery and investment are taken from "U.S. and U.S.S.R.: Comparisons of GNP", Table 2 and applied respectively to the output and fixed capital series in Panel I.

COMMENT: Bergson's methods calls for the pricing of Soviet quantities in dollars. The values in panel II therefore are the appropriate measures for the purposes at hand.

Table 7.A6   Factor and Product Statistics for the American Machine Building and Metalworking Sector 1960-85 (1982 Prices)

	1960	1965	1970	1975	1980	1985
Output (Billions of Dollars)						
A. Manufacturing GNP						
a. Durables	231.3	255.7	284.8	303.3	393.1	481.5
1. Lumber and Wood-Products						20.6
2. Furniture and Fixtures						11.6
3. Stone, Clay, Glass Products						22.2
B. MBMW	205.2	226.8	252.6	269.0	348.7	427.1
Gross Fixed Capital (Billions of Dollars)						
A. Manufacturing: Equipment, Structures	290.2	248.6	461.2	553.4	674.1	770.5
a. Durables	14.9	16.7	19.9	26.3	32.4	30.8
1. Lumber and Wood-Products	4.3	4.7	6.6	8.4	9.9	10.8
2. Furniture and Fixtures	27.8	32.5	38.5	45.4	52.7	52.7
3. Stone, Clay, Glass Products	243.2	294.5	396.2	473.3	579.1	676.2
B. MBMW						
Labor (Millions of Man Years)						
A. Manufacturing						
a. Durables	9.4	10.4	11.3	10.5	12.0	11.4
1. Lumber and Wood-Products	.6	.6	.6	.6	.7	.7
2. Furniture and Fixtures	.4	.4	.5	.4	.4	.5
3. Stone, Clay, Glass Products	.6	.6	.6	.6	.7	.6
B. MBMW	7.8	8.8	9.6	8.9	10.2	9.6

SOURCES: *Survey of Current Business*, Vol. 66, No. 7, July 1986, Table 6.2, p. 63 Table 6.7B, p. 66, *Survey of Current Business*, Vol. 64, No. 7, July 1984, Table 6.2, p. 69, Table 6.8, p. 73; *Survey of Current Business*, Vol. 59, No. 7, July 1979, Table 6.2, p. 52, Table 6.2, p. 55, *Survey of Current Business*, Vol. 51, No. 7, Part 1, July 1971, Table 6.4, p. 36; Tables 1.21, p. 20, *Survey of Current Business*, Vol. 49, No. 7, July 1969, Table 1.21, p. 24, *Survey of Current Business*, Vol. 44, No. 7, July 1964, Table 7, p. 13 and Table 52, p. 29; *Fixed Reproducible Tangible Wealth in the United States 1925-85*, Bureau of Economic Analysis, US Department of Commerce, Washington, D.C. June 1987, Table A1, pp. 7-9.

METHOD: Output: Manufacturing durables are converted from current to constant 1982 prices with the implicit durable chain price indexes constructed in Table A8. The series calculated in this way differs by a few percent from one extrapolated with the industrial production indexes (base

1967) reported in *Economic Indicators*, July 1985, p. 17. MBMW output entry B for observations 1960-80 are calculated by assuming that the ratio of manufacturing durables national income to MBMW GNP reported in 1985 is constant for the full period 1960-85.

COMMENT: The coverage of manufactured durables is narrower than GNP durables generally. The former is defined conformably with the capital and labor series and is therefore the appropriate output measure for this study.

Table 7.A7   Factor and Product Statistics for the American Machine Building and Metalworking Sector 1960-85 (Constant Prices)

(Billions of 1976 Dollars)	1960	1965	1970	1975	1980	1985
Output	141.4	156.3	174.0	185.3	240.3	294.3
Gross Fixed Capital	151.3	183.2	246.4	294.0	360.2	420.6
Labor (Man Years Full Time Equivalents)	7.8	8.8	9.6	8.9	10.2	9.6

SOURCES: Tables A6, A8.

METHOD: Output is converted from 1982 to 1976 prices with the implicit chain price deflators in Table A8.

Gross fixed capital is reported in current and constant 1982 prices. The constant series in 1982 prices was converted to a 1976 price base by computing an implicit price index. This was accomplished by deriving the current gross fixed capital value of machinebuilding and metalworking according to the procedure shown in Table A6 and dividing by the analogous figure reported in 1982 prices. This ratio was then applied to the other years designated. See *Fixed Tangible Wealth in the United States 1925-85*, Bureau of Economic Analysis, US Department of Commerce, June 1987, Tables 1 and 2, pp. 7-9, and 60-63.

Table 7.A8   Implicit Price Deflators for GNP by Major Product Chain Index

Durables	1960	1965	1970	1972	1975	1976	1980	1982	1985
1958 Series (1958=100)	100.9	102.3	115.6	119.1	144.9	153.1	197.6	222.7	230.7
1972 Series (1972=100)	85.7	85.9	97.1	100.0	121.9	128.9	165.9	187.0	193.7
1982 Series (1982=100)	45.8	45.9	51.9	53.5	65.2	68.9	88.7	100.0	103.6

SOURCES: *Survey of Current Business*, Vol. 66, No. 7, July 1986, Table 7.2, p. 75. *Survey of Current Business*, Vol. 63, No. 7, July 1983, Table 7.3, p. 81; *Survey of Current Business*, Vol. 59, No. 7, July 1979, Table 7.3, p. 62; *Survey of Business*, Vol. 54, No. 7, July 1974, Table 8.3, p. 45; *Survey of Current Business*, Vol. 45, No. 8, August 1965, Table 17, p. 53.

METHOD: The durable price index is reported separately for final and total sales. The series differ slightly. Since our concern is with final durable goods production, the final sales series is utilized in constructing the chain index above. N.B. The implicit movement in manufactured durable prices between 1982 and 1985 in the GNP series (*Survey of Current Business*, Vol. 66, No. 7, July 1986, Tables 6.1 and 6.2) differ from the official durable price index. The discrepancy is concentrated in "machinery except electrical" and may be related to foreign exchange fluctuations. In any event the GNP data in 1982 prices are used in Table A.6.

Table 7.A9   Index Numbers of Factors and Output: Machine Building and Metalworking 1975

	Employed Man Years (1)	Reproducible Fixed Capital (2)	Output (3)
United States	100.0	100.0	100.0
USSR (Soviet Quantity Weights)			
1. Official: 1966 I-O Table	155.1	75.5	149.7
2. Official: 1972 I-O Table	155.1	75.5	163.7
3. CIA/Official: Purchasers I	155.1	75.5	120.9
4. CIA/Official: Purchasers II	155.1	75.5	136.3
USSR (US Quantity Weights)			
1. Official: 1972 I-O Table	155.1	75.5	101.9

SOURCES: Tables A4, A5, A7, and note 8 this paper.

COMMENT: The accuracy of the output estimates can be checked by comparing them with the CIA's USSR/US machinery and equipment ratio: 141.4 reported in Edwards, Hughes and Noren, "U.S. and U.S.S.R.: Comparisons of GNP", Table 1, p. 378. Bergson's estimates rely on these data.

**Table 7.A10   Index Numbers of Factor and Output: Machine Build-
ing and Metalworking 1960-85 (US=100)**

USSR (Soviet Quantity Weights)	1960	1965	1970	1975	1980	1985
1. Official: 1972 I-O Table						
Employed Man Years		112.5	125.0	155.1	148.0	164.6
Reproducible Fixed Capi-tal		46.9	56.0	75.5	96.7	117.5
Output		54.0	82.8	163.7	175.7	205.9
2. CIA/Official: Purchasers II						
Employed Man Years		112.5	125.0	155.1	148.0	164.6
Reproducible Fixed Capi-tal		46.9	56.0	75.5	96.7	117.5
Output		45.0	68.9	136.3	146.3	171.2

SOURCES: Tables A4, A5 and A7.

8 Industrial Growth and Efficiency in the United States and the Former Soviet Union

Robert S. Whitesell

Introduction

The Russian revolution in 1917 began a grand experiment in which a new economic system was developed. Rapid industrialization and high growth rates in the 1930s and in the early post-WWII period seemed to imply the formation of a successful alternative to a market economy. But growth rates fell steadily from the late 1950s, and by the early 1980s it was apparent that the system was experiencing extreme difficulties. Nevertheless, few predicted the complete collapse of Soviet-type socialism that began in Poland in 1989, quickly spread throughout Eastern Europe, and finally led to the fall of the Soviet Union in 1991.

From the early 1970s much academic research employing diverse methodologies attempted to explain the growth slowdown in the Soviet Union. It was argued that the basic economic system was inefficient and unable to reform itself successfully (Goldman, 1983; Hewett, 1988). Limitations in the level and rate of improvement in technology were demonstrated (Amann and Cooper, 1977, 1982 and 1986). Deficiencies in the published data were highlighted as explained in the Introduction, Chapter 2 and 7, and it was argued that the Soviet economy had never reached the high income levels generally believed (Birman, 1981). Econometric estimates of aggregate production functions were used to explain the slowdown in growth (Weitzman, 1970; Whitesell, 1983). Each of these approaches has given us insights into the process of decay, but have not explained fully the technical factors underlying the Soviet Union's apparently inexorable decline. This chapter attempts to redress this deficiency, assuming that data deficiencies affect the level of outputs and inputs more than growth and productivity trends.

Standard, 'average', aggregate production function estimates have been used widely to analyze economic growth in the United States and the former Soviet Union. The literature on U.S. growth was stimulated by Solow's (1957) original article in which he found that most U.S. economic growth was caused by increases in factor productivity rather than from input accumulation. This stimulated a body of research which attempted to find the underlying causes of this factor productivity growth, such as human capital development, economies of scale, embodied technological change, etc.[1] Recent research in this field (Jorgenson et al., 1987) has argued that most U.S. economic growth is explained by input growth if inputs are properly adjusted for changes in quality.

Similar research on the Soviet economy has attempted to analyze the causes of the slowdown in economic growth which occurred from the late 1950s. This literature has resulted in a debate over the relative importance of decreasing technological change and diminishing returns to capital. These two interpretations hinge on the use of aggregate Cobb-Douglas or CES production functions. Estimation of the Cobb-Douglas function leads to the conclusion that falling total factor productivity growth is the primary cause of the growth slowdown, and estimation of the CES function leads to the conclusion that diminishing returns to capital is the best explanation. Unfortunately, it seems to be impossible to choose between these two explanations on statistical grounds, and strong theoretical cases can be made for both interpretations in the context of the Soviet economy.[2]

A potential additional cause of economic growth, which has not been tested previously, is that there have been changes in economic efficiency over time. Increases in efficiency might have contributed to rapid economic growth in the post-war U.S. economy, and decreases in efficiency might have been part of the explanation of the growth slowdown in the Soviet Union. To test this hypothesis it is necessary to separate the growth effect of changes in efficiency from the effect of other changes in factor productivity. The purpose of this chapter is to investigate these hypotheses through the estimation of frontier rather than 'average' production functions.

Frontier Production Functions

The notion of intertemporal variations in technical efficiency is clear in the abstract, reflecting deviations from a dynamic production possibilities frontier. The estimation of these deviations from time series data, however, is clouded by the difficulty of accurately measuring the frontier at any moment and for all observations in question. In a disaggregated, microeconomic context the meaning of frontier production function estimates is relatively clear. An industry production function is estimated, in which the data points are individual firms in an industry. The frontier is defined by the most productive firm, in the set, but not necessarily the most productive in all systems. This firm is considered to be efficient, even though in the Soviet case it is apt to be command constrained, and supply may not optimally satisfy demand, and all other firms are considered inefficient by comparison. The level of efficiency for each firm is defined by the ratio of actual to potential output, where potential output is established by the estimated production frontier. Average efficiency is computed for all the firms in the industry. The accuracy of these estimates, however, depends on whether the most productive firm is really on the command constrained, the domestic competitive, or still better this intersystemic frontier. If it is not, static microeconomic efficiency will be understated and the intertemporal trend may be distorted in these various senses.

The most productive firm could deviate from the ideal for many reasons. For example, factors might be internally misallocated (Rosefielde and Pfouts, 1988).[3] Discussions of the frontier production function estimates usually disregard this possibility because the focus is on single product firms. However, data usually pertain to multi-product firms and the output measure is an aggregate index of all the products being produced in the firm. Changes in measured efficiency could occur by input reallocation, so the measure of efficiency may depend on allocative as well as technical efficiency.

This is illustrated in Figure 8.1. Assume a certain firm is producing two goods X and Y with $\overline{K}$ and $\overline{L}$ amounts of capital and labor. Assume the firm begins by producing at point A and then reallocates inputs such that it begins to produce at point B. If the measure of the firm's output is an aggregate index of commodities X and Y, this change would look like a change in technical efficiency because more of the aggregate output is being produced with a fixed amount of inputs, and the fact that this is caused by a reallocation of inputs among individual products is not observed.

Another difficulty which occurs is the distinction between changes in efficiency and technological change. In microeconomic theory it is assumed that all firms have access to the same technology, which makes this distinction clear. In reality, however, the diffusion of technology is slow and costly, and all firms do not have access to the same technology. A firm could be producing efficiently -- in the sense that it is producing the maximum output with given inputs and technology -- but be less productive than the frontier defining firm because of a lower technological level. Frontier production function estimates would categorize this productivity differential as inefficiency. Diffusion of technology would be considered improvements in efficiency rather than technological change.

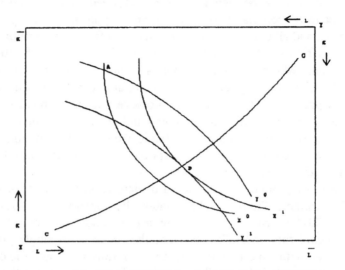

Figure 8.1   Allocational Change and Technical Efficiency

The same problems arise in the aggregate time-series context. The measure of efficiency includes both technical and allocative efficiency. In addition to the effect of intraenterprise factor allocation, interenterprise factor allocation will effect efficiency.

The difficulty of distinguishing technological change and changing efficiency also exists. In 'average' production function estimation techniques, the time trend term picks up all changes in production that are not attributable to input growth. Production is always assumed to be efficient. The time trend is usually specified such that the rate of total factor productivity growth is some variation of $\lambda + 2\mu t$, where t is time and λ and μ are estimated parameters. Factor productivity growth is increasing, decreasing or constant over time depending on whether μ is positive, negative, or zero. It is well known that total factor productivity growth measured in this way is attributable to a large number of possible causes. These include, but are not restricted to, neutral and non-neutral technological change, improvements in the quality of capital and labor, improvements in the organization of production and/or management techniques, the diffusion of technology to new firms in the industry, increases in technical efficiency of firms, improvements in transport and communications, economies of scale, improvements in the allocation of resources among and within firms, etc. If μ is negative, the rate of growth of factor productivity is getting slower over time. This could be caused by reductions in the rate of improvement in all or some of these factors, but it could also be caused by an absolute deterioration in some of these factors, i.e., decreasing efficiency. If the entire factor productivity term, $\lambda + 2\mu t$, is negative, then either all of these factors are deteriorating in absolute terms, or the effects of those that are deteriorating are larger than the effects of those that are improving. Since estimates of some industrial sectors show negative rates of factor productivity growth, this is a case that must be considered. It seems unlikely that all of these factors could be negative. But, if the introduction and diffusion of new technology is slow and getting slower over time, and efficiency is deteriorating over time, this could explain a negative rate of factor productivity growth.

Suppose we estimate frontier production functions rather than 'average' production functions, but include a time trend term. What is being measured by the time trend and what is being measured by the efficiency term? Clearly, the time trend term is going to pick up any effects on factor productivity growth that are occurring continuously over time. If improvements in technological change are occurring smoothly over time, and changes in efficiency are variable, then the time trend term would represent technological change and the one-sided residual from the frontier estimate would show changes in efficiency. But if changes in efficiency are occurring continuously in one direction that would be measured by the time trend term, even in frontier production function estimates. For example, suppose the true rate of technological change were positive and constant, and efficiency was decreasing at a relatively constant rate. Then, the time trend term would be an amalgam of the effects of this constant rate of decrease in efficiency and the constant rate of improvement in technology. The one-sided residual would also be an amalgam. It would measure deviations from the mean in the rate of deterioration in efficiency, and deviations from the mean in the rate of change of new technology. If the constant rate of deteriorating efficiency were greater than the constant rate of technological change the estimated factor productivity growth would be negative.

Estimating frontier production functions does not result in a clean separation between changes in efficiency and other changes which affect factor productivity. What can be gained from the estimation of aggregate frontier production functions that is different from the results of aggregate 'average' production functions? First, the efficiency term shows the effect of macroeconomic and microeconomic fluctuations which change the economic environment facing the firms in an industry. Such fluctuations in the economic environment will alter aggregate efficiency because firms do not instantaneously adjust in an optimal way to such changes, regardless of the economic system. These measures of efficiency can give us a measure of the magnitude of these fluctuations, and an indication of the speed of adjustment. In a market context other measures such as rates of unemployment are measures of changes in efficiency, but in the old Soviet-type economy these economic variables were held artificially constant by the economic system. Frontier production function measures of efficiency are an alternative measure of the size of economic fluctuations.

Second, the measure of efficiency does measure changes in efficiency that are not continuous over time. For example, suppose that efficiency improves over part of the time series and then deteriorates over another part of the time series. This will be captured by the frontier measure of efficiency because the Solow residual only captures a trend in efficiency which continues in one direction over time.

Data

Industrial output for the Soviet Union is the official measure of the gross value of output (GVO) obtained from official statistical sources and are in 1975 industrial wholesale ruble prices, which contain some relatively insignificant turnover tax charges. These should not cause serious distortion, and are available for the period 1951-86.[4] Interest has not been imputed in lieu of profits, nor have other factor cost adjustments been made in accordance with the findings in chapter 2. Output is classified by establishment principle, and includes both finished and semifabricated goods, and the repair of old goods. Intermediate inputs produced and consumed internally are not counted. The inadequacies of the official GVO measure are well known. They include biases due to double counting of intermediate inputs, the vagaries of Soviet prices and taxes, and the exclusion of some services. The capital data are derived from the official statistical yearbooks and are in

1973 prices.[5] The labor series are the number of hours worked computed by Rapawy (1976) for the period 1950-75 and updated using his methodology.

The data for the United States come from Jorgenson, et al. (1987).[6] The data are indexes of gross output, capital stock, and intermediate inputs for industrial sectors for the period 1948-79, and hours worked in those industrial sectors. Jorgenson, et al. (1987) also compute indexes with qualitative change in the inputs. This study uses their data series unadjusted for quality so that the data are as comparable as possible with the Soviet data.

The U.S. and Soviet data are not comparable in several ways. One difference arises from the definition of output based on GDP in the U.S. data and GVO in the Soviet data. Another difference is that the U.S. data on industrial sectors were aggregated from the underlying disaggregated data using translog indexes. The Soviet data were aggregated using a more traditional additive aggregation procedure. Third, the data for the U.S. are more disaggregated and there are more industrial sectors than are available for Soviet industry. Soviet statistics are valued in rubles; American data in dollars; which deliberately sidesteps various issues of index number relativity that are superfluous for the efficiency analysis with respect to firm's perceptible frontiers, as distinct from intersystemic comparisons of globally best practice efficiency. Tables 8.1 and 8.2 list the available sectoral data for U.S. and Soviet industry. Finally, data were available on intermediate inputs for the United States but not for the Soviet Union. It was decided to estimate production functions for the U.S. both with and without intermediate inputs. This was done because it was hoped that the difference in the results of the two kinds of estimates would provide additional information about the meaning of the results. The implications of this are discussed later.

Model Specification

Possible approaches to the estimation of production frontiers include the non-parametric programming approach, the parametric programming approach and the parametric statistical, or stochastic, approach. The third technique has been adopted because it is less sensitive to outliers and measurement error, and provides statistical information for goodness of fit measures and hypothesis testing.

Table 8.1   U.S. Industrial Sectors

1.	METMIN	Metal mining
2.	COALMIN	Coal mining
3.	PETGAS	Crude petroleum and natural gas
4.	NMETMIN	Nonmetallic mining and quarrying
5.	FOOD	Food and kindred products
6.	TOB	Tobacco manufacturers
7.	TEX	Textile mill products
8.	APP	Apparel and other fabricated textile products
9.	PAPER	Paper and allied products
10.	PRINT	Printing and publishing
11.	CHEM	Chemicals and allied products
12.	PETPROD	Petroleum and coal products
13.	RUB	Rubber and miscellaneous plastic products
14.	LEATH	Leather and leather products
15.	WOOD	Lumber and wood products, except furniture
16.	FURN	Furniture and fixtures
17.	GLASS	Stone, clay and glass products
18.	PRIMET	Primary metal industries
19.	FABMET	Fabricated metal industries
20.	MACH	Machinery, except electrical
21.	ELMACH	Electrical machinery, equipment and supplies
22.	TRANS	Transportation equipment and ordnance, except motor
23.	VEH	vehicles
24.	PHOTO	Motor vehicles and equipment
25.	MISC	Professional photographic equipment and watches
26.	ELUT	Miscellaneous manufacturing industries
27.	GASUT	Electric utilities
28.	WATER	Gas utilities
		Water utilities

Table 8.2   Soviet Industrial Sectors

1.	TOTAL	Total industry
2.	POWER	Electric power
3.	FUELS	Fuels
4.	CHEM	Chemicals
5.	MBMW	Machine building and metal working
6.	CONST	Construction materials
7.	WOOD	Wood working
8.	LIGHT	Light industry
9.	FOOD	Food processing

The general form of the stochastic frontier production function is:

$$Y = f(K,L,M) \exp(v - u),$$

where Y is a measure of output, K is a measure of capital, L is a measure of labor and M is a measure of intermediate inputs. Since all functional forms estimated in this study assume constant returns to scale this function can be rewritten

$$y = f(k,m) \exp(v - u),$$

where $y = Y/L$, $k = K/L$ and $m = M/L$. Several forms of the Cobb-Douglas production function with constant returns to scale are used to specify $f(k,m)$. For all specifications v is a normally distributed error term, with each element independently and identically distributed as $N(0,\sigma_v^2)$, which makes the frontier stochastic and accommodates measurement error, etc.; and u is a one-sided error term, in which the individual elements are the absolute value of variables independently and identically distributed as $N(0,\sigma_u^2)$, and represents the distance to the frontier, or inefficiency. This specification of the error term, $\epsilon = v - u$, was selected because it has been widely utilized, the density function has been derived and its statistical properties are well established in the literature.

Eight Cobb-Douglas frontier production functions with constant returns to scale expressed in logarithmic terms are used. Four of these include intermediate inputs and four exclude intermediate inputs. Specifically:

(FRONM1) $\ln(y) = \gamma + \lambda t + \mu t^2 + \alpha_K \ln(k) + \alpha_M \ln(m) + \epsilon$

(FRONM2) $\ln(y) = \gamma + \lambda t + \alpha_K \ln(k) + \alpha_M \ln(m) + \epsilon$

(FRONM3) $\ln(y) = \gamma + \mu t^2 + \alpha_K \ln(k) + \alpha_M \ln(m) + \epsilon$

(FRONM4) $\ln(y) = \gamma + \alpha_K \ln(k) + \alpha_M \ln(m) + \epsilon$

(FRON1) $\ln(y) = \gamma + \lambda t + \mu t^2 + \alpha_K \ln(k) + \epsilon$

(FRON2) $\ln(y) = \gamma + \lambda t + \alpha_K \ln(k) + \epsilon$

(FRON3) $\ln(y) = \gamma + \mu t^2 + \alpha_K \ln(k) + \epsilon$

(FRON4) $\ln(y) = \gamma + \alpha_K \ln(k) + \epsilon$

In all eight specifications t is time and ϵ is the composite error term, $\epsilon = v - u$. The α_i parameters are elasticities of output with respect to capital and intermediate inputs. If factors are paid the value of their marginal products these would be equal to the corresponding factor shares. The assumption of constant returns to scale means that the share of labor is $\alpha_L = 1 - \alpha_K - \alpha_M$.

The literature on frontier estimation suggests that frontiers cannot always be fitted to the data. Two problems may arise. First the frontier may be fitted from the wrong side. In terms of Figure 8.2 this means that there may be several observations defining the frontier (Q_f) with the remainder lying above it rather than below it, as in the figure. The implied σ_u is negative and this is sometimes referred to as a Type I failure; the probability of it happening is larger when σ_u/σ_v is small.[7] This may be detected by examining the estimate of the third moment of the density function of ϵ.[8] If this is the case it is usually assumed that the entire set of observations is defining the frontier. This means that the OLS estimates are interpreted as providing an accurate representation of the frontier and there is no inefficiency.

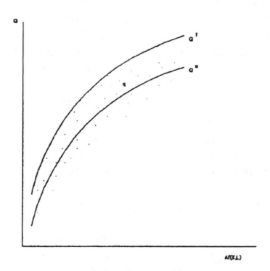

Figure 8.2   Technical Efficiency and Curve Fitting

The second problem that may arise is that the estimated σ_v may be negative. This certainly calls into question the validity of the error specification and is sometimes referred to as a type II failure.[9] The probability of this occurring increases when σ_u/σ_v is large. When σ_u/σ_v is small we have a high probability of Type I failure, i.e., OLS is essentially estimating the frontier, and when σ_u/σ_v is very large we have a high probability of a Type II failure and specification error.

These problems may mean that the functional form being estimated is misspecified. The requirements for the proper identification of the production frontier are more stringent than for the standard average production function. Essentially, the statistical technique is to find the shape of the production function from data points which are mostly inefficient relative to the frontier, and graft that shape onto the outer edge of the data points, subject to the condition that no data points be above the frontier, i.e, no data points should be more than 100 percent efficient. Given a particular functional form, it is often the case that no reasonably shaped production function can fulfill these conditions. For example, if the 'true' production function is characterized by constant factor productivity growth over time, a specification which imposes variable factor productivity growth over time may not be computable. With a standard average production function such a function could be computed because the only condition is to minimize the sum of squared errors of the regression. Of course, the estimate would not yield statistically significant results, but an estimate would be computable.

Once reasonable frontier production function estimates have been obtained the average level of inefficiency may be estimated as:

$$\text{INEF} = E(u) = \left(\sqrt{2/\pi}\right)\hat{\sigma}_u.$$

This is reported in the tables of results and discussed in the next section.

The level of inefficiency for each annual observation is calculated as in Jondrow, et al. (1982). Specifically, the level of inefficiency for each annual observation is estimated as

$$E(u|\epsilon) = \mu_* + \sigma_* \frac{f\left(-\mu_*/\sigma_*\right)}{1-F\left(-\mu_*/\sigma_*\right)}$$

where f and F represent the standard normal density and the cumulative density function, respectively; and $-\mu_*/\sigma_* = \epsilon\sigma_u/\sigma\sigma_v$, where $\sigma^2 = \sigma_u^2 + \sigma_v^2$.

Only estimates of frontier production functions which produced economically meaningful parameter estimates are reported in the tables. Economically meaningful estimates mean that neither Type I nor Type II failure occurred, the residuals are skewed in the correct direction, the distribution of the error term is reasonably well behaved, and the estimated factor shares are between zero and one. This latter restriction ensures that marginal products of capital, labor and intermediate inputs are positive. When no frontier functional forms produce meaningful results OLS results are reported. Finally, these functions are nested and a likelihood ratio procedure is used to choose a best estimate for each industrial branch.[10]

Results

Table 8.3 presents parameter estimates of aggregate frontier production functions for sectors of Soviet industry and for total Soviet industry. This table also gives estimates for the average rate of inefficiency for the entire period. Table 8.4 presents yearly rates of inefficiency based on the estimates given in Table 8.3. Reasonable frontier production function results were obtained for only four of the eight Soviet sectors--electric power, wood products, light industry and food processing. Food processing had decreasing factor productivity growth, and electric power, light industry and wood products have zero factor productivity growth throughout the period. Ordinary least squares estimates are presented for the other sectors and total industry. The chemical branch has zero factor productivity growth and the fuel sector has rapidly decreasing factor productivity growth which is negative by the 1980s. Total industry also has diminishing factor productivity growth which is negative by the end of the period. The surprising results are in the MBMW and construction materials sectors which have high and constant rates of productivity growth. With the exception of these two sectors these results are consistent with earlier studies showing that factor productivity in Soviet industry was stagnant and rapidly deteriorating.

In general, rates of inefficiency are low. The absence of reasonable frontier estimates for four sectors plus total industry is evidence of little variation in efficiency over time in those sectors. Wood products and food processing have very low measured rates of inefficiency. Only electric power and light industry have significant inefficiency, but even these are low to moderate compared to most U.S. sectors. Those two sectors appear to show a trend in which inefficiency is relatively high in the 1960s, low in the 1970s, and high and increasing in the 1980s.

The combination of low measured rates of inefficiency, and zero or declining, and sometimes negative, rates of factor productivity growth for most Soviet sectors is an interesting result. Negative estimates of the rate of factor productivity growth must be a result of declines in efficiency. Surely, Soviet technological change, though it may be very low and close to zero, cannot be negative. Zero factor productivity growth is an indication of either zero technological change, or a combination of slow technical change and a steady deterioration in efficiency over time. On the other hand, the low estimates of inefficiency are an indication of relatively minor year-by-year fluctuations in efficiency around this declining trend.

Table 8.3   Soviet Union, 1956-86

SECTOR	EQ #	γ	λ	μ	α_k	α_m	INEF
TOTAL	OLS1	-1.5159 .9044 1.68	.0417 .0156 2.67	-.0007 .0001 7.66	.5389 .1960 2.75		
POWER	FRON4	-1.4337 .0175 81.94			.7702 .0123 62.81		5.51
FUELS	OLS1	-1.6132 .6120 2.64	.0641 .0176 3.65	-.0015 .0002 9.20	.6283 .1605 3.92		
CHEM	OLS4	-.4460 .0323 13.79			.7883 .0121 65.11		
MBMW	OLS2	-4.7136 .0954 49.43	.0692 .0029 23.98		.0039 .0165 0.24		
CONST	OLS2	-3.9581 .0752 52.61	.0446 .0024 18.84		.1282 .0287 4.47		
WOOD	FRON4	-.9916 26.7730 0.04			.6049 .0133 45.39		0.18
LIGHT	FRON4	-.1081 .0650 1.66			.5346 .0147 36.31		4.64
FOOD	FRON1	-1.1910 .3727 3.20	.0268 .0067 4.03	-.0003 .0001 4.51	.3439 .0788 4.37		1.71

NOTE: γ is an efficiency term, $\lambda + 2\mu t$ is the rate of factor productivity growth, α_k is the share of capital, α_m is the share of intermediate inputs, $1 - \alpha_k - \alpha_m$ is the share of labor, and INEF is the average level of inefficiency for the entire time period expressed as a percentage. For each sector the first row is the estimated coefficient, the second row is the standard error, and the third row is a t-statistic. The functional form of the equations is given in the text. Data sources are *Narodnoe Khoziaistvo, SSSR*, 1956 and 1958-86; *Promyshlenost' SSSR*, 1958-86.

Table 8.4   Rates of Inefficiency Soviet Union, 1956-86

YEAR	POWER FRON4	WOOD FRON4	LIGHT FRON4	FOOD FRON1
1956	3.47	0.18	9.16	1.87
1957	2.78	0.19	6.71	1.09
1958	0.96	0.18	5.21	2.13
1959	7.16	0.17	3.87	1.04
1960	9.33	0.17	1.14	1.10
1961	9.43	0.18	0.67	0.88
1962	12.08	0.18	5.91	1.27
1963	9.10	0.18	7.06	1.46
1964	7.83	0.18	9.11	4.27
1965	5.70	0.18	13.39	1.06
1966	5.56	0.18	8.97	1.77
1967	6.13	0.18	5.93	1.54
1968	5.15	0.18	3.59	2.02
1969	4.06	0.18	2.87	2.46
1970	5.06	0.17	0.76	2.03
1971	4.14	0.17	0.24	1.54
1972	2.96	0.17	0.60	1.75
1973	2.87	0.17	1.69	1.35
1974	2.24	0.17	2.34	0.73
1975	2.16	0.17	0.82	0.52
1976	1.03	0.17	1.24	0.98
1977	1.64	0.17	1.38	0.87
1978	1.54	0.18	0.89	1.26
1979	2.15	0.18	2.53	1.67
1980	2.26	0.18	2.18	3.21
1981	4.14	0.18	2.81	4.07
1982	5.05	0.18	5.85	3.46
1983	6.74	0.18	7.68	1.62
1984	4.69	0.18	9.26	1.64
1985	5.87	0.18	8.84	1.68
1986	21.98	0.18	9.75	0.66

NOTE: These are rates of inefficiency for each year expressed as a percent, i.e., they express the percentage by which output was less than potential output due to inefficiency. The computation of this statistic is explained in the text.

The absence of large changes in efficiency from year to year is consistent with a planning system which did not make rapid changes in the economic environment facing firms. The Soviet economic system avoided large changes in supplies and demands because this complicated planning and administrative processes. Since large fluctuations did not occur from year to year there was no stimulus to large fluctuations in efficiency. These estimates do not provide support for the hypothesis that there was a large deterioration in efficiency in the 1970s and early 1980s which precipitated the crisis in Soviet society. Rather, there appears to be a long term failure to improve productivity, and probably, a gradual long-term deterioration of efficiency throughout the post-WWII period.

Tables 8.5 and 8.6 present parameter estimates of aggregate frontier production functions for sectors of U.S. industry. The estimates in Table 8.5 include intermediate inputs, and the estimates in Table 8.6 use capital and labor only. These tables also give estimates for the average rate of inefficiency for the entire period. Tables 8.7 and 8.8 present yearly rates of inefficiency based on the estimates given in Tables 8.5 and 8.6. Ordinary least squares estimates are presented for those sectors for which no reasonable frontier estimates were obtained.

Table 8.5   U.S., 1948-79 with Intermediate Inputs

SECTOR	EQ #	γ	λ	μ	α_k	α_m	INEF
METMIN	OLS4	1.1136 .1226 9.09			.1815 .0174 10.40	.5126 .0620 8.27	
COALMIN	FRONM4	1.3891 .3016 4.61			.0169 .4317 0.04	.8092 .5165 1.57	25.31
PETGAS							
NMETMIN	FRONM4	1.1734 .0580 20.22			.2837 .0346 8.20	.5190 .0575 9.03	4.26
FOOD							

SECTOR	EQ #	γ	λ	μ	α_L	α_m	INEF
TOB	FRONM3	1.6739 .2902 5.77		.0003 .0001 6.19	.3224 .1061 3.04	.1186 .0543 2.18	6.93
TEX	FRONM1	.7079 .3139 2.26	.0264 .0063 4.22	-.00002 .0001 0.45	.1055 .1183 0.89	.4784 .1551 3.09	3.07
APP	FRONM1	1.1783 .1329 8.87	.0107 .0052 2.08	-.0001 .0001 0.62	.2072 .1085 1.91	.4157 .1072 3.88	2.49
PAPER	FRONM4	.7710 .1548 4.98			.4636 .2142 2.16	.3861 .1660 2.33	3.30
PRINT	OLS2	1.8712 .2290 8.17	.0137 .0017 8.14		.0099 .0951 0.10	.1874 .0569 3.29	
CHEM	OLS1	.8148 .7765 1.05	.0302 .0099 3.07	-.0003 .0001 2.90	.2744 .2713 1.01	.3768 .1477 2.55	
PETPROD	OLS2	.5621 1.1361 0.50	.0241 .0083 2.89		.6239 .2468 2.53	.0809 .0870 0.93	
RUB	OLS3	1.3044 .2145 6.08		.0003 .0001 3.87	.1071 .0848 1.26	.4392 .1076 4.08	
LEATH	FRONM4	1.4194 .1560 9.10			.4690 .1323 3.55	.1933 .1566 1.23	4.93
WOOD	OLS1	1.0921 .1080 10.11	.0348 .0039 8.82	-.0004 .0001 4.81	.3212 .0745 4.31	.0849 .0580 1.47	
FURN	OLS4	1.0550 .0218 48.39			.0918 .0409 2.24	.6567 .0315 20.83	
GLASS	OLS3	1.2889 .1119 11.52		.0001 .00004 2.86	.0595 .0785 0.76	.5777 .0525 11.01	
PRIMET							
FABMET	OLS4	.7494 .0478 15.66			.0665 .0482 1.38	.8751 .0443 19.77	
MACH	OLS4	1.1253 .0298 37.72			.0166 .0359 0.46	.7671 .0336 22.86	

SECTOR	EQ #	γ	λ	μ	α_k	α_m	INEF
ELMACH	FRONM1	.7319	.0092	.0001	.0747	.7381	1.56
		.2052	.0028	.0001	.0574	.0995	
		3.57	3.29	1.76	1.30	7.42	
TRANS	FRONM2	1.3654	.0082		.0118	.5720	3.01
		.0637	.0012		.0248	.0360	
		21.45	6.63		0.48	15.91	
VEH							
PHOTO	FRONM4	1.0877			.4486	.3502	4.22
		.0482			.0390	.0540	
		22.57			11.49	6.48	
MISC	FRONM2	.9673	.0083		.1183	.5981	3.67
		.1084	.0067		.1486	.0782	
		8.93	1.24		0.80	7.65	
ELUT							
GASUT	OLS1	.8362	.0639	-.0013	.3735	.1668	
		1.0262	.0264	.0005	.2458	.0605	
		0.82	2.42	2.70	1.52	1.04	
WATER	OLS2	-.2528	.0294		.7030	.0916	
		.6480	.0020		.2049	.0276	
		0.39	14.80		3.43	3.31	

NOTE: Data are from Jorgenson, Gollop and Fraumeni (1987).

Table 8.6   **U.S., 1948-79 without Intermediate Inputs**

SECTOR	EQ #	γ	λ	μ	α_k	INEF
METMIN	FRON4	2.1594			.2782	8.36
		.2121			.0218	
		10.18			12.76	
COALMIN	OLS3	1.1115		-.0004	.8301	
		.2235		.0002	.1484	
		4.97		1.88	5.59	
FUEL	FRON3	-.4761		-.0002	.8916	11.67
		.3587		.0001	.0875	
		1.33		2.21	10.19	
NMETMIN	FRON4	1.8018			.4542	15.34
		.1196			.0621	
		15.07			7.32	
FOOD	FRON2	2.5128	.0302		.0412	0.54
		.3381	.0028		.1229	
		7.43	10.89		0.34	

SECTOR	EQ #	γ	λ	μ	α_k	INEF
TOB	FRON3	1.6141 .3921 4.12		.0004 .0001 4.12	.4235 .1360 3.12	6.66
TEX	FRON2	1.5185 .2379 6.38	.0398 .0048 8.34		.0472 .1666 0.28	5.29
APP	FRON1	1.6879 .0703 24.02	.0251 .0023 10.74	-.0002 .0001 2.30	.1803 .0958 1.88	1.27
PAPER	FRON3	2.0220 .4333 4.67		.0006 .0002 3.82	.2324 .1976 1.18	5.44
PRINT	OLS1	1.9286 .2183 8.84	.0252 .0022 11.30	-.0003 .0001 3.27	.0930 .1090 0.85	
CHEM	OLS1	2.0803 .6537 3.18	.0458 .0085 5.42	-.0002 .0001 2.03	.0752 .2842 0.27	
PETPROD	OLS2	1.3669 .7344 1.86	.0310 .0039 8.02		.4789 .1909 2.51	
RUB	FRON3	2.0306 .1874 10.84		.0004 .0001 4.66	.1330 .1170 1.14	4.83
LEATH	FRON4	1.5913 .1240 12.84			.5905 .1088 5.43	4.51
WOOD	OLS1	1.1382 .1054 10.80	.0369 .0038 9.79	-.0004 .0001 4.51	.3312 .0756 4.38	
FURN	FRON4	1.1628 .0759 15.32			.8789 .0551 15.94	11.31
GLASS	FRON4	.4022 .1219 3.30			.9706 .0542 17.92	9.92
PRIMET	FRON4	1.3001 .7204 1.81			.6457 .2385 2.71	13.89
FABMET	FRON4	.8439 .2277 3.71			.8811 .1096 8.04	7.72
MACH	FRON4	1.1182 .1371 8.16			.7619 .0606 12.58	8.52
ELMACH	FRON2	1.8769 .1870 10.04	.0287 .0042 6.89		.0770 .1403 0.55	6.22

SECTOR	EQ #	γ	λ	μ	α_k	INEF
TRANSEQ	FRON4	1.8201 .3843 4.74			.5386 .1755 3.07	25.29
VEH	FRON3	2.8685 .3462 8.29		.0008 .0002 4.86	.1524 .1759 0.87	13.35
PHOTO	OLS3	1.7551 .0756 23.21		.0007 .0001 10.73	.1107 .0583 1.90	
MISC	FRON4	1.2439 .0578 21.51			.8434 .0447 18.87	10.31
ELUT						
GASUT	OLS1	1.1471 .9831 1.17	.0840 .0180 4.68	-.0017 .0003 4.95	.3835 .2460 1.56	
WATER	FRON1	1.5203 .9420 1.61	.0423 .0039 10.92	-.0006 .0002 3.90	.1411 .3055 0.46	4.14

NOTE: Data are from Jorgenson, Gollop and Fraumeni (1987).

The first thing that strikes one when looking at Tables 8.5 and 8.6 are the large number of estimates which imply zero rates of factor productivity growth. This is consistent with the results in Jorgenson et al. (1987). However, the estimates presented here use their data series which have not been adjusted for quality change rather than the quality adjusted data which they used. My prior expectation was that these estimates would obtain much higher rates of measured factor productivity growth than those obtained by Jorgenson and his colleagues. This was sometimes but not often the case. On the other hand, negative rates of factor productivity growth are rare. They occur for only two estimates -- coal mining and fuels, without intermediate inputs. In several other sectors a declining rate of factor productivity growth is estimated, but in all of these the rate of factor productivity growth is still positive by the end of the period.

Table 8.7   Rates of Inefficiency U.S., 1948-79 with Intermediate Inputs

YEAR	COALMIN FRONM4	PETGAS FRONM2	NMETMIN FRONM4	TOB FRONM3	TEX FRONM1	APP FRONM1	PAPER FRONM4	LEATH FRONM4	ELMACH FRON1	TRANS FRON2	PHOTO FRON4	MISC FRON2
1948	29.72	20.29	7.19	8.09	0.71	5.19	2.45	4.78	1.01	1.05	6.42	3.19
1949	32.78	32.83	4.46	4.48	0.01	2.92	3.55	10.37	1.31	2.45	8.77	6.24
1950	28.82	21.69	3.49	5.07	5.30	3.86	1.81	13.56	1.87	1.29	3.19	3.54
1951	25.33	3.40	2.26	7.68	8.28	4.18	2.04	15.00	1.72	6.67	1.87	3.14
1952	25.82	6.25	3.07	5.34	3.51	2.78	3.58	9.98	0.53	2.90	2.74	1.73
1953	26.43	5.67	4.51	12.43	2.79	1.67	2.66	6.48	1.06	1.20	2.08	4.15
1954	20.54	4.01	5.17	19.36	2.86	2.58	3.06	7.06	1.29	0.72	3.07	3.88
1955	19.30	2.59	4.09	16.92	2.19	1.00	2.65	4.15	1.91	2.04	1.60	1.19
1956	14.36	1.57	3.82	13.61	2.45	1.15	3.43	3.73	2.27	6.32	3.57	2.14
1957	15.41	4.19	4.86	10.50	2.63	0.02	5.62	3.86	1.56	6.10	9.37	1.98
1958	10.19	23.07	6.20	6.64	0.02	0.001	7.14	4.18	1.22	5.21	10.35	2.98
1959	13.55	15.75	6.04	6.03	0.01	0.16	4.93	4.53	0.99	6.13	5.60	0.50
1960	11.64	12.12	3.73	0.03	1.93	0.57	5.47	4.07	1.60	6.19	6.68	2.08
1961	8.22	14.13	4.29	1.35	0.82	1.09	4.58	4.43	2.25	4.01	8.94	1.30
1962	10.35	18.17	3.66	2.34	1.31	1.03	3.90	3.48	1.94	2.99	3.04	1.96
1963	7.55	12.63	2.57	0.04	1.80	1.28	3.47	2.71	1.80	0.97	3.34	3.69
1964	8.84	11.89	2.17	3.02	1.71	1.77	2.83	1.66	1.23	0.45	4.49	3.22
1965	2.82	13.28	3.79	2.77	1.11	0.78	2.47	1.37	0.62	0.95	1.62	3.22
1966	1.33	13.05	3.21	4.85	0.41	1.69	2.39	1.76	1.16	1.09	0.92	2.85
1967	3.25	5.27	2.80	4.43	1.80	2.01	3.23	1.50	1.73	2.05	2.73	3.46
1968	4.58	4.27	3.89	4.72	3.55	1.49	2.64	1.17	1.56	1.07	2.59	1.73
1969	8.04	6.82	2.81	4.83	3.23	3.63	2.21	2.26	0.78	3.72	1.23	1.03
1970	6.66	3.24	3.01	3.81	0.73	7.41	3.11	4.27	1.43	2.98	7.20	2.15
1971	19.12	4.24	2.75	0.49	0.01	6.74	3.02	4.32	0.63	1.62	6.89	0.72
1972	26.18	6.30	2.66	0.04	1.81	4.32	1.98	5.98	0.49	2.15	3.49	0.51
1973	28.21	1.68	1.27	2.41	6.32	4.86	1.40	5.64	1.19	0.46	1.56	1.57
1974	50.63	6.11	3.49	4.97	12.06	6.22	1.80	5.21	4.72	1.71	2.69	6.66
1975	62.83	8.40	12.56	5.79	6.26	2.66	5.36	2.44	3.60	2.14	7.27	3.53
1976	67.88	6.18	7.85	6.63	6.86	2.63	3.55	2.37	3.08	4.02	3.70	2.61
1977	65.46	20.93	3.01	14.05	2.20	0.73	3.37	2.99	0.89	5.23	2.33	2.70
1978	63.17	17.61	4.43	15.41	3.15	0.05	2.71	3.91	0.92	6.10	2.22	6.86
1979	62.49	15.63	6.18	19.52	0.01	0.01	3.05	6.23	1.31	5.21	4.22	18.42

Table 8.8 **Rates of Inefficiency U.S., 1948-79 without Intermediate Inputs**

YEAR	METMIN FRON4	PETGAS FRON3	MNETMIN FRON4	FOOD FRON2	TOB FRON3	TEX FRON2	APP FRON1	PAPER FRON3	RUB FRON3	LEATH FRON4
1948	4.12	9.56	42.14	0.74	9.15	19.96	1.66	15.71	11.02	2.77
1949	10.51	31.21	41.90	0.45	2.24	6.99	0.74	13.64	11.17	8.36
1950	7.01	19.37	30.23	0.54	1.89	6.42	1.36	3.84	4.56	10.53
1951	5.64	1.50	26.44	0.64	6.72	8.69	2.15	4.21	4.92	12.28
1952	9.44	5.43	26.94	0.59	6.91	7.28	1.75	9.01	6.25	10.30
1953	9.11	6.90	27.42	0.58	12.33	5.14	1.37	3.13	5.82	6.05
1954	14.89	4.71	13.66	0.67	19.40	6.03	1.18	2.94	5.11	8.13
1955	9.33	4.30	12.64	0.53	17.40	2.69	0.96	1.38	4.68	4.70
1956	7.52	2.66	13.24	0.47	14.27	2.86	0.91	2.57	7.12	3.96
1957	7.86	5.67	15.48	0.47	11.23	2.87	0.75	4.83	8.61	4.55
1958	16.34	33.99	16.04	0.42	6.80	1.82	0.87	7.09	5.30	4.73
1959	13.56	21.21	10.97	0.43	5.56	0.95	1.03	3.73	3.06	3.64
1960	6.74	16.06	9.56	0.46	0.86	2.94	1.15	5.77	2.69	3.86
1961	7.43	17.16	7.19	0.48	1.26	1.32	1.12	5.28	2.20	4.06
1962	7.35	22.22	6.71	0.48	2.68	0.98	1.38	3.67	2.13	3.41
1963	5.69	15.28	4.36	0.46	3.26	0.87	1.13	2.66	1.88	3.33
1964	4.52	14.97	3.65	0.42	3.09	0.46	1.16	1.82	1.56	1.93
1965	4.76	17.91	3.40	0.58	3.13	1.51	1.28	1.24	1.66	1.55
1966	5.33	15.85	3.70	0.70	4.39	3.02	1.74	1.39	2.92	1.72
1967	8.57	6.52	7.46	0.51	4.06	3.65	1.29	3.85	3.01	1.61
1968	8.87	5.01	10.71	0.57	5.13	5.12	1.18	3.87	2.74	1.28
1969	6.96	10.66	6.48	0.65	6.19	7.11	1.27	3.31	3.15	2.15
1970	6.36	3.68	6.29	0.63	5.93	6.62	2.14	5.75	4.61	4.44
1971	8.68	4.06	8.48	0.53	1.84	4.14	1.41	6.00	3.22	4.87
1972	6.74	8.75	10.42	0.41	0.87	4.02	1.01	3.43	1.75	4.10
1973	4.01	1.81	8.12	0.56	3.16	10.12	1.09	1.60	2.20	4.01
1974	5.26	2.78	20.38	0.50	3.10	13.94	1.90	0.94	4.00	5.01
1975	14.64	7.22	23.70	0.62	3.26	8.50	1.12	8.77	7.07	3.20
1976	8.05	6.48	17.50	0.47	3.37	8.50	1.50	7.34	10.10	2.77
1977	13.24	18.69	17.85	0.53	10.71	3.49	0.75	11.06	7.36	2.95
1978	11.75	18.81	19.27	0.59	11.79	5.24	1.03	11.21	6.90	3.41
1979	7.57	15.65	20.63	0.61	16.58	1.88	1.17	12.16	7.32	3.75

YEAR	FURN FRON4	GLASS FRON4	PRIMET FRON4	FABMET FRON4	MACH FRON4	ELMACH FRON2	TRANS FRON4	VEH FRON3	MISC FRON4	WATER FRON1
1948	29.57	25.92	10.42	15.25	10.03	11.78	94.66	45.39	18.56	4.04
1949	27.72	21.84	14.69	16.87	14.44	4.59	80.78	25.40	14.80	2.37
1950	10.32	4.85	20.59	5.38	6.94	9.35	70.81	10.81	2.32	8.87
1951	20.52	2.22	6.87	5.28	3.02	2.37	45.73	25.24	14.31	3.77
1952	20.30	8.51	15.39	10.82	4.84	2.25	19.08	29.93	19.53	1.69
1953	12.94	6.84	9.62	6.16	5.90	2.29	8.58	18.30	8.29	1.35
1954	13.88	10.91	28.11	12.31	13.84	6.89	18.29	20.29	18.39	3.03
1955	3.47	2.13	12.50	7.39	8.05	4.63	25.05	3.63	9.63	2.61
1956	4.47	4.84	9.48	8.94	6.86	8.07	26.32	16.72	11.85	3.41
1957	11.48	16.82	18.02	10.18	12.92	14.79	22.75	11.70	20.06	5.51
1958	15.72	25.85	39.96	14.67	21.68	15.98	31.89	23.14	23.81	8.75
1959	8.07	12.78	29.39	8.28	12.51	14.40	26.92	11.75	7.14	2.44
1960	13.04	17.61	21.59	8.70	15.69	15.39	28.24	6.25	9.10	2.61
1961	14.79	19.79	25.76	10.33	16.31	11.54	23.31	11.31	8.75	5.16
1962	8.10	16.89	21.17	6.73	10.71	8.56	20.30	3.25	5.27	2.19
1963	6.04	10.83	13.89	5.90	9.89	6.99	16.76	2.45	6.55	3.01
1964	4.43	7.95	8.96	5.12	5.66	5.30	14.45	3.53	4.24	1.05
1965	1.32	3.77	6.40	4.01	4.72	2.24	10.71	1.58	1.01	2.43
1966	1.54	3.13	5.41	3.60	3.31	3.48	4.41	3.67	1.34	1.28
1967	5.82	9.83	10.60	3.47	5.19	5.52	6.90	10.94	3.57	6.92
1968	6.50	7.09	11.17	2.99	7.00	4.11	10.88	5.82	2.58	3.57
1969	4.15	5.56	8.61	3.60	5.60	4.30	13.39	7.76	2.13	7.36
1970	14.98	11.91	14.71	6.22	9.40	5.25	22.41	18.38	9.13	9.25
1971	14.74	10.53	18.18	6.90	12.93	4.39	19.27	3.71	11.45	11.51
1972	1.39	2.31	9.08	4.81	5.88	2.01	17.39	6.97	1.97	6.33
1973	2.17	1.38	4.48	3.47	3.19	1.97	7.10	6.09	5.36	5.44
1974	17.53	3.17	3.81	5.52	3.35	5.32	8.90	15.31	15.83	3.72
1975	3.18	16.36	11.57	14.95	11.62	9.83	10.65	18.95	28.06	1.02
1976	19.28	12.35	12.53	9.93	8.26	4.93	14.30	10.81	15.19	1.75
1977	9.44	9.03	9.40	7.68	5.22	2.27	11.84	11.37	12.16	3.24
1978	5.66	3.68	6.00	6.29	4.52	2.72	4.67	15.30	15.53	3.88
1979	5.12	5.00	5.65	6.12	4.77	2.45	2.55	23.21	15.83	2.77

Two observations about the average rates of measured inefficiency are striking. First, the estimated rates of inefficiency are much lower when intermediate inputs are included in the regression than when they are excluded. This result is easy to interpret. Implicitly, the production function estimates without intermediate inputs assume that intermediate inputs are being used in fixed proportion with output. If they are not,[11] changes in efficiency may reflect changes in the use of intermediate inputs not accompanied by corresponding changes in the use of capital and labor. Figure 8.3 illustrates an example that will clarify this point. Let us make the reasonable assumption that in the short run capital and labor inputs are more fixed than intermediate inputs. Suppose a shock occurs which increases the cost of intermediate inputs relative to capital and labor and increases the cost of production (for example, there is an increase in the price of oil). Figure 8.3a represents the production function estimate without intermediate inputs. Before the shock, the firm produces Q_1 efficiently at point A. After the shock, the firm decreases output to Q_0 by reducing the use of intermediate inputs but leaving capital and labor unchanged. The result is that the firm now appears to be producing inefficiently because less output is being produced with the same amount of capital and labor inputs. Figure 8.3b illustrates the same scenario when the estimation uses intermediate inputs. Now the shock results in a change from point A to point B, and the shock no longer results in inefficiency.

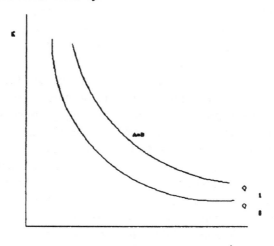

Figure 8.3A   Inefficiency Estimates Excluding Intermediate Inputs

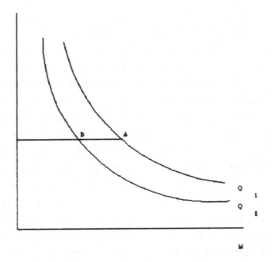

Figure 8.3B   Inefficiency Estimates Including Intermediate Inputs

Second, the U.S. rates of inefficiency are generally, but not universally, larger than the Soviet rates of inefficiency. Before discussing this result compare the trends in inefficiency in Table 8.4 with those in Tables 8.7 and 8.8. Compared to the Soviet results the U.S. trends over time are much less clear. Soviet rates of inefficiency tend to gradually and rather smoothly change from relatively low to relatively high and vice-versa. Such smooth transitions are not apparent in the U.S. results. On the contrary, the U.S. rates of inefficiency change much more dramatically from year to year and show less of a long term pattern.

This result has to do with the existence of and the response to demand and supply shocks in the two economic systems. In the U.S. market economy changes in output demand and input supply prices result in both short run and long run responses. As firms respond to these changes, levels of efficiency will change. Figure 8.4 illustrates another example to clarify the mechanism by which responses to changed economic conditions can change efficiency. Again assume a supply shock such as the increase in the price of oil. This increases the cost of production and induces firms to decrease production. However, in the short run some inputs will be more variable than others.[12] In Figure 8.4 the firm is producing Q_2 units of output at point A before the change in the price of oil. In the short run the firm reduces output to Q_0 using the input combination at point B. This implies that the firm is now producing inefficiently. This occurs because firms' responses take time and different inputs will have different time frames in which they can be changed. After a period of time the firm will be able to reallocate inputs more fully, moving to point C and producing Q_1 units of output efficiently. The idea is that a large change in the economic environment is likely to lead to a dramatic change in efficiency as firms attempt to adjust to the new environment. But in a market economy they will adjust rather quickly and once again produce relatively efficiently.

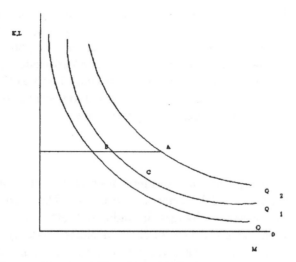

Figure 8.4   Demand Shock and Efficiency

In the Soviet-type economic system changes in the economic environment occurred less frequently and were less dramatic than in a market economy, and the responses of firms to those changes which did occur were much slower. This interpretation is consistent with the econometric results presented here. The low estimated rates of inefficiency mean that fluctuations in inefficiency were small over time, and the absence of large changes from year to year means that levels of efficiency did not change dramatically from one year to the next. This was a result of the relatively stable economic environment provided by the Soviet system of administrative orders. These orders did not change dramatically from year to year because such changes disrupted the planning process. In addition, firms were shielded from demand and supply shocks that occurred because of changes in consumer demand or from changes in the international market place. On the other hand, the long term trends in rates of inefficiency are consistent with the view that the economy did not respond rapidly to those changes in the economic environment that did occur. The trends seem to be consistent with the interpretation that relatively high rates of inefficiency occurred in periods of change, not of economic variables in the normal sense, but rather changes in the mode of operation of the system. Inefficiency is relatively low during periods in which little of interest was occurring in the Soviet economic system -- the early 1950s, the mid to late 1970s and the early 1980s. Inefficiency is relatively high during those periods in which changes in the system were attempted -- during the Khrushchev period, the Kosygin reforms, and Andropov's attempts to increase labor discipline. These changes do seem to have had some negative effect on efficiency, probably caused by disruption to established patterns of behavior, but the effect is not large. Moreover, these effects lingered for a substantial period of time since the economic system did not respond easily to change.

Conclusion

In this study frontier production functions have been estimated for industrial sectors in the United States and the former Soviet Union. The major purpose was to investigate whether changes in industrial efficiency had any substantial effect on industrial growth rates in either economy. Before concluding remarks are made, three caveats need to be reemphasized. First, the inefficiency which has been calculated in this study is the result of both technical and allocative inefficiency, as these terms are normally used in microeconomic theory, and do not settle the further question of economic efficiency. Second, efficiency is not calculated in an absolute sense, i.e., it is calculated with respect to observed best domestic practice, not relative to an engineering norm, or to a domestic or internationally competitive standard. Third, the levels of efficiency in the two economies directly compared, i.e., the absolute level of efficiency in the Soviet Union is not being compared with the level of efficiency in the U.S.[13] The methodology used here shows the effect on growth of changes in efficiency over time, but does not identify the absolute level of efficiency.

The results indicate that changes in efficiency have had very little long term effect on U.S. growth, but that short run growth is often affected by rather large changes in efficiency from year to year. In the Soviet Union, on the other hand, short run changes in efficiency were much smaller and there is little evidence of a dramatic decrease in efficiency in the late 1970s and early 1980s that would have precipitated the Soviet economic crisis. There is evidence of a serious long-term decline in factor productivity growth, probably caused by a low rate of technological change combined with a gradual deterioration in efficiency throughout the entire post-war period. Both of these results seem consistent with standard interpretations about the operation of a market and a Soviet-type economic system.

Notes

1. See Denison (1985), Kendrick (1985), and others.

2. See Brada (1985), Weitzman (1983), Whitesell (1983), and Kemme and Whitesell (1988).

3. See Fare, Grosskopf and Lovell (1985) for a thorough discussion of the distinctions between various kinds of efficiency in microeconomic theory.

4. *Narodnoe Khoziaistvo, SSSR,* 1956 and 1958-86; and *Promishleost' SSSR,* 1958-86.

5. *Narodnoe Khoziaistvo, SSSR,* 1956 and 1958-86.

6. See Jorgenson, Gollop and Fraumeni (1987) for a detailed description of the data.

7. See Olson, Schmidt and Waldman (1980).

8. See Aigner, Lovell and Schmidt (1977), *inter alia,* for an explanation. If the third moment is negative the frontier is being fitted to the wrong side of the data. In software packages like LIMDEP™ the resulting frontier is not reported. It is then assumed that the entire set of observations make up the frontier isoquant - there is no inefficiency - and the OLS estimates are accurate estimates of the stochastic frontier.

9. Again see Olson, Schmidt and Waldman (1980) on the Type I and Type II errors.

10.   See Whitesell (1983) and Mizon (1977) for a more detailed description of the selection procedure. Since the difference between the results with and without intermediate inputs is important in the discussion of results, the best equation for each specification is given in the tables above.

11.   Jorgenson et al. (1987) explicitly tests this assumption and finds that it does not hold. This means that the estimates without intermediate inputs are not completely legitimate. They have been used here in order to make comparisons with the Soviet estimates, for which data on intermediate inputs are not available. It seems likely that the necessary conditions for this assumption do not hold in the Soviet case either, although one might expect the deviation to be smaller.

12.   Again, it seems reasonable to expect that capital and labor will be less variable than intermediate inputs in the short run.

13.   See Bergson (1987 and 1990) and Rosefielde (1990) for thorough discussions of the difficulties of making such comparisons.

Bibliography

Aigner, D.J., C.A.K. Lovell and Peter Schmidt, "Formulation and Estimation of Stochastic Frontier Production Function Models", *Journal of Economtrics*, Vol. 6, 1977, 21-37.

Amann, Ronald and Julian Cooper, eds., *The Technological Level of Soviet Industry*, Yale University Press, 1977.

_____, *Technical Progress and Soviet Economic Development*, Basil Blackwell, 1986.

_____, eds., *Industrial Innovation in the Soviet Union*, Yale University Press, 1982.

Barreto, Humberto and Robert Whitesell, "Estimation of Output Loss from Allocative Inefficiency: Comparison of the Soviet Union and the U.S"., *Economics of Planning*, 25, 1992, 219-36.

Bergson, Abram, "Comparative Productivity: The USSR, Eastern Europe, and the West", *American Economic Review*, June 1987, 77, 342-57.

_____, "Comparative Productivity: Reply", *American Economic Review*, September 1990, 80, 955-56.

_____, "The Communist Efficiency Gap: Alternative Measures", *Comparative Economic Studies*, 36(1), Spring 1994, 1-12.

Bergson, Abram, and Herbert S. Levine, eds., *The Soviet Economy: Toward the Year 2000*, London: George Allen & Unwin, 1983.

Birman, Igor, *Secret Incomes of the Soviet State Budget*, Boston: Martinus Nijhoff, 1981.

Block, Herbert, "Soviet Economic Performance in a Global Context", in Joint Economic Committee, *Soviet Economy in a Time of Change*, Washington: U.S. Government Printing Office, 1979, 121-46.

Brada, Josef C., "The Slowdown in Soviet and East European Economic Growth", *Osteuropa-Wirtschaft*, 30(2), 1985, 116-28.

_____, "Technical Progress and Factor Utilization in Eastern European Economic Growth", *Economica*, 56, November 1989, 433-48.

CIA, *Handbook of Economic Statistics 1984*, CPAS 84-10002, September 1984.

Danilin, V.I., Ivan S. Materov, Steven S. Rosefielde and C.A.K. Lovell, "Measuring Enterprise Efficiency in the Soviet Union: A Stochastic Frontier Analysis", *Economica*, 52, May 1985, 225-33.

Denison, Edward F., *Trends in American Economic Growth, 1929-1982*, The Brookings Institution, 1985.

Fare, Rolf, Shawna Grosskopf and C.A.K. Lovell, *The Measurement of Efficiency of Production* (Boston: Kluwer-Nijhoff Publishing), 1985.

Forsund, F.R., C.A.K. Lovell, and P. Schmidt, "A Survey of Frontier Production Functions and of their Relationship to Efficiency Measurements", *Journal of Econometrics*, 13:1, May 1980, pp. 4-27.

Goldman, Marshall I., *USSR in Crisis: The Failure of an Economic System*, New York: W.W. Norton, 1983.

Hewett, Ed A., *Reforming the Soviet Economy: Equality versus Efficiency*, Washington: The Brookings Institution, 1988.

Joint Economic Committee, *Allocation of Resources in the Soviet Union and China -- 1985*, Washington: U.S. Government Printing Office, 1986.

Jondrow, James, C.A.K. Lovell, Ivan Materov, and Peter Schmidt, "On the Estimation of Technical Inefficiency in the Stochastic Frontier Production Function Model", *Journal of Econometrics*, 19, August 1982, 233-238.

Jorgenson, Dale W., Frank M. Gollop, and Barbara M. Fraumeni, *Productivity and U.S. Economic Growth*, Harvard University Press, 1987.

Kemme, David M., and John Neufeld, "The Estimation of Technical Efficiency in Polish Industry: 1961-85", Paper presented at the 20th National Convention of the AAASS, Honolulu, November, 1988.

Kemme, David M., and Robert S. Whitesell, "Changes in Technical Efficiency and the Economic Slowdown in Eastern Europe and the Soviet Union", Report for the National Council for Soviet and East European Research, December 1988.

Kendrick, John W., *Interindustry Differences in Productivity Growth*, American Enterprise Institute, 1983.

Mizon, Grayham E., "Inferential Procedures in Nonlinear Models: An Application in a UK Industrial Cross Section Study of Factor

Substitution and Returns to Scale", *Econometrica*, 45(5), July 1977, 1221-42.

Narodnoe Khoziaistvo SSSR, Moscow: Central Statistical Administration, 1956, 1958-85.

Nishimizu, M. and J.M. Page, "Total Factor Productivity Growth, Technological Progress and Technical Efficiency Change: Dimensions of Productivity Change in Yugoslavia, 1965-1978", *Economic Journal*, 92(368), December 1982, 920-36.

Olson, J., P. Schmidt, and D. Waldman, "A Montecarlo Study of Estimators of Stochastic Frontier Production Functions", *Journal of Econometrics*, 13, 1980. pp. 67-82.

Promyshlennost' SSSR (Moscow: Central Statistical Administration, 1956 and 1958).

Rapawy, Stephen, *Estimates and Projections of the Labor Force and Civilian Employment in the USSR--1950-99*, Foreign Economic Report no. 10, Washington: U.S. Department of Commerce, Bureau of Economic Analysis, 1976.

Rosefielde, Steven, "Comparative Productivity: Comment", *American Economic Review*, September 1990, 80, 946-54.

Rosefielde, Steven and R.W. Pfouts, "Economic Optimization and Technical Efficiency in Soviet Enterprises Jointly Regulated by Plans and Incentives", *European Economic Review*, 32(6), 1988, 1285-99.

Sato, Ryuzo, "The Impact of Technical Change on the Holotheticity of Production Functions", *Review of Economic Studies*, 47(4), July 1980, 767-76.

Solow, Robert M., "Technical Change and the Aggregate Production Function", *Review of Economics and Statistics*, August 1957, 312-20.

Weitzman, Martin L., "Soviet Postwar Economic Growth and Capital-Labor Substitution", *American Economic Review*, 60(4), September 1970, 676-92.

_____, "Industrial Production", in Bergson and Levine (1983), 178-190.

Whitesell, Robert S., "The Contribution of Production Function Analysis to the Interpretation of Industrial Growth in the Soviet Union and Eastern Europe", unpublished Ph.D. dissertation, University of North Carolina, Chapel Hill, 1983.

_____, "The Influence of Central Planning on the Economic Slowdown in the Soviet Union and Eastern Europe: A Comparative Production Function Analysis", *Economica*, 52, May 1985, 235-44.

9 Command Constrained Efficiency in Soviet Cotton-Refining and the Kaunasskoi Candy Factory

Mikhail Iu. Afanas"ev
Translated by Steven S. Rosefielde

Introduction

Sectoral and aggregate studies as shown in chapters 7 and 8, subject to the qualifications elaborated in chapters 1 and 2 provide valuable insight into comparative productive potential and efficiency, but shed little light on the microeconomic aspects of the phenomena. This chapter delves into these matters by applying stochastic production frontier techniques to measure the efficiency of cotton refining semifabricates and more ambitiously to discern efficiency differentials in Soviet multiproduct candy firms. Cotton refining is a relatively simple manufacturing process, with a well established technology. There is a single enterprise wholesale ruble price and inputs are compensated identically across firms. Variations in performance therefore should not be great and efficiency differences should be primarily attributable to managerial competence. Multiproduct firms constitute a greater challenge. Managers not only oversee general operations, but are supposed to allocate factors to the best uses indicated by their bonus functions, subject to diverse planning constraints. Inefficiency variations under these circumstances are apt to be greater due both to increased complexity and the proliferation of planning constraints.

Methodology

The command constrained efficiency of cotton refining firms and multiproduct enterprises in the confection industry can be computed using a production function with parameters θ, which portrays $F(X,\theta)$ as an upper, technologically determined output frontier, given assigned resources X. It encompasses a set of n enterprises, producing homogeneous goods, each of which is characterized by a vector of resource costs X_i, i=1,...,n and an output value Y_i. If the general form of the production function is specified, it can be estimated by discovering parameter values θ^* that yield

$$\overset{\infty}{\theta} \overset{n}{\underset{j=1}{\Sigma}} \left[F\left(X_i, \theta\right) - Y_i \right]$$

given the constraints

$$F\left(X_i, \theta\right) \geq Y_i, \quad i = 1,...,n. \tag{9.1}$$

Inefficiency is

$$\epsilon = F\left(X_i, \theta^*\right) - Y_i,$$

the deviation of output from the frontier technology $F(X, \theta^*)$. The constraints (9.1) indicate that only deviations "below" the frontier are possible.

This deterministic approach is rarely used in practice because the parameters θ^* are affected by random errors $\{X_i, Y_i\}$ and technology.

The stochastic approach to estimating a production functions provides a good alternative. It describes the average aggregate technological potential of the enterprise. Least squares techniques are usually employed to estimate this potential. The vector of parameters θ^* is chosen to obtain

$$\theta^* \overset{n}{\underset{j=1}{\Sigma}} \left[F\left(X_i, \theta\right) - Y_i \right]^2.$$

The random variable ϵ

$$\epsilon = F\left(X_i, \theta^*\right) - Y_i,$$

measures productive efficiency. It is assumed to be normally distributed with a mathematically expected value of zero.

Production potential where exogenous disturbances affect individual enterprises differently, can be defined with respect to the stochastic production frontier $F(X_i, \theta) \, e^{v_i}$. The subscript i refers to a specific enterprise; $F(X_i, \theta)$ is the production potential, v_i is the share of the estimated production potential attributable to random events and measurement errors. The stochastic frontier production function by assumption reflects the maximum output achievable from the existing technology.

Production may lie on the stochastic frontier, or lie inefficiently below it. The gap between the achieved level of production and the maximum is assessed with the aid of a one-sided probability distribution. To identify efficiency a random variable u_i is introduced measuring deviations "below" the stochastic frontier. The output of enterprise i can be expressed as:

$$Y_i = F(X_i, \theta) e^{\epsilon_i}, \tag{9.2}$$

where $\epsilon_i = v_i - u_i$, $u_i \geq 0$.

This formulation separates out ordinary random effects from efficiency. The coefficient μ_i expresses efficiency as a ratio of the observed and potential level of output on the stochastic production frontier

$$\mu_i = \frac{Y}{F(X_i, \theta) \, e^{v_i}}.$$

From equation (9.2), we have $\mu_i = e^{-u_t}$.

For every i, $i = 1,...,n$, from the condition $0 \geq u_i < \infty$, it follows that $0 < \mu_i \geq 1$.

Estimates of enterprise efficiency depend on assumptions about the distribution of the random variables v_i and u_i. The most natural assumption is that variables are normally distributed.

v_i is normally distributed with parameters $(0, \sigma_v^2)$; u_i is truncated at 0, and normally distributed with parameters (μ, σ_u^2). v_i, u_i are independent, $i = 1,...,n$.

If for every firm, Y_i depends on the quantity of inputs X_i, and the production function can be written:

$$F(Y_i, X_i, \theta) \equiv 0 \qquad i = 1,...,n. \tag{9.3}$$

Estimating the stochastic production frontier and efficiency requires the identification of a vector of production parameters θ, σ_u^2, σ_v^2, and μ. The vector of parameter estimates $\beta^* = [\theta^*, \sigma_u^2, \sigma_v^2, \mu]$ is estimated by maximizing the logarithmic likelihood function

$$\ln L = -n\left[a + \frac{\ln(2\pi)}{2} + \frac{\ln\sigma^2}{2}\right]$$

$$-\frac{1}{2\sigma^2}\sum_{i=1}^{n}(\epsilon + \mu)^2 + \sum_{i=1}^{n}b_i$$

given the restrictions in (9.3), where

$$\sigma^2 = \sigma_v^2 + \sigma_u^2$$

$$a = \ln\left[1 - G\left(1 - \mu/\sigma_u\right)\right]$$

$$b_i = \ln\left[1 - G\left(\frac{\epsilon_i\sigma_u^2 - \mu\sigma_v^2}{\sigma_u\sigma_v\sigma}\right)\right]$$

and G is a distribution function of standardized normally distributed random variables.

The maximum values a vector of parameters β^* are attained when

$$\partial \ln L/\partial\beta_{\beta=\beta^*} = 0.$$

The method of maximum likelihood is the best because it allows the statistical significance of each estimate β to be determined asymptotically by the covariance matrix

$$B = \left[\frac{-\partial^2\ln L}{\partial\beta\partial\beta'}\right]^{-1}$$

The value S_i, determined by the formula $S_i \sqrt{B_{ii}}$, is the standard error of the estimated parameter, and $t_i = \beta_i/S_i$, are the t statistics.

Production potential is estimated with the function

$$c_1 \left[Ye^{-\epsilon} \right]^{\gamma_1} K^{-\rho} + c_2 \left[Ye^{-\epsilon} \right]^{\gamma_2} L^{-\rho} \equiv 1, \tag{9.4}$$

the most general form of the class of two-factor production functions, that exhibit constant elasticity of substitution. Here K is the average annual fixed capital stock; L is the number of industrial workers, $\theta = (c_1, c_2, \gamma_1, \gamma_2, \rho)$ is a vector of parameters. The CES and Cobb-Douglas production functions are special cases of this general function.

Estimates were computed with a nonlinear program developed for the EVM series ES [Afanas"ev and Skokov, 1984], with n+8 variables and nonlinear constraints. The task was reduced to unconditionally maximizing the objective function with respect to the parameter vector β by using a separable functional form for the constraints in equation (9.3) regarding $\epsilon_i = v_i - u_i$. In each iteration of the calculation of the function and its gradient, ϵ_i was computed from equation (9.4) using the Newtonian method for homogeneous nonlinear equations. The task of maximizing the function ln L for the parameters β was solved with the program package PAOEM [Skokov, et al., 1980]. The program provides an effective method for estimating the reduced gradient, using a combination of the quasi-Newtonian method and the conditional gradient.

The stochastic deviations ϵ_i are derived from the β parameters, and v_i and u_i are estimated in the second stage of the identification procedure.

If the density of the distribution $P_u(\bullet)$ and $P_\epsilon(\bullet)$ are known, the average values of u_i can be estimated as the expected values $E(u_i/v_i - u_i)$. The estimates v_i, u_i can be determined by the maximum probability of their joint distributions. In Materov [1981], it is shown that the most expected values v_i and u_i are attained when

$$\min_{v_i, u_i} \left[\left(\frac{\hat{v}_i}{\sigma_v} \right)^2 + \left(\frac{\hat{u}_i - \mu}{\sigma_u} \right)^2 \right]$$

is satisfied; given the restrictions

$$\hat{v}_i - \hat{u}_i = \hat{e}, \ \hat{u}_i \geq 0$$

and have the form

$$[\hat{v}_i, \hat{u}_i] = \begin{cases} \hat{e}_i \geq 0 \\ \dfrac{\hat{e}_i + \mu}{\sigma_v^2 + \sigma_u^2}, \ \sigma_v^2, \ \mu - \dfrac{\hat{e}_i + \mu}{\sigma_v^2 + \sigma_u^2} \end{cases}, \ \text{if } \hat{e}_i > \mu \sigma_v^2 / \sigma_u^2. \qquad (9.5)$$

Command Constrained Efficiency in Cotton-Refining Semifabricates

The application of these methods requires information on outputs and factor costs. Output can be measured in natural terms in single product firms, otherwise they must be valued at prevailing enterprise wholesale ruble prices.

Capital normally is valued at industrial ruble wholesale prices, but labor is expressed in norm-hours.

These data form three vectors:

$$Y = \{Y_i\}_{i=1}^n, \qquad K = \{K_i\}_{i=1}^n, \qquad L = \{L_i\}_{i=1}^n.$$

n is the number of enterprises in each sector; Y_i is the volume of output of each enterprise i (in natural or value terms); K_i is the value of fixed capital; L_i is labor costs in man years.

The performance of each enterprise is evaluated annually, and the data is processed sequentially $\{Y_i\}_{i=1}^n$, $\{K_i\}_{i=1}^n$, $\{L_i\}_{i=1}^n$.

For convenience Y_i, K_i, L_i are normalized, allowing the sum of the parameter estimates C, and C_2 to approximate 1 without altering the meaning of the other parameters. The calculations are performed with

$$Y'_i = \frac{Y_i}{Y_n}, \qquad K'_i = \frac{K_i}{K_n}, \qquad L'_i = \frac{L_i}{L_n},$$

and

$$Y'_n = K'_n = L'_n = 1.$$

The results of these computations have the form illustrated in Table 9.1.

Table 9.1   **Normalization of Y_i, K_i, L_i**

Enterprise	Output	Fixed Capital	Labor	Deviation e	Deviation e^ϵ	Efficiency e^{-u}
1	Y_1'	K_1'	L_1'	ϵ_1	e^{ϵ_1}	e^{-u_1}
•	•	•	•	•	•	•
•	•	•	•	•	•	•
•	•	•	•	•	•	•
n	Y_n'	K_n'	L_n'	ϵ_n	e^{ϵ_n}	e^{-u_n}

The information which is contained in the ith row describes enterprise i, i=1,...,n. The Y_i', K_i', L_i' are normalized output fixed capital and labor respectively. The deviation ϵ_i is estimated from equation (9.4) given the parameters θ^* corresponds e^{ϵ_i} is the ratio of observed output to the estimated potential Y_i, determined by costs and the production function

$$c_1^* \, \hat{Y}_i^{\gamma_1^*} + c_2^* \, \hat{Y}_i^{\gamma_2^*} \, L_i^{-\rho^*} \equiv 1. \tag{9.6}$$

(9.6) follows from (9.4) given $\epsilon = 0$. The magnitudes v_i and u_i, which satisfy the condition $\epsilon_i = v_i - u_i$, are determined from (9.5).

The function $\hat{Y}e^v$, computed from $\hat{Y}e^{v_i}$ reflects enterprise production potential. $\bar{v}$ derived from v_i, i=1,...,n measures the random disturbances in the production process and measurement errors. The deviation in the composite $\hat{Y}$ is measured by e^{v_i}. The random value $\bar{u}$, computed from u_i represents the output deviation from the potential $\bar{Y}e^v$, and e^{-u} measures efficiency.

The production and disturbance parameters gradient and estimated by maximizing the likelihood functions are:

$$\beta_1 = c_1, \ \beta_2 = c_2, \ \beta_3 = \gamma_1, \ \beta_4 = \gamma_2,$$

$$\beta_5 = e, \ \beta_6 = \sigma_u^2, \ \beta_7 = \sigma_v^2, \ \beta_8 = \mu.$$

The symmetric matrix of the second derivatives of the log likelihood function is derived from

$$A(\beta) = \frac{\alpha^2 \ln L}{\alpha_\beta \ \alpha_{\beta'}}$$

and the covariance matrix of parameter estimates is

$$B(\beta) = \left[-A(\beta) \right]^{-1}$$

$S = \sqrt{B_{ii}}$ provide the standard errors of the parameter estimates, where B_{ii} are the diagonal elements of the matrix B; $t_i = \beta_i / S_i$ and t_i are t statistics.

The following information should also be taken into account:

-the significance of the logarithm of the likelihood function.

-the average coefficient of technical efficiency, $e - \int_0^\infty u \, dp(u)$.

-the elasticity of input substitution, $\dfrac{1}{1 + e}$.

-the elasticity of heterotheticity, $\dfrac{\gamma_1 - \gamma_2}{1 + e}$.

-the elasticity of output with respect to increased capital capacity, γ_i / e.

-the elasticity of output with respect to labor, γ_2 / e.

Enterprises can be divided into two groups: those with negative deviations ϵ and those in which $\epsilon \geq 0$. The number of enterprises with negative deviations should exceed those where $\epsilon \geq 0$ because potential associated with the stochastic frontier exceeds the estimate.

If $\epsilon_i \geq 0$, the enterprise is efficient, and in accordance with (9.5) $u_i = 0$. The value of the coefficient e^{-u} is 1. Output can exceed the frontier $\hat{Y}$, defined by (9.6) because of positive random deviations. If $\epsilon < 0$, either:

　　a) $u_i = 0$
　　b) $u_i > 0$

In the first case production is efficient. The fact that the output is less than the $\hat{Y}$, is interpreted is attributable to the negative random disturbance ($v_i < 0$) in the production process.

Where $\epsilon < 0$ and $u > 0$, output is inefficient. The negative effect of the random variable, and the systematic factor reinforce each other, with the output shortfall determined by e^{-u} (or u percent). Table 9.2 presents gradient and β^* parameter estimates for 151 enterprises in the Soviet cotton-refining industry, illustrating these various possibilities.

Table 9.2   **Gradient and β^* Parameter Estimates for 151 Soviet Cotton-Refining**

The optimum value of the function ln L is -36.38.	
Gradient	**Functional Parameter**
1. -3.81469727E+00	7.51296100E-03
2. 1.66893005E+00	4.36051960E-01
3. 1.43051147E+00	4.32705438E-01
4. 0.00000000E+00	2.26090440E+00
5. -9.53674317E-00	2.23765706E+00
6. -1.43051147E+00	3.65123005E-00
7. -2.14576721E+00	4.57538820E-02
8. -2.38418579E-01	9.55278743E-01

The θ parameters provide estimates of the elasticity of substitution, heterotheticity, and other important production characteristics. 125 enterprises have negative ϵ_i values and 26 positive values. In the letter case $v_i = e_i$ and $u_i = 0$.

Negative values of ϵ_i can be expressed as v_i-u_i. 98 of the 125 enterprises for which $\epsilon_i < 0$, had positive values of u_i. 27 enterprises were completely efficient.

The expected value of the random variable u_i was $E(u_i/\epsilon_i) = .2089$. The average value of the indicator u where $\epsilon_i < 0$ was $E(u_i/\epsilon_i = .2089$. The average value of the indicator u where $\epsilon_i < 0$ was $\Sigma u_i/125 \geq 0.2080$.

The closeness of these values demonstrates that the method used to decompose ϵ_i into u_i and v_i is effective. The aggregate efficiency coefficient was $\mu = e^{-0.2089} = 0.81$, indicating that managers were able to produce near their command constrained best practice frontiers.

For comparative purposes an experiment was performed using the very same data to estimate the θ^* parameters from function (9.3) using least squares. The following parameter estimates were obtained.

$c_1 = 0.001$
$c_2 = 0.617$
$\gamma_1 = 1.452$
$\gamma_2 = 4.240$
$p = 4.368$

The normally distributed random values of the deviations ϵ_i for v_i and u_i are $(0; 0.104)$.

As expected nearly half -70 enterprises-displayed negative deviations $\epsilon_i < 0$, and 81 were positive.

The stability of the parameters should also be noted. The exclusion of three enterprises changed the estimated values within the narrow range 10^{-3}.

Efficiency can also be assessed dynamically both with respect to the initial frontier and the performance of individual firms. A comparison of the results for 108 cotton refining enterprises in Uzbekistan between 1977 and 1982-1983 revealed that production potential increased by 3 percent (9.7) [Afanas"ev, 1988]. However, the efficiency of individual enterprises did not change proportionally because the number of efficient enterprises fell by 8. Their efficiency growth apparently lagged the leading firm's.

Sectoral rates of scientific and technical progress are endogenized into the computation of the stochastic frontier by modifying equation (9.2):

$$y = F(X, \theta)\, e^{\epsilon + \lambda(t - t_i)}$$

where λ is the sectoral rate of scientific and technological progress; t is the year being investigated; and t_i is the year the enterprise was founded. Data on the vintage of the capital stock $\{t\}_{i \leq 1}^{n}$ is added to identify the effect capital improvements have on technological progress. The maximum value of the likelihood function is then estimated with 9 parameters, one of which is λ.

The estimated rate of scientific and technological progress for 151 cotton-refining enterprises was:

$\lambda = 0.0088$
$\quad (0.0018)$

The Efficiency of Candy Manufacturing in Soviet Multiproduct Firms

The techniques elaborated above for estimating the static efficiency of cotton-refining can be extended from semifabricates to the production of each and every individual finished good in multiproduct firms.

Estimates of these sorts were computed for 141 different kinds of confectionery products manufactured at the Kaunasskoi confectionery factory (using data for 1982).

The following data were employed.

-Output valued in enterprise wholesale ruble prices.

-Normed employment statistics obtained from the labor input schedules (kart trudoemkosti).

-Normed capital use statistics.

The calculations generated the following results:

The optimal value of the likelihood function ln L = -91.30; the parameter estimates are

$$\beta^* \begin{bmatrix} 0.6808; & 0.3172; & 0.0227; & 0.0029 & 0.161; & 0.5061; & 0.0781; & -0.2812 \\ (0.012) & (0.013) & (0.015) & (0.010) & (0.0085) & (0.0654) & (0.0011) & (0.35) \end{bmatrix}$$

The elasticities of substitution, heterotheticity and other important characteristics of production can be derived from the θ production function parameters, but attention here is focused on the efficiency estimates.

For the multiproduct firm as a whole, 121 of the 141 product lines displayed negative values of ϵ_i, and 20 had positive values imputed to measurement errors and random disturbances.

113 of the 121 product lines were $\epsilon_i < 0$, had positive values of u_i. Eight were almost fully efficient.

Aggregate confectionery production at the Kaunasskoi candy factory can be grouped into six categories: boxed candy (konfety), wrapped candy, chocolates, candy drops (drazhe), toffee (iris), marmalade-pastila (fruit fudge).

The dispersion of efficiency across the product lines in the first group is shown in Table 9.3. As might be expected efficiency is positively correlated with capital returns and labor productivity.

Table 9.3   Dispersion of Efficiency Across Product Lines in the Kaunasskoi Multiproduct Candy Factory

Group $u_i > 0$	Efficiency $\mu = e^{-M}$	Product Lines
1. $0.0 < u_i \le 0.1$	.95	10
2. $0.1 < u_i \le 0.3$	.82	24
3. $0.3 < u_i \le 0.5$	.67	33
4. $0.5 < u_i \le 0.7$	.55	24
5. $0.7 < u_i \le 0.9$	.45	9
6. $0.9 < u_i < 1$	.39	2
7. $1.0 < u_i$	.28	11

Average technical efficiency coefficients were also calculated for the other groups and are illustrated in Figure 9.1. Candy drops (drazhe), marmalade-pastila products, candy and boxed candy are relatively inefficient; chocolate is the most efficient. This dispersion reveals that aggregate efficiency could be substantially enhanced by shifting resources from inefficient to efficient product lines, and suggests that planning constraints prevent bonus maximizing managers from doing so.

These command constrained efficiency losses however may not be entirely detrimental because demand for boxed candy is strong. In this instance the best course of action might be to improve productivity and efficiency by semi-automating boxing as has been done for the most efficient candy sampler "Assorti" in this subgroup.

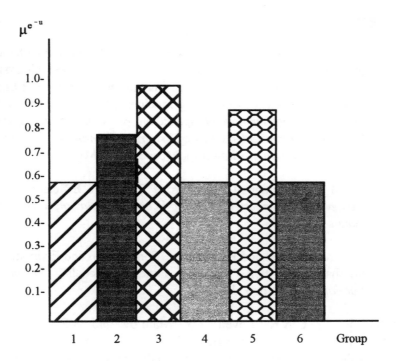

Figure 9.1   Average Group Efficiency in Candy Manufacturing

Conclusion

Stochastic production frontier estimates of command constrained efficiency in the Soviet cotton-refining semifabricate industry using data for 1977 showed as expected that most firms operated near the best practice frontier. Apparently where the manufacturing task is comparatively simple, managers are able to achieve a high level of performance.

The efficiency of individual product lines in multiproduct candy firms by contrast was far more diverse, with some activities operating at a small fraction of potential. This suggests that command planning constraints prevented bonus maximizing managers from allocating factors to best use, or phenomenon concealed in sectoral and aggregate efficiency studies that rely on best practice to identify efficiency frontiers.

Bibliography

Afanas"ev, M., V. Skokov, "Programma otsenki effektivnosti funktsionir-ovaniia predpriiatii na osnove rascheta stokhasticheskikh granits proizvodstva", (A Program for Estimating the Efficiency of Enter-prises on the Basis of Computing Stochastic Production Frontiers), in *Sistemy programmnovo obespecheniia resheniia zadach optimal 'novo planirovaniia* (*Systems of Program Techniques for Solving the Task of Optimal Planning*), Moscow, TsEMI, 1984.

Afanas"ev, M., "Experimental Estimates of Enterprise Efficiency in the Cotton Refining Industry", *Atlantic Economic Journal*, unpublished manuscript, 1988.

Aigner, D., C.A.K. Lovell and P. Schmidt, "Formulation and Estimation of Stochastic Frontier Production Function Models", *Journal of Econometrics*, No. 5, 1977.

Danilin, V. I., C.A.K. Lovell, I.S. Materov and S.S. Rosefielde, "Normativnye i stokhasticheskie metody izmereniia i kontrolia effektivnosti raboty firmy i predpriiatiia", (Normative and Stochastic Methods for Measuring and Controlling the Efficiency of Labor in Firms and Enterprises), *Ekonomika i matematicheskie metody*, T. XUSH, No. 1, 1982.

Materov, P., "K probleme polnoi identifikatsii modeli stokhasticheskikh granits proizvodstva" ("Concerning the Problem of the Full Identification of the Model of Stochastic Production Frontiers", *Ekonomika i matematicheskie metody*, T.XUII, No. 4, 1981.

Skokov, V., Iu. Nesterov, and I. Purmal', *Paket analiza optimizatsionnykh ekonomicheskikh modeli PPP. "PAO M ES EVM"*. (*A Package for the Analysis of Optimal PPP Economic Models "PAO M ES EVM"*. *Nonlinear Programming*, Moscow, TsEMI, 1980.

Suvorov, Boris P., ed., *Osnovy optimizatsii tekushevo otraslevovo planirovaniia*, (Principles of Optimization for Current Sectoral Planning), Moscow, Nauka, 1987.

10 Efficiency at Different Stages of Production in the Soviet Union

Joseph M. Nowakowski

Complexity and Performance

The sectoral and aggregate efficiencies reported in chapters 7 and 8 are not only overstated by the command planning constraints impairing the performance of Soviet multiproduct firms revealed in chapter 9, but by the same sorts of restrictions which apply at different stages of fabrication, and among final goods produced in independent enterprises. In both these instances bonus incentives play only a marginal role in factor allocation and input use, so that wide efficiency differentials are likely to be the fault of administrative command planning, including aberrations of price setting. This chapter probes the dimensions of these concealed inefficiencies by examining the performance of textile manufactures at different stages of production.[1] Special attention is devoted to evaluating Banerjee's and Spagat's hypothesis that command constrained efficiency may be inversely correlated with complexity.[2] It extends previous studies by introducing a new element to the analysis, an estimation of the efficiency levels of two sets of enterprises involved in the ultimate production of cotton goods, but operating at different stages in the production process. Strictly speaking, efficiency levels should not be compared across samples. Since the estimates are relative to an estimated frontier, meaningful comparisons must be made relative to a single frontier. Therefore, data on vertically integrated enterprises are pooled below into a single data set. This has the disadvantage of restricting the data to a single technology, which may not accurately reflect the technology of either set of enterprises. Since there is no reason to assume a common technology, care will be taken to allow for adjustments in parameter estimates across sectors. While the shortcomings of the pooling procedure (and results) should be taken seriously, pooling does permit inferences to be made on the issue of interest: relative efficiency levels in these integrated sectors.

The Relative Efficiency of Vertically Associated Enterprises

The complexity hypothesis can be investigated by studying efficiency differentials in vertically associated cross-sections. The term vertical association refers to enterprises involved in operations at different stages of production of a good or service. One stage may be extractive, another distributive. Oil wells and gasoline pumps, for example, represent activity at two particular stages of production in the automobile fuel industry.

The analysis here examines cross-sections of enterprises involved in the refining and processing stages of production. Specifically, the performance of raw cotton refining enterprises will be compared to that of cotton textile weaving enterprises. Enterprises are assumed to have no ties to one another, and to ship output to central receiving warehouses. Refining cotton fibers is known to be a relatively simple process, but weaving these fibers into fabrics can be a much more complicated. There are various types of cotton yarn that can differ with respect to construction, count (weight), warp, weave, and finishing, and each variation in the yarn itself leads to several different possible variations in the fabric. When one component of the basic yarn is changed, a new and possibly more complex fabric is produced.[3] While the variety of cotton fabrics is not expected to be as wide in the Soviet economy as it is in a Western market economy, different applications of the final good necessitate some degree of variety. Since the options in fabric construction are more numerous than those in fiber refining, the latter stage of production is assumed to be more complex.

In studies of manufacturing overhead costs, complexity in the manufacturing process is recognized as a factor responsible for increasing costs and decreasing the level of efficiency.[4] The higher level of complexity makes it simultaneously more difficult for managers to proctor the process, and easier for workers to minimize efforts, or to go astray in their efforts. Furthermore, in the Soviet setting, passive acceptance of plans, as opposed to active pursuit of bonus payments, could lead to severe reductions in technical efficiency due to bottlenecks in intermediate goods and ministry-level mistakes. This suggests that cotton refining should be more efficient than weaving. Previous studies confirm that cotton-refining indeed is fairly efficient, but the results briefly reviewed below as a baseline indicate that estimates are sensitive to the methods employed and vary from one data set to another.

1974 Cotton Refining Activity

Danilin, *et al.* studied 151 cotton refining enterprises operating in five Soviet republics in 1974. They report a high average efficiency level, 92.9 percent. Older enterprises (constructed prior to 1961) were estimated to have had a slight disadvantage in the technological level of equipment available to them, but to have operated somewhat more efficiently.[5]

1977 Cotton Refining Activity

An additional cross-section of enterprises producing refined cotton in five Union republics in 1977 has been analyzed in two previous papers. Afanas"ev and Skokov initially examined the data. Their results indicate that several enterprises operated on the technically efficient frontier, while the average efficiency level was .86; in other words, the typical enterprise operated about 14 percent below its technically efficient level, given the inputs available to it. According to Afanas"ev and Skokov, the least efficient enterprise operated at 28 percent of its efficient production potential.[6]

Concerned with the consistency of results based on different approaches, Lovell and Wood undertook another examination of these enterprises, using two additional estimation procedures. Average levels of efficiency were below Afanas"ev and Skokov's in both of Lovell and Wood's procedures. Using a fairly restrictive, non-stochastic ray-homothetic approach, the average level of efficiency was estimated to be .33, with a high of 1.00 and a low of .06. Their other approach, based on linear-programming techniques, produced nine fully efficient enterprises and a mean efficiency level of .77. The lowest score in the linear-programming results was .16. Although the average level of efficiency estimated via each approach differed due to different assumptions made concerning the causes of deviations below the technically efficient frontier, and due to the flexibility of the model employed, the relative rankings within the cross-section were very consistent. As Lovell and Wood point out, although the absolute estimators of technical efficiency may vary according to techniques, attempts to identify above- and below-average performers would remain consistent.[7] Here the data provided by Afanas"ev and Skokov, as well as newly available data concerning Soviet cotton-weaving enterprises, are reexamined.[8] One estimation model, based on a linearized Cobb-Douglas production function, is of the form

$$q_i = \alpha + \beta_1 k_i + \beta_2 l_i + e_i; \qquad\qquad (10.1)$$

the other model, based on Kmenta's linear approximation to the CES production function,[9] is of the form[10]

$$q_i = \alpha + \beta_1 k_i + \beta_2 l_i + \beta_3 (k_i - l_i)^2 + e_i; \qquad\qquad (10.2)$$

where q_i, k_i and l_i are the ith output, capital and labor respectively with a normal distributed error term e_i.

In addition, for each available data set, a standard production function for the best-fit form of the model was also estimated by OLS. The OLS models are of the same form as (10.1) and (10.2) above, with the exception that the error term is assumed to be normally distributed without truncation. This enables one to compare 'average' parameter estimates with frontier estimates. The average production function was estimated with corrections for heteroskedasticity and spatial autocorrelation. The results are included in Tables 10.10-10.13.

For the frontier production functions, the following parameters were estimated by maximum likelihood techniques (MLE): α, β, λ, and σ, where λ is the ratio of distortion caused by enterprise-specific and exogenous factors, and σ is the sum of the variances of two types of disturbance. From these estimates, individual estimates of the components of the composed error term can be derived, again using maximum likelihood techniques as discussed above. The results for the 1977 data are reproduced in Table 10.1, along with partial results of Afanas"ev and Skokov's and Lovell and Woods' analyses of the data.

Although the coefficient of the capital variable was not significant in the frontier CES model, this model appears to perform better than the Cobb-Douglas model. This conclusion is based on the significance of the capital-labor ratio variable, and on the log-likelihood ratio. The Cobb-Douglas model is a restricted form of the CES model. The significance of the restriction can be tested by examining twice the difference of the log likelihood values, which is distributed as a Chi-square variable, with degrees of freedom equal to the number of restrictions.[11] The statistic is then $2[\log(L_U) - \log(L_R)]$, where the subscripts U and R refer to the unrestricted and restricted models, respectively. The calculated statistic in this case is 12.912, significant at the $\alpha = .005$ level. The null hypothesis that the restricted (CD) form of the model is the best available is therefore rejected.

One somewhat surprising result of both frontier models is the suggestion of increasing returns to scale, although the results generate a picture of an over-capitalized industry. The coefficient on labor is large and positive, that on capital is negative but not significant at $\alpha=5$ percent, and the coefficient on the square of the capital-labor ratio is extremely significantly negative. The parameter estimates on the capital coefficients are sensitive, of course, to measurement error. The full data set was retained, despite the possibility of mismeasured observations resulting in outliers, to maintain a consistent data set for comparisons. The parameter $\lambda > 1$ indicates that more of the composite distortion in production is caused by inefficiencies than by random factors.

For the 1977 cotton refining enterprises, the OLS estimates of the linearized CES production function also indicated increasing returns to scale, slightly higher at the frontier than in the interior. The coefficients on capital and the squared capital-labor ratio variables were both more strongly negative than the frontier model's estimates. The difference in coefficients can be interpreted as indicating that capital was even less marginally productive in the interior than at the frontier. Labor, on the other hand, was marginally more productive internally that at the frontier.

The mean level of efficiency estimated via the frontier model, .7375, is somewhat below Afanas"ev and Skokov, but somewhat above the linear programming estimate of Lovell and Wood. It is also above the estimate generated by the stochastic frontier Cobb-Douglas model, which was .692. According to the estimates generated by the linearized production functions, no enterprise achieved its full potential frontier production level. The highest recorded level of efficiency was .9479 based on the Cobb-Douglas model, and .9397 based on the CES model. All three of the previous studies indicate that at least one enterprise achieved its full potential. At the other end of the scale, the Cobb-Douglas and ray-homothetic models both indicate a worst-practice enterprise producing around 6 percent of its potential. The CES,

LP, and linearized CES models all give about the same low efficiency score, between roughly 24 percent and 30 percent of potential.

Table 10.1   1977 Cotton Refining Activity (n=151)

Results of Linearized Cobb-Douglas (CD) and CES (LCES) Standard (OLS) and Stochastic Frontier (MLE) Production Function Estimates and Previous CES, Ray-homothetic and Linear Programming Analyses

Variable (t-ratio)	CES (OLS)	CD (MLE)	LCES (MLE)	CES (MLE)	Rayhomo-thetic	LP
Z High Low Avg.		.9479 .0611 .6920	.9397 .2468 .7375	1.00 .28 .86	1.00 .06 .33	1.00 .30 .64
λ		1.94*** (6.246)	1.33*** (4.045)			
σ		.585*** (15.77)	.504*** (10.77)			
Intercept	.221 (2.96)	.601*** (7.457)	.572*** (5.926)			
k	-.160* (-1.66)	.174** (1.940)	-.0697 (-.633)			
l	1.26*** (14.23)	.962*** (10.21)	1.197*** (18.09)			
$(k-l)^2$	.428*** (-5.402)		-.362*** (-6.20)			
$\bar{R}^2$/log(L)	.67	-77.063	-70.607			

SOURCES: *CES-OLS, CD-MLE* and *LCES-MLE*: Original estimates. *CES*: Afanas"ev and Skokov, "The Estimation of the Efficiency of Enterprise Activity". *Ray-homothetic and LP*: Lovell and Wood, "Progress Report".

---

*Significant at 10 percent level.
**Significant at 5 percent level.
***Significant at 1 percent level.

1982 Refining Activity

Data describing a cross-section of cotton refining enterprises in operation in 1982 were obtained and analyzed by Lovell and Wood, who shared the data. This same data was previously examined by Afanas"ev, whose results are summarized in Lovell and Wood.[12]

According to Lovell and Wood, Afanas"ev employed a stochastic CES frontier production function, estimated via MLE techniques, and estimated the mean efficiency level to be 87.8 percent for a sample of 108 Soviet cotton-refining enterprises. Lovell and Wood report an average efficiency level of 62.2 percent for the same enterprises, using linear programming techniques. They also report that most enterprises operated in the region of diminishing returns to scale.

The data were reexamined using linearized stochastic frontier models of the Cobb-Douglas and CES production functions, as above. Output was expressed as tons of cotton refined, capital as thousands of rubles of fixed capital, and labor as thousands of man-days. Results of these new analyses, as well as reported findings of Afanas"ev and Lovell and Wood are reproduced in Table 10.2.

The Cobb-Douglas model seems to fit the data better, based on the insignificance of the coefficient of the capital-labor ratio variable. The Chi-square value for the test of the restriction on the model was .1312, not significant at $\alpha = .10$. In the Cobb-Douglas model results, all of the coefficients estimated, except λ, were significant at the 5 percent level. (λ was significant at the 10 percent level.) It is interesting to note, however, that the estimates of primary interest here, the estimates of efficiency, were not statistically different in either model: the mean level of efficiency estimated using the Cobb-Douglas model was .83228 (standard deviation = .072963); the average level of efficiency based on the estimates of the CES model was .83397 (.071478). The minimum and maximum scores were also very similar: efficiency scores ranged from .5798 to .9558 using the Cobb-Douglas model, and from .5872 to .9553 using the CES model.

Table 10.2   1982 Cotton Refining Activity (n=108)

Results of Linearized Cobb-Douglas (CD) and CES (LCES) Standard(OLS) and Stochastic Frontier (MLE) Production Function Estimates and Previous CES and Linear Programming Analyses

Variable (t-ratio)	CD (OLS)	CD (MLE)	LCES (MLE)	CES (MLE)	LP
Z High Low Avg.		.9558 .5798 .83228	.9553 .5872 .83397	 .878	 .622
λ		1.3158* (1.815)	1.2914* (1.744)		
σ		.297*** (5.885)	.296*** (5.736)		
Intercept	-.973** (-2.316)	15.59*** (37.242)	13.22* (1.957)		
k	.1138** (2.222)	.1311** (2.460)	.686 (.437)		
l	.7398*** (12.432)	.7074*** (13.229)	.707*** (13.21)		
$(k-l)^2$			-.0323 (-.356)		
R^2/log(L)	.66	6.1660	6.2316		

SOURCES: *CD-OLS, CD-MLE* and *LCES-MLE*: Original estimates. *CES and LP*: Lovell and Wood, "Progress Report".

---

*Significant at 10 percent level.
**Significant at 5 percent level.
***Significant at 1 percent level.

The estimate of λ produced by the Cobb-Douglas model was 1.31580; the estimate using the CES model was 1.29141; again, there was little difference between the two estimates. The sum of performance-related and exogenous deviation, σ, was .297252 in the Cobb-Douglas model and .295596 in the CES model. It seems that the differences between Afanas"ev, Lovell and Wood, and these results may lie in the technique rather than the model; maximum likelihood estimation of linearized versions of the models results in very similar outcomes. Finally, the results of the frontier analysis indicate decreasing returns to scale, consistent with the findings of Lovell and Wood.

The Cobb-Douglas parameter estimates produced by OLS are not very different from the MLE frontier estimates: capital is slightly less productive in the interior, labor slightly less so. Both frontier and average models exhibit diminishing returns to scale.

1983 Refining Activity

Afanas"ev, and Lovell and Wood continued their separate analyses of cotton refining enterprises operating in 1983 as well. The data set examined in this stage of their investigations consisted of 108 enterprises. The studies were performed by each set of authors in the same way as their respective previous studies: Afanas"ev used the general CES model formulated by Materov, while Lovell and Wood employed linear programming techniques. As before, in this study the data was examined using both linearized Cobb-Douglas and linearized CES production functions. Results of these estimations are reported in Table 10.3. To be consistent with Afanas"ev and Lovell and Wood, all observations were retained.

The Chi-square statistic for the test on the restriction in this case was .588, insignificant at $\alpha = .10$. In addition, the coefficient on the capital-labor ratio was not significant. Again, the Cobb-Douglas model fit the data better, and the technology estimated exhibited decreasing returns to scale. The coefficients on capital and labor suggest either mismeasurement of the capital stocks or severe over-capitalization: the capital coefficient was only slightly positive, but not significantly different from zero. The capital output elasticity suggested by the maximum likelihood estimates is only .06, which indicates that a one percent increase in fixed capital would result in only six one-hundredths of a percent increase in output. The output elasticity for the labor coefficient, on the other hand, indicates that a percentage increase in the labor input would result in an increase in output of almost three-quarters of a per cent. Again, the accuracy of the measurement of capital stocks will affect the estimates in these procedures.

Afanas"ev (as reported by Lovell and Wood) finds an average efficiency score of 87.5 percent for the 1983 data set. Lovell and Wood report an average efficiency of 70.3 percent. The linearized Cobb-Douglas model yields a mean efficiency level of 82.3 percent, with a low score of 51.46 percent and a high score of 94.23 percent. The same values from the CES model were 83.65 percent, 57.5 percent, and 94.23 percent, respectively. The ratio of performance-related to exogenous disturbances, λ, in the Cobb-Douglas model is 1.65233 (CES: 1.40495), which indicates more performance-related fluctuations than exogenous disturbances.

Again, there are no striking differences between interior and frontier parameter estimates. Labor is slightly more marginally productive in the interior, capital slightly less so, with evidence of diminishing returns to scale.

1988 Cotton Textile Production Activity

The final set of observations is from the year 1988. The data describe a cross-section of 86 cotton textile producing enterprises, as opposed to cotton refining enterprises. The 86 textile producers were located throughout the Soviet Union. As received, the data contain information on output expressed in thousands of rubles worth of cotton fabric produced, in wholesale prices; the value of fixed capital in thousands of (1982) rubles; and the average number of production personnel employed by the enterprise. In order to begin formulating one consistent pooled data set it was necessary to make certain adjustments to the output and labor variables. The adjustments to output are discussed in detail below. A rather simple and straightforward adjustment was made to the labor input. According to the annual economic yearbook, the average work-year consisted of 229.9 days in 1988 for an industrial production worker. Based on this information, the labor variable was converted to thousands of man-days by multiplying the number of production line workers given in the original data by 229.5 and then dividing by one thousand. This was a preliminary step in creating a pooled data set.

Table 10.3   1983 Cotton Refining Activity (n=108)

Results of Linearized Cobb-Douglas (CD) and CES (LCES) Standard (OLS) and Stochastic Frontier (MLE) Production Function Estimates and Previous CES and Linear Programming Analyses

Variable (t-ratio)	CD (OLS)	CD (MLE)	LCES (MLE)	CES (MLE)	LP
Z High Low Avg.		.9427 .5146 .82299	.9423 .5749 .83654	.875	.703
λ		1.65233* (1.739)	1.40495 (1.452)		
σ		.2942** (6.051)	.281*** (5.072)		
Intercept	-.3753 (-.956)	6.594*** (17.17)	1.3859 (.237)		
k	.0234 (.466)	.0601815 (1.118)	1.2744 (.941)		
l	.7796*** (12.602)	.7302*** (16.161)	.731*** (15.94)		
$(k-l)^2$			-.071 (-.907)		
$\bar{R}^2/\log(L)$	.66	13.927	14.221		

SOURCES: *OLS-CD, MLE-CD* and *MLE-LCES*: Original estimates. *CES and LP*: Lovell and Wood, "Progress Report".

---

*Significant at 10 percent level.
**Significant at 5 percent level.
***Significant at 1 percent level.

Table 10.4   1988 Cotton Textiles Activity (n=86)

Results of Linearized Cobb-Douglas (CD) and CES (LCES) Standard (OLS) and Stochastic Frontier (MLE) Production Function Estimates

Variable (t-ratio)	CD (OLS)	CD (MLE)	LCES (MLE)
Z High Low Avg.		.9606 .771 .91333	.9607 .7700 .91301
λ		.878245 (.970)	.882782 (.963)
σ		.17353*** (4.541)	.173710*** (4.506)
Intercept	-2.945*** (-3.48)	2.34183*** (6.759)	2.41637*** (3.527)
k	.160037 (1.499)	.131965 (1.498)	.02377 (.028)
l	.76574*** (7.312)	.753962*** (7.064)	.863592 (.999)
$(k-l)^2$			.006813 (.124)
$\bar{R}^2$/log(L)	.45	42.642	42.648

SOURCE: Original data obtained by the author from Goskomstat.

---

*Significant at 10 percent level.
**Significant at 5 percent level.
***Significant at 1 percent level.

Once again, regressions were run with linear approximations of the Cobb-Douglas and CES production functions. The results are summarized in Table 10.4. The Cobb-Douglas production function yielded the best results in terms of fitting the data. The Chi-square value here was an insignificant .012. Furthermore, the t-test on the capital-labor ratio coefficient did not indicate rejection of the null hypothesis. The inclusion or deletion of outliers did not affect the results of these statistical tests.

Maximum likelihood estimation of the stochastic frontier Cobb-Douglas production function gave a very small and insignificant coefficient on capital (.131965) and a significant output elasticity for the labor input (.753962). Again, decreasing returns to scale are evident.

There are small differences between the standard and frontier model parameter estimates. There are no sign changes except for the intercept term, but the output elasticity of capital is higher in the interior than at the frontier (although still not significant at $\alpha=10$ percent), and that of labor is slightly larger. Enterprises near the frontier exhibited diminishing returns to scale more severe than the returns to scale for interior enterprises.

The ratio of variation below the frontier to variation in the frontier itself, .8782, was lower than analogous estimates for cotton refiners. At the same time, the estimated levels of average industrial efficiency were higher than for cotton refiners. This cannot, however, be interpreted as evidence of a higher level of overall efficiency. Each group of data was evaluated within itself; that is, for each cross-section a separate frontier was estimated, and, for each enterprise, only deviations below that cross-section-specific frontier were estimated. This procedure produced, for the data available, a set of four stochastic production frontiers with estimates of efficiency for the represented enterprises. The question of a single unified frontier incorporating vertically integrated features is addressed below. Before the question of the unified frontier can be addressed, however, a consistent data set must be formulated from the various sets of observations.

Pooling the Data

As mentioned above, the original data were expressed in a variety of units for output and inputs. In order to create one single, consistent data set, a number of conversions were necessary. Data for enterprises operating in 1977 posed a problem. For this year, output and inputs were expressed as a fraction of the last enterprise in the cross-section, which generated three variables (output, labor, and capital) normalized around the values for the last enterprise. The nature of the 1977 data made it impossible to establish reliable estimates for the actual levels of outputs and inputs. For this reason, as well as for the distance in time from the 1988 cotton textile producers, the 1977 data set was unsatisfactory for constructing a unified data set.

Values for input levels for each of the three remaining data sets were fairly consistent. Information on the levels of fixed capital available to each enterprise operating in the 1980's was consistently expressed in 1982 ruble values. Labor inputs were made uniform by transforming the individual personnel units reported for 1988 enterprises into estimates of man-days worked, using Soviet statistics on workers and work-time. (See above.)

Output is expressed in tons produced. The 1988 data, originally expressed in thousands of rubles received by the enterprises, were converted as follows: The average retail price of a meter of cotton cloth in 1988 was R1.73. Of this price, 21.8 percent was retained by the government as a turnover tax ("nalog s oborota"), and 78.2 percent was returned to the enterprises to cover costs and profits. This indicates that each meter of cotton fabric brought the enterprise 1.35 rubles. With this information, it is straightforward to calculate that each 1000 rubles received by an enterprise indicates an output of 580 linear meters, on average. (Different qualities of cotton fabric had different prices attached to them; R1.73 is used as an average of what Soviet consumers paid for one running meter of cloth.) In order to make the conversion from running meters to square meters, it was necessary to determine the width of the fabric sold at retail outlets. The *Young Family's Encyclopedia* (*Ensiklopedia molodoy semi*) gives two standard widths of fabric, 90-100 cm. and 140 cm. An average of these two widths was used to make the final adjustment into square meters. The result of these calculations is that 1000 rubles' worth of output translates into approximately 681.5 square meters of output. Square meters were then translated into tons of output according to the formula employed by the International Cotton Advisory Committee, which equates one ton with 6500 square meters.

Empirical Analysis of Pooled Data

According to the original data, in 1982 each worker in the cotton refining enterprises accounted for 93.32 tons of refined cotton and each thousand rubles of fixed capital had an average product of 3.03 tons of refined cotton. The figures for 1983 are 90.55 tons and 2.72 tons, respectively. The cotton textile output figures yield an average product of labor of 21.52 tons of fabric per worker, and .7123 tons of fabric per thousand rubles of fixed capital.

Both the 1982 and 1983 cross-sections of cotton refiners were fairly similar to the 1988 cross-section of cotton textile producers with respect to labor and capital inputs.   The 1983 cross-section was selected for comparison to the 1988 cross-section. The 1983 refining enterprises and the textile producing enterprises were combined into a single data set of 194 observations for analysis. It is obvious from the figures cited above that refining enterprises, in terms of tons of output, had far higher average product figures than weaving enterprises. With similar levels of inputs, textile output was only about twenty-five percent of refined cotton output by weight.

Frontier Cobb-Douglas and CES production functions for the combined data set were initially difficult to estimate. In the Cobb-Douglas model, only one input coefficient was significant at the 5 percent level. (Results of the estimations are reported in Table 10.5.) An ordinary least squares regression (OLS) run on the same model had an adjusted R^2 of approximately .07.   The CES model performed even worse, with no significant input coefficients at the 10 percent level. The OLS results of the same model had an adjusted R^2 of .06. The test of the restriction on the capital-labor ratio variable yielded an insignificant Chi-square value of 1.32. The frontier production function estimates of technical efficiency yielded an average level of 47 percent efficiency for the complete data set for both models, with the refiners averaging 71 percent and the textile manufacturers averaging 18 percent, again in both models (see Table 10.8).   Not surprisingly, the refiners were estimated to be much more efficient. They were also more consistent, in that there was relatively less variations around the mean level of efficiency. The coefficients of variation for both the CD and CES models were only a bit over half as large for the refiners as the same coefficients for the textile producers.

Table 10.5   Refining vs. Weaving Enterprise Performance (n=194)

Maximum Likelihood Results of Linearized CD and CES Stochastic Frontier Production Function Estimates

Variable (t-ratio)	CD	CES
Intercept	-.992 (-1.250)	-3.793 (-1.078)
k	.1839 (1.455)	1.2622 (.992)
l	.6677*** (7.419)	-.40697 (-.327)
$(k-l)^2$		-.103399 (-.873)
λ	18.5793* (1.673)	18.8334* (1.675)
σ	1.2595*** (14.066)	1.25584*** (14.139)
log(L)	-193.05	-192.39

SOURCE: Lovell and Wood, "Progress Report", and original data obtained from Goskomstat.

NOTE: Of the 194 observations, 108 were cotton refining and 86 cotton weaving enterprises.

---

*Significant at 10 percent level.
**Significant at 5 percent level.
***Significant at 1 percent level.

Table 10.6   Refining vs. Weaving Enterprise Performance (n=194)

Maximum Likelihood Results of Linearized CD and CES Stochastic Frontier Production Function Estimates with Slope and Intercept Dummy Variables

Variable (t-ratio)	CD	CES
Intercept	-.1751 (-.296)	-5.1895* (-1.708)
k	.0365 (.505)	1.98463* (1.782)
l	.74455*** (10.06)	-1.21089 (-1.089)
$(k-l)^2$		-.187276* (-1.819)
D_1 (=0 if refiner, 1 if weaver)	-2.24008*** (-2.919)	3.12544 (.865)
$k*D_1$	.08942 (.942)	-2.02387 (-1.472)
$l*D_1$	.0124465 (.123)	2.13753 (1.553)
$(k-l)^{2}*D_1$		.204557 (1.546)
λ	1.03695** (2.165)	.904057* (1.784)
σ	.338286** (8.833)	.323586*** (.03975)
log(L)	-25.756	-23.430

SOURCE: Lovell and Wood, "Progress Report", original data obtained from Goskomstat.

NOTE: Of the 194 observations, 108 were cotton refining and 86 cotton weaving enterprises.

---

*Significant at 10 percent level.
**Significant at 5 percent level.
***Significant at 1 percent level.

Table 10.7   Refining vs. Weaving Enterprise Performance (n=194)

Maximum Likelihood Results of Linearized CD, CES and Translog (TL)
Stochastic Frontier Production Function Estimates with Intercept Dummy
Variable

Variable (t-ratio)	CD	CES	TL
Intercept	-.467949 (-1.289)	-3.2949*** (-2.843)	-6.24852 (-1.097)
k	.0700174 (1.564)	1.19075*** (2.655)	3.16109*** (2.582)
l	.748727*** (14.586)	-.377442 (-.832)	-3.37509*** (-3.525)
$(k-l)^2$		-.110371** (-2.489)	
k^2			-.241127*** (-3.467)
l^2			.217527* (1.876)
kl			.291112*** (2.675)
D_1 (=0 if refiner, 1 if weaver)	-1.42143*** (-28.689)	-1.42705*** (-28.653)	-1.42589*** (-27.755)
λ	1.12323*** (2.686)	.927356** (2.054)	.912788* (1.697)
σ	.346002*** (10.649)	.327778*** (9.423)	.311795*** (7.595)
log(L)	-26.215	-24.775	-15.771

SOURCE: Lovell and Wood, "Progress Report", and original data obtained
from Goskomstat.

NOTE: Of the 194 observations, 108 were cotton refining and 86 cotton
weaving enterprises.

---

*Significant at 10 percent level.
**Significant at 5 percent level.
***Significant at 1 percent level.

Table 10.8   **Descriptive Statistics of Efficiency Estimates**

Variable	Mean	Std. Dev.	Minimum	Maximum	St. Dev/Mean
All Enterprises (n=194)					
ZCD	.47221	.28790	.05219	.9666	.60969
ZCES	.47365	.28792	.05352	.9700	.60786
ZCD$\alpha\beta$	.82658	.063372	.4915	.9364	.07667
ZCES$\alpha\beta$	.84314	.052596	.5468	.9375	.06238
ZCDα	.81766	.069716	.4465	.9390	.08526
ZCESα	.83944	.054607	.5210	.9378	.06505
ZTLα	.84783	.051568	.5266	.9421	.06082
Refining Enterprises (n-108)					
ZCD	.70780	.14167	.2998	.9666	.20016
ZCES	.70945	.14014	.3314	.9700	.19753
ZCD$\alpha\beta$	.83163	.04971	.6371	.9086	.05977
ZCES$\alpha\beta$	.84732	.03892	.7317	.9158	.04593
ZCDα	.82346	.05525	.6021	.9049	.06709
ZCESα	.84377	.04105	.7040	.9124	.04865
ZTLα	.85264	.03594	.7561	.9126	.04215
Weaving Enterprises (N=86)					
ZCD	.17635	.06203	.0522	.3831	.35714
ZCES	.17752	.06425	.0535	.3927	.36193
ZCD$\alpha\beta$	.82024	.07704	.4915	.9364	.09392
ZCES$\alpha\beta$	.83790	.06576	.5468	.9375	.07848
ZCDα	.81038	.08424	.4465	.9390	.10395
ZCESα	.83400	.06779	.5210	.9378	.08128
ZTLα	.84179	.06592	.5266	.9421	.07831

NOTE: Results of maximum likelihood estimation of stochastic frontier production functions, where $Z = \exp(-U)$, and $U \equiv$ the one-sided residual indicating inefficiency; CD denotes a Cobb-Douglas model, CES a constant elasticity of substitution model, and TL a transcendental logarithmic model; $\alpha\beta$ denotes the use of dummy variables allowing the slope and intercept estimates to vary according to type of enterprise; and α denotes a single dummy variable allowing only the intercept to vary.

In absolute terms, then, the cotton refiners operated much closer to the hypothetical production frontier, as measured by tons of output produced. The simple model employed may present too strict a test, however, as it is acknowledged that cotton textile producers undertook a more difficult task. In the first set of estimations, the textile producers were constrained to have the same production frontier as the refining units, which was obviously not the case. Allowing the production function to adjust for different types of activities yields a more accurate picture of efficiency levels taking into consideration the relative differences in the activities, while the above models describe efficiency levels without accounting for varying degrees of difficulty.

A new set of estimates includes dummy variables which allow the slopes and intercepts terms for textile weavers to vary. The remainder of the procedure is as outlined above. The results are reported in Tables 15 and 16. As the values in Table 10.6 indicate, the only significant dummy variable was attached to the intercept term.   Since the coefficients on the slope coefficient dummy variables did not indicate a statistically significant difference between the refining and weaving enterprises, the estimation was done again, this time deleting the dummy variables on inputs and retaining that on the intercept. (See Table 10.7.)

Table 10.7 presents the results of the stochastic frontier estimates. The significance of the capital-labor ratio coefficient indicates that the CES model fits the data better than does the CD model. Given this, it seemed appropriate to estimate an even less restrictive production function, the linearized transcendental logarithmic model. This model is of the form

$$q_1 = \alpha + \beta_1 k_i + \beta_2 l_i + \beta_3 k_i^2 + \beta_4 l_i^2 + \beta_5 k_i l_i + e_i, \tag{10.3}$$

where all definitions are retained. Results of this procedure are presented in Table 10.7, Column 4. A test of the hypothesis that the coefficient on the capital-labor ratio is zero again allows us to compare the Cobb-Douglas and CES models. Here the Chi-square value, 2.88, is significant at the $\alpha = 10$ level only. The t-test on the ratio's coefficient led to rejection of the null hypothesis at the $\alpha = .05$ level, however. Testing the restricted models against the translog form, however, suggests that the flexible model performed best. To test the translog model against the Cobb-Douglas model, three linear restrictions are imposed, i.e., that the coefficients on variables other than labor and capital are all zero. The Chi-square value in this test was 20.88, high enough to reject the null hypothesis at the $\alpha = .005$ level. Testing translog against CES imposes one linear restriction, $\beta_{kk} + \beta_{ll} - 2\beta_{kl}$ $= 0$. The Chi-square value for this test was 20.88, again high enough to reject the null hypothesis at the $\alpha = .005$ level.

Supporting the conclusions of the Chi-square tests, the coefficients on each input variable were significant at at least the $\alpha = .10$ level. The translog model seemed to be the best performer. Examination of the variables and results is somewhat troubling, however. Not surprisingly, the capital-labor term was correlated with the input variables. This multicollinearity produced some odd signs on coefficient estimates, but estimates of the residuals appeared to be unaffected: the Spearman correlation coefficient between z-scores generated by the Cobb-Douglas and CES models was .9914; between Cobb-Douglas and translog, .9494; and between CES and translog, .9617. These results indicate that efficiency estimates, the parameter of primary interest here, were robust in the presence of multicollinearity. Efficiency estimates based on this model, as well as the other two frontier models with intercept-dummies, are reported in Table 10.8.

Analysis of Efficiency Estimates

It is obvious, and not surprising, from Table 10.8 that the simplest forms of the models show the textile enterprises in the worst light. In the basic CD and CES models, the average efficiency of refining enterprises is estimated to be over four times that of weaving enterprises. If dummy variables are included in the models allowing both slope and intercept estimates to differ across enterprise types, the difference is reduced dramatically. Generally, this seems to be the appropriate approach, since the job of the weaving enterprises is inherently more difficult than that of the refiners. The dummy variables can be thought of as indicating how much more difficult weaving is than refining. The slope coefficients did not differ significantly. This result led to the next step, estimating the models with only intercept dummy variables. Here, increasingly flexible models were estimated: first Cobb-Douglas, then CES, and finally translog. Not surprisingly, the increased flexibility of the models allowed the estimates of overall efficiency to rise. Compensating textile-producing enterprises for their more difficult task did not, however, make them equal in efficiency to refiners. Although the average levels of efficiency were similar according to all three intercept-dummy models, the variation among the enterprises was larger for weavers than for refiners. The complexity of the process led to much greater fluctuations in the performance of the weavers. For the intercept-dummy models, although average levels of efficiency were slightly lower for weavers than for refiners, the weavers had both the lowest and highest rated enterprises under all three intercept-dummy production function specifications. Comparisons of the coefficients of variations indicate that refiners were more tightly packed around the mean level of efficiency.

Although the differences between the mean efficiency estimates for refiners and weavers were not significantly different at the 5 percent level in all three intercept-dummy models, F-tests of the variance ratios indicated that the null hypotheses of equal variances under all three models had to be rejected at the 5 percent level. A glance at the coefficients of variation shows that weaving enterprises were nearly twice as varied in their performance as refining enterprises. Finally, it bears repeating that the three frontier models employed yielded consistent estimates of individual enterprise efficiency levels.

Conclusions

Statistical analysis was performed on several individual sets of Soviet enterprises, and then on a pooled data set of two vertically integrated sets of enterprises involved in the production of cotton goods. One set of enterprise refined raw cotton fiber into cotton yarn for later use by the second set of enterprises, which wove yarn into fabrics. This latter stage of production was assumed to be inherently more complex, because of the larger number of decisions to be made and processes to be monitored. This suggested that performance in this latter stage of production, as measured by estimated efficiency levels, would likely be lower, since the degree of difficulty was higher. As a test of the ability of Soviet managers to maintain high levels of performance given a more complex production process, the performance of refining enterprises operating in 1983 were compared to textile weavers operating in 1988. Initial results indicated a substantially lower level of efficiency among the textile producers, but controlling for the inherent difficulty of their production process yielded similar levels of efficiency for the cross-sections overall. However, while the average textile-producing enterprises did manage to perform at efficiency levels similar to refining enterprises, given the degree of difficulty, they were unable to perform as consistently as the fiber refiners. The complexity of the production process was reflected in the higher variance in performance among the textile weaving enterprises.

These findings broadly confirm that the rigidities of administrative command planning impair factor allocation to best interfirm use. Consequently achieved produciton for the industry as a whole is below potential. Efficiency judged from this standpoint i. The average performance of firms in the sector may appear satisfactory, but these results conceal the inefficiencies detected here by close microeconomic inspection.

Notes

1. A short list of studies concerning these issues include Abram Bergson, "Comparative Productivity: The USSR, Eastern Europe, and the West", *American Economic Review* 77 (June 1987):342-57; Padma Desai, "The Production Function and Technical Change in Postwar Soviet Industry: A Reexamination", *American Economic Review* 66 (June 1976):372-81, and "Total Factor Productivity in Postwar Soviet Industry and Its Branches", *Journal of Comparative Economics* 9 (March 1985):1-23; David M. Kemme, "Productivity Growth in Polish Industry", *Journal of Comparative Economics* 11 (March 1987):1-20; Steven Rosefielde, "Comparative Productivity: Comment", and Abram Bergson, "Reply", *American Economic Review*, 80 (September 1990):946-54 and 955-6; Judith Thornton, "Value-Added and Factor Productivity in Soviet Industry", *American Economic Review* 60 (December 1970):863-71; Robert S. Whitesell, "The Influence of Central Planning on the Economic Slowdown in the Soviet Union and Eastern Europe: A Comparative Production Function Analysis", *Economica* 52 (May 1985):235-44.

2. Abhijit V. Banerjee and Michael Spagat, "Productivity Paralysis and the Complexity Problem: Why Do Centrally Planned Economies Become Prematurely Gray?" *Journal of Comparative Economics* 15 (December 1991):657.

3. Debbie Ann Gioello, *Profiling Fabrics: Properties, Performance, and Construction Techniques* (New York: Fairchild Publications, 1981), pp. 2-3.

4. George Foster and Mahendra Gupta, "Manufacturing Overhead Cost Driver Analysis", *Journal of Accounting and Economics* 12 (January 1990):311.

5. V.I. Danilin, Ivan S. Materov, Steven Rosefielde, and C.A. Knox Lovell, "Measuring Enterprise Efficiency in the Soviet Union: A Stochastic Frontier Analysis", *Economica* 52 (May 1985), p. 230.

6. M. Afanasiev and V. Skokov, "The Estimation of the Efficiency of Enterprise Activity", in *Proceedings of the 6th Finnish- Soviet*

Symposium in Economics, edited by Pekka Sutela. Helsinki, n.p., 1985, p. 89.

7.   C.A. Knox Lovell and Linda Wood, "Soviet Cotton Refining Revisited: A Progress Report". Chapel Hill, North Carolina, June, 1990, p. 10. (Mimeographed manuscript.)

8.   Each cross-section contains outliers. There were three reasons for not deleting the outliers: the previous studies did not delete them, and it was desirable to make as close a comparison as possible between previous studies and the results in this study; deletion of enterprises producing far below their estimated outputs would inflate efficiency estimates; finally, results from full data sets and trimmed data sets produced very similar parameter estimates. Since the frontier was the object of primary interest, estimation with the maximum amount of information on enterprises seemed the best choice. The largest outliers typically had negative residuals; retention of enterprises with observed values below predicted values therefore suggests a lower bound on efficiency estimates. Compare the trimmed cotton data set of Table 3, Chapter 2 with the full 1988 cotton data set used here; deletion of four outlying enterprises noticeably reduced average efficiency estimates. The significance of this difference in efficiency levels and its implications for the robustness of the model are discussed in Chapter 6 below.In the case of cotton, two outliers were below and two above predicted (OLS) levels of output.

9.   Jan Kmenta, *Elements of Econometrics*, 2nd ed. New York: Macmillan Publishing Company, 1986, p. 515.

10.   Attempts to estimate the parameters of a transcendental logarithmic production function were not successful at this stage. The translog production function is, however, used below.

11.   George G. Judge, William E. Griffiths, R. Carter Hill, and Tsoung-Chao Lee, *The Theory and Practice of Econometrics*, Wiley Series in Probability and Mathematical Statistics, New York: John Wiley & Sons, 1980, p. 758.

12.   Lovell and Wood, "A Progress Report".

Bibliography

Afanasiev, M. and V. Skokov, "The Estimation of the Efficiency of Enterprise Activity", in *Proceedings of the 6th Finnish- Soviet Symposium in Economics*, edited by Pekka Sutela. Helsinki, n.p., 1985, p. 89.

Banerjee, Abhijit V. and Michael Spagat, "Productivity Paralysis and the Complexity Problem: Why Do Centrally Planned Economies Become Prematurely Gray?" *Journal of Comparative Economics* 15 (December 1991):657.

Bergson, Abram, "Comparative Productivity: The USSR, Eastern Europe, and the West", *American Economic Review* 77 (June 1987):342-57.

_____, "Reply", *American Economic Review*, 80 (September 1990):955-6.

Danilin, V.I., Ivan S. Materov, Steven Rosefielde, and C.A. Knox Lovell, "Measuring Enterprise Efficiency in the Soviet Union: A Stochastic Frontier Analysis". *Economica* 52 (May 1985), p. 230.

Desai, Padma, "The Production Function and Technical Change in Postwar Soviet Industry: A Reexamination", *American Economic Review* 66 (June 1976):372-81.

_____, "Total Factor Productivity in Postwar Soviet Industry and Its Branches", *Journal of Comparative Economics* 9 (March 1985):1-23.

Foster, George and Mahendra Gupta, "Manufacturing Overhead Cost Driver Analysis", *Journal of Accounting and Economics* 12 (January 1990):311.

Gioello, Debbie Ann, *Profiling Fabrics: Properties, Performance, and Construction Techniques* (New York: Fairchild Publications, 1981), pp. 2-3.

Judge, George G., William E. Griffiths, R. Carter Hill, and Tsoung-Chao Lee, *The Theory and Practice of Econometrics*, Wiley Series in

Probability and Mathematical Statistics, New York: John Wiley & Sons, 1980, p. 758.

Kemme, David M., "Productivity Growth in Polish Industry", *Journal of Comparative Economics* 11 (March 1987):1-20.

Kmenta, Jan, *Elements of Econometrics*, 2nd ed. New York: Macmillan Publishing Company, 1986, p. 515.

Lovell, C.A. Knox and Linda Wood, "Soviet Cotton Refining Revisited: A Progress Report". Chapel Hill, North Carolina, June, 1990, p. 10. (Mimeographed manuscript.)

Rosefielde, Steven, "Comparative Productivity: Comment", *American Economic Review*, 80 (September 1990):946-54.

Thornton, Judith, "Value-Added and Factor Productivity in Soviet Industry", *American Economic Review* 60 (December 1970):863-71.

Whitesell, Robert S., "The Influence of Central Planning on the Economic Slowdown in the Soviet Union and Eastern Europe: A Comparative Production Function Analysis", *Economica* 52 (May 1985):235-44.

11 Russian Enterprise Inefficiency: An Elasticity Test for Incomplete Profit Maximization

George B. Kleiner
Edited by Steven S. Rosefielde
Appendix by Ralph W. Pfouts

Introduction

The abolition of administrative command planning which accompanied the fall of the Soviet Union one might have supposed, should have generated a surge in production as competitive market processes eradicated the concealed efficiency losses of the old regime, but the response has been just the reverse. Output has fallen precipitously exacerbating past inefficiencies. A comprehensive investigation into the causes of the perverse behavior has yet to be undertaken, but the techniques developed in chapter 6 are harnessed here to show that enterprise inefficiency has increased in part because some managers may not be profit maximizing. The legacy of command constrained inefficiency apparently is still impairing Russian economic performance.

Incomplete Profit-Maximizing

The null hypothesis that some Russian managers are operating their enterprises inefficiently despite the dismantling of administrative command planning can be tested using a production function with a constant disparate mobility of factor productivity elaborated in chapter 6. The data for these tests were obtained from the State Committee on Statistics of Russia (Roskomstat) for the years 1991 and 1992 for twenty enterprises subject to anti-monopoly price regulation. The information provided for two of these enterprises, both in the defense sector, was inadequate, and they were dropped from the sample.[1]

Parameters c_1, ..., c_5 were estimated using ordinary least squares (OLS) for the two factor normalized CDMP function.

$$y = c_1 \left(c_2 + \left(1 - c_2\right) x_1^{c_3}\right)^{1/c_3} \left(c_4 + \left(1 - c_4\right) x_2^{c_5}\right)^{1/c_5}$$

where y is output in current prices, x_1 is the value of fixed capital, and x_2 is the number of workers employed.

The following estimates were obtained.

Table 11.1   Mobility of Factor Productivity 1991-92

Year	c_1	c_2	c_3	c_4	c_5	Coef. of Var.
1991	0.4523	0.6435	-0.3405	0.6691	0.1090	14.38%
1992	1.1173	0.9833	1.8892	0.3493	-0.5221	12.25%

As it is evident from the Table 11.1 estimates are statistically significant: the coefficients of variation are 14.4 percent and 12.2 percent respectively. The mobility values of factors x_1 and x_2 are

MFP_1 (1991) = 0.7460, MFP_2 (1991) = 1.1223,
MFP_1 (1992) = -1.1246, MFP_2 (1992) = 0.6570.

These mobility of factor productivity statistics suggest a significant shift in activity level in response to changed conditions. The mobility of both capital and labor productivity decline sharply between 1991 and 1992, and in the former case becomes intensely negative clearly indicating that managers failed to profit maximize even though potential gains were large and easily garnered.

Atomistic Disorganization

The disordered behavior of Russian managers indicated by these findings is easily explained and has broad systemic significance. The traditional forces channeling managerial self seeking (more neutrally personal utility maximizing) in socially constructive ways including managerial identification with the establishment have eroded, and have not been replaced by competitive markets based on individual private ownership (or derivative western corporate forms). Managers recognizing that their claims on revenues, profits and assets may be transitory under Chubais's ownership scheme, in the absence of external and internal controls have pillaged state and collective "private" assets for their own venal ends without regard for the public good. In the process they have antagonized their workers, hastening their enterprises' productive decline.

This atomistic disorganization which has resulted in extreme income inequality where managers often earn 100 times more than their employees, is the outgrowth of a gradual institutional evolution that has spawned intra enterprise dysfunction, corruption at all levels of power and control, criminalization of economic relations, inefficient interenterprise factor allocation and is thwarting the transition to competitive market capitalism. The principal stages of this evolution from the forties onward are outlined in Table 11.2. They show how decentralization has spread conceptually from regionalization to ministerial and departmental control, to augmented enterprise autonomy within the framework of the automatic system of management, to spontaneous small enterprise collectivist privatization, culminating in disordered, managerial opportunism.

This degenerate state obviously cannot persist forever. On one hand normal forms of property rights may emerge as ownership coalesces in the hands of opportunistic managers. On the other hand the state may tire of its laissez-faire policies and move to reassert its authority. Yavlinsky's and Luzhkov's new industrial privatization plan for Moscow which employs industrial associations in the form of financial industrial groups to regulate enterprise activities provides an example of how this may be accomplished.

These tendencies are encouraging, but it is premature to be optimistic. Opportunistic managers can be expected to staunchly defend their privileges, and the conflicting interests of other market participants and the government may unwittingly further their cause. Likewise, if the new regulatory associations exclude workers they may well degenerate into cartels pursuing monopoly rents at the expense of free competition. Economic recovery undoubtedly will occur, but the complex cross tendencies revealed in this investigation suggest that it will not happen very soon.

Table 11.2   **The Atomization of Soviet Productive Authority**

N	Period	Cause of Changes	Type of Management	Main Independent Units	Conventional Name of Period
1	2	3	4	5	6
1.	40s-50s	Industrial management reform 1940-41	Centralized	State	"Command Economy"
2.	End of the 50s-mid 60s	Khrushchev's 1957 economic reforms	Regional	Regional committees of national economy	"Regional Decentralization"
3.	Mid 60s-mid 70s	Brezhnev's 1965 economic reforms	Industrial	Industrial ministries	"Ministerial Administrative Command Planning"
4.	Mid 70s-mid 80s	Brezhnev's 1973 industrial management reforms Various schemes of industrial management	Subindustrial	Main boards of ministries, all-union All- Union Industrial corporations	"Departmental Administrative Command Planning"
5.	Mid 80s-1992	Gorbachev's perestroika reforms, state enterprise law of 1987	Enterprise	Large enterprises, corporations, enterprises	"All-Union Industrial Combines" VPO
6.	1992-1993	Spontaneous Privatization	Divisional	Enterprises, small enterprises	"Economy of small Enterprises"
7.	1993-1994	Chubais's voucher privatization	Individual, group	Enterprise managers, clique of self-seeking individuals	"Unrestrained Managerial Opportunism"

Note

1.   The data are confidential.

Appendix   Mobility of Factor, Productivity: Economic Regions and Homogeneity

The purpose of this note is to render Kleiner's coefficient of the mobility of factor productivity into terms more familiar to Western economists. To do this assume a production function

$$y = f\left(x_1, x_2\right) \tag{11.1}$$

Assume further that the production function reaches a clearly defined maximum. This, of course, simply says that we cannot go on increasing the output of an existing plant indefinitely. We cannot, by increasing seed, fertilizer and labor, produce on a single acre of Kansas wheatland enough wheat to supply the world's yearly consumption of flour.

Making use of the usual textbook device, we assume one of the factors, say x_2, is used in some fixed amount, while the amount of x_1 is varied. This permits us to adopt the usual textbook diagram, Figure 11.A1, in which total product reaches a maximum which gives rise to the stages of production. Stage I begins at the origin and ends at the point where marginal product (MP) intersects average product (AP), stage II begins where stage I ends and ends where MP is zero, which is also the point at which total product (TP) is largest. Stage III lies to the right of this point.

Economic production takes place only in stage II according to usual textbook presentation. Stage I for x_1, which is the stage I shown in Figure 6.1, is also stage III for x_2 and stage III for x_1 is stage I for x_2. For a derivation and discussion of this see (Vaughn and Pfouts, 1972).

Kleiner's coefficient of the mobility of factor productivity, his equation (6.3), may be written in terms of (6.1) as

$$MFP_1 [f] = \frac{x_1 f_1^2 - f f_1}{x_1 f f_{11}}, \tag{11.2}$$

where subscripts on f indicate partial differentiation. For our purpose the right hand member of (11.2) may be more conveniently shown as

$$MFP_1 [f] = \frac{f_1 \left(x_1 f_1 - f\right)}{x_1 f f_{11}}. \tag{11.3}$$

It can now be demonstrated that $MFP_1[f]$ will be positive only in stage II. In stages I and III it will be negative. Thus its sign indicates whether the firm is operating efficiently or not.

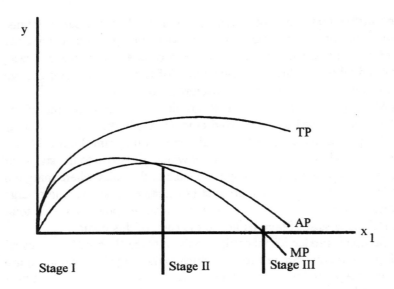

Figure 11.A1   Stages of Factor Productivity

As a matter of preparation we note first that $MP_1 = f_1$ and $AP_1 = f/x_1$. Thus it follows easily that if $MP_1 > AP_1$, the quantity in parentheses, $x_1 f_1 - f$, will be positive, but if $AP_1 > MP_1$ it will be negative. We also notice that because of the concavity of TP_1, f_{11} will be negative.

Looking now at stage II, one may see that $AP_1 > MP_1$ thus the quantity in parentheses in (6.39) will be negative and $MFP_1[f]$ will be positive.

For stage I $MP_1 > AP_1$ and the quantity in parentheses is positive. Thus $MFP_1[f]$ will be negative. In the case of stage III the quantity in parentheses will be negative but so will f_1. As a consequence $MFP_1[f]$ will be negative. Thus $MFP_1[f]$ will be positive only in stage II. In summary it may be said that economic production occurs if $MFP_1[f] > 0$.

Since $MFP_1[f]$ had different signs in stages I and II at the demarcation point between these stages it is zero. The same is true of the demarcation point between stages II and III. This can be verified directly from (6.39).

There is an important qualification to be attached to Kleiner's coefficient of the mobility of factor productivity: It is valid only if the production function is linear homogenous. For non-homogenous production functions it will not locate economic production with complete accuracy.

To see that homogeneity of degree one is required observe that at the beginning of stage II, the economic stage of production,

$$x_1 \, f_1 = f,$$

and since x_2 is held constant

$$f_2 = 0.$$

Multiplying the second equation by x_2 and adding them gives us

$$x_1 \, f_1 + x_2 \, f_2 = f,$$

which assuming continuous differentability throughout, requires that f be homogeneous of degree one. This seriously limits the scope of the mobility of factor productivity as a measure of economic efficiency.

The question of economic production can be simply and effectively handled by defining the economic region of production as that in which all factors have positive, or at least a non-negative, marginal products. Thus in the case of two factor inputs the area on and within the ridgelines in the isoquant map is economic. The areas outside the ridgelines have one factor which has a negative marginal product (Vaughn and Pfouts, 1972; Pfouts and Vaughn, 1973). This is a very simple and unobjectionable definition of economic production. Figure 11.A2 gives a graphical presentation of this definition.

The coefficient of mobility of factor productivity will meet the definition just given if and only if the production function is linear homogeneous. To demonstrate this in terms of isoquants and ridgelines consider two input points $\left(x_1^0, \, y_1^0\right)$ and $\left(\lambda \, x_1^0, \, \lambda \, y_1^0\right)$ were λ is slightly larger than unity. Using Taylor's expansion we can write

$$f\left(\lambda \, x_1^0, \, \lambda \, x_2^0\right) = f\left(x_1^0, \, x_2^0\right) + f_1 \, x_1^0 \, (\lambda - 1)$$

$$+ \, f_2 \, x_2^0 \, (\lambda - 1),$$

$$(11.4)$$

with the partial derivatives evaluated at $\left(x_1^0, \, x_2^0\right)$.

Now define a new variable u,

$$f\left(\lambda\, x_1^0,\ \lambda\, x_2^0\right) - \lambda\, f\left(x_1^0,\ x_2^0\right) = u. \tag{11.5}$$

Clearly if $u = 0$, f is homogeneous of the first degree. If $u > 0$, f shows increasing returns and the opposite for $u < 0$, and f is not necessarily homogeneous.

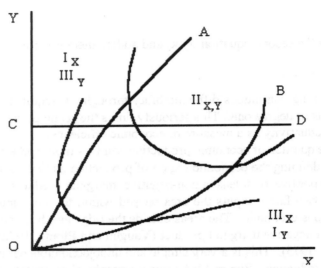

Figure 11.A2   Regions of Efficient Economic Production

Since we are concerned with ridgelines we assume we are on a ridgeline with x_1 variable. In this case $f_2 = 0$ on the ridgeline. Making use of this and substituting (11.5) into (11.6), yields,

$$\frac{f\left(x_1^0,\ x_2^0\right)}{x_1^0} + \frac{u}{x_1^0\left(\lambda - 1\right)} = f_1. \tag{11.6}$$

It is clear from the last equation that the quantity in parentheses in Kleiner's coefficient will be zero if and only if $u = 0$, that is if f is linear homogeneous.

If $u \neq 0$, then Kleiner's coefficient will show as economic input combinations that are not economic and vice versa. This is because the traditional stages of production as opposed to those in Figure 11.A2 are not accurate for identifying economic production unless the production function is linear homogeneous. If $u > 0$, then as (11.6) shows, the ridgeline which contains (11.6) will not lie at the point where traditional stage II begins but will fall in stage I. Thus some economic points may be erroneously considered uneconomic by Kleiner's rule. On the other hand if $u < 0$, $AP_1 >$ MP_1 and the ridgeline falls in traditional stage II. Some input combinations that are actually uneconomic may be considered economic.

Bibliography

Pfouts, R.W. and K.I. Vaughn, "Symmetry of Production Stages and Economic Production: Reply", *Southern Economic Journal*, *XXXX*, 1973, 334-5.

Vaughn, K.I. and R.W. Pfouts, "The Symmetry of Production Stages and Uneconomic Production", *Southern Economic Journal*, XXXVIII, 1972, 403-6.

Part III Russia's Economic Recovery Potential

Steven S. Rosefielde

Synopsis

The microeconomic inefficiencies empirically established in Part II show that Russia's production potential was lower than prior authoritative estimates indicated, and that inefficiencies, especially incomplete profit maximizing impede post-Soviet economic recovery. Part III amplifies on this theme by reexamining Russia's position in the global development hierarchy, and by assessing its recovery potential from this perspective. Chapter 12 suggests that instead of being in the first tier, Russia is actual in the fourth tier of the global development hierarchy, just above Thailand, and that even if incomplete profit maximization and other command inefficiencies vanished, the dead hand of communism continues to severely restrain recovery potential because its products are obsolete and its inherited embodied technologies are infungible. Chapters 13 and 15 explore various systemic barriers to recovery, and chapter 14 provides some preliminary evidence that market forces are beginning to enhance the efficiency of Russian foreign trade, suggesting that while prosperity is further away than some analysts suppose, Russia may eventually achieve the living standards enjoyed in the west.

12 Capital Infungibility and Production Potential in Post-Soviet Russia

Steven S. Rosefielde

Introduction

The empirically verified efficiency theory elaborated in this volume indicates that the Soviet Union was only able to realize a small portion of its global best practice production potential. Barriers to technology transfer and diffusion, together with administrative command planning constraints severally impaired physical productivity and consumer welfare. This deficiency was widely recognized in the descriptive literature, but comparative international statistical studies told a very different story. Soviet GNP measured in dollars was often calculated to be more than two thirds of America's (Table 12.A1) purportedly making the USSR the world's second largest economy.[1] The per capita gross national product of the Russian Soviet Federated Socialist Republic (RSFSR) was estimated to be 68 percent of the US standard, on a par with the European Community average (Table 12.1).

      The Russian Statistical Agency, Roskomstat has partially acknowledged that its prior purchasing power estimates were significantly overstated by paring them 39 percent, but a huge gap still remains between the revised figures and much lower ones computed through the exchange rate.[2] As a consequence, students of transition find themselves in a quandary. If the purchasing power parity estimates are accepted, Russia's economic recovery prospects are bright. Since market economies are supposed to outperform command regimes, Russia should be able to quickly regain economic superpower status, and relative affluence with the capital stock at its disposal either by fully employing resources as in the past, or by redeploying them in accordance with market demand. But, if Roskomstat's revised purchasing power parity estimates are rejected Russia's recovery potential is cast in a different light. Russian GDP in 1995 was 245 billion dollars, a figure supported by Emil Ershov, former head of Roskomstat's research division,[3] roughly one tenth the CIA's figure for 1991. Some of this disparity is explained by Russia's hyperdepression, but most is attributable to a radically reduced estimate of production potential (cf. Ericson, 1994, 1996). More or less the same story can be told if the 245 billion dollar estimate is adjusted for the 40 percent ruble appreciation engineered by the government in 1995.[4] Given this contradictory evidence, how should Russia's economic recovery potential be evaluated?

Table 12.1   Gross Domestic Product per Capita

	1989
OECD[a]	
United States	100.0
Australia	72.8
Canada	87.7
Japan	76.4
Sweden	77.0
Switzerland	94.8
European Community	69.3
Belgium	72.2
France	77.4
Germany[b]	80.9
Italy	70.7
Netherlands	69.6
Russia	**68.0**
Spain	51.9
United Kingdom	71.1
Selected East European[c]	
Bulgaria	25.9
Czechoslovakia	37.3
Hungary	29.8
Poland	22.1
Romania	17.6
Former Yugoslavia	24.8

Russia's gross domestic product per capita is computed in three steps. First the CIA's dollar estimate of Soviet GDP in 1989 is computed by multiplying America's GNP in 1989 valued at 1991 prices by the CIA's dollar size ratio of Soviet to U.S. GNP, 67 percent. See Table 12.A1 and (CIA, 1990a,b). (5,659.2 billion dollars) (.67) = 3,791.7 billion dollars. Second, the Russian GDP in 1989 valued in 1991 dollars is calculated from its ruble share of Soviet GNP reported by the CIA. (.609) (3,791.7 billion dollars) = 2,309 billion dollars. See *Narodnoe khoziaistvo SSSR*, 1990. Third, Russian GDP per capita is calculated by dividing the figure from step 2 by the population in 1989. (2,309 billion dollars)/(147.6 million people) = 15,631 dollars per capita.

The size ratio of Russian GDP per capita to American GDP per capita is computed by dividing the former by the later (15,631 dollars)/(22,977 dollars) = .680. See CIA, *Handbook of International Economic Statistics*, CPAS 92-10005, September 1992, Table 7, 21, and 31, pp. 24, 38 and 59. A detailed explanation of the CIA's sizing methodology is provided in Imogene Edwards, Margaret Hughes, and James Noren, "U.S. and U.S.S.R.: Comparisons of GNP", in *Soviet Economy in a Time of Change*, Vol. 1, Joint Economic Committee, U.S. Congress, Washington, DC, 1979, pp. 369-401, and *Consumption in the USSR: An International Comparison*, Joint Economic Committee, U.S. Congress, Washington, DC, 1981. Detailed estimates for 1987 are provided in Table 12.A1. The dollar parity for 1989 was computed from the CIA's statement that the geometric mean in 1989 was about 50 percent. It is possible that the dollar parity was closer to 66 than 67. See CIA, "The Soviet Economy Stumbles Badly in 1989", paper presented to the Joint Economic Committee, U.S. Congress, April 20, 1990, p. A.5.

---

[a]GDP figures to compute these data were converted to US dollars by purchasing power parties calculated by the OECD.

[b]Western area only.

[c]See Table 7, footnotes c and d for an explanation of the methodology used to estimate GDP.

Ruble-Dollar Ratios and Capital Fungibility

The answer reposes in the assumptions underpinning prior estimates of Russia's comparative economic size, and their subsequent disconfirmation. All involve the estimation of dollar-ruble ratios to convert ruble to dollar values, rather than the preferability of various kinds of ruble prices because conversion parities can be tailored to each ruble price standard. The assumptions in question are straightforward. First where microdata are concerned, practioners assumed that qualitative matching based on a few physical indicators yielded reliable conversion parities. Second, it was assumed that the qualitative and structural mix of sectoral aggregates were similar in Russia and the United States when aggregate conversion parities were applied. And finally, if tastes differed significantly in the east and the west, then this difficulty could be overcome by assuming that the capital stock was fungible (putty rather than clay), and therefore capable of producing goods that would satisfy western preferences.

This last assumption seldom made explicit, was the most important because it could be invoked to mitigate disputes regarding the first two potential sources of error. If qualities were not perfectly matched because socialist and capitalist tastes diverged, or because structures differed, fungibility meant that embodied technologies allowed modifications of characteristics and assortments that would remedy the problem. Thus while it was freely acknowledged that dollar estimates of Soviet GNP had to be treated with greater caution than similar estimates for Western Europe, the fungibility assumption justified their use in the appraisal of comparative economic performance.

Revealed Infungibility

The liberalization of the post-Soviet Russian economy has provided an opportunity to test the fungibility assumption. Presumably, if product characteristics were easily transformed, profit maximizing entrepreneurs and collectives should have harnessed the potential of the existing capital stock to produce a new set of goods that validated the old purchasing power parity ratios. As has already been demonstrated this has not happened, even allowing for the effects of Russia's hyperdepression. It follows directly, making generous allowances for other factors including ruble undervaluation that Russia's capital stock is largely infungible, implying that its recovery potential is correspondingly restricted. While the findings in chapter 10 confirm that resources can be transformed into various Soviet era goods in multiproduct firms, infungibility means that they cannot be fabricated into world standard products with the prevailing embodied technology. As a consequence, the old capital stock which has become obsolete in the new competitive environment can only make a relatively modest contribution to Russia's future prosperity.

Obsolescence and Socialist Inefficiency

This deduction illuminates an otherwise concealed aspect of Soviet inefficiency: deficient adaptivity. Soviet planners and designers operated in a stable environment with assured state demand. This encouraged them to disregard the competitive requirements of the global market both with respect to product characteristics and the fungible technologies needed to produce them. Change was controlled and obsolescence risk was small as long as the system endured, but when it collapsed the benefits of insularity vanished leaving Russia with an enormous, but largely worthless capital stock.

During the Soviet period the command and managerial inefficiencies described and estimated in this volume properly took pride of place in scholarly assessments of central planning. Obsolescence shock vivifies the magnitude of these losses, but also reveals that the consequences of administrative command planning have outlived the system. Russian managers and entrepreneurs who seek to adapt to the new environment find themselves fettered by past infungible technological choices that neither adequately foresaw present contingencies, nor the long term needs of global competition. The infungibility of their obsolete equipment impedes modernization, compelling them to scrap what otherwise might have been a key ingredient in the process of rapid recovery. In this regard it seems that Bolshevism's greatest failure was not its misindustrialization, but the adoption of infungible technologies that precludes painless adaptation.

Baseline for Recovery and Development

Obsolescence and infungibility taken together do not bar economic recovery, they merely codetermine the starting point for Russia's third attempt at finding a viable path for self sustaining industrial growth and modernization. Prospects will depend more on the characteristics of the new emergent system, given the Soviet legacy, than the old operational inefficiencies besetting administrative command planning. The methods developed in this volume do not allow this sort of prognostication because the empirical evidence, Kleiner's study aside, is primarily derived from the Soviet experience. But some useful insights can be gleaned about past performance, and the present starting point for the next great leap forward.

First and foremost, the theoretical and quantitative evidence suggest as Roskomstat's now tacitly admits that the Soviet Union was not the second largest economy in the world as prior estimates indicated. The assumptions underlying the old dollar-ruble ratios are simply untenable. The dollar estimates they generate, judging from contemporary calculations of Russia's GDP through what remains a managed exchange rate appear to be overstated by a factor of 4.6.[5] This implies that Soviet GNP in 1989 was nearer 9 percent of the American level rather than the 40.8 percent asserted,[6] before taking account of index number relativity either directly, or through the computation of geometric Fisher ideals. The hyperdepression that ensued has cut this figure to 3.9 percent.[7]

These comparisons need to be adjusted for population. Although the Soviet and American populations were similar in 1989, Russia's population now is only 60 percent of America's. On a per capita basis Russia's GDP was 15,631 dollars, or 68 percent of the United States's in 1989 valued at the old dollar-ruble ratio.[8] It is 3,388 dollars or 14.7 percent at the new ones.[9] Again adjusted for the subsequent hyperdepression, Russia's current GDP per capita is roughly 7 percent of the American standard by the beginning of 1996. Alternative estimates by the World Bank which suffer from arithmetic errors and dubious adjustment methods show a decline of about one third less, but this is partly offset by further subsequent declines in GDP from the second half of 1995 to the end of 1996 (Rossiiskaia Federatsiia, 1995).[10]

These changes have drastically revised perceptions of Russia's position in the world's development hierarchy, demoting it from the second tier in per capita GDP along with Israel, New Zealand, Spain and the United Arab Emirates into the fourth tier, with China, Cuba, Iraq and Thailand. Table 12.2 provides a summary view of Russia's fall given the 1991 standings,[11] and its current GDP. It demonstrates plainly how the use of overvalued dollar-ruble ratios misguided informed impressions of Russia's achievements. This possibility was implied by the CIA's frequent use of geometric ruble-dollar mean estimates, which were misleadingly reported as dollar figures, that placed Russia in the upper part of the third tier at 8,941 dollars per capita along with Saudi Arabia and Kuwait, but failed to convey the full dimensions of the disparity in 1991 when Russia's per capita GDP was actually 2,820 dollars.[12]

Recovery Potential

The proceeding calculations provide the basis for calibrating Russia's recovery potential with the aid of sensitivity analysis. Taking the new dollar-ruble ratios as a point of departure, and putting current capital formation aside, the best case scenario would require a full return to the activity levels of 1989, plus a 10 percent improvement in managerial efficiency in line with the empirical findings for the Soviet period reported on this volume (Cf. *Ekonomicheskii Monitoring Rossii*, 1996). Some additional gains might also accrue from the elimination of command constraints, but they are apt to be offset by the depreciation of the undermaintained Soviet capital stock. Thus Russia's GDP on this count, expressed in 1991 dollars would be 550 billion dollars, with a corresponding per capita figure of 3,679 dollars, placing it in the lower tail of the third development tier, below Mexico,[13] at 16.0 percent of the U.S. standard.

Table 12.2   Gross Domestic Product per Capita, 1991 (in 1991 US $)

More Than $15,000			
Australia	Finland	Liechtenstein	San Marino
Austria	France	Luxembourg	Sweden
Belgium	Germany	Monaco	Switzerland
Bermuda	Iceland	Netherlands	United Kingdom
Canada	Italy	Norway	United States
Denmark	Japan	Qatar	
$10,001 to $15,000			
Andorra	Guam	New Zealand	United Arab Emirates
Aruba	Hong Kong	**Russia (Dollar)**	Virgin Island, British
Cayman Islands	Ireland	Singapore	Virgin Island, US
Faroe Islands	Israel	Spain	
$2,001 to $10,000			
Algeria	Estonia	Mauru	Serbia & Montenegro
American Samoa	Falkland Islands	Man, Isle of	Seychelles
Anguilla	French Guiana	Martinique	Slovenia
Antigua & Bermuda	French	Mauritius	South Africa
Argentina	Polynesia	Mexico	South Korea
Armenia	Gabon	Moldova	Suriname
Azerbaijan	Georgia	Montserrat	Syria
Bahamas, The	Gibraltar	Netherlands Antilles	Taiwan
Bahrain	Greece	New Caledonia	Tajikistan
Barbados	Greenland	Northern Mariana Islands	Trinidad & Tobago
Belarus	Grenada	Oman	Turkey
Bosnia & Hercegovina	Guadeloupe	Pacific Islands, Trust Territory	Turkmenistan
Botswana	Hungary	of	Turks & Caicos Islands
Brazil	Kazakhstan	Panama	Uruguay
Brunei	Kuwait	Poland	Uzbekistan
Bulgaria	Kyrgyzstan	Portugal	Venezuela
Chile	Latvia	Puerto Rico	
Cook Islands	Lithuania	Reunion	
Croatia	Libya	Romania	
Cyprus	Macau	**Russia (Geometric)**	
Czechoslovakia	Macedonia	St. Kitts & Nevis	
Dominica	Malaysia	St. Pierre & Miquelon	
	Malta	Saudi Arabia	

$501 to $2,000			
Albania	Egypt	Mauritania	Solomon Islands
Angola	El Salvador	Mayotte	Swaziland
Belize	Fiji	Micronesia, Federated States of	Thailand
Bolivia	Gaza Strip	Mongolia	Tokelau
Burma	Guatemala	Morocco	Tonga
Cameroon	Honduras	Namibia	Tunisia
Cape Verde	Indonesia	Niue	Tuvalu
China[a]	Iran	North Korea	Vanuatu
Colombia	Iraq	Papua New Guinea	Wallis & Futuna
Comorons	Ivory Coast	Paraguay	West Bank
Congo	Jamaica	Peru	Western Samoa
Costa Rica	Jordan	Philippines	Yemen
Cuba	Kiribati	Russia (Exchange Rate)	Zambia
Djibouti	Lebanon	St. Lucia	Zimbabwe
Dominican Republic	Maldives	St. Vincent & the Grenadines	
Ecuador	Marshall Islands	Senegal	

Less Than $501			
Afghanistan	Gambia, The	Madagascar	Sierra Leone
Bangladesh	Ghana	Malawi	Somalia
Benin	Guinea	Mali	Sri Lanka
Bhutan	Guinea-Bissau	Mozambique	Sudan
Burkina	Guyana	Nepal	Tanzania
Burundi	Haiti	Nicaragua	Togo
Cambodia	India	Niger	Uganda
Central African	Kenya	Nigeria	Vietnam
Republic	Laos	Pakistan	Zaire
Chad	Lesotho	Rwanda	
Equatorial Guinea	Liberia	Sao Tome & Principe	
Ethiopia			

SOURCE: CIA, *Handbook of International Economic Statistics*, **CPAS** 92-10005, September 1992, Figure 1, p. 10.

COMMENTS: Per capita Russian GDP in 1991 was $11,981 computed by adjusting the figure for 1989 in Table 12.1 for the negative growth 1989-1991 shown in Table 12.A2. The geometric mean pseudo dollar estimate is .50/.67 ($11,981) = $8,941. Russian GDP in 1995 was 260 billion dollars; and 220 billion dollars annualized through year's end. Per capita GDP in current dollars is 1,739. See *Russian Economic Trends 1995*, 1996, Table A1, p. 112; Table A17b, p. 140. See note 2. Cf. "The Russian Economy-Stabilization at Last?", *Transition*, World Bank, Vol. 6, No. 5-6, May-June, 1995, p. 20. Russian GDP per capita further adjusted to 1991 dollars is 1,327.

---

*Estimates of China's per capita GDP range from $315 to over $3,000. The wide discrepancy among the figures is in part due to the difficulty of assessing the size and rates of growth for various economic sectors as Beijing attempts to reform its socialist structure, and the poor quality of much of China's data. Nonetheless, many studies have placed China's per capita GDP within the $500 to $2,000 range.

The worst case scenario assumes that the entire decline in Russia's production since 1989 is attributable to the obsolescence and depreciation of its capital stock, and that the alleviation of past inefficiencies, given technological infungibility puts a conjectured ceiling at 20 percent above the current achieved level. Russia's recovery potential in this instance would be 300 billion dollars with a corresponding per capita estimate of 1,994 dollars, placing it in the fourth development tier, near Thailand, at 8 percent of America's level.

Clearly in either scenario, prospects for Russia achieving West European and Japanese standards of living in the first tier depend entirely on new capital formation and the creation of an efficient, competitive market economy; processes that are likely to take decades before full convergence becomes thinkable.

More optimistic forecasts are possible. Should the old Soviet capital stock ultimately prove to be fungible, obsolescence can be overcome by producing new globally competitive goods that validate the old dollar-ruble ratios. In the limit with complete fungibility and competitive efficiency, Russia could attain first tier status, swiftly rivaling the U.S., but this seems extremely improbable. The disagreeable reality appears to be that the inefficiencies of the command system extended to infungibility, impoverished Russia and now confront her with a daunting development problem viewed from the vantage point of what Soviet attainments were; not what they previously seemed to be.[14]

Notes

1.   CIA, *Handbook of International Economic Statistics*, CPAS92-10005, September 1992, Table 7, p. 24.

2.   Personal interview May 17, 1996, Moscow.

3.   Alexander Bulatov, *Ekonomika vneshnykh sviazei Rossii*, 1995.

4.   *Russian Economic Trends, 1995*, Vol. 4, No. 4, 1996, p. 33.

5.   Russia's GDP for 1995 was 96 percent of 1994, or 586,580 rubles in 1994 prices. The average exchange rate in 1994 before the conversion "corridor" was imposed in the Spring of 1996 to appreciate the ruble in real terms was 2,205 rubles per dollar (*Russian Economic Trends*, 1996, Table A1, p. 112; Table A17b,

p. 140). The dollar value of Russia's GDP in 1995 therefore was 266 billion in 1994 dollar prices and 250 dollars in 1991 prices. Cf. "The Russian Economy-Stabilization at Last?", *Transition*, World Bank, Vol. 6, No. 5-6, May-June, 1995, p. 20. The Russian GDP declined by 49.4 percent 1990 through 1994, with a further fall of 9 percent predicted for 1995. See *Economic Survey of Europe in 1993-1994*, Economic Commission for Europe, United Nations Publication, New York and Geneva, 1994; and *Economic Survey of Europe in 1994-1995*, p. 70. Cf. *Rossiiskaia Federatsiia: Doklad o natsional'nykh schetakh*, 1995, pp. xxi. The total contraction 1989 through 1995 is approximately 50 percent, implying a GDP of 532 billion dollars in 1989 before adjustment for U.S. dollar price inflation. The implicit GDP deflator in the first quarter of 1995, 1987=100, was 127.6. See *Survey of Current Business*, U.S. Department of Commerce, Vol. 75, No. 5, May 1995, Table 7.1, p. 23. The implicit index for 1991 was 117.6, and Russian GDP in 1989 valued in 1991 dollars therefore is 532/1.063 = 500 billion dollars. See *Survey of Current Business*, Vol. 74, No. 8, August 1994, Table 7.1, p. 32. The CIA estimated Soviet GNP in 1989 valued in 1991 prices to be 67 percent of the American GNP, or 3,791.7 billion dollars. Russia's GNP, based on its official ruble share of Soviet GNP was (.609) (3,791.7) = 2,309 billion dollars. See CIA, *Handbook of International Economic Statistics*, CPA592-10005, September 1992, Table 7, 21 and 31, pp. 24, 38, and 59. A detailed explanation of the CIA's sizing methodology is provided in Imogene Edwards, Margaret Hughes and James Noren, "U.S. and U.S.S.R.: Comparisons of GNP", in *Soviet Economy in a Time of Change*, Vol. 1, Joint Economic Committee, U.S. Congress, Washington, D.C., 1979, pp. 369-401.

The disparity between the CIA's 1989 Russian GNP (GDP) estimate using the old dollar-ruble ratios and the contemporary one computed through the current exchange rate is 2,309/500 billion dollars = 4.6.

6.   Russian GNP in 1989 computed with the 1994 dollar-ruble ratios explained above is 490 billion dollars in 1991 prices. The corresponding American GNP figure was 5,659.2 report in CIA, *Handbook of International Economic Statistics*, September 1992. The ratio is 490/5,659.2 billion dollars = 0.087. The CIA's estimate

of Russian GNP in 1989 was 2,309 billion dollars, or 2309/5,659.2 billion dollars = .408 of the American level.

7. American GDP in the first quarter of 1995 was 5,470 billion dollars valued at 1987 prices, and 6,979.7 in current prices and 6432.9 in 1991 prices. Russian GDP in 1994 prices is 266 billion dollars and 250 in 1991 prices (see note 5), and the ratio is 250/6,432.9 billion dollars = 0.039. See *Survey of Current Business*, Vol. 75, No. 5, May 1995, Table 2, p. 2.

8. Russia's per capita GNP in 1989 estimated by the CIA was 2,309 billion dollars/.1476 billion people = 15,631 dollars. America's per capita GDP was 22,997 dollars.

9. Russia's per capita GNP in 1989 computed at the 1995 exchange rate expressed in 1995 dollars is 531 billion dollars/.1476 billion people = 3,604 dollars.

10. Russia's per capita GDP 1995 in 1991 prices was 250 billion dollars/.1495 billion people = 1,672 dollars. America's per capita GDP in 1991 prices is 24,514 dollars. See *Survey of Current Business*, Vol. 75, No. 5, May 1995, Table 8.2, p. 29. The ratio is 1,672/24,514 dollars = 0.068.

11. Russia's GDP in 1995 derived through the current exchange rate, and expressed in 1991 dollars is 532/1.063 = 500 billion dollars. Russian GDP fell 40.4 percent 1991 through the first quarter of 1995. See *Economic Survey of Europe in 1994-1995*, Table 3.1.1, p. 70, reproduced in Table S2. Its GDP in 1991 therefore was 1.676 (500) = 838 billion dollars, and on a per capita basis 838 billion dollars/.1476 billion people = 5,678 dollars.

12. *Economic Survey of Europe in 1993-1994*, Economic Commission for Europe, United Nations Publication, New York and Geneva, 1994, p. 33.

13. Russia's GNP in 1989 before its hyperdepression was 500 billion dollars in 1991 prices. A 10 percent boost from enhanced managerial efficiency would raise this figure to 550 billion dollars, or 7.9 percent of America's GDP. The per capita figure 550 billion dollars/.1495 billion people = 3,679 dollars. Mexico per capita

GDP in 1991 value in 1991 prices is 3,198 dollars. See CIA, *Handbook of International Economic Statistics*, 1992, Tables 7 and 24, pp. 25 and 39.

14. If Russia reverts to administrative command planning, and western institutions like the CIA revert to their old dollar ruble values, then Russian GNP could recover to past Soviet levels. This might be heralded by all concerned governments as a grand accomplishment if expediency dictated, but our findings indicate that the victory would be hollow because the real competitive international value of the additional output would be far less than the value of resources squandered.

Bibliography

Afanas"ev, Mikhail, "Command Constrained Efficiency in Soviet Cotton-Refining and the Kaunasskoi Candy Factory", in Steven Rosefielde, ed., *Efficiency and the Economic Recovery Potential of Russia*, forthcoming 1996.

Åslund, Anders, *How Russia Became a Market Economy*, Washington, DC: Brookings Institute, 1995a.

_____, "Russia's Sleaze Sector", *The New York Times*, 11, July 11, 1995b.

_____, "Lessons of the First Four Years of Systemic Change in Eastern Europe", *Journal of Comparative Economics*, 19, 22-38, March 1994.

_____, "How Small Is Soviet National Income?". In Henry Rowen and Charles Wolf, Jr. Eds., *The Impoverished Superpower: Perestroika and the Soviet Military Burden*, 13-62. San Francisco, CA: ICS Press, 1988.

Bergson, Abram, "The Communist Efficiency Gap: Alternative Measures". *Comparative Economic Studies* XXXVI, 1:1-12, Spring 1994.

_____, *Planning and Performance in Socialist Economies*, Boston: Unwin Hyman, 1989.

_____, "Comparative Productivity: the USSR, Eastern Europe and the West", *American Economic Review*, 77, 3:342-357, June 1987.

_____, *Productivity and the Social System--The USSR and the West*, Harvard University Press, Cambridge, Massachusetts, 1978a.

_____, *Soviet Postwar Economic Development*, Almqvist and Wiksell, Stockholm, 1978b.

_____, "National Income", in Bergson and Simon Kuznets, Eds., *Economic Trends in the Soviet Union* 1-37. Cambridge, MA: Harvard University Press, 1963.

_____, *Soviet National Income and Product in 1937*, New York, NY: Columbia University Press, 1953.

Birman, Igor, *Ekonomika nedostach*, New York: Chalidze Publishers, 1983.

Blanchard, Olivier J., Maxim Boycko, Marek Dabrowski, Rudiger Dornbusch, Richard Layard, and Andrei Shleifer, *Post-Communist Reform*, MIT Press, Cambridge, Massachusetts, 1994.

Blanchard, Olivier J., Rudiger Dornbusch, Paul Krugman, Richard Layard, and Lawrence Summers, *Reform in Eastern Europe*, MIT Press, Cambridge, Massachusetts, 1994.

Brada, Josef C. and Arthur E. King, "Is There Still a J Curve for the Economic Transition from Socialism to Capitalism", *Economics of Planning*, Vol. 25, No. 1, 1992, pp. 37-53.

Bulatov, Alexander S., *Ekonomika vneshnykh sviazei Rossii*, Beck, Moscow, 1995.

Campbell, Robert W., *The Postcommunist Economic Transformation: Essays in Honor of Gregory Grossman*, Boulder, CO: Westview, 1994.

CIA, *USSR: Measures of Economic Growth and Development, 1950-80*, Joint Economic Committee of Congress, 175-250, December 8, 1982.

_____, *Handbook of International Economic Statistics*, CPAS 88-10001, September 1988.

_____, *Measuring Soviet GNP: Problems and Solutions*, SOV90-10038, September 1990a.

_____, "The Soviet Economy Stumbles Badly in 1989", paper presented to the Joint Economic Committee, U.S. Congress, April 20, 1990b.

_____, *Handbook of International Economic Statistics*, CPAS 92-10005, September 1992.

Cohen, Ariel, "Crime and Corruption in Eurasia: A Threat to Democracy and International Security", *Transition*, World Bank, 6, 5-6:7-10, May-June, 1995.

Dornbusch, Rudiger, Wilhelm Nölling, and Richard Layard (eds.), *Postwar Economic Reconstruction and Lessons for the East Today*, MIT Press, Cambridge, Massachusetts, 1994.

Edwards, Imogene, Margaret Hughes, and James Noren, *Consumption in the USSR: An International Comparison*, Joint Economic Committee, U.S. Congress, Washington, DC, 1981.

_____, "U.S. and U.S.S.R.: Comparisons of GNP", in *Soviet Economy in a Time of Change*, Joint Economic Committee, U.S. Congress, Washington, DC, 1:369-401, 1979.

Ekonomicheskii Monitoring Rossii: Global'nye tendentsii i kon'iunktura v otrasliakh promyshlennosti, Institut Narodnokhoziaistvennovo prognozirovaniia, RAN, Bulletin 7, Moscow, April 1996.

Ellman, Michael, "Transformation, Depression, and Economics: Some Lessons", *Journal of Comparative Economics*, Vol. 19, No. 1, August 1994, pp. 1-21.

Ericson, Richard, "The Classical Soviet-Type Economy: Nature of the System and Implications for Reform", *Journal of Economic Perspectives*, Vol. 5, No. 4, Fall 1991, pp. 11-28.

_____, "Cost Trade-Offs in Activity Shutdowns: A Note on Economic Restructuring During Transition", in R. Campbell and A. Brzeski, ed., *Issues in the Transformation of Centrally Planned Economies*, Bloomington, IN: Indiana University Press, 1994, pp. 195-217.

_____, "Note on the Input-Output Tables of Centrally Planned Economies", preprocessed March 1996.

Gomulka, Stanislaw, "The Causes of Recession Following Stabilization", *Comparative Economic Studies*, Vol. 33, No. 2, Summer 1991, pp. 71-89.

Hewett, Ed A., *Reforming the Soviet Economy*, The Brookings Institute, Washington DC, 1988.

Intriligator, M., "Privatization in Russia Has Led to Criminalisation", *The Australian Economic Review*, 106:4-14, 1994.

Kaufman, Richard F., "The 'Good' in the Bad Russian Economic Statistical System", *Russia Business Watch*, 14 and 26, August 1994.

Kleiner, George, "Russian Management: A Test for Incomplete Profit Maximization", *Comparative Economic Studies*, XXXVI, 4:101-118, Winter 1994.

Kornai, János, "Transformational Recession: The Main Causes", *Journal of Comparative Economics*, Vol. 19, No. 1, August 1994, pp. 39-63.

Layard, Richard, Oliver J. Blanchard, Rudiger Dornbusch, and Paul Krugman, *East-West Migration*, MIT Press, Cambridge, Massachusetts, 1994.

Leamer, Edward E., and Mark P. Taylor, "The Empirics of Economic Growth in Previously Centrally Planned Economies", April 1994, unpublished manuscript.

Leijonhufvud, Axel, "The Nature of the Depression in the Former Soviet Union", *New Left Review*, 1220-26, May-June 1993.

McFaul, Michael and Tova Permutter, *Privatization, Conversion and Enterprise Reform in Russia*, Boulder, CO: Westview Press, 1995.

Murrell, Paul and Mancur Olson, "The Devolution of Centrally Planned Economies" in Christopher Clague and Gordon C. Rauser (eds.) *The Emergence of Market Economies in Eastern Europe*, Basil Blackwell, Cambridge, Massachusetts, 1992.

Murrell, Peter, "The Transition According to Cambridge, Mass"., *Journal of Economic Literature*, XXXIII, 1:164-178, March, 1995.

Nowakowski, Joseph, "Efficiency at Different Stages of Production in the Soviet Union", *Comparative Economic Studies*, XXVI, 4:79-100, Winter 1994.

OECD, *The Russian Federation 1995*, Paris, 1995.

Osband, Kent, "Economic Crisis in a Shortage Economy", *Journal of Political Economy*, Vol. 100, No. 4, August 1992, pp. 673-89.

Rosefielde, Steven", "The Soviet Economy in Crisis: Birman's Cumulative Disequilibrium Hypothesis", *Soviet Studies* XL, 1:23-43, April 1988.

_____, "Comparative Productivity: The USSR, Eastern Europe and the West: Comment", *American Economic Review* 80, 4:45-54, September 1990.

_____, "Russia's Economic Recovery Potential: Optimizing the Residual Productivity of the Soviet Capital Stock", *Comparative Economic Studies*, XXXVI, 4:119-42, Winter 1994.

_____, Eastern Economic Reform: Transition or Mutation?", *Atlantic Economic Journal*, Vol. 23, No. 4, December 1995a, pp. 323-332.

_____, "Review of Robert Campbell, ed., *The Postcommunist Economic Transformation: Essays in Honor of Gregory Grossman*", *Journal of Economic Literature*, Vol. XXXIII, December 1995b, pp. 2023-2024.

Rosefielde, Steven, and R.W. Pfouts, Economic Optimization and Technical Efficiency in Soviet Enterprises Jointly Regulated by Plans and Incentives, *European Economic Review* 32, 6:1285-1299, 1988.

_____, "Neoclassical Norms and the Valuation of National Product in the Soviet Union and Its Postcommunist Successor States", *Journal of Comparative Economics*, December 1995, pp. 375-389.

Rossiiskaia Federatsiia: Doklad o nationalinykh schetakh, World Bank and Roskomstat, Moscow, October 1995.

Russian Economic Trends 1995, Russian European Centre for Economic Policy, Whurr Publishers, London, Vol. 4, No. 4, 1996.

Rutland, Peter, "Privatisation in Russia: One Step Forward: Two Steps Back?", *Europe-Asia Studies*, Vol. 46, No. 7, 1994.

Sachs, Jeffrey D., "Prospects for Monetary Stabilization in Russia", in Anders Åslund, ed., *Economic Transformation in Russia*, London: Pinter Publishers, 1994.

_____, "Russia's Struggle with Stabilization", *Transition*, World Bank, Vol. 5, No. 4, May-June 1994b, pp. 7-10.

Sterling, Claire, *Thieves' World*, Simon and Schuster, 1994a.

_____, "The Mafia Privatized 50 to 80 Percent of All Shops, Hotels and Services in Moscow", *Transition*, World Bank, Vol. 5, No. 4, April 1994b, pp. 6-7.

Stiglitz, Joseph E., *Whither Socialism*, MIT Press, Cambridge, Massachusetts, 1994.

Taylor, Lance, "The Market Met Its Match: Lessons for the Future from the Transition's Initial Years", *Journal of Comparative Economics*, Vol. 19, No. 1, August 1994, pp. 64-87.

Van Selm, Gijsbertus and E. Dölle, "Soviet Interrepublican Capital Transfers and the Republics' Level of Development, 1966-91", *MOST, Economic Journal on Eastern Europe and the Former Soviet Union*, 1:133-49, 1993.

Van Selm, Gijsbertus and H.J. Wagener, "Soviet Republics' Economic Interdependence", *Osteuropa Wirtschaft*, 1:23-39, 1993.

Williamson, John, "A Persuasive Theory of State Collapse", *Transition*, World Bank, Vol. 5, No. 4, May-June 1994, pp. 11-12.

Winiecki, Jan, "The Inevitability of a Fall in Output in the Early Stages of Transition to the Market: Theoretical Underpinning", *Soviet Studies*, 43, 4:669-76, 1991.

World Bank, *Russian Federation: Report on the National Accounts* (prepared by the Joint Roskomstat-World Bank Team), Confidential, unpublished, 1995.

_____, "The Russian Economy-Stabilization at Last?", *Transition*, 6, 5-6, May-June 1995.

Yavlinsky, Grigory, and Serguey Braguinsky, "The Inefficiency of *Laissez-Faire* in Russia: Hysteresis Effects and the Need for Policy-Led Transformation", *Journal of Comparative Economics*, Vol. 19, No. 1, August 1994, pp. 88-116.

Table 12.A1   Gross National Product, by End Use, in the US and the USSR, 1987[a]

	Billion 1982 Rubles			Billion 1982 US $			Geometric Mean of the Comparisons in Dollars and Rubles
	USSR[b]	US	USSR as a Percent of US	USSR	US	USSR as a Percent of US	USSR as a Percent of US
GNP	766	1,857	41	2,608	3,797	69	53
Of which: Consumption	408	1,536	27	1,253	2,637	48	36
New Fixed Investment	217	233	93	928	776	120	106

SOURCE: CIA, *Handbook for Economics Statistics, 1988*, CPAS 88-10001, September 1988, Table 8, p. 32.

---

[a]The preferred procedure for making international economic comparisons is to convert each country's GNP to the currency of the other. Two comparisons can then be made, one in rubles and one in dollars. The two comparisons will yield different answers. This phenomenon is commonly known as the "index number problem", and it results from differences in the relative price and quantity structures found in each country. Goods produced in relatively large quantities in either country tend to sell at relatively low prices in the country, and vice versa. Soviet GNP is, therefore, a large share of US GNP when comparisons are made in dollars since dollars place a greater weight than ruble prices do on investment and defense goods, which account for larger shares of output in the Soviet Union than in the United States.

The important point about index numbers is that valuations in either rubles or dollars are equally correct. When a single comparison of US and Soviet GNP is required, economists by convention often use the geometric mean of the ruble and dollar comparisons as a reasonable compromise that falls between the two.

The geometric mean comparison is presented here, although the reader is cautioned that it is used for its presentational convenience and does not, strictly speaking represent a more valid result than that presented in either currency.

The estimate of Soviet GNP in dollars presented here is different from that given in Table 7, which uses the geometric mean of the comparisons for consistency with the other data in that table. The approach used in this table, however, is theoretically preferable.

ᵇThe above Soviet GNP data in established prices should not be used in conjunction with Soviet foreign trade data appearing in Tables 138-140. These latter tables use official foreign exchange rates to derive dollar values for trade; we have yet to estimate the value of Soviet foreign trade in terms of actual purchasing power, which would allow for an estimate of the share of foreign trade in Soviet national income.

The magnitudes for the Soviet end-use components were calculated to measure value of output compared with the United States but not the cost in resources. The share of total economic resources devoted to particular end use (such as defense) or the share of total output originating in an individual sector (for example, agriculture or industry) in the USSR should be measured in internal ruble prices and costs.

The identified end uses of GNP are defined as follows: (1) Consumption includes personal expenditures for goods and services for all purposes and noninvestment outlays by government for goods and services for health and education. (2) New fixed investment is defined as the sum of expenditures for gross private domestic investment net of inventories for public construction other than that for military facilities; and for equipment purchased by the government except that for defense. Since part of Soviet capital repair is considered new investment in the Western sense, a portion of Soviet expenditures on capital repair is included in Soviet new fixed investment.

Other uses of GNP include defense, space, research and development, inventory change, administration, net exports, and a statistical discrepancy. The total value for these expenditures cannot be derived for the USSR by subtraction, however.

Table 12.A2   European Transition Countries: Economic Activity, 1990-93 (Percentage Change over Same Period of Preceding Year)

	NMP* or GDP^a					Gross Industrial Output			1993				
	1990	1991	1992	1993	1994 Fore-cast	1990	1991	1992	Jan.-March	Jan.-June	Jan.-Sept.	Jan.-Dec.	1994 Fore-cast
Albania	-13.1	-29.4	-6.0	11.*	8	-7.8	-30.0	..	..	..	..	-1.*	..
Bulgaria^a	-9.1	-11.7	-7.7	-6.*	..	-17.2	-22.2	-16.2	-10.9	-8.2	-8.5	-9.3*	..
Bosnia-Herzegovina	1.6	..	..	..	..	0.9	-10.5	-25	..	..	..	..	..
Croatia^b	-8.5	-29	-8	-8.*	-	-11	-28.5	-14.6	-1.1	-1.5	-3.7	-6.0*	..
Czech Republic^a	-1.2	-14.2	-7.1	-0.5	1.5-2.5	-3.3	-24.4	-10.6	-7.3^c	-6.7^c	-7.4	-7.1^c	-(0-2)
Hungary^a	-3.3	-11.9	-5.0	-2.*	..	-4.5	-19.1	-9.8	0.1	2.4	4.2	3.8	..
Poland^a	-11.6	-7.6	1.5	4.0	4.5	-24.2	-11.9	4.2	7.1	9.3	8.3	7.4	..
Romania^a	-8.2	-13.7	-15.4	1	1.5	-19.0	-18.7	-22.1	-16.0	-6.7	-1.2	1.3	2.0
Slovakia^a	-2.5	-14.5	-7.0	-4.7	..	-4.0	-25.4	-12.9	-26.2	-18.2	-14.7	-15.4	..
Slovenia^a	-4.7	-9.3	-6.0	1	1	-10.5	-12.4	-13.2	-7.4	-6.7	-4.8	-2.8	-2
The FYR of Macedonia^b	-10.2	-12.1	-13.4	-15.0*	-8	-11.0	-17.4	-15.8	-2.3	-7.5	-12.4	-15.0*	-12
Yugoslavia (FR)^b	-8.4	-11.2	-26.1	-30.3	-10	-11.7	-17.6	-22.4	-39.8	-41.1	-38.7	-37.4	..
Eastern Europe	-7.9	-12.3	-7.4	-3	1*	-15.1	-18.1	-10.0	-7.6	-4.6	-3.6	-4*	..
CETE-4	-7.5	-10.2	-2.2	1	3*	-15.3	-16.8	-2.4	0.2	2.2	2.1	2*	..
SETE-8	-8.6	-15.0	-14.5	-8	-2*	-15.0	-19.6	-19.2	-16.7	-12.9	-10.5	-10*	..

	NMP* or GDP[a]					Gross Industrial Output			1993				
	1990	1991	1992	1993	1994 Forecast	1990	1991	1992	Jan.-March	Jan.-June	Jan.-Sept.	Jan.-Dec.	1994 Forecast
Armenia	-8.2	-11.4	-46.0	-9.9	..	-7.5	-7.7	-52.5	-58.4	-51.4	-39.9	-11.1	..
Azerbaijan	-11.3	-0.4	-28.1	-13.3	..	-6.3	4.7	-24.0	-20.4	-12.4	-11.6	-6.8	..
Belarus	-3.2	-1.9	-10.6	-10	..	2.1	-1.0	-9.4	-16.5	-16.3	-14.9	-10.9	..
Georgia	-4.3	..	-43.4	-35	..	-5.7	..	-45.8	..	..	..	-26.6	..
Kazakhstan	-0.9	-10.3	-14.2	-12.8	..	-0.8	-0.9	-14.8	-11.3	-10.7	-11.8	-16.1	..
Kyrgyzstan	4.8	-5.2	-19.0	-17.4	..	-0.6	-0.3	-26.8	-22.4	-24.6	-26.0	-24.2	..
Moldova	-1.5	-18.0	-21.3	-4	..	3.2	-11.1	-21.7	0.2	0.9	7.0	-10[d]	..
Russia	-4.0	-14.3	-22.0	-13	..	-0.1	-8.0	-18.0	-19.3	-18.0	-16.7	-16.2	-12
Russia*	-2.0	-12.9	-18.5	-12	-(8-10)	..	..	..	..	..	..	..	..
Tajikistan	0.2	-8.4	-31.0	-21	..	1.2	-3.6	-24.3	-28.2	-30.5	-24.5	-19.5	..
Turkmenistan	1.8	-4.7	..	7.8	..	3.2	4.8	-16.7	5.1	16.9	15.9	5.3	..
Ukraine	-3.6	-11.2	-16	-16	..	-0.1	-4.8	-9.0	-15.0[d]	-18.0[d]	-18.0[d]	-22.4[d]	..
Uzbekistan	4.3	-2.4	-12.9	-3.5	..	1.8	1.5	-6.2	-3.5	-1.9	4.7	-7[d]	..
CIS	-3.4	-12.2	-19.9	-13	-10*	-1.1	-7.	-18.2	-17.5	-16.1	-14.9	-14.6	..
Estonia[a]	-8.1	-10.0	-14.4	-2*	..	-5.6	-9.0	-38.9	-39.8	-34.9	-31.8	-26.6	..
Latvia[a]	2.7	-8.3	-33.8	-19.9	..	-0.2	-0.6	-35.1	-41.9	-40.9	-38.4	-34.6	..
Lithuania[a]	-6.9	-13.1	-37.7	-17*	..	-2.8	-4.9	-51.6	-52.0	-51.9	-48.5	-46.0	..
Baltic States	-3.9	-10.8	-31.5	-14.8*	-2*	-2.5	-4.2	-43.3	-45.2*	-44.7	-41.7	-38.2	..
Total Transition Economies	-4.8	-12.3	-16.9	-10.0	-6*	-3.6	-8.8	-15.7	-16.3	-15.0	-13.8	-13.8	..
Ex-GDR Länder[a]	-15.5	-29.1	9.7	7.0	6-7	-27.3	-49.1	-6.2	-2.3	2.2	4.4	5.5*	..

SOURCES: *Economic Survey of Europe in 1994-19954*, Economic Commission for Europe, United Nations Publication, New York and Geneva, 1995, p. 70; national statistical publications and statistical office communications to ECE; IMF estimates for Albania; non-governmental forecasts. Aggregates for eastern Europe, the Baltic states and total transition economies are ECE secretariat computations based on 1992 weights and some estimates for missing components. Forecasts for 1994 are generally end-1993 forecasts of national conjunctural institutes.

NOTES: Aggregates are *Eastern Europe* (the 12 countries above that line), with sub-aggregates *CETE*-4 ("central European transition economies": Czech Republic, Hungary, Poland, Slovakia) and *SETE*-8 ("south European transition economies": Albania, Bulgaria, Romania, and the 5 Yugoslav successor states); *CIS* (12 member countries of the Commonwealth of Independent States); *Baltic states* (Estonia, Latvia, Lithuania), and *total transition countries*.

*Net material product (produced) unless otherwise noted.

[a] Gross domestic product.

[b]Gross material product (value added of the material sphere including depreciation).

[c]Enterprises with 25 or more employees.

[d]Sample of physical output indicators. Since March 1993, the Russian Ministry of Statistics publishes two industrial output indicators: one based on deflated gross output value analogous to those shown for other CIS countries, and one based on an aggregation of physical indicators. The former shows much more moderate rates of output contraction in 1993 (5 percent for January-June, 8 percent for January-September, 7.4 percent for January-December), but may be affected by inadequate deflation procedures during a period of rapidly accelerating inflation. Similar physical indicator measures of industrial output for the full year 1993 were also published for Moldova (-10 percent, vs. 4.2 percent growth in deflated output value) and Uzbekistan (-7 percent, vs 4.1 percent growth). The physical indicator values are recorded in the table.

13 Egalitarianism and Production Potential in Postcommunist Russia

Ralph W. Pfouts and Steven S. Rosefielde

Introduction

The legacy of the Soviet Union's labor policies, like the infungibility of its capital stock has profound implications for Russia's economic recovery potential. Under the new economic arrangements instituted by Yeltsin workers can be retrained, reallocated and competitively remunerated which should improve efficiency and production potential, accelerating recovery and modernization. But the various potentials formed in these ways are strongly restricted by the dead hand of the past (Connor, 1996). The privatization program devised by Chubais, and continued under his successor is strongly collectivist, at least on paper. Likewise the job rights guarantees which were the hallmark of Soviet labor policy although diminished continue with the state finding ever changing ways of assisting managers in retaining idle employees. This chapter examines one aspect of Russia's collectivist legacy, egalitarianism, and explains why its revival in the pursut of social justice (Rawls, 1971; Nozick, 1974; Phelps Brown, 1988; Sen, 1995) would likely impair labor efficiency, production potential and recovery, if the community is non-altruistic (Samuelson, 1993).[1]

Egalitarianism

The term egalitarianism denotes a state in which workers are equally remunerated, regardless of occupation, ability, need or effort. It is sometimes used less stringently to describe states that approximate this ideal.[2] To avoid confusion, egalitarianism is reserved here solely for the first usage. The term semi-egalitarianism is employed when income equalization is incomplete.

Egalitarianism may be voluntary or involuntary. In the voluntary case altruism may prevent workers from reserving their effort, thereby assuring that sharing does not immiserate the community. Otherwise, selfish considerations may encourage some individuals to reserve, or even minimize their exertion.

Russian Collectivism

The Russian economy today is collectivist in two senses. First, 75 percent of the 11,463 joint stock companies registered on 31 December 1993 exhibited a large degree of worker ownership and potential control under options of the mass privatization program law promulgated June 1992 and December 1993 (Bornstein, 1994, pp. 423, 436). Workers and managers combined in these firms are entitled to buy 51 percent of the charter capital, giving them absolute control. The majority of these inside shares are in the workers' hands, an advantage which can be enhanced by the purchase of additional shares at voucher auctions (Bornstein, 1994, p. 444). Although the authority of workers as intended by the leadership is circumscribed in many ways including residual state ownership, workers nonetheless are in a position to affect their wages and continue egalitarian traditions carried over from communism (Boyco, Schleifer and Vishny, 1993a,b; Chubais and Vishnevskaya, 1993; Clarke, et.al., 1994; Rutland, 1994; Lainela and Sutela, 1993; Malle, 1994).

Second, the Russian government continues to favor strongly progressive taxation, large welfare transfers especially, through collectivist services, and vocally champions a social safety net. Neither of these two conditions separately or together indicate that the Russian economic system is wholly, or even predominantly collectivist given other aspects of privatization and marketization, but the phenomenon is pronounced enough to warrant treating collectivism as an important feature of the emerging post-transition regime.

The relationship between collectivism and egalitarianism also warrants clarification. Although collective control does not require equal renumeration, the concept of collectivism implies sharing. As a consequence it seems more plausible and consistent for advocates of collectivism to support income equalization within and among firms than advocates of free capitalist enterprise. Collectivism from this perspective can be interpreted as a weak precondition for the adoption of staunchly egalitarian programs.

Egalitarian Collectivist Optimization

Egalitarianism can be achieved in a collectivist economy by requiring that workers in all occupations, and industries receive the same remuneration, or if any income differentials exist, that they be eliminated through taxation. The pure example of the first type to which Russia may be inclined under option 2 of the Chubais privatization program is an egalitarian labor managed commonwealth (Bernstein, 1895), where the net income of firms is distributed equally to members of egalitarian labor managed firms (ELMFs) and the community (ELMC) alike.

This specification has the advantage of subsuming two aspects of collectivism, labor management and social sharing, consistently in a unified framework. If for the sake of realism, it is assumed that the per worker dividends paid members of individual firms in lieu of wages vary from firm to firm due to differences in demand, technology, skill and fixed costs; economy wide income equalization must be accomplished through the use of taxes and transfers. Thus firms earning a dividend per worker greater than the national average pay taxes equal to the product of this difference and the number of enterprise workers, while those with dividends per worker less than average receive a comparable subsidy.

As a context for our arguments we assume a strictly concave production function for each firm. Thus for the ith firm we write

$$x_i = f_i \left(x_{1i}, \ldots, x_{i-1,i}, x_{i+1,i}, \ldots, x_{ni}, y_i \right). \quad \forall_{i=1}^m \qquad (13.1)$$

Here the x's indicate goods and services including all productive factors except labor. Thus x_{ji}, indicates the quantity of good j used in the production of i while y_i indicates the amount of labor used by firm i.

The profit before labor payments, the pie to be divided among the workers, is

$$\pi_i = p_i x_i - \sum_{k \neq i} p_k x_{ki} - F_i, \quad \forall_{i=1}^m$$

where the p's are prices and F is fixed costs. The dividend per worker before interfirm transfers is

$$P_i = \frac{\pi_i}{y_i}, \quad \forall_i \tag{13.2}$$

and the post-transfer egalitarian wage paid all workers regardless of place of employment is the average dividend per worker,

$$\bar{P} = \frac{\sum\limits_{i=1}^{m} P_i \, y_i}{\sum\limits_{i=1}^{m} y_i} = \frac{\sum\limits_{i} \pi_i}{\sum\limits_{i} y_i}. \tag{13.3}$$

For later reference we also record the equilibrium conditions for a ELMF that maximizes dividend per worker (Pfouts and Rosefielde, 1986):

$$P_i \frac{\partial x_i}{\partial x_{ki}} = P_k, \quad \forall_{i=1,k\neq i}^{m} \tag{13.4}$$

$$P_i \frac{\partial x_i}{\partial y_i} = P_i. \tag{13.5}$$

We turn now to certain problems that can arise under an egalitarian regime. First it may be noted from (13.3) that it is necessary that $\sum \pi_i > 0$ for a reasonable outcome. Usually, of course, one would expect that this would be the case, but there is nothing that assures the desired outcome.

Even if $\sum \pi_i$ is sufficiently large there are still serious problems. How should the firms that earn a larger than average dividend behave? Should they try to maximize their dividends per worker even though these will be reduced to the average for the benefit of those who are less productive? Surely they would do this only if they were committed to egalitarianism. History however suggests that unreserved altruism is rare and seldom universal.

Egalitarianism cannot escape this problem. The payment per worker must be the arithmetic mean since this is the only numerical value for which the positive deviations and the negative deviations are equal in absolute amount. The productive must give up part of their earnings to support the less productive. Are the productive willing to face a lifetime of this?

If we assume that the workers are utility maximizers and that altruism plays a limited role in their utility functions then they have no motivation to earn beyond the overall average. Consequently we use the following behavioral rule: (i) *Firms whose dividend per worker is larger than the overall average in time period τ will reduce their dividends per worker in time period τ + 1. Firms where the dividend per worker is equal to or less than the overall average will maintain the same dividend per worker in the next time period.*

The second part of (i) may well impute more altruism to the less productive firms than would actually be warranted. But as will be seen it is not necessary to impose a stronger condition.

We assume further that: (ii) *Both product and non-labor factor prices are fixed either by efficient markets or by the state and remain unchanged during all time periods covered by the discussion.* This postulate serves as a simplifying device which highlights the broad applicability of the approach.

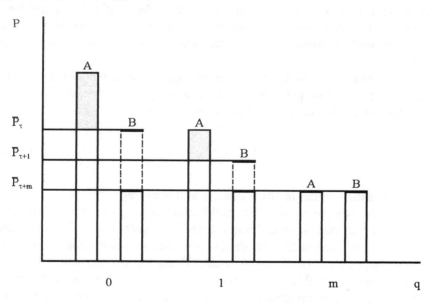

Figure 13.1 Egalitarian Convergence to the Output Minimum: The Two Firm Case

COMMENT: The above mean income in firm A is transferred to the below mean income firm B in each round until a commonwealth-wide egalitarian dividend is achieved.

An examination of (i) and (ii) clearly shows that they lead to a degenerate situation. Firms with per worker dividends above average have considerable latitude to reduce their effort. Since they cannot, or at least, may not be able to judge the overall average of the next time period the size of their dividend reductions cannot be accurately predicted. Consequently, the overall mean might change either rapidly or slowly, perhaps taking a large number of time periods to change appreciably. We therefore have no basis for judging the dividend per worker of each firm in any given time period, or the movements of the system as a whole.

To deal with this complication we modify (i) slightly, imposing a lagged adjustment rule (i'): *Firms whose dividends per worker are larger than the overall average will reduce their dividend per worker in the next time period so that it equals the overall average of the current time period. Those whose dividends are equal to or less than the overall average will maintain the same dividend per worker in the next time period.*

Thus if a firm has an above average dividend per worker in time period τ, its dividend per worker in time period $\tau+1$ must equal the overall average per worker in τ. Or, in an obvious notation

$$P_i \left(\tau + 1 \right) = \overline{P} \left(\tau \right), \qquad \forall_{i=1}^{\psi} \tag{13.6}$$

where ψ is the number of firms that are above average.

Our consideration of the equilibration process can start in any time period in which the system is disequilibrated. At such a time, firms that are above $\overline{P}(\tau)$ will reduce their dividends per worker so that in time period $\tau+1$, they will equal $\overline{P}(\tau)$ i.e. (13.6) will hold. These adjustments will reduce the overall average or $\overline{P}(\tau + 1) < \overline{P}(\tau)$. This may cause some of the firms where per worker dividends were lower than $\overline{P}(\tau)$ to be greater than $\overline{P}(\tau + 1)$ and they along with other above average firms will have to reduce their per worker dividend in $\tau + 2$ so that it equals $\overline{P}(\tau + 1)$. The process will continue to reduce $\overline{P}(\tau + q)$, but there is some firm or firms where the dividend per worker is the lowest. As the overall average falls it will approach this lower bound. It can never go below the minimum dividend per worker. Clearly $\bar{P}(\tau+q) \to \min_{i \in m} P_i(\tau+q)$ as q increases.

Thus (i') and (ii) imply that the firms will equilibrate at a dividend per worker equal to the lowest dividend per worker. This is clearly undesirable and could easily result in economic collapse.

These outcomes of course, hold if (i') and (ii) apply. Clearly other axioms could be developed that would give somewhat different, possibly slightly more favorable, results. But egalitarianism implies using a mean value so that the taxes levied on the more productive firms will provide a sufficient subsidy for the less productive firms. If the more productive firms are permitted to choose their level of output they will be motivated to regress toward the mean and the result will invariably be a diminished national product.

The process of serial contraction can be analyzed further if a rule for organizing production can be suggested. Maximizing the per worker dividend is inappropriate for firms curtailing their activities to levels generating last period's commonwealth-wide per worker dividend.

Suppose these firms decide instead to minimize non-labor costs. They need a logical framework to organize production and minimizing non-labor costs gives them a feasible basis. It is difficult to visualize any other basis because they are in a process of reducing workers' dividends which precludes the usual optimization goal, dividend maximization. Minimizing non-labor cost provides a defensible alternative because it conserves society's resources. Thus if the firms minimize non-labor costs while generating a dividend equal to the overall dividend of the last period, the Lagrangian, using a time index, is

$$L_i(\tau) = \sum_{k \neq i} p_k x_{ki}(\tau) - F_i - \mu_i(\tau) \left(\frac{p_i x_i(\tau) - \sum_{k \neq i} p_k x_{ki}(\tau) - F_i}{y_i(\tau)} - \bar{P}(\tau - 1) \right). \quad \forall_{i=1}^m$$

The relevant first order conditions are

$$\frac{\partial L_i(\tau)}{\partial x_{ki}(\tau)} = p_k - \mu_i(\tau) \left(\frac{p_i \frac{\partial x_i(\tau)}{\partial x_{ki}(\tau)} - p_k}{y_i(\tau)} \right) = 0$$

or

$$p_k \left(1 + \frac{y_i(\tau)}{\mu_i(\tau)} \right) = p_i \frac{\partial x_i(\tau)}{\partial x_{ki}(\tau)}, \qquad \forall_{i=1, k \neq i}^{m} \qquad (13.7)$$

and

$$\frac{\partial L_i(\tau)}{\partial y_i(\tau)} = -\mu_i(\tau) \left(\frac{p_i \dfrac{\partial x_i(\tau)}{\partial y_i(\tau)}}{y_i(\tau)} - \frac{p_i x_i(\tau) - \sum\limits_{k \neq i} x_{ki}(\tau) p_k - F_i}{y_i(\tau)^2} \right) = 0$$

or

$$p_i \frac{\partial x_i(\tau)}{\partial y_i(\tau)} = P_i(\tau). \qquad (13.8)$$

The quantities in the parentheses in (13.7) are positive, and hence comparing (13.7) and (13.4) reveals that contracting firms will reduce their non-labor factors, while employment rises, according to (13.8) because $P_i(\tau) < P_i(\tau-1)$.

But can this excess labor demand be satisfied? Not likely. Workers have no incentive to change because their dividends are the same regardless of their employer. The authorities could compel workers to move from low to high productivity firms in order to generate a stable pan-commonwealth egalitarian per worker dividend above the unconstrained minimum, but any attempt of this sort undoubtedly would encounter formidable locational and practical difficulties.

Of course if there were a pool of unemployed labor then workers would be available. But unemployment and egalitarianism are mutually exclusive concepts, implying injustice for one group or the other. If all workers are to be treated fairly, they must be employed regardless of the need for their services, forcing us to conclude that productivity cannot be stabilized at a high level and that the system will be plagued by inefficiency as workers in more productive enterprise are thwarted in their efforts to minimize non-labor factor costs. Under these conditions (13.7) would hold and (13.8) would be impossible. Fewer non-labor factors would be used with the same amount of labor, and the relative scarcity of non-labor factors would force workers to reserve their efforts.

Semi-Egalitarianism

The perverse behavioral potential of non-altruistic ELMCs can be traced to the tax-transfer rules which require participants to subordinate considerations of income, utility and social welfare to the higher goal of equality. Rewards in this system are uncorrelated with effort, and are largely outside the control of individual participants. This suggests that egalitarians should consider tolerating some income differentiation in collectively privatized eastern firms to maintain acceptable living standards. One way to bolster production within the framework of the egalitarian commonwealth is to raise the ceiling on confiscatory taxation so that fewer firms reserve their effort. However, in doing so, some workers must earn more than others even if all subsidized firms receive the same after-transfer per worker dividend because the cap exempts some firms with per worker incomes above the commonwealth mean from taxation. The magnitude of this inequality will depend on the scale of exemption on average, and special concessions to selected enterprises, if any. Semi-egalitarian income disparities can be narrowed by increasing the scope of taxation, and widened by diminishing it. Our analysis thus points to a continuous tradeoff between equity and income when members of the community are non-altruistic.

This result can be softened by replacing confiscatory with graduated taxation on per worker dividends. The step function in Diagram 2 illustrates the approach, where the tax rates, the r's, are arrayed on one scale and the dividend per worker on the other.

The tax per worker paid by firm j is given by

$$t_j = \sum_{i=1}^{q-1} r_i \left(P_{j,i+1} - P_{ji} \right) + r_q \left(P_{jq} - P_{j,q-1} \right)$$

where $0 < \max r_j < 1, \forall_j$.

Thus the total tax paid by the firm is

$$T_j = y_j \, t_j \tag{13.9}$$

and the total paid by all taxed firms is

$$T = \sum_j T_j. \qquad (13.10)$$

Consequently the after-tax dividend per worker in firm j is

$$\hat{P}_j = P_j - t_j > 0. \qquad (13.11)$$

Maximization of the after-tax dividend requires that (13.4) and (13.5) be satisfied.

The taxes, of course, would be used to provide subsidies for the firms that earn smaller dividends per worker. The decision regarding which firms should be taxed and which subsidized is determined by the authorities using whatever standards they deem appropriate. But one rule they might find appealing, in the spirit of our previous axioms, is that the dividend of the firm or firms with the lowest after-tax dividend should exceed that of the firm or firms with the largest subsidized dividend. The authorities must decide how great the difference can be and still prevent or minimize effort reservation by the more productive firms. Indeed a skeptic might question the existence of such a difference. This decision must be based on subjective considerations and thus may appear to be without a solid foundation. Yet it is evident that any government that imposes a graduated income tax makes a comparable decision and often, but not always, the decision is successful.

If we let

$$\overset{v}{P}_k = P_k + s_k,$$

where s_k is the subsidy per worker in firm k, then the preceding rule requires that

$$\min \hat{P}_j \geq \max \overset{v}{P}_k + h \qquad (13.12)$$

i.e., j indexes the more profitable firms and k the less profitable and h represents a difference the authorities believe will prevent idling by the more productive workers. Since the inequality holds for the firm with the smallest after-tax dividend, it holds for all the tax paying firms. Hence

$$\hat{P}_j \geq \max_k \overset{v}{P_k} + h \quad \forall_j.$$

We may substitute from (13.11) into the last inequality and rearrange obtaining

$$t_j \leq P_j - \max_k \overset{v}{P_k} - h \quad \forall_j$$

which sets a bound on the tax levied on each worker's dividend. This also implies a bound on the tax paid by each firm:

$$T_j = y_j t_j \leq y_j \left(P_j - \max_k \overset{v}{P_k} - h \right)$$

or using (13.2)

$$T_j \leq \pi_j - y_j \left(\max_k \overset{v}{P_k} + h \right).$$

A bound on the total tax payment is also implied:

$$T = \sum_j T_j \leq \sum_j \pi_j - y_j \left(\max_k \overset{v}{P_k} + h \right). \tag{13.13}$$

To pursue the analysis further we need to consider how the subsidies are allocated among the less profitable firms. No doubt there are many ways that this could be done, but one that would appeal to egalitarian minded authorities would be to require that all subsidized firms have the same after subsidy dividend. In other words

$$\max_k \overset{v}{P_k} = \overset{v}{P_k}. \quad \forall_k$$

We need also to note that the total tax revenue must be sufficient to cover the subsidies and the administrative costs of the tax-subsidy program. We assume for simplicity that the subsidies and administrative costs are met from annual taxes. In other words no fund is accumulated to permit larger subsidies or lesser taxes at some future time although some of the tax might be used for unrelated purposes. Thus in an obvious notation

$$T \gtreqless S + A, \tag{13.14}$$

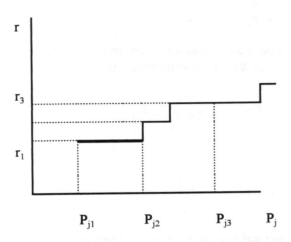

Figure 13.2   Graduated Taxation and Semi-egalitarian Dividend Maximization

If $\overset{v}{P}_k$, the after subsidy dividend, is to be the same for all subsidized workers, it cannot be less than max P_k. The largest member of the set cannot be taxed because it is excluded from the category of taxed firms, and therefore with min s_k added must be the subsidized dividend for each member of the group. Also it is clear that min s_k could be zero.

Thus equal subsidized dividends require

$$\sum_k y_k \left(\max P_k + \min s_k - P_k \right) = S \lesseqgtr T - A,$$

where use is made of (13.14). Using (13.2), the last inequality may be written as

$$T \overset{v}{\geq} \max P_k \sum_k y_k - \sum_k \pi_k + A,$$

which gives a lower bound for T.

The inequality immediately above may be combined with (13.13) to yield

$$\max \overset{v}{P_k} \sum_k y_k - \sum_k \pi_k + A \leq T \leq \sum_j \pi_j - \left(h + \max \overset{v}{P_k} \right) \sum_j y_j$$

thus giving a lower and upper bound for T. From the last we have

$$\max \overset{v}{P_k} \leq \frac{\sum_j \pi_j + \sum_k \pi_k - h \sum_j y_j - A}{\sum_k y_k + \sum_j y_j}.$$

The inequality immediately above could be used to estimate the greatest acceptable value of max $\overset{v}{P}$ because the quantities on the right would be known or could be estimated. Obviously the largest acceptable value of max $\overset{v}{P}$ would be that for which the equality holds.

Another possible way of overcoming the labor reservation problem posed by egalitarianism is to offer managers bonuses based on the outputs of their firms. For this to succeed it is necessary that the managers be able, by whatever means, to induce the workers to make a maximum labor effort in spite of the taxation of their dividends.

If the managers can do this then a managerial bonus based on the worker's pre-tax dividend will cause the managers to produce at a dividend maximizing level of output because this is also the bonus maximizing level of output. Or bonuses might be made to depend on the profit before labor dividends are paid, the variable denoted by π in earlier discussion. If this is done, labor will be used to the point where its marginal product is zero. This is the case because managers now want to maximize π and no longer care about the dividend for individual workers, thus it pays them to produce more than in the case where the workers' dividend is maximized.

Any use of managerial bonuses to sustain labor effort depends, as was noted, on the managers abilities to motivate the workers to put forth a maximum effort for which they will be penalized. This needs no further comment.

Conclusion

Egalitarianism is an enticing ideal which despite obvious defects has long attracted intellectual attention. It therefore comes as no surprise that while Russia is trying to empower its economy through collectivist privatization, it is simultaneously endeavoring to curb its inegalitarian consequences. Close analysis at the level of the ELMC reveals however that egalitarianism is apt to degrade efficiency, production potential and Russia's recovery prospects if the community is not altruistic, regardless of its professed convictions. It follows directly that if Russia persists in institutionalizing collectivist and egalitarian elements of its Soviet past, prosperity may prove elusive.

Notes

1. Altruism is a term first coined by the positivistic followers of Comte, meaning unselfish concern for others. It is the antonym for egoism. In the present context the term means a willingness to work for the benefit of others without personal compensation, interpreted broadly to include cases where the altruist's utility function is dependent or independent of the utility of other members of the community.

2. The requirement of equal remuneration does not imply that all members of society enjoy the same utility in consumption, although it may often be supposed that this is so. Compensatory schemes that satisfy this higher standard raise intractable issues of measurement, veracity and social consensus which go beyond the scope of this essay.

Bibliography

Aganbegyan, Abel, *Inside Perestroika: The Future of the Soviet Economy*. Harper and Row, New York, 1990.

_____, *The Economic Challenge of Perestroika*, Indiana University Press, Bloomington, 1988.

Aleksashenko, Sergei and Leonid Grigoriev, "Privatisation and the Capital Market", *Communist Economies and Economic Transformation*, Vol. 3, No. 1, 1991, pp. 41-56.

Allocation of Resources in the Soviet Union and China, Joint Economic Committee of Congress, April 14, 1989.

Andreoni, James, "Privately Provided Public Goods in a Large Economy: The Limits of Altruism", *Journal of Public Economics*, Vol. 35, No. 1, February 1988, pp. 57-73.

_____, "Impure Altruism and Donations to public Goods: A Theory of Warm-Glow Giving?", *Economic Journal*, Vol. 100, No. 401, June 1990, pp. 464-77.

Bergson, Abram, "Socialist Economics", in Bergson, *Essays in Normative Economics*, Belknap, Cambridge, Mass., 1966.

_____, "Comparative Productivity: The USSR, Eastern Europe and the West", *American Economic Review*, Vol. 77, No. 3, June 1987, pp. 342-357.

Bernstein, Edward, *Cromwell and Communism*, Schocken, New York, 1895.

Bim, Aleksandr S., Derek C. Jones and Thomas E. Weisskopf, "Hybrid Forms of Enterprise Organization in the Former USSR and the Russian Federation", *Comparative Economic Studies*, Vol. 35, No. 1, Spring 1993, pp. 1-37.

Bonin, John, and Louis Putterman, *Economics of Cooperation and the Labor-Managed Economy*, Harwood, London, 1987.

Bornstein, Morris, "Privatisation in Eastern Europe", *Communist Economies and Economic Transformation*, Vol. 4, No. 3, 1992, pp. 282-320.

Boycko, Maxim and Andrei Shleifer, "The Voucher Programme for Russia" in Anders Aslund and Richard Layard (eds.), *Changing the Economic System in Russia*, Pinter Publishers: London, 1993, pp. 100-111.

Boycko, Maxim, Andrei Shleifer and Robert W. Vishny, "Privatizing Russia", *Brookings Paper on Economic Activity*, No. 2, 1993, pp. 139-192.

Bradley, Michael and Stephen Smith, "On Illyrian Macroeconomics", *Economica*, Vol. 55, No. 218, May 1988, pp. 249-59.

Buchanan, James M. and Gordoni Tullock, *The Calculus of Consent*, Ann Arbor: University of Michigan Press, 1962.

Chubais, Anatolii and Maria Vishnevskaya, "Main Issues of Privatization in Russia" in Anders Aslund and Richard Layard (eds.), *Changing the Economic System in Russia*, Pinter Publishers: London, 1993, pp. 89-99.

CIA and DIA, *Gorbachev's Economic Program: Problems Emerge*, DDB-1900-187-88, Washington, D.C., 1988.

Clarke, Simon, et.al, "The Privatisation of Industrial Enterprises in Russia", *Europe-Asia Studies*, Vol. 46, No. 2, 1994, pp. 179-214.

Coate, Stephen, "Altruism, The Samaritan's Dilemma, and Government Transfer Policy", *The American Economic Review*, Vol. 85, No. 1, pp. 46-57.

Cohen, G.A., "On the Currency of Egalitarian Justice", *Ethics*, Vol. 99, No. 4, July 1989, pp. 906-44.

Conner, Walter, *Tattered Banners: Labor, Conflict and Corporatism in Postcommunist Russia*, Boulder, CO: Westview Press, 1996.

De Jouvenel, Bertrand, *The Ethics of Redistribution*, Liberty Press, 1990.

Domar, Evsey, "The Soviet Collective Farm as a Producer Cooperative", *American Economic Review*, Vol. 56, No. 4, September 1966, pp. 734-757.

"Draft Constitution of the Federation Published", FBIS SOV92 063, 1 April 1992.

Estrin, Saul, and V. Perotin, "Cooperatives and Participating Firms in Great Britain", *International Review of Applied Economics*, Vol. 1, 1987, pp. 152-76.

Filtzer, Donald A., "The Contradictions of the Marketless Market: Self-Financing in the Soviet Industrial Enterprise, 1986-90", *Soviet Studies*, Vol. 43, No. 6, 1991, pp. 989-1009.

Frydman, Roman, Andrzej Rapaczynski and John Earle, *The Privatization Process in Central Europe*, CEU Press, London, 1993.

Gorbachev, Mikhail, *On the Tasks of the Party in the Radical Restructuring of Economic Management*, Novosti, Moscow, 1987.

Hanson, Philip, "Property Rights and the New Phase of Reforms", *Soviet Economy*, Vol. 6, No. 2, April-June 1991, pp. 95-124.

Ireland, Norman, and Peter Law. *The Economics of Labor-managed Enterprises*. New York, St. Martins Press, 1982.

Isaev, Aleksandr, "Reforma i oboronnye otrasli", *Kommunist*, No. 5 (1339), March, 1989, pp. 24-30.

Jones, Anthony and William Moskoff, *Ko-ops: The Rebirth of Entrepreneurship in the Soviet Union*, Indiana University Press: Bloomington, IN, 1991.

Kang, Suk, "Fair Distribution Rule in a Cooperative Enterprise", *Journal of Comparative Economics*, Vol. 12, No. 1, March 1988, pp. 89-92.

Keren, Michael, "Privatization in Eastern Europe and the Soviet Union", *Jahrbuch det Wirtschaft Osteuropas*, Vol. 14, No. 2, 1990, pp. 159-185.

Lainela, Seija and Pekka Sutela, "Russian Privatization Policies" in Pekka Sutela (ed.), *The Russian Economy in Crisis and Transition*, Bank of Finland: Helsinki, 1993, pp. 81-110.

Lange, Oscar, "On the Economic Theory of Socialism", in   Benjamin Lippincott, ed., *On the Economic Theory of Socialism*, McGraw Hill, New York, 1964.

Le Grand, Julian, *The Strategy of Equality*, George Allen and Unwin, London, 1982.

_____, "Equity as an Economic Objective", *Journal of Applied Philosophy*, Vol. 1, No. 1, 1984 pp. 39-51.

Le Grand, Julian and Saul Estrin, *Market Socialism*, Clarendon Press, Oxford, 1989.

Lindbeck, Assar and Jorgen W. Weibull, "Altruism and Time Consistency: The Economics of Fait Accompli", *Journal of Political Economy*, Vol. 96, No. 6, December 1988, pp. 1165-82.

Malle, Silvana, "Developments in the Cooperative and Private Sector" in Reiner Weichhardt (ed.), *The Soviet Economy Under Brezhnev*, NATO: Brussels, 1991, pp. 39-67.

_____, "Privatization in Russia: A Comparative Study in Institutional Change" in László Csaba (ed.), *Privatisation, Liberalisation, and Destruction: Creating the Market in Central and Eastern Europe*, Dartmouth Publishing Company: Aldershot, 1994, pp. 71-101.

Mason, David and Svetlana Sydorendo, "Perestroika, Social Justice, and Soviet Public Opinion", *Problems of Communism*, Vol. XXXIX, November-December, 1990, pp. 34-43.

McAuley, Alastair, "Social Welfare Under Socialism: A Study of Soviet Attitudes Toward Redistribution", in Collard, et al., *Income Distribution: The Limits of Redistribution*, Halsted Press, John Wiley and Sons, New York, 1980.

Meade, James, *Efficiency, Equality and the Ownership of Property*, Harvard University Press, 1965.

_____, *Alternative Systems of Business Organization and Workers' Remuneration*, George Allen and Unwin, London, 1986.

Meyer, Monique, "Vouchers and the Financing of the Russian Economy", *Moct-Most*, 3, November 1993, pp. 95-125.

Miller, David, *Market, State and Community: Theoretical Foundations of Market Socialism*, Oxford University Press, Oxford, 1990.

Moulin, Herve, "Egalitarianism and Utilitarianism in Quasi- linear Bargaining", *Econometrica*, Vol. 53, 1985, pp. 49-67.

_____, "Equal or Proportional Division of a Surplus, and Other Methods", *International Journal of Game Theory*, Vol. 16, 1987, pp. 161-186.

Nove, Alec, *The Economics of Feasible Socialism*, George Allen and Unwin, London, 1983.

Nozick, Robert, *Anarchy, State, and Utopia*, Basic Books, New York, 1974.

Nuti, Domenico Mario, "Market Socialism: The Model That Might Have Been, But Never Was", Paper presented at the IV World Congress of Soviet and East European Studies, Harrogate, England, July 21-27, 1990.

Organization for Economic Cooperation and Development (OECD), *Valuation and Privatization*, Paris, 1993.

Pfouts, Ralph W., and Steven Rosefielde, "The Firm in Illyria: Market Syndicalism Reconsidered", *Journal of Comparative Economics*, Vol. 10, No. 2, June 1986, pp. 160-170.

Phelps Brown, Henry, *Egalitarianism and the Generation of Inequality*, Clarendon Press, Oxford, 1988.

Plant, Raymond, *Equality, Markets and the State*, Fabian Pamphlet No. 494, Fabian Society, London, 1984.

Plokker, Karin, "The Development of Individual and Cooperative Labour Activity in the Soviet Union", *Soviet Studies*, Vol. 42, No. 3, 1990, pp. 403-429.

Prasnikar, Janez, Jan Svejnar, Dubravko Mihaljek and Vesna Prasnikar, "A Test of Enterprise Behavior Under Labor-Management", Working Paper No. 247, Department of Economics, University of Pittsburgh, July 1989.

Rawls, John, *A Theory of Justice*, Harvard U.P., Cambridge, 1971.

Romer, John, "A Future For Socialism", Harvard University Press, Cambridge, MA, 1994.

Rose-Ackerman, Susan, "Altruism, Nonprofits, and Economic Theory", *Journal of Economic Literature*, Vol. XXXIV, No. 2, June 1996, pp. 701-728.

Rosefielde, Steven, "Comparative Productivity: Comment", *American Economic Review*, Vol. 80, No. 4, September 1990, pp. 45-54.

_____, "Democratic Market Communism: Gorbachev's Design for Utopia", *Shogaku Ronshu, (Fukushima Journal of Commerce, Economics, and Economic History)*, Vol. 59, No. 3, March 1991a, pp. 15-23.

_____, "The Illusion of Material Progress: The Analytics of Soviet Economic Growth Revisited", *Soviet Studies*, Vol. XXXIII, No. 2, July 1991b, pp. 597-611.

_____, "Beyond Catastroika: Prospects for Market Transition in the Commonwealth of Independent States", *Atlantic Economic Journal*, Vol. 20, No. 1, March 1992 pp. 2-9.

Rosefielde, Steven and R.W. Pfouts, "Economic Optimization and Technical Efficiency in Soviet Enterprises Jointly Regulated by Plans and Incentives", *European Economic Review*, Vol. 32, No. 6, 1988, pp. 1285-1299.

_____, "Towards the Privatization of the CIS Weapons Industry: The `Collectivist Option'", *Economics of Planning*, Vol. 26, No. 2, 1993, pp. 143-160.

Russian Federation (RF), "Statute on the Commercialization of State-Owned Enterprises with Simultaneous Conversion into Public-Type Stock Corporations" (approved by Presidential edict 721, 1 July 1992), FBIS, USR-92-098, August 5, 1992, pp. 38-48. (Translated from *Rossiiskaya Gazeta*, July 7, 1992, pp. 4-5.)

_____, "Special Features in the Privatization and Reorganization of State Enterprises and Production and Scientific-Production Associations in the Oil and Refining Industries and Industries Providing Petroleum Products into Joint-Stock Companies" (Presidential edict 1403, November 17, 1992), FBIS, USR-92-163, December 23, 1992, pp. 44-46. (Translation from *Rossiiskie Vesti*, December 5, 1992, p. 4.)

_____, "Changeover to Joint-Stock Companies and Privatization of State Enterprises, Associations, and Organizations of the Russian Federation Gas Industry" (Presidential edict 1559, December 8, 1992), FBIS, USR-93-006, January 15, 1993, pp. 42-44. (Translation from *Rossiiskaya Gazeta*, January 5, 1993, p. 5.)

Rutgaizer, V., "Privatizatsiya v Rossii: dvizhenie 'na oshchup'", Part I, *Voprosy ekonomiki*, 10, October 1993, pp. 48-63.

Samuelson, Paul, "Altruism as a Problem Involving Groups Versus Individual Selection in Economics and Biology", paper presented at the American Economics Meetings, Anaheim, California, January 6, 1993.

Sen, Amartya, "Rationality and Social Choice", *The American Economic Review*, Vol. 85, No. 1, March 1995, pp. 1-24.

Shlapentokh, Vladimir, "Privatization Debates in Russia: 1989-1992", *Comparative Economic Studies*, Vol. 35, No. 2, Summer 1993, pp. 19-32.

Shleifer, Andrei and Maxim Boycko, "The Politics of Russian Privatization" in Olivier Blanchard, et.al., *Post-Communist Reform: Pain and Progress*, MIT Press: Cambridge, MA, 1993, pp. 37-80.

Sutela, Pekka, "Rationalizing the Centrally Managed Economy: Probing for the Limit", Paper presented at the IV World Congress of Soviet and East European Studies, Harrogate, England, July 21-27, 1990.

Svejnar, Jan, "On the Theory of a Participatory Firm", *Journal of Economic Theory*, Vol. 27, 1983, pp. 313-30.

Vanek, Jaroslav, *The General Theory of Labor-Managed Market Economies*, Ithaca, NY: Cornell University Press, 1970.

Ward, Benjamin, "The Firm in Illyria: Market Syndicalism", *American Economic Review*, Vol. 48, No. 4, September 1958, pp. 566-589.

Weisskopf, Thomas, "Democratic Self-Management: An Alternative Approach to Economic Transformation in the Former Soviet Union", in Silverman et.al., ed., *Double Shift, Transforming Work in Post-Socialist and Post-Industrial Societies*, M.E. Sharpe, Armonk, 1993.

Weitzman, Martin, "Some Macroeconomic Implications of Alternative Compensation Systems", *Economic Journal*, Vol. 93, 1983, pp. 763-83.

_____, *The Share Economy*, Harvard University Press, Cambridge, 1984.

Wiles, Peter, *The Political Economy of Communism*, Oxford University Press, Oxford, 1964.

Yanowitch, Murray, "The Problem of Egalitarianism: Continuities and Changes in Soviet Attitudes", in Silverman, et.al., ed. *Double Shift, Transforming Work in Post-Socialist and Post-Industrial Societies*, M.E. Sharpe, Armonk, 1993.

14 Trade and Production Potential: Evidence from the Changing Embodied Factor Proportions of Russia's Trade with Japan

Steven S. Rosefielde

Introduction

Whether Russia's leaders decide to scrap the old Soviet capital stock, or maximize the recovery and modernization of the nation's production potential by adopting an optimal retirement program, the efficiency of transition will depend significantly on their handling of foreign trade. Little will be gained if Russia replaces one obsolete capital stock with another, or the pace of transition is impeded by the inefficient conduct of international trade. Russia needs to maximize its gains from trade, using this mechanism to realize its long run generally competitive production potential.

This chapter attempts to shed light on Russia's prospects by studying the embodied factor content of its trade with Japan. It will be shown using Heckscher-Ohlin theory and Leontief statistics that after years of deterioration, the pattern of trade in the nineties has become more rational, providing some hope that Russian efficiency is improving, and its production potential has begun to converge toward the global norm.

The Heckscher-Ohlin Foreign Trade Efficiency Test

According to the Leontief variant of Heckscher-Ohlin theory for a single country, imports (exports) should intensely embody scarce (abundant) domestic factors, if the productivities of domestic technologies are the same across sectors, rents of all sorts do not distort the pattern of factor embodiment, and the sectoral structure of foreign technologies is not offsetting,[1] regardless of whether the multinational requirements for commodity and factor price equalization elaborated by Samuelson are satisfied.[2] If imports and exports are governed by factor availabilities under these circumstances, and price data are consistent with the composition of trade then it can be inferred that commerce is rational (but not necessarily efficient). If they are not, then trade is either ambiguously rational (proper factor proportions, but improper trade composition), or even irrational in the sense that production potential and/or welfare decline absolutely because under the prevailing regime the high opportunity cost factor may not only be inefficiently exported, but the derivative profits if any many not compensate for the domestic income foregone.[3] Theoretians should also note that factor and commodity prices cannot be globally and competitively equalized in accordance with factor availabilities if any nation exports its scarce factor intensive and imports its abundant factor intensive products. The violation of the Leontief variant of Heckscher-Ohlin rationality if it occurs, thus serves as a proof that the Samuelson variant is empirically falsified.

This same methodology can also be harnessed to assess variations in foreign trade performance. Trends in Leontief statistics and comparative international price advantage can illuminate whether foreign commerce is becoming more or less rational and/or efficient, subject to diverse qualifications. This property is especially useful for appraising the consequences of epochal changes like the collapse of communism on foreign trade performance.

Soviet/Russian Foreign Trade

The hypothesis that foreign trade performance improved under postcommunism is not intuitively compelling. Official data presented in Tables 14.1 and 14.2 reveal that imports and exports expressed in current dollars have fallen drastically since 1990, implying that the new system has been trade destroying rather than market creating. The only ostensible counter-evidence is the relatively good performance of Russian exports to the developed west which declined less precipitously than the gross domestic product, especially in 1993. The same picture holds for Russian imports from Japan, with exports seeming to behave unusually well because of the appreciation of the yen against the dollar. The data in Table 14.3 confirm a strong rebound in 1993 from the low levels of the preceding year, but provide little evidence of deeper structural transformation.

Table 14.1 **Foreign Trade of Transition Countries, by Direction, 1991-1993 (Value in billion US dollars: growth rates in percentages)[a]**

	Exports				Imports			
	VALUE	GROWTH RATES			VAL-UE	GROWTH RATES		
Country or Country Group[b]	1992	1991	1992	1993[c]	1992	1991	1992	1993[c]
Eastern Europe, to or from:								
World	53.3	-6.9	-4.8	-13.5	60.6	-4.1	1.1	6.7
Transition Economies	12.3	-24.6	-21.2	-11.9	15.2	-19.8	-3.2[e]	0.5[e]
Soviet Union/Successor States	5.4	-25.1	-31.7[e]	-17.6[e]	8.8	-9.3	-6.5[e]	4.8[e]
Eastern Europe[d]	3.0	-20.1	-9.7[e]	-8.0[e]	2.8	-25.8	-4.4[e]	1.8[e]
Developed Market Economies	34.9	6.6	0.4	-14.3	39.6	7.8	9.2	11.2
Developing Countries	6.1	-11.8	8.1	-12.0	5.8	-9.2	-22.1	-6.4
Russia/Soviet Union,[f] to or from:								
	38.1	-24.6	-25.2	-0.8	35.0	-35.9	-21.3	-45.6
World	11.3	-35.0	-25.8	-11.8	8.0	-43.4	-42.8	-43.4
Transition Economies[d]	7.8	-40.8	-32.7[g]	-15.4[g]	5.5	-51.6	-	-54.9[g]
Eastern Europe[d]	22.9	-16.2	-20.3	4.3	22.5	-31.0	49.7[g]	-48.6
Developed Market Economies	3.9	-29.0	-44.0	0.9	4.5	-35.8	-13.0	-36.1
Developing Countries							-2.6	

SOURCES: Secretariat of the United Nations Economic Commission for Europe, based on national statistical publications and direct communications to the NATIONS secretariat from national statistical offices. Table 3.1.1, United Nations Economic Commission for Europe, *Economic Bulletin for Europe*, Vol. 45, 1993.

NOTE: Eastern Europe: 1992 value and growth rates for 1992 and 1993 exclude trade of Bosnia-Herzegovina and the FYR of Macedonia, for which no data are available.

---

[a]Growth rates are calculated on values expressed in US dollars. Trade with "transition" and east European countries in 1990 was revalued on the basis of an adjusted dollar measure reflecting consistent rouble/dollar cross-rates. For details of the revaluation, see the note to table 2.1.3 in United Nations Economic Commission for Europe, *Economic Bulletin for Europe*, Vol. 45, 1993; and the discussion in box 2.1.1 and section 2.1 (iii) in United Nations Economic Commission for Europe, *Economic Bulletin for Europe*, Vol. 43, 1991, New York, 1991. All trade values for 1992 and 1993 were either originally reported in dollars or were converted to dollars at the appropriate national conversion coefficient.

[b] "Eastern Europe" refers to Albania, Bulgaria, Czechoslovakia (through 1992) or the Czech and Slovak Republics (for 1993), Hungary, Poland, Romania and Yugoslavia (SFR Yugoslavia for 1991; Croatia, Slovenia and FR Yugoslavia for 1992-1993). The partner country grouping follows the practice until recently prevalent in the national statistical sources, which differs from the breakdown usually employed in United Nations publications. Thus, "transition economies", cover the ex-socialist trade partners, in addition to the east European countries, the Soviet Union, and the Asian centrally planned economies, including Yugoslavia and Cuba. "Developed economies" differs from the aggregate used in section 3.3.2 below by the exclusion of Turkey and the inclusion of Australia, New Zealand and South Africa.

[c] January-June 1993 from January-June 1992.

[d] Excluding Yugoslavia.

[e] Data from four reporting countries only (Bulgaria, Czechoslovakia, Hungary and Romania).

[f] 1991 growth rates refer to the former Soviet Union.

[g] Trade with all former CMEA members (i.e., including Cuba, Mongolia, Vietnam). It can be assumed that trade with the non-European CMEA members fell more steeply than that with the east European CMEA members.

Table 14.2   Russian Trade by Groups of Countries (Millions of Dollars)

	1990	1991	1992	1993
Total Imports; including Baltic States	---	---	36984	26807
Baltic States	---	---	333	172
Total Exports	71148	50911	41697	43707
Former CMEA Countries	30714	11661	8093	6587
China, North Korea, Laos, Yugoslavia	4885	3588	4258	3543
Developed Countries	25884	28764	24563	28260
Less Developed Countries	9965	6898	4784	5317
Total Imports	81751	44473	36651	26635
Former CMEA Countries	36293	10917	5347	2707
China, North Korea, Laos, Yugoslavia	5189	3080	3082	2884
Developed Countries	32480	25857	23055	16767
Less Developed Countries	7789	4619	5167	4277
Total Exports	100.0	100.0	100.0	100.0
Former CMEA Countries	43.2	22.9	19.4	15.1
China, North Korea, Laos, Yugoslavia	6.9	7.0	10.2	8.1
Developed Countries	36.0	56.5	58.9	64.7
Less Developed Countries	14.0	13.5	11.5	12.2
Total Imports	100.0	100.0	100.0	100.0
Former CMEA Countries	44.4	24.5	14.6	10.2
China, North Korea, Laos, Yugoslavia	6.3	6.9	8.4	10.8
Developed Countries	39.7	58.1	62.9	63.0
Less Developed Countries	9.5	10.4	14.1	16.1

SOURCE: Shinichiro Tabata, "Trends in Foreign Trade of Russia: Volumes, Composition, and Geographic Distribution", paper prepared for the 26th National Convention for the AAASS, Philadelphia, November 17-20, 1994

Table 14.3   Soviet/Russian Trade with Japan 1989-93

| | Thousands of American Dollars | | | | | Percent 1989 | | | |
	1989	1990	1991	1992	1993	1990	1991	1992	1993
Imports	2954415	2413922	2010473	1038476	1471279	81.7	68.0	35.1	49.8
Exports	3035277	3343241	3131507	2393245	2709066	110.1	103.2	78.8	89.3

SOURCE: MITI.

Comparative Advantage

The trade participation rate, however, only tells part of the story. Trade should be optimized, not maximized; that is, both the level and the assortment of imports and exports must be consistent with competitive profit maximization. Excess trade participation will occur if imports and/or exports exceed the bounds of profit maximizing; and undertrading holds in the opposite case.

Profit maximizing import and export behavior in turn are governed by the principle of comparative advantage. Goods which are relatively cheap (due to low factor costs and/or technology) computed at the prevailing competitive market exchange rate will be exported, while those which are expensive will be imported. The advantage in question is comparative rather than absolute, because nations produce a wide array of similar goods whose international cheapness (dearness) depends on relative domestic factor costs and the exchange rate. Most goods are tradeable, and their volumes and composition depend on relative costs evaluated through the exchange rate. The specific source of advantage in competitive economies without government controls may lie primarily in the structure of factor costs or technology, but as is widely understood in accordance with Heckscher-Ohlin theory if technologies are internationally homogeneous, plant and installed capital immobile, labor migration restricted and tradeables are commodities, the pattern of trade will be determined by factor proportions. The same outcome can occur in controlled economies in accordance with the less stringent Leontief variant of Heckscher-Ohlin theory if the productivity of various technologies are similar across sectors, prices reflect factor costs and the sector structure of foreign technologies is not offsetting. Empirical tests of this version of the Heckscher-Ohlin hypothesis in the Soviet case surprisingly revealed that the embodied factor content of traded goods was rational from this standpoint, although exports became increasingly and excessively capital intensive over time for Soviet trade with the developed countries of the West (Finland, France, United Kingdom, West Germany).[4]

This excessive capital intensity was primarily explained by the underpricing of Soviet industrial durables in trade with CMEA and less developed countries, and the increased share of fuels and metals exported to the West, a distortion which should be partly rectified under postcommunism by the emergence of a competitive price mechanism.[5] It follows directly therefore that if competitive forces are developing in the Russian foreign trade sector, they should manifest themselves visibly in an adjusted trade pattern which is more consistent with latent competitive comparative advantage reflected in the embodied factor content of trade flows.

Heckscher-Ohlin Rationality

The usefulness of embodied factor flows to evaluate the responsiveness of Russian foreign commerce to market forces is circumscribed. It should be obvious that the formal correspondence of embodied factor proportions in a controlled economy with those predicted by either the narrow or extended version of Heckscher-Ohlin theory does not imply that the assumptions of Heckscher-Ohlin theory (henceforth only the Leontief variant) are satisfied, or that trade is Pareto-efficient.[6] Such an outcome may be fortuitous. For example, it will be shown that in the case of Soviet trade with Japan, the commodity composition appears to be best explained by absolute advantage; the export of unique, or unusually abundant natural resources, and the importation of superior goods that cannot be duplicated domestically. This pattern of commodity exchange generates a Heckscher-Ohlin (H-O) rational pattern of embodied factor flows, which is initially consistent with relative domestic prices (comparative advantage). But, the commodity trade pattern on closer inspection is insensitive to sharp changes in relative domestic prices, suggesting that the correspondence with H-O rationality may be partly coincidental.

Furthermore, it must be clearly understood that even if the commodity trade pattern had been responsive to changing domestic prices, the planners may not have chosen a trade mix that maximized their or consumers' welfare. This is generally assumed to be a fundamental consequence of controlled economies. H-O rationality in the Soviet case therefore serves merely as a test of constrained efficiency. If trade is H-O irrational (exports are scarce factor intensive, and imports abundant factor intensive), the implication is that the pattern is not only inefficient, but could indicate that the Soviets actually diminished production potential and social welfare by trading the wrong product mix.

H-O rationality may also differ in degree. By comparing Soviet and Russian embodied factor proportions, and the commodity composition of traded goods judgments can be made regarding their relative congruency with comparative advantage and H-O rationality, and Russia's future trade potential.[7]

The Leontief Statistic

Embodied factor flows can be computed and appraised with a methodology first developed by Wassily Leontief. The idea as he formulated it was to compute the embodied factor content of standard units of imports and exports (a dollar's worth) to evaluate domestic opportunity costs at the margin. The factors in question are always those of the home country used in the production of import substitutes and exports. The calculation is at best approximate because it is impossible from a practical point of view to accurately match Soviet/Russian import substitutes with their western counterparts. Presumably western goods are superior which implies that import substitutes produced in Russia if properly standardized would require more inputs than similar goods designed for domestic consumption. Following Leontief it is assumed that this will not distort factor proportions, only total factor content.

The computation of the Leontief statistic is simple:

$$\Omega = \frac{km/\ell m}{kv/\ell v}$$

The first term in the numerator is km. k is a vector of coefficients representing the direct plus indirect capital k_j required to produce 1 unit of the import substitute m_j. The vector k itself is computed by multiplying a vector of direct capital coefficients for each intermediate input by the Leontief inverse.[8] This vector multiplication can be illustrated as follows for the four import substitute case:

$$k = \begin{bmatrix} k_1, & k_2, & k_3, & k_4 \end{bmatrix}$$

so

$$m = \begin{bmatrix} m_1, & m_2, & m_3, & m_4 \end{bmatrix}$$

$$km = \begin{bmatrix} k_1, & k_2, & k_3, & k_4 \end{bmatrix} \begin{bmatrix} m_1 \\ m_2 \\ m_3 \\ m_4 \end{bmatrix}$$

where k is measured in rubles per unit of import substitute and km is the direct plus indirect ruble expenditure on capital required to produce all Russia's import substitutes.

The same vector k is used to compute capital embodied in exports, v_i.

The labor vector ℓ is defined similarly, and the value of Ω is merely the result of four simple vector products, that is;

$$\Omega = \frac{\begin{bmatrix} k_1, & k_2, & k_3, & k_4 \end{bmatrix} \begin{bmatrix} m_1, & m_2, & m_3, & m_4 \end{bmatrix}'}{\begin{bmatrix} \ell_1, & \ell_2, & \ell_3, & \ell_4 \end{bmatrix} \begin{bmatrix} m_1, & m_2, & m_3, & m_4 \end{bmatrix}'} \Bigg/ \frac{\begin{bmatrix} k_1, & k_2, & k_3, & k_4 \end{bmatrix} \begin{bmatrix} v_1, & v_2, & v_3, & v_4 \end{bmatrix}'}{\begin{bmatrix} \ell_1, & \ell_2, & \ell_3, & \ell_4 \end{bmatrix} \begin{bmatrix} v_1, & v_2, & v_3, & v_4 \end{bmatrix}'}$$

The Data

The statistics required to appraise Russian foreign trade performance all have special characteristics that warrant extended comment. The core data in this study are Japanese historical series on trade with the Soviet Union and Russia from 1965 to 1993, expressed in dollars. Statistics for individual Japanese ports are also employed to gauge regional variations. All the data are obtained from customs receipts and should be more reliable than alternatives, especially during the current period when Russian data are distorted by high-inflation, tax evasion and smuggling. According to Shinichiro Tabata, Russian foreign trade statistics are being compiled by different agencies, using diverse methods that vary by region, and are all incompatible with prior Soviet statistical series.[9] The magnitudes of the discrepancies moreover are extremely large precluding a definitive assessment of the real trends. The Japanese data obviate these problems and provide a reasonable basis for historical compositional comparisons after adjustment to constant 1966 dollar values, and conversion into 1966 rubles to assure compatibility with the 1966 Soviet input-output table (see Appendix I). The trade data, modified in these ways however still do not accurately reflect total intertemporal flows in physical terms because the yen has fluctuated against the dollar.

Since the Leontief statistic depends solely on commodity and factor proportions, not total real flows, this shortcoming is unimportant for the purposes at hand. But anyone interested in total flows should adjust the data further for variation in the yen/dollar exchange rate.

The second data set employed in the study is import and export price ratios computed by the American Bureau of Economic Analysis which compare the domestic ruble prices of tradeables with their foreign prices expressed either in current foreign trade rubles (essentially dollars), or dollars in 1966. These ratios can be used to directly assess the nominal comparative advantage and efficiency of Soviet trade, given the internal disequilibrium associated with planning controls.

These same ratios also enable Japanese foreign trade data valued in dollars to be converted into rubles by deflating dollars with sectoral dollar price indices to the 1966 price base of the input-output table (see Appendix I). The conversion which is essential for computing embodied factor flows, is computed solely with the BEA's export purchasing power parity coefficients because the import data from Japanese sources do not include the turnover taxes and retail mark ups reflected in the BEA's import coefficients. The resulting ruble foreign trade data are consistent with the 1966 input-output table. Although this table is relatively old it has various advantages. It is not thought to be distorted by open and hidden inflation like subsequent tables. Missing sectors have been meticulously reconstructed by Vladimir Treml, and comprehensively adjusted for turnover tax by Steven Rosefielde, in an 11 aggregate sector format that is compatible with MITI's data. Also, prior studies of embodied factor flows were keyed to this and earlier tables, facilitating scholarly comparison.[10]

The Pattern of Soviet-Japanese Commodity Trade

The commodity composition of imports and exports traded between the Soviet Union and Japan 1965-1991 was distinctive. The Soviets primarily exported fuels (coal, petroleum), metals (platinum, palladium, aluminum), construction materials (timber), food (fish) and agricultural products (raw cotton) in exchange for finished metal products (pipes), machinery (general, electrical, transport), chemicals (plastics) and light industrial products (textiles). The export bundle was dominated by natural resources and raw materials with relatively little advanced technological and skilled labor value-added. The quality of these goods was intrinsic, rather than the consequence of superior design and processing. Demand depended principally on price, which in turn, according to Soviet price-fixing rules depended on the factor costs of extraction and transportation.[11] Since these costs were usually low by world standards (see Table 14.6), and the Soviets were notoriously bad at producing globally competitive finished goods (they were high cost producers of world standard products),[12] this export pattern was consistent with prevailing comparative advantage as it was shaped by the closed communist economic system. The embodied factor content of this export mix as shown by the direct plus indirect I-O factor coefficients,[13] was predominantly capital intensive, especially the fuels sector. Timber (forestry) was the only exception.

The composition of Soviet imports from Japan was just the reverse. The USSR imported finished industrial goods, which were comparatively expensive to produce domestically. Here too presumably the trade pattern was broadly consistent with comparative advantage, although there is not enough detailed information to be sure that the goods imported were always cost justified. The embodied factor content of Soviet imports from Japan was primarily labor intensive, especially light industrial goods, but this was partially offset by substantial imports of finished metal goods. Other things equal, therefore it should be anticipated that Soviet trade with Japan would be Heckscher-Ohlin irrational (assuming that Japan was comparatively well endowed with superior, world-standard capital) because the communist system prevented the Soviet Union from producing cheap, labor intensive industrial goods, forcing it to import them from abroad. Exports which should have been labor intensive as a consequence were capital intensive, and imports which should have been capital intensive were labor intensive.

This expectation (see Appendix II) however was not fulfilled because of the extraordinary labor intensity of timber exports which overwhelms all other influences, although with significant fluctuations. There were two dominant subperiods: 1965-1980; 1981-1991. Using Heckscher-Ohlin rationality as the norm, Soviet-Japanese trade was always rational (export labor intensive), but during the first period export labor intensity rose dramatically, peaking in 1976. During the second period it fell until 1991 to near irrational levels (Figure 14.1). These fluctuations are associated with structural changes in the commodity composition of imports and exports displayed in Tables 14.4 and 14.5. With regard to imports, the main structural shift occurs between 1972 and 1973, when the metals share jumps 67 percent, while light industry declines pari passu sharply increasing the capital intensity of the import aggregate and raising the Leontief statistic.

Table 14.4   Soviet (Russian) Trade with Japan Import Composition (Shares Valued in 1966 Rubles)

	Fuels	Metals	Machinery	Chemicals	Food	Light Industry
1965	3.2	26.9	25.3	16.9	0.2	27.6
1966	1.8	20.4	29.2	13.9	0.2	34.5
1967	1.5	16.5	21.2	16.0	0.2	44.5
1968	1.2	20.3	17.1	13.7	0.3	47.3
1969	2.5	19.8	17.0	16.9	0.2	43.5
1970	1.3	19.2	20.4	15.7	0.1	43.3
1971	1.2	23.2	20.5	19.4	0.2	35.6
1972	0.5	24.1	27.0	13.9	0.1	34.5
1973	0.6	38.5	25.2	12.7	0.1	22.9
1974	0.7	49.1	15.3	12.5	0.1	22.4
1975	0.7	40.7	25.8	13.3	0.1	19.7

	Fuels	Metals	Machinery	Chemicals	Food	Light Industry
1976	0.6	55.7	22.7	8.4	0.0	12.6
1977	0.3	37.1	30.5	10.5	0.0	21.1
1978	0.5	39.3	37.4	10.9	0.1	11.9
1979	0.7	50.0	25.0	11.3	0.0	13.0
1980	0.6	42.9	23.9	15.2	0.0	17.4
1981	0.7	48.6	24.1	9.9	0.0	16.6
1982	0.4	50.9	27.9	9.3	0.1	11.4
1983	0.5	45.9	24.4	11.9	0.0	17.3
1984	0.6	47.4	22.6	13.3	0.0	16.1
1985	0.9	42.0	29.1	14.4	0.0	13.7
1986	0.5	47.8	30.1	11.2	0.0	10.4
1987	0.6	47.4	22.7	18.7	0.1	10.5
1988	0.6	48.0	25.8	16.2	0.1	9.3
1989	1.0	34.2	35.2	17.0	0.2	12.4
1990	0.9	24.2	42.4	16.6	0.3	15.6
1991	0.6	26.2	47.0	17.2	0.9	8.1
1992	1.2	15.2	55.1	12.8	2.2	13.5
1993	0.7	33.8	43.7	11.7	0.8	9.2

SOURCES: MITI.

METHOD: MITI's dollar data have been converted to 1966 rubles as explained in Appendix I.

Export shares also vary. The labor intensive agriculture share rises from 1965 to a peak in 1976, and is reinforced by the sharp decline in the fuel share. Other similar variations 1972-1980 have the same effect causing the labor intensity of exports to drastically rise. The strengthening

Heckscher-Ohlin rationality of this pattern thus is attributable to both the importation of increasingly capital intensive goods, and the exportation of increasingly labor intensive products.

After 1980, the capital intensity of Soviet exports rises markedly with the fuel and metal shares expanding and fish and timber declining. The capital intensity of Soviet imports by contrast remains more or less constant with some upward trend caused by a declining light industrial share. The reversal back to a weak Heckscher-Ohlin pattern through 1990 thus is attributable in this instance mostly to the altered export composition, especially the fall in timber sales.

Although, as previously noted, the overall pattern of Soviet-Japanese trade is consistent with prevailing communist comparative advantage, the fluctuations 1965-1991 do not have an obvious explanation. Table 14.6 reveals that the domestic price was below the mean parity for all primary exports except metallurgy (although its possible that the comparative international cost of palladium, platinum and aluminum are also below the mean), and above it for all principal imports. But as shown in Table 14.7 Russian enterprise wholesale prices fell relatively rapidly 1965-1979 in machine-building and the chemical sector. Presumably, this made these products more internationally competitive, but this appears to have had no impact whatsoever on exports to Japan. Similarly, domestic metals prices rose, but this did not deter expanded metals exports. The story for imports is the same. As Soviet machinery became cheaper, machinery imports should have contracted but they expanded. Light industrial imports should have risen as domestic prices climbed, but instead they fell (see Appendix III).

Table 14.5   Soviet (Russian) Trade with Japan Export Composition (Shares Valued in 1966 Rubles)

	Agriculture	Fuels	Metals	Machinery	Chemicals	Food	Light Industry	Construction Materials	TOTAL*
1965	3.4	31.8	36.2	0.7	4.9	1.8	0.3	20.8	100.0
1966	5.4	29.8	35.3	0.5	4.2	1.9	0.7	22.3	100.0
1967	9.1	20.7	40.4	0.5	3.7	1.6	0.8	23.2	100.0
1968	11.9	19.6	31.2	0.5	3.5	1.3	1.0	30.9	100.0
1969	18.5	14.1	34.7	0.6	2.7	1.4	1.0	27.1	100.0

	Agriculture	Fuels	Metals	Machinery	Chemicals	Food	Light Industry	Construction Materials	TOTAL*
1970	10.2	15.1	33.9	0.8	3.5	1.7	1.5	33.2	100.0
1971	13.3	14.8	32.4	1.2	4.6	1.5	1.0	31.2	100.0
1972	22.6	11.1	31.1	0.7	3.9	1.3	1.8	27.6	100.0
1973	16.5	9.3	37.4	0.5	3.3	1.8	2.5	28.7	100.0
1974	23.7	12.3	21.7	0.5	4.2	2.3	7.6	27.6	100.0
1975	27.0	13.7	20.6	0.4	4.4	2.3	2.9	28.7	100.0
1976	22.7	13.8	20.3	0.5	3.7	3.2	5.3	30.6	100.0
1977	27.0	8.1	20.2	0.8	3.5	3.8	5.1	31.5	100.0
1978	21.9	6.7	27.5	0.3	3.4	4.3	7.5	28.5	100.0
1979	18.1	6.4	25.1	3.1	2.7	4.1	8.9	31.6	100.0
1980	13.3	5.4	26.8	2.5	4.1	3.9	11.1	33.0	100.0
1981	18.4	4.4	45.9	1.7	2.9	3.9	3.9	18.8	100.0
1982	19.8	3.9	42.4	0.4	3.1	4.5	6.0	19.9	100.0
1983	12.5	4.8	36.0	0.4	4.5	5.6	11.0	25.2	100.0
1984	13.1	5.4	34.6	0.7	4.9	7.9	10.2	23.2	100.0
1985	5.8	7.7	41.1	0.7	6.6	7.1	7.3	23.8	100.0
1986	6.4	6.1	49.8	0.4	3.7	6.2	8.0	19.5	100.0
1987	4.8	7.1	56.8	0.3	2.8	6.7	6.6	14.8	100.0
1988	3.2	8.0	50.8	0.3	3.2	9.4	5.4	19.7	100.0
1989	4.8	8.3	51.5	0.3	3.3	7.3	5.7	18.8	100.0
1990	1.7	7.7	59.6	0.3	2.8	8.0	5.9	14.0	100.0
1991	2.6	5.9	60.8	0.4	3.0	9.5	5.2	12.5	100.0
1992	0.7	6.5	45.9	0.2	2.8	20.6	5.9	17.5	100.0
1993	0.8	4.5	47.8	0.2	2.4	21.5	3.6	19.3	100.0

SOURCE: MITI.

METHOD: MITI's dollar data have been converted to 1966 rubles as explained in Appendix I.

*Totals rounded to 100 percent.

Table 14.6   Foreign Trade Ruble/Dollar Conversion Coefficients, by Branch 1966

Industry	Exports	Imports
Metallurgy	1.33	1.33
Fuels	0.92	1.38
Power	0.94	(X)
Machine-building and Metalworking	0.71	0.71
Chemicals	1.30	1.30
Woodworking and Paper	1.29	1.29
Construction Materials	0.80	0.80
Glass	1.00	1.00
Textiles and Apparel	1.34	4.28
Food	0.85	1.67
Industry N.E.C.	1.05	1.53
Agriculture	0.95	1.51
Other Branches of Material Production	1.00	1.00
Mean	1.04	

(X) = Not applicable, power is not imported by the Soviet Union.

SOURCE: Barry Kostinsky and Vladimir Treml, *Foreign Trade Pricing in The Soviet Union: Exports and Imports in the 1966 Input-Output Table*, U.S. Department of Commerce Bureau of Economic Analysis, Foreign Economic Report No. 8, March 1976, p. 11.

COMMENT: The numerator of each coefficient is the domestic ruble price at the point of purchase. This means that most export prices are wholesale before the imposition of retail turnover taxes, and most imports include retail turnover tax. The mean ruble/dollar conversion coefficient can be used as a bench mark for assessing competitiveness. Ratios less than the mean indicate that goods are relatively cheap and vice versa.

**Table 14.7   Indices of Enterprise Wholesale Prices
(Net of Turnover Taxes: 1949=100)**

	1955	1965	1970	1975	1979
All Industries	68	70	77	75	73
Heavy Industry	61	55	64	59	57
Electricity	74	62	83	83	79
Fuel	77	76	132	131	131
Ferrous Metals	60	60	90	90	93
Chemicals	67	66	66	63	62
Machinery	52	41	39	33	30
Woodprocessing	80	95	114	113	115
Construction Materials	57	57	68	67	67
Light Industry	80	81	86	93	93
Food	90	126	126	129	129

SOURCE: *Narodnoe khoziaistvo SSSR, 1979*, p. 164.

These responses obviously reflect the qualitative noncompetitiveness of Soviet goods and other demand priorities, which illustrate how communist controls prevented the system from responding to latent comparative advantages attainable in a competitive market regime.

Soviet Embodied Factor Flows

The consequences of repressed market competition which shackled the Soviet Union with a primitive trade pattern where natural resources were exchanged for processed goods is clearly revealed in its embodied factor content. Table

14.8 presents Leontief statistics, which are ratios of the capital/labor content of Soviet imports compared with the capital/labor content of its exports. They reveal that for the entire period under review the Soviets on balance specialized in the right goods. The labor intensity of exports, and hence the corresponding Leontief statistics however were unusually high after 1967, judged by Rosefielde's earlier findings illustrated in Figure 14.2. This extraordinary labor intensity cannot be attributed to Japan's capital endowment and per capita GNP because they were below France's, West Germany's and the United Kingdom's in 1968. The high labor intensity is attributable to a single commodity, timber which was abundant in the Russian Far East and easily exported. This special factor suggests that the extraordinary labor intensity of Soviet (Russian) trade with Japan may have been locationally justified, but it would probably be wrong to assume further that it was Pareto efficient because as shown in Table 14.7 shifts in the trade pattern including timber sales were negatively correlated with changes in relative domestic prices.

Table 14.8   Soviet (Russian) Trade with Japan Leontief Statistics

	Full Import Capital Content	Full Import Labor Content	Full Export Capital Content	Full Export Labor Content	km/lm	kv/lv	Ω
1965	376893	56674	599655	101338	6.6502	5.9174	1.1239
1966	439605	72718	682772	124577	6.0453	5.4807	1.1030
1967	330088	57279	927685	191869	5.7628	4.8350	1.1919
1968	380524	65642	805110	213578	5.7969	3.7696	1.5378
1969	556839	92414	876923	236562	6.0255	3.7069	1.6255
1970	638569	108928	812773	233946	5.8623	3.4742	1.6874
1971	709591	113681	815726	231729	6.2419	3.5202	1.7732
1972	859611	141402	937475	279447	6.0792	3.3548	1.8121
1973	827608	119845	1554614	451545	6.9056	3.4429	2.0058
1974	1700527	228898	1643909	517633	7.4292	3.1758	2.3393
1975	2009022	283243	1191916	383350	7.0929	3.1092	2.2813
1976	2751915	351278	1024235	335461	7.8340	3.0532	2.5658
1977	2028468	299567	1064477	400373	6.7713	2.6587	2.5468

	Full Import Capital Content	Full Import Labor Content	Full Export Capital Content	Full Export Labor Content	km/lm	kv/lv	Ω
1978	2351215	331496	1053846	350981	7.0927	3.0026	2.3622
1979	2306905	301868	1151289	411960	7.6421	2.7947	2.7345
1980	2280942	312271	999410	359074	7.3044	2.7833	2.6244
1981	2477669	332791	1297808	311610	7.4451	4.1649	1.7876
1982	2838460	372184	1040997	266808	7.6265	3.9017	1.9547
1983	2011397	274213	783027	222161	7.3352	3.5246	2.0811
1984	1746661	232899	737188	198961	7.4996	3.7052	2.0241
1985	1771529	241476	754825	180955	7.3363	4.1713	1.7587
1986	2137561	282672	1211254	259340	7.5620	4.6705	1.6191
1987	1816644	232698	36966	275276	7.8069	5.5834	1.3982
1988	2026979	260445	1555387	313954	7.7828	4.9542	1.5709
1989	1716000	242335	1651109	326559	7.0811	5.0262	1.4088
1990	1268886	194510	1978608	329603	6.5235	6.0030	1.0867
1991	1023550	151414	1909595	310584	6.7600	6.1484	1.0995
1992	465966	76355	1256623	241785	6.1026	5.1973	1.1742
1993	759521	109269	1391440	282052	6.9509	4.9333	1.4090

NOTE: The Leontief statistics above are computed using full factor coefficients for the fish and timber subsectors where appropriate.

The Postcommunist Russian Commodity Trade Pattern

Insofar as market forces superseded administrative command planning controls in the late stages of perestroika, and during Yeltsin's transition 1990-1993, the pattern of Soviet and Russian commodity trade should have shifted in accordance with competitive comparative advantage. The data in Tables 14.4 and 14.5 demonstrate that several significant changes indeed have occurred. On the export side the most dramatic divergence from the trends 1973-1989 was the contraction of the fuel share (especially coal), and the expansion of the food (fish) and timber shares after 1990. They increased the labor intensity of aggregate exports to Japan.

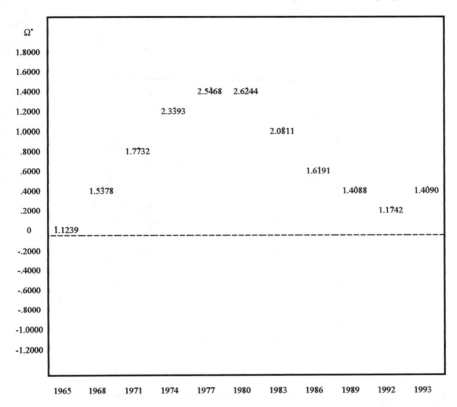

Figure 14.1   **Leontief Statistics: Soviet (Russian) Trade with Japan 1965-93**

Ω^* designates the conventional Leontief statistic rescaled so that the factor proportions neutrality point is 0, rather than 1. Capital intensive import biases are then computed as $\Omega^* = \Omega - 1$ while capital intensive export biases are calculated as $\Omega^* = -(1/\Omega - 1)$. The reciprocal form used when $\Omega < 1$ transforms the inverse numeric scaling of capital intensive export biases to the same numeric form used in scaling capital intensive import biases. As a result of this transformation, factor proportions bias is indicated by a sign convention which preserves symmetric scaling. Conventional Leontief statistics, however, are also provided directly on the figures and in the relevant tables.

SOURCE: Table 14.8.

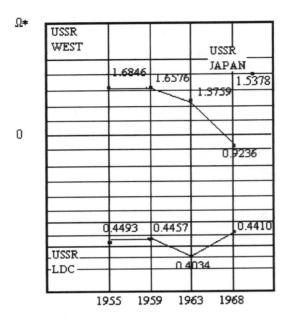

Figure 14.2   The Embodied Factor Proportions Structure of Soviet Trade with the West, CMEA, and LDC, 1955-68

SOURCE: Steven Rosefielde, *Soviet International Trade in Heckscher-Ohlin Perspective*, Lexington Books, 1973, p. 49, and Table 14.8.

The shift in the commodity composition of imports was also pronounced. The machinery share roughly doubled after 1987, and chemicals (mainly plastics) fell reciprocally. Since both activities are capital intensive the net effect was a modest increase in the capital intensity of imports, reflecting the larger share of machinery in the trade mix.

The correlation between these trends and the adjustment of Russian relative prices to world ratios is mixed. Tables 14.9 and 14.10 show that fuel and metals exports should have contracted and did. Timber exports likewise should and did expand. However, machinery imports should have slightly contracted, but did not, and chemical imports should have increased, but decreased.

The interpretation of these variations is clouded partly because the sample is small, and partly because the hyper depression overwhelming Russia has temporarily reduced its export capacity. Strikes in the coal sector and declining petroleum production may well co-explain the contraction of the fuel export share.[14] The changes in fish and timber exports however are clearly consistent with market logic and comparative advantage. Authorities and traders in the Russian Pacific Far East apparently responded to the superior profit opportunities provided by fish and timber sales to Japan, once domestic quotas were relaxed. Changes in the import pattern are less obvious. Perhaps falling demand for Japanese plastics reflects the decline in aggregate Russian production. Similar trends are apparent in general and electrical machinery. The only exceptions are transportation (mostly cars), and precision instruments. The former as is widely understood is a clear response to market opportunities. The Russians have been purchasing huge volumes of used Japanese cars that are no longer road worthy for resale at home where there are not any restrictions on auto service lives. However, this behavior strictly speaking does not reflect comparative production costs. It is an artefact of Japanese government policy and public dispreference for old things. The behavior of precision instruments could signal Russia's desire to recapitalize with superior Japanese equipment. If so, this is certainly compatible with comparative advantage, and bodes well for the future.

The Embodied Factor Content of Russian Trade

The data in Table 14.8 reveal that the changes in the commodity composition of Soviet and Russian trade with Japan 1991-1993 associated with the Yeltsin transition have once again resulted in high Leontief statistics. From a formal standpoint the Russian trade pattern with Japan is now plausibly Heckscher-Ohlin rational. This rationality moreover seems more consistent with Pareto efficiency (consumer demand) than was the case in the past. But it is equally obvious that traditional forces continue to play a major role. There is no evidence whatsoever suggesting that Russia's manufacturing sector has adjusted to the latent comparative advantages afforded by its abundant and skilled labor force. On balance therefore one must conclude with one cheer for Yeltsin. A competitive foreign trade market does appear to be emerging with Japan, but as yet its impact remains feeble compared with the enormous potential.

Robustness

It was mentioned at various points in the text that the Soviets and Russians exported a very narrow range of goods to Japan, and that this may have affected embodied factor proportions.   Perhaps the postcommunist improvement in Russia's foreign trade is a quirk associated with the embodied factor proportions of a few products. This contingency is easily tested. Suppose that the Soviets exported a wider range of goods. Instead of selling raw timber and fish assume they exported a variety of construction materials, and food products. In this instance, the full factor coefficients for the fish and timber sectors should be replaced by those for food and construction materials. The corresponding counterfactual Leontief statistics are presented in Table 14.11. The trends are broadly the same as before, but the scale has shifted. Instead of being uniformly Heckscher-Ohlin rational, the statistics are only spottily so.   Soviet (Russia) trade with Japan is strongly irrational 1965 to 1972, and 1989-92. But the postcommunist improvement in foreign trade performance is unmistakable with the Leontief statistic rising from .8060 to 1.0330 1990-1993. Market forces thus appear to be moving Russia in the right direction, regardless of the micro peculiarities of its export mix.

Generalization

Strictly speaking this finding holds only for bilateral trade been Japan and Russia. If the study were extended to other countries the outcomes might be different. Without prejudging the issue however it is worth observing that the trend toward excessively capital intensive exports exhibited in Soviet trade with Finland, West Germany, England and France by prior studies for the fifties and sixties is echoed a decade later in Soviet trade with Japan. This suggests that the bilateral Japanese experience with the Soviet Union is not unique, and that the improvements in postcommunist performance identified in Table 14.8 may well be indicative of the broader trend.

Table 14.9   **Russia: Structure of Industrial Output using Alternative Price Sets (In Percent, at Current Prices)**

	1992	1993	1994 Jan.-Sept.	1991 World Prices
Electric Energy	6.4	9.2	13.1	12.4
Fuel	18.5	17.2	17.3	25.7
Metallurgy	16.7	17.1	16.2	7.9
Chemistry	8.0	7.2	7.3	2.2
Machine-Building	20.1	20.0	18.5	19.0
Forestry, Timber-Processing Pulp and Paper	4.8	3.9	4.0	13.5
Construction Materials	3.3	3.3	3.9	5.4
Light Industry	7.1	5.2	3.0	2.9
Food Industry	10.3	12.4	12.2	8.2
Other	4.9	4.6	4.4	2.8
TOTAL	100.0	100.0	100.0	100.0

SOURCES: Goskomstat, Evgeny Gavrilenkov, "Macroeconomic Crises and Transformation of Price Structure in Russia", paper presented at the 26th AAASS conference, Philadelphia, November 19, 1994.

NOTE: The output data is for 1991.

COMMENT: The trends in relative sectoral ruble prices 1992-94 can be assessed by comparing sectoral value shares in these years, given 1991 output weights. Their relationship to world prices is shown in the last column.

Table 14.10   Structure of Russian Industrial Output in 1991 at World and Domestic Prices (In Percent)

	World Prices	Domestic Prices
Ferrous Metallurgy	3.53	4.30
Non-Ferrous Metallurgy	4.34	4.92
Coal Industry	2.23	0.99
Oil-and-Gas Industry	23.38	7.78
Other Fuel	0.09	0.04
Electric Power	12.43	3.01
Mechanical Engineering	19.00	23.12
Chemistry	2.16	6.84
Timber, Wood-Working, Pulp and Paper Industries	13.54	5.83
Construction Materials	5.36	4.18
Light Industry	2.90	16.09
Food Industry	8.20	18.61
Other Manufacturing	2.83	4.32
INDUSTRY TOTAL*	100.00	100.00

SOURCES: Goskomstat, and Gavrilenkov. See Table 14.12.

*Totals rounded to 100 percent.

Table 14.11   Soviet (Russian) Trade with Japan Counter-factual Leontief Statistics

	Full Import Capital Content	Full Import Labor Content	Full Export Capital Content	Full Export Labor Content	km/lm	kv/lv	Ω Leontief Statistic
1965	376819	56765	680915	70233	6.6382	9.6951	0.6847
1966	439509	72836	785708	85168	6.0343	9.2254	0.6541
1967	330023	57358	1086955	130569	5.7537	8.3248	0.6912
1968	380402	65792	1011771	133384	5.7819	7.5854	0.7622
1969	556734	92542	1081750	157301	6.0160	6.8769	0.8748
1970	638505	109007	1049374	142396	5.8575	7.3694	0.7948
1971	709444	113863	1039147	145147	6.2307	7.1593	0.8703
1972	859558	141467	1176860	186626	6.0760	6.3060	0.9635
1973	827476	120008	1961647	294465	6.8952	6.6617	1.0350
1974	1700413	229039	2075186	352367	7.4241	5.8894	1.2606
1975	2008966	283312	1518012	258225	7.0910	5.8786	1.2062
1976	2751868	351336	1323452	221557	7.8326	5.9734	1.3112
1977	2028412	299636	1419939	265683	6.7696	5.3445	1.2666
1978	2351067	331677	1352446	238955	7.0884	5.6598	1.2524
1979	2306859	301925	1528742	269352	7.6405	5.6756	1.3462
1980	2280902	312319	1343496	228566	7.3031	5.8779	1.2425
1981	2477626	332844	1505613	235085	7.4438	6.4046	1.1623
1982	2838210	372492	1222747	200268	7.6195	6.1056	1.2480
1983	2011327	274299	963959	155788	7.3326	6.1877	1.1850
1984	1746597	232979	888312	145769	7.4968	6.0940	1.2302
1985	1771453	241569	902731	128100	7.3331	7.0471	1.0406
1986	2137487	282763	1396874	193440	7.5593	7.2212	1.0468
1987	1816535	232832	1700011	220186	7.8019	7.7208	1.0105
1988	2026847	260608	1783484	237629	7.7774	7.5053	1.0362
1989	1715627	242796	1882638	248681	7.0661	7.5705	0.9334
1990	1268412	195093	2167653	268720	6.5016	8.0666	0.8060

	Full Import Capital Content	Full Import Labor Content	Full Export Capital Content	Full Export Labor Content	km/lm	kv/lv	Ω Leontief Statistic
1991	1022528	152672	2068560	263662	6.6976	7.8455	0.8537
1992	464706	77906	1405216	207350	5.9649	6.7770	0.8802
1993	758815	110138	1579155	236757	6.8897	6.6699	1.0330

Conclusion

Despite the sharp decline in foreign trade turnover precipitated by the collapse of the Soviet Union, and the absence of structural modernization, market forces appear to have improved Russia's international economic performance. A careful investigation of the embodied factor proportions and competitiveness of Russian-Japan trade has revealed striking gains in rationality and constrained efficiency. Leontief statistics have risen and the commodity composition has become more responsive to prices which are no longer fixed by the state, but are set at least in part by the market.

The effect of Soviet-Japanese trade on Soviet command constrained production potential and social welfare for most of the postwar era appears to have been restrictedly beneficial contrary to earlier irrational findings for Soviet trade with Finland, West Germany, England and France in the late sixties. Soviet-Japanese embodied factor proportions were consistently rational, but the trend in the Leontief statistic in the eighties was verging toward the irrational, while changes in the composition of traded goods were negatively correlated with price fluctuations. Had Soviet communism endured, and these trends persisted, production potential and social welfare might well have been diminished by Soviet-Japanese trade due to the perverse embodied factor content and composition of the commodities exchanged, given Leontief's assumptions about technology, factor immobilities and rents.

The liberalization of prices and entrepreneurial autonomy associated with Yeltsin's postcommunist reforms however seems to have arrested and reversed these tendencies. Soviet-Japanese trade as a consequence, even though it is still partly command constrained has become more strongly Heckscher-Ohlin rational, and partly responsive to competitive demand, augmenting production potential and social welfare, and providing a ray of hope for a more comprehensive market transition.

Finally, it should be observed that since trade between Russia (Soviet Union) and Japan has not violated the Leontief variant of Heckscher-Ohlin theory, it follows directly that Samuelson's global factor and commodity price equalization hypothesis is not disconfirmed on this narrow ground.

Notes

1. The textbook version of Heckscher-Ohlin usually requires technologies to be globally homogeneous, and markets generally competitive, where products are commodities that do not earn quasi-rents. The purpose of these assumptions is to assure that prices are determined solely by factor proportions and costs. Also labor and capital are sometimes specified to be transnationally immobile, although these latter criteria can be relaxed for non-installed machinery and equipment, and some labor migration so long as these flows do not cause endowed factor proportions to become globally equalized (in which case there would be no basis for trade).

2. Wassily Leontief, "Domestic Production and Foreign Trade: The American Capital Position Re-examined", *Proceedings of the American Philosophical Society*, September 1953, pp. 332-49; Leontief, "Factor Proportions and the Structure of American Trade: Further Theoretical and Empirical Analysis", *Review of Economics and Statistics*, November 1956, pp. 386-407. Cf. Paul Samuelson, "International Trade and the Equalization of Factor Prices", *Economic Journal*, June 1948, pp. 181-97, and Samuelson, "International Factor-Price Equilization Once Again", *Economic Journal*, June 1949, pp. 181-97.

3. The likelihood that international trade will degrade production potential and welfare when a nation exports scarce factor intensive and imports abundant factor intensive goods depends on the particular situation. With respect to short run production potential what counts is the net flows of materials which affect the location of the production possibilities frontiers. If a nation disregards comparative advantage and has fewer materials after trade, production potential will decline. Likewise, if the utility generated by the commodities imported are the same as their domestic

substitutes, and a nation trades against its comparative advantage social welfare must decline. But neither of these immizerizing possibilities is easy to ascertain in practice because the composite goods used to appraise comparative advantage are seldom homogeneous and may misindicate value and factor cost. Where foreign goods cannot be easily duplicated, a nation may benefit even though it exports what appear to be the wrong goods, with the wrong embodied factor proportions.

4. Steven Rosefielde, *Soviet International Trade in Heckscher-Ohlin Perspective*, Heath-Lexington, August 1973, 193 pp.; "The Embodied Factor Content of Soviet International Trade: Problems of Theory, Measurement and Interpretation", *Association of Comparative Economic Systems Bulletin*, Vol. XV, No. 2-3, Summer-Fall, 1973, pp. 3-12; "Factor Proportions and Economic Rationality in Soviet International Trade 1955-1968", *American Economic Review*, Vol. LXIV, No. 4, September 1974, pp. 670-81; "Foreign Trade Ruble Prices and the Heckscher-Ohlin Interpretation of Soviet Foreign Trade", *Association for Comparative Economic Systems Bulletin*, Vol. 8, No. 3, Fall 1976, pp. 31-38; and "Is the Embodied Factor Content of Soviet Foreign Trade Hyper-Irrational?", *Association for Comparative Economic Systems Bulletin*, Vol. 21, No. 2, Summer 1979, pp. 19-52.

5. Evgeny Gavrilenko, "Macroeconomic Crises and Transition of Price Structure in Russia", paper presented at the 26th AAASS Conference, Philadelphia, November 19, 1994.

6. International trade provides a mechanism through which natural resources, technology, capital durables, labor, skills, intermediate inputs, final goods and services can be globally allocated to best competitive use. Flows of technology and inputs broadly construed alter the production potential of all participating nations by improving factor availabilities and enhancing productivity. This potential reflected in best practice production possibilities frontiers defines the efficiency boundary for globally generally competitive supply. If the point of production, consumption and trade on any nation's frontier under these conditions equilibrates supply and demand neoclassical theory describes it as being economically, or

Paretian efficient. If for institutional reasons prevailing prices do not reflect purchasers' preferences, but still determine profit maximizing supply, the production point is referred to as being technically efficient, a term also conventionally applied by neoclassical theorists to the closely related case where input and output prices are distorted, causing factors to be suboptimally allocated and production to occur consequently on a lower, production feasibility frontier. And, of course, production potential can be further degraded if supply including intermediate inputs is additionally constrained because managers cannot profit maximize at prevailing prices.

The potentialities elaborated above for a competitive international market can be classified variously under the categories of short run 1) economic efficiency, 2) technical efficiency, 3) allocationally constrained technical efficiency, and 4) command constrained technical efficiency. The same set of concepts also can be applied to imperfectly competitive markets. For a fuller analysis see Steven Rosefielde, "Russia's Economic Recovery Potential: Optimizing the Residual Productivity of the Soviet Capital Stock", *Comparative Economic Studies*, forthcoming 1995; "Neoclassical Norms and the Valuation of National Income in the Soviet Union and Its Post-Communist Successor States", *Journal of Comparative Economics*, forthcoming 1995.

The foreign trade efficiency of controlled economies like the Soviet Union thus can be calibrated in principle by measuring the degree to which international commerce enables the nation to attain its command constrained production potential, since it is, or should be, obvious that higher orders of efficiency were unattainable under communism. This inference, however, cannot be extended to postcommunist Russia. Insofar as domestic consumer preferences in the emerging transitionary market affect import supplies and exports, international commerce may involve economic efficiency.

The inefficiency of Soviet foreign commerce can be measured in theory by computing pre and post trade production potentials adjusted for domestic technological progress. Calculations of this sort are necessarily approximative to the extent that the perceived domestic production potential deviates from the true unobserved potential, but presumably the gap can be gauged by controlled micro-experimentation. The same procedures can be applied in the

Russian case, recognizing the greater role played by the market.

No empirical calculations of these sorts have ever been attempted. Therefore there is no way to definitively assess how inefficient the Soviet Union was, or, Russia is, with respect to their foreign trade. The only evidence available comes indirectly from studies of the embodied factor content of Soviet and Russian international commerce. Leontief statistics computed in the seventies for trade flows in 1959 and 1968 revealed that the pattern of factor embodiment was initially bilaterally consistent with the requirements of comparative advantage, given the assumptions of Heckscher-Ohlin theory which make trade depend on factor availabilities, but not strictly so thereafter. In 1968 Soviet trade with the developed West paradoxically entailed the export of capital intensive goods and the importation of products whose substitutes were labor intensive.

Setting aside the possibility that trade flows were properly governed by comparative advantages wrongly excluded by the assumptions of Heckscher-Ohlin theory, the results just described indicate that the Soviet foreign trade pattern did not degrade the nation's production potential in 1959, and could have augmented the Soviet Union's command constrained production potential to the fullest extent possible given the gains attainable from foreign trade. The exact degree to which trade enhanced production potential, cannot be discerned because the Leontief test is not sufficiently powerful. But the paradox that emerged after 1959 strictly implies that Soviet bilateral trade with the west degraded the USSR's production potential. It was worse than inefficient and hence irrational.

As previously noted these inferences are predicated on the assumptions of Heckscher-Ohlin theory. Perhaps the irrationality of Soviet Russia's trade was not as perverse as it seems judged from the standpoint of command constrained technical efficiency because the productivity of capital intensive export sector greatly exceeded that of its labor intensive import substitute sector, but this rationalizing conjecture is not sufficient in its own right to override the presumption of partial irrationality.

7.   During the last 5 years much of Russia's capital stock has become obsolete because state demand for the products manufactured from

its assets has fallen drastically, and few alternative uses have materialized.

This means that compared with the Soviet period Russia is labor (especially skilled labor) rich and capital poor. Excluding natural resources H-O theory therefore would predict that Russia should import capital intensive goods and export labor intensive products.

Natural resources can be viewed as something of an exception because of their relative abundance, but even here H-O theory requires that the share of labor intensive non natural resource exports should rise relative to capital intensive non natural resources, and probably relative to natural resources as well.

As a consequence, changes in embodied factor proportions should provide a significant clue about the efficiency of Russian marketization.

8.   Steven Rosefielde, *Soviet International Trade in Heckscher-Ohlin Perspective*, Heath-Lexington, August 1973, p. 173.

9.   Shinichiro Tabata, "Trends in Foreign Trade of Russia: Volumes, Composition, Geographic Distribution", paper presented at the 26th AAASS Conference, Philadelphia, November 18, 1994.

10.   The computation of Russian embodied factor proportions using Soviet production relationships that prevailed in 1966 has the following limitations.

1.   The BEA's purchasing power parity ratios may misestimate the sectoral conversion rates actually used by the Soviets.

2.   Input-output relationships may have changed substantially over time due to sectoral disparities in technological progress, and the dismemberment of the Soviet Union.

3.   Input-output relationships for any year may misrepresent embodied factor content because Russia is in the midst of a hyper-depression and is not fully utilizing its fixed capital.

If exact calculation were essential, any of the deficiencies identified above might render the calculation of Leontief statistics pointless. The purpose of the present exercise however is less demanding. An impression of the general magnitude of the Leontief statistic, and its trend 1989-1993 in Russian-Japanese bilateral trade will suffice. For this purpose, it is assumed that

1.   The BEA's purchasing power parity ratios adequately approximate internal Soviet conversion rates. This assumption is probably acceptable because the BEA employed the same sorts of information the Russians did. Also the adjustment for turnover tax eliminates an important potential source of distortion (using export coefficients).

2.   Changes in input-output relations in the past thirty odd years have not been drastic because technological progress has been slow, and evenly dispersed. It is generally true that I-O relations change slowly but it is nonetheless acknowledged that altered structural relations could be a source of significant distortion.

3.   Input-output analysis assumes that production functions have rectangular isoquants and are linear homogeneous. If capital is idled by depression labor and other factor use must fall proportionally. It is assumed here either that this so, or that factor substitution has been sectorally unbiased. If these assumptions are false, computed Leontief statistics can be interpreted as reflecting the factor embodiment that would have occurred absent the depression. Although imperfect this latter measure should still be suggestive of how changes in Russia's trade pattern with Japan should normally affect embodied factor proportions.

11.   Morris Bornstein, "The Soviet Price System", *American Economic Review*, Vol. 52, No. 1, March 1962, pp. 64-103; "Soviet Price Statistics", in Treml and Hardt (eds.), *Soviet Economic Statistics*, Duke University Press, Durham, NC, 1972, pp. 355-96; "The Administration of the Soviet Price System", *Soviet Studies*, Vol. 30,

No. 4, October 1978, pp. 466-90.

12.   Vladimir Treml, "Foreign Trade and the Soviet Economy" in Neuberger and Tyson (eds.), *Transmission and Response: The Impact of International Disturbances on the Soviet Union and Eastern Europe*, Pergamon Press, New York, 1980.

13.   Vladimir Treml, *The Structure of the Soviet Economy*, Praeger, New York, 1972, pp. 513-551.

14.   Leslie Dienes, "The Oil and Gas Industries in the New Corporate Russia", paper presented at the 26th AAASS meetings, Philadelphia, November 19, 1994.

Bibliography

Bornstein, Morris, "The Soviet Price System", *American Economic Review*, Vol. 52, No. 1, March 1962, pp. 64-103.

_____, "Soviet Price Statistics" in Treml and Hardt (eds.), *Soviet Economic Statistics*, Duke University Press: Durham, NC, 1972, pp. 355-96.

_____, "The Administration of the Soviet Price System", *Soviet Studies*, Vol. 30, No. 4, October 1978, pp. 466-90.

Dienes, Leslie, "The Oil and Gas Industries in the New Corporate Russia", paper presented at the 26th AAASS meetings, Philadelphia, November 19, 1994.

Gavrilenko, Evgeny, "Macroeconomic Crisis and Transition of Price Structure in Russia", paper presented at the 26th AAASS Conference, Philadelphia, November 19, 1994.

Leontief, Wassily, "Domestic Production and Foreign Trade: The American Capital Position Re-examined", *Proceedings of the American Philosophical Society*, September 1953, pp. 332-49.

_____, "Factor Proportions and the Structure of American Trade: Further Theoretical and Empirical Analysis", *Review of Economics and Statistics*, November 1956, pp. 386-407.

Rosefielde, Steven, *Soviet International Trade in Heckscher-Ohlin Perspective*, Heath-Lexington, August 1973, 193 pp.

_____, "The Embodied Factor Content of Soviet International Trade: Problems of Theory, Measurement and Interpretation", *Association of Comparative Economic Systems Bulletin*, Vol. XV, No. 2-3, Summer-Fall 1973, pp. 3-12.

_____, "Factor Proportions and Economic Rationality in Soviet International Trade 1955-1968", *American Economic Review*, Vol. LXIV, No. 4, September 1974, pp. 670-81.

_____, "Foreign Trade Ruble Prices and the Heckscher-Ohlin Interpretation of Soviet Foreign Trade", *Association for Comparative Economic Systems Bulletin*, Vol. 8, No. 3, Fall 1976, pp. 31-38.

_____, "Is the Embodied Factor Content of Soviet Foreign Trade Hyper-Irrational?", *Association for Comparative Economic Systems Bulletin*, Vol. 21, No. 2, Summer 1979, pp. 19-52.

_____, "Russia's Economic Recovery Potential: Optimizing the Residual Productivity of the Soviet Capital Stock", *Comparative Economic Studies*, Vol. XXXVI, No. 4, Winter 1994, pp. 111-116.

_____, "Neoclassical Norms and the Valuation of National Income in the Soviet Union and Its Post-Communist Successor States", *Journal of Comparative Economics*, Vol. 21, No. 3, December 1995, pp. 375-389.

Samuelson, Paul, "International Trade and the Equalization of Factor Prices", *Economic Journal*, June 1948, pp. 181-97.

_____, "International Factor-Price Equilization Once Again", *Economic Journal*, June 1949, pp. 181-97.

Tabata, Shinichiro, "Trends in Foreign Trade of Russia: Volumes, Composition, Geographic Distribution", paper presented at the 26th AAASS Conference, Philadelphia, November 18, 1994.

Treml, Vladimir, *The Structure of the Soviet Economy*, Praeger: New York, 1972, pp. 513-551.

_____, "Foreign Trade and the Soviet Economy" in Neuberger and Tyson (eds.), *Transmission and Response: The Impact of International Disturbances on the Soviet Union and Eastern Europe*, Pergamon Press: New York, 1980.

Appendix I   Sample Computation of Soviet (Russian)-Japanese Leontief Statistics

Foreign Trade Statistics

A. Conversion of Japanese Trade Statistics into 1966 Ruble Producers Prices (Deflated for Turnover Tax)

The first three quadrants of the 1966 Soviet Input-Output table (intermediate input flows I, final demand II, factors III), adjusted by Steven Rosefielde are valued at enterprise wholesale prices, net of turnover taxes and subsidies. Exports and import substitutes must be valued in the same metric to avoid distortion. For example, if relative traded goods prices computed in dollars differ from their domestic ruble counterparts

$$
\begin{bmatrix} P_1/P_n \\ P_2/P_n \\ \cdot \\ \cdot \\ \cdot \\ P_n/P_n \end{bmatrix}
\neq
\begin{bmatrix} P_1^*/P_n^* \\ P_2^*/P_n^* \\ \cdot \\ \cdot \\ \cdot \\ P_n^*/P_n^* \end{bmatrix}
$$

where P_i is the dollar and P_i^* the ruble price, the weighted measure of embodied capital and labor in the Leontief statistic will be biased because the dollar estimates misindicate the structural output input ratios, i.e., $pm/k \neq p^*m/k$.

$$\Omega = \frac{kpm/lpm}{kpv/lpv} \neq \frac{kp^*m/lp^*m}{kp^*v/lp^*v}$$

where k and l are vectors of capital and labor valued in rubles, and m and v are imports and exports expressed in physical units.

This potential bias would not pose a problem, if data on traded goods published in the Soviet Union, Russia and Japan were valued in rubles, but they are not. The available data for the most part are expressed in dollars or disguised dollars called foreign trade rubles (because the Soviets bought and sold goods in the West for hard currency).

Dollar statistics therefore must be converted into internal rubles, but the task is complicated. The Soviet exchange rate was fixed arbitrarily by the planners without regard for competitive equilibrium, and the Russian exchange rate is distorted by quantity controls. The only solution is to compute product and sectoral ruble dollar ratios, that is, micro purchasing power parity ratios for traded goods. This task has been undertaken by various scholars and institutions. The most exhaustive studies have been conducted by the American Bureau of Economic Analysis. These are presented in Table 14.6, and have been computed directly from Soviet input-output sources.

These conversion ratios are multiplied by MITI's dollars statistics adjusted to a 1966 base. The American dollar deflators are reported in Table 14.A1, and sample dollar imports and exports for 1993 in 1966 dollar prices are shown in Table 14.A2, where they are converted to rubles in 1966 prices.

Table 14.A1   Dollar Price Deflators (1966 = 1)

	Fuel[a]	Metal[a]	Machinery[a]	Construction Materials[a]	Chemical[b]	Food[c]	Construction Transp.[a,d]	Heavy Industry	Light Industry
1965	1.05	1.01	1.03	1.03	1.00	1.05	1.02	1.00	1.04
1966	1.00	1.00	1.00	1.00	1.00	1.00	1.00	1.00	1.00
1967	0.97	0.99	0.97	0.99	0.99	0.99	0.97	0.98	0.98
1968	1.05	0.97	0.94	0.93	1.00	0.96	0.94	0.95	0.95
1969	1.03	0.92	0.91	0.89	0.99	0.91	0.91	0.92	0.90
1970	0.93	0.86	0.87	0.88	0.97	0.86	0.86	0.88	0.86
1971	0.89	0.81	0.84	0.83	0.96	0.84	0.82	0.85	0.83
1972	0.84	0.77	0.82	0.78	0.96	0.80	0.81	0.83	0.81
1973	0.76	0.73	0.79	0.71	0.90	0.70	0.79	0.81	0.74
1974	0.59	0.55	0.69	0.61	0.68	0.61	0.71	0.75	0.65
1975	0.45	0.49	0.60	0.57	0.55	0.57	0.65	0.68	0.60
1976	0.34	0.46	0.56	0.53	0.53	0.55	0.59	0.64	0.58
1977	0.25	0.43	0.53	0.48	0.52	0.51	0.55	0.60	0.55
1978	0.23	0.39	0.50	0.43	0.50	0.47	0.53	0.57	0.51
1979	0.18	0.35	0.46	0.39	0.45	0.42	0.46	0.51	0.45
1980	0.13	0.32	0.41	0.37	0.37	0.39	0.39	0.47	0.40
1981	0.10	0.30	0.37	0.35	0.33	0.36	0.35	0.43	0.37
1982	0.09	0.29	0.35	0.34	0.34	0.35	0.33	0.41	0.35
1983	0.08	0.29	0.34	0.33	0.35	0.34	0.33	0.39	0.35
1984	0.09	0.28	0.33	0.32	0.35	0.33	0.31	0.37	0.34
1985	0.09	0.28	0.32	0.32	0.35	0.32	0.30	0.36	0.33
1986	0.11	0.29	0.32	0.32	0.37	0.31	0.32	0.36	0.34
1987	0.12	0.28	0.31	0.31	0.36	0.30	0.31	0.36	0.33
1988	0.13	0.25	0.30	0.30	0.32	0.29	0.30	0.35	0.31
1989	0.12	0.25	0.29	0.29	0.30	0.27	0.28	0.35	0.30
1990	0.12	0.25	0.29	0.29	0.30	0.25	0.27	0.34	0.28
1991	0.12	0.26	0.28	0.28	0.30	0.25	0.26	0.33	0.27
1992	0.12	0.26	0.27	0.28	0.31	0.24	0.26	0.33	0.26
1993	0.12	0.25	0.27	0.27	0.31	0.24	0.25	0.32	0.26

[a]Cost of Living indexes by the U.S> Bureau of Labor Statistics.
[b]*U.S. Presidential Economic Report*. Producer price index.

        [c]*Business Statistics*, Vol. 60, No. 5, Section 2, 1994, U.S. Department of
Commerce.
        [d]*Statistical Abstract of U.S. 1993*, U.S. Department of Commerce, Bureau of the
Census, p. 714 (for the 1993 estimate).

Table 14.A2   Russian Imports and Exports with Japan in 1993 (Conversion to Rubles in 1966 Prices)

I-O Sector	Current Dollars			1966 Dollars			1966 Rubles	
	Imports	Exports	Deflator	Imports	Exports	Ruble/Dollar	Imports	Exports
	(1)	(2)	(3)	(4)	(5)	(6)	(7)	(8)
Agriculture		23368	0.24		5602	0.95		5322
Fuels	25774	292958	0.12	2995	34047	0.92	2756	31324
Metals	375825	983415	0.25	94604	247549	1.33	125824	329243
Machinery & Equip-ment	847284	6812	0.27	229156	1842	0.71	162701	1308
Construction Materials		61464	0.27		165943	0.80		16300
Chemicals	109238	40749	0.31	33612	12538	1.30	43695	148343
Food	15117	728030	0.24	3624	174521	0.85	3080	24691
Light Industry	98041	70923	0.26	25472	18426	1.34	34132	132755

SOURCES: Tables 14.2, 14.7, 14.8, 14.9.

Classification from MITI nomenclature:

Fuels	= petroleum products and synthetic rubber.
Metals	= metal goods.
Machinery	= machinery.
Chemicals	= chemicals.
Food	= foodstuffs.
Light Industry	= light industrial goods.

Table 14.A3   Direct Plus Indirect Factor Coefficients for the Turnover Tax Deflated Producers Price Valued 1966 Soviet Input-Output Table
(Ruble Cost per Unit of Ruble Output Value)

Sector	Capital	Labor
Agriculture	1.3197	0.5336
Fuels	4.1653	0.2608
Metals	2.6264	0.2530
Machinery and Equipment	1.6078	0.3131
Weapons	1.9775	0.3431
Construction Materials	1.9369	0.3754
Forestry (Timber)	0.2669	1.0317
Chemicals	2.1400	0.2564
Food	1.6298	0.5260
Fish Products	1.8589	0.2440
Light Industry	1.6628	0.4049
Construction	1.3625	0.4544
Transportation and Communications	2.7828	0.3065
Trade	2.7828	0.4972

SOURCES: Steven Rosefielde, *The Transformation of the 1966 Soviet Input-Output Table From Producers to Adjusted Factor Cost Values*, GE75TMP-47, Center for Advanced Studies, Washington, DC, 1975. Vladimer Treml, *The Structure of the Soviet Economy*, Praeger, New York, 1972, pp. 513-551.

NOTE: The fish products and forestry coefficients are from the 1966 purchasers price table reconstructed by Treml.

Table 14.A4   The Numerator of the Leontief Statistic for Russia's Trade with Japan: Embodied Factor Content of Import Substitutes from Japan 1993

	1993
lm	109269
km	759200
km/lm	6.9509

SOURCES: Tables 14.A2 and 14.A3.

METHOD: The direct plus indirect labor and capital coefficients are multiplied by their corresponding sector import coefficients for each year displayed in Table 14.A3.

Table 14.A5   The Denominator of the Leontief Statistic for Russia's Trade with Japan: Embodied Factor Content of Russian Exports to Japan 1993

	1993
lv	282052
kv	1391440
kv/lv	4.9333

SOURCES: Tables 14.A3 and 14.A4.

METHOD: The direct plus indirect labor and capital coefficients are multiplied by their corresponding sector export coefficients for each year displayed in Table 14.A3.

Table 14.A6   The Leontief Statistic for Russia's Trade with Japan: Embodied Factor Proportions 1993

	1993
km/lm	6.9509
kv/lv	4.9333
Ω	1.4090

SOURCES: Tables 14.A2 and 14.A3.

Leontief Statistics

The Leontief statistics as explained in the text are computed by premultiplying the trade vectors Table 14.A3, columns 7 and 8 by the vectors of direct plus indirect factor coefficients displayed in Table 14.A4.
Sample calculations for 1993 are shown in Tables 14.A4-14.A6.

Appendix II   The Mechanics of Underpricing in the Soviet Machine Building Sector

Official Soviet machine building prices reported in *Narodnoe khoziaistvo SSSR* (National Economy of the Soviet Union) routinely declined several percent annually during the postwar era (Table 14.9). These decreases were attributed to declining unit production costs brought about by technological progress (Table 14.A7). Prices fell in other sectors, but the decline in machinebuilding prices was far and away the most rapid. Insofar as the official explanation of these price trends is correct, the factor cost of machinery decreased, and its comparative advantage increased throughout the period. Although the capital intensity of machine building production was an important element in determining comparative advantage, the price trend implies that its influence was outweighed by technological progress.

Many western scholars however believe that the official explanation of Soviet price behavior may be erroneous. They argue that productivity in the machinery sector was not really rising exceptionally fast; that it only seemed to increase quickly because the value of machinery output was overstated by illegal price increases that were not accounted for in the official productivity statistics. The source of these illegal price increases was the overestimation of the cost of producing new and improved products. It is alleged that managers in the privileged machine building sector, protected by their political network, routinely deceived the State Price Committee by telling it that they were producing expensive new and improved goods which allowed them to raise prices, when they were really manufacturing the same old products with some superficial modifications. Managers are alleged to have deceived the State Price Committee in this way because their bonuses would increase proportionally. See Steven Rosefielde, "The Meaning and Measurement of Hidden Inflation in Demand Insensitive Economic Systems", in *Economic Statistics for Economies in Transition: Eastern Europe in the 1990's*, Washington, DC, 1994, Chapter 7, pp. 190-200.

From the government's standpoint profits appeared to continuously increase because costs were falling as technology progressed. These benefits were passed on to buyers with a lag, by cutting the prices on all machinery several percent annually, a procedure which had the additional advantage of keeping profit margins stable in the long run. From the critics' viewpoint, the decline in unit costs was illusory, and caused the Ministry of Foreign Trade to misassess the comparative advantage of its machinery. They contend that capital intensive machinery was not becoming cheaper and cheaper, and should not have been exported to the west. If they are correct, then Soviet and Russian trade with Japan is more consistent with constrained comparative advantage; if the government is right, it failed to expand machinery exports as profit maximizing required.

Table 14.A7   Labor Productivity Growth 1965-79
(Gross Output per Worker: 1940=100)

	1965	1970	1975	1979
All Industry	372	492	657	749
Electricity	359	470	625	692
Fuel	268	374	544	583
Chemicals	630	908	1344	1586
Machinery	645	938	1419	1824
Wood Products	269	348	450	481
Construction Materials	516	678	896	939
Light Industry	220	292	359	402
Food	238	281	353	368

SOURCE: *Narodnoe khoziaistvo SSSR 1979*, p. 148.

Appendix III   The Irrationality of Russia's Trade with the Developed West

The pattern of every nation's international trade, according to the Heckscher-Ohlin theory, depends primarily on its factor endowments. In the two-factor neoclassical model, assuming internationally homogeneous technology, immobile plant and installed equipment, restricted labor migration and that tradeables are commodities, countries abundantly endowed with capital will have comparative export advantages in capital intensive production and countries with relatively abundant labor will export labor intensive products. Both sets of countries will benefit from exchanging goods according to their respective comparative advantages.

This hypothesis, in a restricted variant that only required domestically homogeneous capital, and a foreign sectoral structure of technology that was not offsetting, without global factor and commodity price equalization, was not tested until 1953 when W. Leontief examined the case of American foreign trade. He used input-output techniques to measure the embodied factor content of U.S. export and import substitutes to verify whether they corresponded with the requirements of Heckscher-Ohlin theory. This was accomplished by calculating the ratio of capital and labor embodied in America's import substitutes divided by the ratio of capital and labor embodied in its export goods.

Leontief unexpectedly discovered that the embodied factor content of American imports was capital biased in U.S. trade with the rest of the world. Since the United States was viewed as capital rich, his finding was deemed paradoxical, and prodded other scholars to investigate the problem further.

Steven Rosefielde applied Leontief's methodology to study the Heckscher-Ohlin rationality of Soviet international trade in 1973. Given the deficiencies of administrative command planning and the suppression of competitive markets it might have been expected that the pattern of Soviet trade would be inconsistent with the profit maximizing logic underlying comparative advantage. The Soviet bilateral trade pattern on average between 1955-1968 with the West, CMEA and LDC, however, was consistent with the dictates of Heckscher-Ohlin theory and hence rational. Leontief statistics indicated that when the Soviets traded with the LDC the embodied factor content of exports was capital intensive, but changed to being labor intensive when the USSR traded with the capital rich economies of the West. As in the case of the irrational American trade pattern, this Heckscher-Ohlin rational outcome puzzled many.

Rosefielde ascribed the Soviet paradox to accounting rules which made output prices depend on administratively fixed factor prices; wages, interest charges, and technical progress. The latter played a role because it affected factor productivity, and was especially pronounced in the capital durables sector. As factor productivity rose over time, output prices were reduced, with capital durable prices declining fastest. On the basis of these rules, goods embodying large amounts of high priced factors like skilled labor were extremely expensive, those embodying low priced factors like capital durables were inexpensive. Dearness, and cheapness in this way were determined by administratively fixed factor prices. As a consequence when the Ministry of Foreign Trade set about deciding which goods to import and export its impression of comparative advantage was governed by factor prices, periodically adjusted for technological progress. The structure of Soviet factor prices at first corresponded by happenstance with factor endowments, but over time capital durables became increasingly underpriced (due either to hidden inflation as discussed in Appendix II, or the low real opportunity cost of capital), misindicating real comparative advantage. This caused the Ministry of Foreign Trade seeking to maximize the profits of trade, to over-export capital intensive goods which seemed cheap and over import goods whose substitutes were labor intensive. These profits were classified as income and included in official national income and product statistics. This resulted in a trade pattern in which the Soviets over-exported underpriced capital intensive heavy industrial goods and imported consumer products whose substitutes were labor intensive. As the underpricing of capital intensive durables increased due to ostensible rapid cost saving in the producer durables sector (Table 14.10), the Soviet pattern of trade with the developed West became increasingly irrational, with the USSR exporting more and more capital intensive and importing more and more goods whose domestic substitutes were labor intensive from the West. This Heckscher-Ohlin irrational pattern appears to have taken hold in the late sixties and beyond, with the exception of Japan where the labor intensity of timber and fish exports dominated other influences.

15 Systemic Change and Recovery Potential During Russia's Economic Transition

Steven S. Rosefielde and Vyachaslav Danilin

Introduction

The early signs of emerging market rationality in the embodied factor content of Russo-Japanese trade documented in chapter 14 may be heralding Russia's imminent ascent from the trough of the J curve. Perhaps as market building progresses the pace of change will accelerate, ushering in a full capitalist transition that will quickly propel Russia's recovery potential to the global frontier, despite the infungibility of the obsolete Soviet capital stock. Schumpeterian and more current variants of general competitive theory strongly support this expectation if the transition as usually implied is toward entrepreneurial capitalism. But suppose as Gerschenkron argued Russia continues to hew its own unique systemic path as it has for a millennium since the time of Olga in Kievan Rus. What about the J curve then?

The microeconomic inquiry into the anatomy of efficiency and production potential under administrative command planning indicates that extreme caution is needed against assuming that all "transitions" generically lead to the same happy outcomes on the global production possibility frontier. For many purposes of course satisfaction of the criterion hardly matters, but for a growing number of systems theorists the consensus is that the new Russian economy may be every bit as dysfunctional as its benighted predecessor, even if existing market mechanisms survive.

This chapter briefly explores these concerns more as an antidote to complacency than as a systems based countertheory because Russian economic institutions are in rapid and unpredictable flux. Opinions among the contributors regarding prospects for a radical, market lead quantum leap in Russia's recovery potential vary on numerous particulars, but they all believe that the peculiarities of the new economic system are discouraging, and expect efficiency and production potential to be substandard well into the twenty first century.

Vestiges of Socialism

The gross domestic product and industrial production continued their uninterrupted decline through 1996. Boris Yeltsin recently asserted in July 1997 that the economy had turned the corner in the first half of 1997, but statisticans familiar with the numbers advise against taking the supporting data too seriously (Tselitschev, 1997).   Perhaps the recent rally in the Russian stock market is heralding a reversal of fortune (Pioneer Securities, 1997), however institutional impediments, capital infungibility aside remain substantial because many of the elements of the old regulatory mechanism, including state purchases and subsidies have endured. Although the statistics are difficult to appraise it appears as if government contracts and subsidies (including exotic policies like the cancellation of interenterprise arrears) account for well over 50 percent of GDP. Capital durables, weapons, municipal transportation, electricity, water, health, housing, recreational and governmental services are all in the main dependent on state demand. As a consequence the "privatization" of enterprises supplying these goods and services has had little impact on their performance. It is a constant complaint among blue and white collar workers that their tasks and routines have hardly changed in the new ownership regime.

The same situation applies to regulation. As principal purchaser the state has a major impact on product design, technology and modernization. The state continues to establish standards, rules of the workplace, imposes import and export controls (McMillan, 1994), manipulates the foreign exchange rate, encourages price discrimination against foreigners in tourist services, regulates the money and credit supply, controls taxes, fees, permits, has imposed rigid property rights forms on denationalized enterprises and has adopted diverse incomes policies including indexing. Indeed, piercing the facade it is easily seen that the state has not abandoned planning, industrial policy, and ministerial supervision. These features of the old landscape have faded into the background but they are still there operating in the collectivist mode, profoundly shaping efficiency, production potential and Russia's recovery possibilities.

Semi-Privatization

The old Soviet arrangements were deemed socialist even though enterprises enjoyed limited autonomy including informal barter and profit based bonus maximizing because nearly all capital assets other than consumer durables were state owned. Yeltsin blurred this distinction by expanding the scope of enterprise autonomy and granting managers partial ownership rights in an effort to harness the efficiency of the market by allowing managers to receive some capital gains as compensation for entrepreneurship. The degree of desocialization, or privatization achieved in this way obviously depends on the breadth of owner-manager autonomy and their share of capital gains. If both are extremely circumscribed then arrangements will remain correspondingly socialized; if autonomy and private ownership are complete then they are capitalist.

The true extent of entrepreneurial independence between these antipodes is unclear. While most new firms are owned by venture capitalists, state assets have been for the most part collectivized with the workers receiving the majority of inside shares, and the state retaining a significant stake, bolstered by the recurrent threat of renationalization. The state as Moscow Mayor Luzhkov has repeatedly made clear reserves the right of eminent domain and can repossess property at its discretion. Needless to say enterprise autonomy is subject to the same capricious curtailment.

Russian enterprises, which were previously owned by the state thus should be best construed as semi-privatized. In principle, they are more responsive to market demand, and therefore more efficient than their Soviet counterparts, but may not perform as effectively as capitalist firms in the West.

Inefficiency and Disorder

The inefficiencies in question might be minor in a well functioning market socialist regime where the limits placed on autonomy and ownership were congruent with society's preferences. Owner-managers in this scenario would operate Paretian optimally, with consumer demand governing supply, subject to appropriate governmental constraints. This causality however could be disordered if the semi-autonomous, owner-managed firms conspired with complicitous governmental officials to fleece the state and society through profiteering contracts and the erection of bureaucratically imposed barriers to competitive entry. Under these arrangements vendors would be able to overcharge state procurement departments for the same old goods, or inferior variants thereof, while the former Soviet supply and service networks like the foreign trade organizations, grain storage operators, energy distributors, Intourist, Aeroflot, etc. were transformed into licensed, mercantilist, monopolies.

In the view of many senior Russian economists the static and dynamic efficiency gains sought through semi-privatization have been subverted by corrupt decontrol and divestiture.   They contend that collectivist-owner managers are primarily concerned with consolidating their sinecures, rather than enhancing efficiency, or creating new ventures. Also because tenures are uncertain, and collectivist ownership rights insecure, managers are prone to asset strip, frequently sending the proceeds abroad with no intention of subsequent repatriation.

These disordered behavioral patterns cast Russian laissez-faire in a revealing light. Many observers have noted that the government has often adopted an exceedingly tolerant attitude toward the machinations of its owner-managers, inferring that enlightened entrepreneurship is sure to follow. But this is only so under competitive capitalism. In the Russia variant of mercantilism it too often is little more than a license to steal.

While a majority of specialists recognize this problem not all are dismayed. Pekka Sutela speculates that collectively owned enterprises will soon become the sole property of individuals, or management groups through subterfuge and fraud, at which time they will outgrow mercantilist constraints and begin behaving like competitive entrepreneurs.

Sylvana Malle foresees a "corporativist" outcome, blending Italian economic organization of the thirties with the Japanese cross-participation structure, both based on protectionism and strong governmental power, and both characterized by concealed lobbying and widespread corruption. In this regard, she considers herself an optimist since postwar Italy and Japan have flourished in their own fashion.

Others are less sanguine about the benefits of corruption, and are concerned that criminal organizations loosely referred to as the Russian mafia will tilt the balance toward permanent depression by stifling competitive entrepreneurship wherever it arises. Apparently the situation is sufficiently protean that analysts can justify their optimism and pessimism regardless of whether Russia's future is perceived to lie with market assisted socialism, kleptocracy, corporatism, robber baron capitalism, mafiocracy, the welfare state or competitive free enterprise.

It is frivolous therefore to characterize Russia's recovery potential in restrictive terms, except to observe that historical precedent and the experience of the Yeltsin years should serve as a strong antidote against infectious optimism. The Bolshevik record as only recently clarified was hardly what idealists hoped it would be, and the postcommunist economic statistics displayed in Tables S1 and S2 as unreliable as they may be speak eloquently for themselves.

Conclusion

Most specialists have concluded that the economic system emerging in Russia is divorced from the Schumpeterian and neoclassical concepts frequently used to appraise the nation's efficiency, production potential and recovery possibilities. Even if Russia avoids reverting to communism, the economy remains encumbered by its socialist institutional legacy, and has shown itself prone to mercantilist, kleptocratic and other exotic systemic disorders. Although some remain optimistic that Russia will muddle through to Italian-Japanese corporatism, or robber baron capitalism, the record suggests that a rapid recovery up the J curve should not be anticipated anytime soon.[1]

Note

1. This was the judgment of Ivan Tselitschev, Pavel Minakir and Alexander Granberg at the Japan and Russia in Northeast Asia Workshop, Economic Research Institute for Northeast Asia, Tainai, Niigata, Japan, July 30, 1997.

Bibliography

Afanas"ev, Mikhail I., "Methods of Estimating Productive Efficiency for the Enhancement of Plan Decision Making", *Atlantic Economic Journal*.

Aganbegyan, Abel, *Inside Perestroika: The Future of the Soviet Economy*, Bessis/Harper and Row, New York, 1989.

Åslund, Anders, *How Small Is Soviet National Income?*, Washington, D.C., 1988.

_____, "Why Goulash-Communism is a Liability Now", *Transition, World Bank*, Vol. 5, May-June 1994a, p. 6.

_____, "Lessons of the First Four Years of Systemic Change in Eastern Europe", *Journal of Comparative Economics*, Vol. 19, No. 1, August 1994b, pp. 22-38.

_____, *How Russia Became a Market Economy*, The Brookings Institution, Washington, DC, 1995.

_____, "Rentoorientirovannoe povedenie v Rossiiskoi perekhodnoe ekonomike (Rent-Seeking Behavior in Russia's Transition Economy)", *Voprosy ekonomiki*, Vol. 8, 1996, pp. 99-108.

Belkin, Viktor, "Vlianie razlichii rynochnovo i nerynochnovo khoziaistvennovo mekhanizma na sopostavleniia makroekonomicheskikh pokazateli", paper presented at the Conference on Comparing the Soviet and American Economics, American Enterprise Institute, April 19-22, 1990.

Belousov, A.R., "Krizis sovremennoi modeli vosproizvodstva ekonomiki Rossii (kratkosrochnyi aspekt)", in Ekonomicheskii monitoring Rossii: global'nye tendentsii i kon"iunktura v otrasliakh promyshlennosti, Institut narodnokhoziaistvennovo prognozirovaniia RAN, Moscow Biuletten' No. 8, January 1997, pp. 1-44.

Bergson, Abram, *Soviet National Income and Product in 1937*, Columbia University Press, NY, 1953.

_____, *Productivity and the Social System-The USSR and the West*, Harvard University Press, Cambridge, Massachusetts, 1978.

_____, "Comparative Productivity: USSR, Eastern Europe and the West: Appendix Sources and methods for Basic Data", unpublished manuscript, 1987.

_____, "The USSR Before the Fall: How Poor and Why", *Journal of Economic Perspectives*, Vol. 5, Fall 1991, pp. 29-44.

_____, "The Communist Efficiency Gap: Alternative measures", *Comparative Economic Studies*, Vol. XXXVI, No. 1, Spring 1994a, pp. 1-12.

_____, "Russia's Economic Reform Muddle", *Challenge*, September-October 1994b, pp. 56-59.

Blanchard, Olivier J., Maxim Boycko, Marek Dabrowski, Rudiger Dornbusch, Richard Layard, and Andrei Shleifer, *Post-Communist Reform*, MIT Press, Cambridge, Massachusetts, 1994.

Blanchard, Olivier J., Rudiger Dornbusch, Paul Krugman, Richard Layard, and Lawrence Summers, *Reform in Eastern Europe*, MIT Press, Cambridge, Massachusetts, 1994.

Blasi, Joseph, Maya Kroumova and Douglas Kruse, *Kremlin Capitalism: Privatizing the Russian Economy*, Cornell University Press, Ithaca, NY, 1997.

Boycko, M., A. Shleifer and R. Vishny, "Privatizing Russia", *Brookings Papers on Economic Activity*, No. 2, 1993, 139-192.

Brada, Josef C. and Arthur E. King, "Is There Still a J Curve for the Economic Transition from Socialism to Capitalism", *Economics of Planning*, Vol. 25, No. 1, 1992, pp. 37-53.

Bush, Keith, *From the Command Economy to the Market*, Dartmouth, Aldershot Brookfield, Vermont, 1991.

Campbell, Robert (ed.), *The Postcommunist Economic Transformation: Essays in Honor of Gregory Grossman*, Westview Press, Boulder, Colorado, 1994.

Chavance, Bernard, *The Transformation of Communist Systems* (translated by Charles Hauss), Boulder, CO: Westview Press, 1994.

Commander, Simon et al., eds., *Enterprise Restructuring and Economic Policy in Russia*, The World Bank, Washington, DC, 1996.

Danilin, V.I., I.S. Materov, S. Rosefielde, and C.A.K. Lovell, "Measuring Enterprise Efficiency in the Soviet Union: A Stochastic Frontier Analysis", *Economica*, Vol. 52, 1985, pp. 225-233.

Dornbusch, Rudiger, Wilhelm Nölling, and Richard Layard (eds.), *Postwar Economic Reconstruction and Lessons for the East Today*, MIT Press, Cambridge, Massachusetts, 1994.

Edwards, Imogene, Margret Hughes, and James Noren, "U.S. and U.S.S.R.: Comparisons of GNP", *Soviet Economy in a Time of Change, JEC*, Vol. 1, 1979, pp. 369-401.

Egorova, N.E., and E.P. Main, "Rol' i funktsii Rossiiskovo malovo biznesa v period stanovleniia rynochnykh otnoshenii", Tsentral'nyi ekonomiko-matematicheskii institut, Rossiiskaia Akademiia Nauk, Moscow, 1995.

Ellman, Michael, "Transformation, Depression, and Economics: Some Lessons", *Journal of Comparative Economics*, Vol. 19, No. 1, August 1994, pp. 1-21.

Ericson, Richard E., "The Classical Soviet-Type Economy: Nature of the System and Implications for Reform", *Journal of Economic Perspectives*, Vol. 5, No. 4, Fall 1991, pp. 11-28.

Ernst, Maurice, Michael Alexeev, and Paul Marer, *Transforming the Core: Restructuring Industrial Enterprises in Russia and Central Europe*, Westview Press, Boulder, CO, 1996.

Estrin, Saul, Alan Gelb, and Inderjit Singh, "Shocks and Adjustment by Firms in Transition: A Comparative Study", *Journal of comparative Economics*, Vol. 21, No. 2, October 1995, pp. 131-153.

Fogel, Daniel S. (ed.), *Managing in Emerging Market Economies*, Boulder, CO: Westview Press, 1994.

Friedman, Thomas, "Yeltsin's Economic Checknya", *The New York Times*, February 1, 1995, p. 5.

Goldman, Marshall, *Russia's Failed Transition: Lost Opportunities*, New York: Norton, 1994a.

_____, *Lost Opportunity*, Norton, New York, 1994b.

_____, "Insider Capitalism: Privatization A Success or Sorry Failure?" Paper presented at the American Association for the Advancement of Slavic Studies, Boston, November 1996.

Gomulka, Stanislaw, "The Causes of Recession Following Stabilization", *Comparative Economic Studies*, Vol. 33, No. 2, Summer 1991, pp. 71-89.

Gosudarstvennyi komitet Rossiiskoi Federatsii po statistike, Sotsial'no-ekonomicheskoe polozhenie Rossii, Moscow, No. 12, 1996.

Hanson, Philip, *From Stagnation to Catastroika*, New York, NY: Praeger Publishers, 1992.

Hewett, Ed A., *Reforming the Soviet Economy*, The Brookings Institute, Washington DC, 1988.

Johnson, Simon and Gary W. Loveman, *Starting Over in Eastern Europe*, Boston, MA: Harvard Business School Press, 1995.

Keren, William S., *From Socialism to Market Economy*, W.E. Upton Institute, Kalamazoo, Michigan, 1992.

Keren, Michael, and Gur Ofer (eds.), *Trials of Transition*, Boulder, CO: Westview Press, 1992.

Kleiner, George, "Average and Marginal Factor Productivity: Interdependencies and Efficiency", in Rosefielde, ed., *Efficiency and the Economic Recovery Potential of Russia*, 1995a.

_____, "Russian Mismanagement: A Test for Incomplete Profit Maximizing", *Comparative Economic Studies*, forthcoming, 1995b.

Kornai, János, "Transformational Recession: The Main Causes", *Journal of Comparative Economics*, Vol. 19, No. 1, August 1994, pp. 39-63.

Kuboniwa, Masaaki and Evgeny Gavrilenkov, *Development of Capitalism in Russia: The Second Challenge*, Maruzen, Tokyo, 1997.

Lange, Oscar, *On the Economic Theory of Socialism*, McGraw-Hill, 1964, 567-97.

Layard, Richard, Oliver J. Blanchard, Rudiger Dornbusch, and Paul Krugman, *East-West Migration*, MIT Press, Cambridge, Massachusetts, 1994.

Leamer, Edward E., and Mark P. Taylor, "The Empirics of Economic Growth in Previously Centrally Planned Economies", April 1994, unpublished manuscript.

Linz, Susan, "Red Executives in Russia's Transition Economy", *Post-Soviet Geography and Economics*, Vol. XXXVII, No. 10, December 1996, pp. 633-652.

Linz, Susan and Gary Krueger, "Russia's Managers in Transition: Pilferers or Paladins?", *Post-Soviet Geography and Economics*, Vol. 37, No. 7, September 1996, pp. 397-425.

Litwack, John, "Corporate Governance, Banks, and Fiscal Reform in Russia", in Masahiko Aoki and Hyung-Ki Kim, eds., *Corporate Governance in Transitional Economies: Insider Control and the Role of Banks*, Economic Development Institute of the World Bank, The World Bank, Washington, DC, 1995, pp. 99-120.

Makarov, V,L., G.B. Kleiner, "Barter v Rossiiskoi ekonomike: osobennosti i tendentsii perekhodnovo perioda", Tsentral'nyi ekonomiko-matematicheskii institut, Preprint WP/96/006, Moscow 1996.

McKinnon, Ronald, *The Order of Economic Liberalization: Financial Control in The Transition to a Market Economy*, Baltimore, MD: Johns Hopkins, 1991.

McMillan, Carl, "The Role of Foreign Direct Investment in the Transition from Planned to Market Economies", *Transnational Corporations*, Vol. 2, No. 3, 1993, 97-119.

_____, "Foreign Investment and Privatization in Russia", 26th AAASS meetings, Philadelphia, PA, November 18, 1994.

Milner, Boris Z. and Dmitry S. Lvov, *Soviet Market Economy: Challenges and Reality*, North Holland, New York, 1991.

Nowakowski, Joseph, "Efficiency at Different Stages of Production" in *Efficiency and the Recovery Potential of the Soviet Union and Its Successor States*, forthcoming.

Olson, Murrell and Mancur Olson, "The Devolution of Centrally Planned Economies" in Christopher Clague and Gordon C. Rauser (eds.) *The Emergence of Market Economies in Eastern Europe*, Basil Blackwell, Cambridge, Massachusetts, 1992.

Osband, Kent, "Economic Crisis in a Shortage Economy", *Journal of Political Economy*, Vol. 100, No. 4, August 1992, pp. 673-89.

Pioneer Securities, *The Russian Equities market in 1997*, Moscow, 1997.

Polterovich, Victor, "Economic Reform in Russia in 1992: The Government Battles Labor Collectives", *Journal of International and Comparative Economics*, Vol. 4, 1995, pp. 265-287.

_____, "Krizis ekonomicheskoi teorii", Nauchnyi seminar "Neizvestnaia ekonomika", Tsentral'nyi ekonomiko-matematicheskii institut RAN, Moscow, 1997.

Poznanski, Kazimierz (ed.), *The Evolutionary Transition to Capitalism*, Boulder, CO: Westview Press, 1994.

Roberts, Bryan, "Welfare Consequences of Price Liberalization", paper presented at the American Economics Meetings, Washington, DC, January 8, 1995.

Rosefielde, Steven, "The Soviet Economy in Crisis: Burman's Cumulative Disequilibrium Hypothesis", *Soviet Studies*, Vol. XL, No. 1, April 1988, pp. 222-244.

_____, "Comparative Productivity: The USSR, Eastern Europe and the West: Comment", *American Economic Review*, Vol. 34, 1990, pp. 1-21.

_____, "The Illusion of Material Progress: The Analytics of Soviet Economic Growth Revisited", *Soviet Studies*, Vol. 43, No. 4, 1991, pp. 597-611.

_____, "Beyond Catastroika: Prospects for Market Transition in the Commonwealth of Independent States", *Atlantic Economic Journal*, 20, 1, March 1992, pp. 1-8.

_____, "Foreword", *Comparative Economic Studies*, Vol. XXXVI, No. 4, Winter, 1994, pp. 41-46.

_____, "Russia's Economic Recovery Potential: Optimizing the Residual Productivity of the Soviet Capital Stock", *Comparative Economic Studies*, Vol. XXXVI, No. 4, Winter 1994, pp. 119-142.

_____, "Corporatism and Kleptocracy in Post-Soviet Russia", Östekonomiska Institute (Stockholm Institute of East European Economics), Working Paper No. 10, March 1996.

_____, "Stalinism in Postcommunist Perspective: New Evidence on Killings, Forced Labor and Economic Growth in the Thirties", *Europe and Asia Studies*, Vol. 48, No. 6, 1996, pp. 959-987.

Rosefielde, Steven, Vyachasla Danilin, and George Kleiner, "Deistvuiushaya Model' Reform i Ugroza Giperdepressii", The Russian Reform Model and the Threat of Hyperdepression, *Russian Economic Journal (Rossiiskii Ekonomicheskii Zhurnal)*, No. 12, 1994, pp. 48-55.

Rosefielde, Steven, and R.W. Pfouts, "Economic Optimization and Technical Efficiency in Soviet Enterprises Jointly Regulated by

Plans and Incentives", *European Economic Review*, Vol. 32, No. 6, 1988, pp. 1285-1299.

Rutland, Peter, "Privatisation in Russia: One Step Forward: Two Steps Back?", *Europe-Asia Studies*, Vol. 46, No. 7, 1994, pp. 1109-1131.

Sacks, Jeffrey, *Poland's Jump to the Market Economy*, MIT Press, Cambridge, Massachusetts, 1994a.

_____, "Russia's Struggle with Stabilization", *Transition*, World Bank, Vol. 5, No. 4, May-June 1994b, pp. 7-10.

Sato, Tsuneaki, "Transition to a Market Economy: Lessons from East European Experiences", unpublished manuscript, 1994.

Schmidt, Klaus M. and Monika Schnitzer, "Privatization and Management Incentives in the Transition Period in Eastern Europe", *Journal of Comparative Economics*, Vol. 17, 1993, pp. 264-87.

Shukhgal'ter, Maya, "Capital Stock in the USSR and USA: Problems of Comparison", paper presented at the Conference on Comparing the Soviet and American Economics, American Enterprise Institute, April 19-22, 1990.

Sinn, Gerlinde, and Hans-Werner Sinn, *Jumpstart: The Economic Unification of Germany*, MIT Press, Cambridge, Massachusetts, 1994.

Smirnov, A.D., "Nelinineinaia dinamika perekhodnykh protsessov v ekonomike", Nauchnoi-issledovatel'skii seminar, teorticheskie i prakticheskie problemy modelirovaniia ekonomiki perkhodnovo perioda, Vysshaia Shkola Ekonomiki, Issue 1, Moscow 1996.

_____, "Infliatsiia i biudzhetnyi defitsit v perekhodnoi ekonomike", Nauchno-issledovatel'skii seminar, teoreticheskie i prakticheskie problemy modelirovaniia ekonomiki perekhodnovo perioda, Vysshaia Shkola Ekonomiki, Issue 1, Moscow 1997.

Sterling, Claire, *Thieves' World*, Simon and Schuster, 1994a.

_____, "The Mafia Privatized 50 to 80 Percent of All Shops, Hotels and Services in Moscow", *Transition*, World Bank, Vol. 5, No. 4, April 1994b, pp. 6-7.

Stiglitz, Joseph E., *Whither Socialism*, MIT Press, Cambridge, Massachusetts, 1994.

Sutela, Pekka (ed.), *The Russian Economy in Crisis and Transition*, Bank of Finland, 1993.

_____, "Insider Privatization in Russia: Speculations on Systemic Changes", *Europe-Asia Studies*, Vol. 46, No. 3, 1994, 417-35.

Taylor, Lance, "The Market Met Its Match: Lessons for the Future from the Transition's Initial Years", *Journal of Comparative Economics*, Vol. 19, No. 1, August 1994, pp. 64-87.

Tinbergen, Jan, "Some Suggestions on A Modern Theory of The Optimum Regime", in C. Feinstein, *Socialism, Capitalism and Economic Growth*, Cambridge University Press, London, 1967, 125-132.

Transformation in Progress, proceedings of the First Roundtable Conference, Budapest, Institute for World Economics, Budapest, 1994.

Whitesell, Robert, "The Influence of Central Planning on the Economic Slowdown in the Soviet Union and Eastern Europe: A Comparative Production Function Analysis", *Economica*, 52, May 1985, pp. 235-44.

_____, "Industrial Growth and Efficiency in the United States and the Former Soviet Union", this volume, Chapter 5, pp. 133-166.

Williamson, John, "A Persuasive Theory of State Collapse", *Transition*, World Bank, Vol. 5, No. 4, May-June 1994, pp. 11-12.

Yavlinsky, Grigory, and Serguey Braguinsky, "The Inefficiency of *Laissez-Faire* in Russia: Hysteresis Effects and the Need for Policy-Led Transformation", *Journal of Comparative Economics*, Vol. 19, No. 1, August 1994, pp. 88-116.

Conclusion

Steven S. Rosefielde

Having revisited the theory and estimation of efficiency and production potential as they apply to the Soviet Union and postcommunist Russia, extended to include the further issue of recovery, we have arrived at a conclusion foreseen sixty years ago by Fredrich Hayek, Ludwig von Mises and Lionel Robbins. Administrative command planning and controlled economies more generally are prone to disaster even though they may succeed temporarily in veiling their inefficiencies and vulnerabilities with a multitude of sophistries and statistics which conflate fiat cost with genuine value added. Although governments can and do effectively manipulate economic activity for their own purposes, including the social good, excessive controls inevitably degrade efficiency, and production potential, causing growth retardation, stagnation, or worse, while suppressing the automatic adjustment processes of the market. These outcomes can be reversed by eliminating the offending controls, but recovery is apt to be impeded by the physical legacy of the old order, and coercive institutions which emerge or adapt to capitalize on market dysfunction.

This finding is significant because had the Soviet Union not collapsed it would have been difficult to prove from the statistical record that command controls had been as destructive as communism's critics had foreseen. The authoritative scholarly literature looking toward the year 2000 from the eighties not only expected the Soviet Union to survive, but to steadily raise living standards one or two percent per annum.

This study has traced the statistical source of this misprediction to a series of factors concealing the inefficiency, low production potential and worthlessness of much of Soviet economic activity. It has been shown that the comparative size of the USSR's GNP was overstated by adopting a factor cost standard which disregarded the competitive unsalability of inferior goods, conflated fiat cost with value added, and winked at the biased use of composite dollar-ruble ratios inadequately adjusted for their qualitative inferiority. Growth estimates were similarly overappraised by assuming that adjusted ruble factor costing formed prices that reliably measured Russian production potential, and were congruent with planners' preferences. Mathematical modeling of input use and output determination in Soviet enterprises proved that adjusted factor costing could not have fulfilled this task, except under circumstances so unlikely that constructed ruble prices could not reasonably be construed as approximate opportunity cost estimators.

Stochastic production frontier studies of different stages of production, and in multiproduct firms, sectors and larger aggregates confirmed these deductions by revealing the extent to which aggregation concealed inefficiencies, and thereby exaggerated performance. Multiproduct firms it was discovered were unable to allocate factors to most technically efficient use, and were oblivious to consumer demand. Aggregate value computed at fiat factor cost given mandatory full and overfull employment under prevailing conventions was necessarily high, but this misleadingly hid the fact that assortments and characteristics were being produced willy-nilly without regard to efficiency and demand.

The evidence thus confirmed the theory that the production potential of administratively planned economies was likely to lie far beneath the Paretian frontier when technologies were identical, and to perform even more poorly when input and output characteristics determined by the system were taken into account.

The misdetermination of input and output characteristics links postcommunist Russia to its Soviet past. Even if Yeltsin had purged Russia of every vestige of the command system on December 21, 1991, he could not have eradicated its heritage of misdesigned capital durables and consumer goods. Transition and recovery as a consequence necessitated more than dismantling the apparatus of administrative command planning. It required society to recognize and bear much of the concealed costs of the old regime, while simultaneously adopting policies vigorously promoting recapitalization responsive to competitive market demand.

Systems theory and some novel empirical evidence on incomplete profit maximization presented in this volume suggest that competitive recapitalization is likely to be more difficult than abolishing central planning. Communist administrators through long experience became adept at turning reform to their own advantage, and their postcommunist successor have displayed similar gifts. The markets which have emerged since 1991 are variously dependent on government largesse, or are controlled by anticompetitive cliques with the result that Russia has failed to benefit either by reemploying mostly obsolete capacities, or competitively recapitalizing. Perhaps the forces thwarting recovery, and modernization will soon be swept away, but the complexities of the Soviet and Russian system revealed by this inquiry suggest that they are more likely to linger.

Index